MAN, TIME, AND FOSSILS

MAN, TIME, AND FOSSILS

The Story of Evolution

by RUTH MOORE

Drawings by SUE RICHERT

NEW YORK   ALFRED A. KNOPF   1953

The universe is not to be narrowed down to the limits of the understanding, which has been man's practice up to now, but the understanding must be stretched and enlarged to take in the image of the universe as it is discovered.

FRANCIS BACON: *Parasceve* (Aphorism 4)

ACKNOWLEDGMENTS

THERE WAS only one way in which I could approach the writing of a book on a subject so deep, so moving, and so all-encompassing as the evolution of man. That was as a reporter. The function of a reporter is to tell about, and in one sense to interpret, the work of the expert for the layman. In this case that was an unequaled assignment.

These were men reaching out for the widest understandings of which we are capable. They have tried to understand and explain the majestic course of life. They have experimented to that end. They have dug into the earth in a search for our earliest forebears, and they have brought the clear light of mathematics to bear upon this infinite and yet nearest problem. To work with material of this magnificent scope was both exciting and humbling. As the late learned Prime Minister of the Union of South Africa, Field Marshal Jan C. Smuts, said: "The story of the evolution of life on this globe is perhaps the most enthralling in all science."

To tell this story I have drawn on the work of many scientists. I have extensively used their own writings and what others have written about them. For the story of the recent developments that have brought a new surge of progress in the study of evolution and have changed many past concepts, I have tried, whenever possible, to talk to the men who were doing the work.

I should like to express my appreciation particularly to Dr. Sherwood L. Washburn, of the University of Chicago. Without his assistance and guidance the writing of this book would have been an almost impossible task. It was heartening too to discover that he did not quail at the idea of the story of evolution being written by a reporter for people generally. I also am indebted to Dr. Washburn for some South African and English material that I might otherwise have had a difficult time obtaining in this country.

I also want to thank Dr. Willard F. Libby, Dr. Sewall Wright, and Dr. Kenneth Page Oakley for their willingness to discuss their work with me and to lend their general assistance. Dr. G. H. R. von Koenigswald was kind enough to reply to my questions and to send me some extremely interesting information about his work in Java.

There are many others whose assistance has contributed invaluably to this book. I should like to mention especially the China Medical Board and its secretary, Miss Agnes M. Pearce. Miss Pearce permitted me to borrow some of the board's file material on Dr. Davidson Black. Jeannette Lowrey and others of the staff of the University of Chicago were constantly helpful. I also relied steadily on the rich resources of the University of Chicago biology library, the Chicago Public Library, and the John Crerar Library.

For another essential kind of assistance I wish to thank my mother and father. They relieved me of a number of responsibilities that would have cut seriously into my time for working on this book. I want to express my thanks too to Milburn P. Akers, executive editor of the *Chicago Sun-Times*, for making it possible for me to obtain a leave of absence from the paper, and for encouragement and co-operation, which I deeply valued.

I could not end a note of this kind without speaking of my sincere appreciation of the counsel and guidance I was given by Harold Strauss, editor-in-chief of Alfred A. Knopf, Inc. His concept of this book and his understanding of its problem are the base upon which it is written.

R. M.

Chicago, Illinois
February 1953

CONTENTS

I. MAN'S ORIGINS

II. MAN'S BURIED RECORD

Contents

III. A CHANGED THEORY OF
MAN'S EVOLUTION

[xi]

LIST OF PLATES

FOLLOW PAGE 236

LIST OF DRAWINGS
IN THE TEXT

Part I

MAN'S ORIGINS

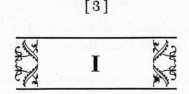

BEGINNINGS AND CHANGES

At a few rare moments in the history of a scientific problem, understanding takes a long leap forward, and so it is at this moment in that most basic of all the sciences, the evolution of man. Understanding suddenly has been increased.

There was a similar moment in the middle of the last century, when Charles Darwin convinced most of the world that living forms are not fixed but changing, and that they had changed by natural process operating over great periods of time. The concept of organic evolution revolutionized biology and profoundly affected thought generally.

There was another such moment in the first year of this century. At that turning-point, the laws that govern physical inheritance from parent to child were discovered, or, it should be said, were re-discovered. The Mendelian laws laid the basis for the modern science of heredity and brought about a major revision in the theory of evolution. Former ideas about evolution had to be reshaped and reinterpreted.

And now in the middle of this century another time has come when new findings are upsetting older theories and opening the way for another rapid surge forward. It is still too early for the final verdict, though even now it is clear that the current and traditional theory of how and when man evolved must be changed. Some long-held and respected beliefs will have to be revised and the textbooks rewritten, for much of what has been said and some of the supposed facts are now found to be incorrect. Darwin's theory of evolution is being modified—though in the end strengthened and reaffirmed. Darwin was wrong, but right.

It was an unplanned and unexpected converging of new materials that brought about the present moment of progress in evolution:

Suddenly new fossil discoveries filled in some of the great gaps in the record of human evolution.

Suddenly wartime research and the precision methods of atomic physics and chemistry made it possible to fix firm dates for some of the highly important but hitherto undatable events of man's past.

Suddenly research answered some of the unanswered questions about how man evolved and the rate at which he evolved.

Much that always had been inexact became exact. Much that had been unclear became clear. Many matters of surmise were turned into certainty.

The gaps in the evolutionary record of man always had been many and marked. Darwin had no sooner published his *Origin of Species,* with its implication that man is descended from some earlier, simpler form than his outraged critics demanded proof. If creatures in between man and his nearest relatives, the anthropoids, had ever lived, where were their remains? Where were the bones? Why were there missing links? Darwin could reply only that the likeliest places on the earth had not been searched for any hidden remains of man's earliest forebears.

The truth was that the theory of human evolution was a deduction. It was a deduction based on strong evidence— upon man's resemblance to all the other forms of life upon the globe; upon some of the strange vestigial structures, such as the appendix, which man carries within him; upon the eerie way in which the human embryo relives the history of the race. This evidence was difficult to deny, but until actual bones could be found to show how human beings had progressed, human evolution had to remain a deduction. Opponents made much of this weakness. The term "the missing link" became a world-wide byword and joke, for in fact the record of human evolution was embarrassingly incomplete and the missing links were many.

And then the search began, the search for man's ancestors. It was to be an exploration as adventurous and as full of incredible happenings as the search for gold, or oil, or man's lost civilizations. One of the first to take it up was a young Dutch physician. He went out to the Dutch East Indies for the avowed purpose of finding the missing link. And he nearly succeeded. From a riverbank in Java he dug up the fossilized bones of *Pithecanthropus erectus,* who in the end proved to be one of the earliest of men, though not the missing link.

And then the search shifted to China. Near ancient Peking two other remarkable physicians, a Canadian who nearly always worked at night, and a thoroughgoing German, dug into a hill from which the Chinese long had quarried "dragon bones." The searchers found the bones of a number of very primitive men, men who traced back to the very beginnings of our kind. Astonishing new light was being shed on man's very early history when World War II not only ended the digging, but caused Peking man to vanish from the world he had so recently re-entered. The disappearance of the fossils of Peking man is one of the most enthralling of modern international mysteries.

And still, it was thought, the missing link had not been found.

A little earlier a startling telegram had flashed out of South Africa. The bones of an ape-man, it said, a being less human than man and more human than the apes, had been blasted from lime workings near Johannesburg. Scientists could not have been more skeptical; the report was hooted down. But another doughty physician, who was convinced that the first report was accurate, took up the search and proceeded to unearth the bones of many more ape-men. By the time the first full impartial scientific study was completed in 1950, the evidence was overwhelming. The verdict was a breath-taking one: the missing link had at long last been found.

Thus at mid-century the biggest gap in man's record was filled in. There were the bones to prove what man had been like at the major stages in his long climb from some anthropoid-like ancestor to his modern guise. Human evolution no longer was purely a deduction. And the theory of evolution as it had been outlined by Darwin and his successors was materially substantiated.

But this was only the beginning. The bones spaded from the Java riverbank, from the Chinese hill and the South African caves, told a new and unanticipated story of how man had developed. When science had not yet found the bones of ape-men or early man, scientists had been compelled to deduce what such creatures might have been like by studying comparatively recent fossils and living man. In this way a picture was drawn of the missing link and primitive man. Both were conceived as hulking apelike creatures who shuffled along with bent knees and head thrust forward.

The actual bones, when they were found, shattered this picture. The fossils revealed that the ape-men walked very much like man and had an upright near-human body long before the brain reached human size. A drastic change must therefore be made in the illustrations and accounts of man's forebears given in nearly all textbooks and scientific volumes. A long-accepted picture must be changed.

Another of evolution's great difficulties lay in the lack of an accurate way of dating man's ancestors. Unfortunately, the fossils taken from the ground bore no dates stamped upon them. There were, of course, some clues to their age. If the bones lay in well-defined geological strata, that told something of when their owners might have lived. But often the bones were not found in such strata.

Sometimes the bones of ancient animals rested beside the

human fossils. That afforded another clue to age, but there was no certainty that the men and the animals were contemporary. Perhaps the human bones had been buried in the deposit at some later time, perhaps some flood or volcanic overflow had swept them from their original burial place and carried them to the spot in which they were found.

It was extremely difficult to be sure. And since there could be no assurance in most cases, serious differences of opinion developed about the age of almost every important human or near-human fossil. One group would contend that the strata and associated bones, if any, indicated an age of, say, a million years. Another would argue that the primitive-looking bones were a burial and hence should be dated at 500,000 years, or perhaps at 100,000.

Despite the disagreements and confusion about when the earliest humans and their predecessors might have lived, man was given an impressive antiquity. Anthropologists drew up timetables that carried him far back into the world's history. In the timetables, and in the trees of life which were devised from them, man was shown branching off from his ancestral anthropoids many millions of years ago.

All of this—the labor of years—was upset abruptly by new scientific methods that removed much of the guesswork in the dating of man.

A young British scientist who was assigned during World War II to study the effect of fluorine in preventing the decay of children's teeth discovered—he would say re-discovered—a way to use fluorine to determine the relative ages of human and animal bones buried in the same deposit. By measuring the amount of fluorine the bones had absorbed from the ground and its waters, it became possible to say authoritatively that these human and animal bones in such a geological bed had lain buried there for approximately the same length of time; or, on the other hand, that the bones had been there for different lengths of time.

When some of the key fossils in man's history were tested, their fluorine content indicated that they were not contemporaneous with the bones of the long-extinct animals with which they rested. On the contrary, they had a fluorine content no greater than the bones of relatively recent animals found in the same deposit.

The great antiquity given man was immediately overthrown. The timetables in the textbooks were outmoded. This time a deduction fell before the new facts.

At about the same period, principally since 1950, a radiochemist at the University of Chicago found a way to measure the actual age in years—up to a maximum of twenty-five thousand years—of any scrap of organic material.

A bit of charcoal that had been buried for, say, twenty thousand years could be dated, or a bit of rope, or a sliver of charred bone. And when it became possible to date such remaining scraps of the past, it became possible to date the eras to which they had belonged. Science at long last could fix accurate dates for the last advance of the glaciers in all parts of the world, and for the first appearance of man in the lands that had been covered with ice. For the first time a start could be made on an exact chronology of man's last twenty-five thousand years.

Even in its earliest stages this new dating—dating with Carbon-14 or radiocarbon—also indicated that man is younger than science had ever dared to think. As man's time was compressed, a new dilemma was created. Could man have evolved in the shorter time set by the new dating? Could the tremendous differences between primitive man and modern man have been achieved in a shorter time?

Almost at this moment, new experimental work in anthropology provided an answer to the dilemma. Ingenious experiments indicated that man may have changed more rapidly than Darwin thought and that he could have evolved in the shorter time allowed by the new dating.

These were major changes that were being made in the understanding of evolution. The new fossils filled in and changed the record of man. The new methods of dating altered all previous estimates of the period of man's existence. And experiment suggested that evolution could have come about in a shorter time.

If the world has heard little of these major developments which have so closely affected and altered the traditional and current theory of evolution, it is not surprising. The new findings are not the work of one man or of one science. They are not even the product of a number of sciences collaborating in the solution of a problem. In the beginning, at least, any collaboration was unplanned and unforeseen. Each group—the fossil-hunters, the radiochemists, the geologists, and the anthropologists—pursued its own studies separately.

In addition, most of the work that is so notably advancing the understanding of evolution at present is too recent to have become widely known. Most of the full scientific reports on the new fossils, the new timing, and the new experimental anthropology have come out since 1949. Nearly all of them have been written for the scientific rather than the lay audience. There has not yet been time for revising the textbooks or for writing the definitive scientific book that will bring together all the new thinking and mold it into a revised theory of evolution.

If I attempt to tell the story of what is happening at this third great moment of change in evolution, I must do it primarily by piecing together the work of many scientists, the early scientific reports, and in some cases the significant interchange that goes on between scientists before new ideas are put into print. Nowhere is the story as a whole now to be found.

To write about the new work in evolution and the men who are doing it, it seems necessary to tell first about those who laid the foundations upon which it stands. This book, therefore, will start with Charles Darwin, the famous English naturalist, with whom scientific evolution begins. And yet that was not the actual beginning of the *idea* of evolution, and the earlier speculations cannot be ignored.

The Greeks caught more than a glimpse of the basic truth of evolution. Thales, who lived from 624 to 548 B.C., looked at the abounding life in the blue Ægean and declared water to be "the mother from which all things arose and out of which they exist." Heraclitus, who was imbued with the idea that all is motion, wrote that everything "is transposed into new shapes." Aristotle saw that there had been a progression, from plants, to plant-animals, to animals, and then by graduated stages to man. And yet this thought, farsighted as it was, still was a nebulous, half-mythical one.

Even this shadowy idea of evolution was largely lost from the end of the Greek era until the revival of science in the seventeenth century.

Milton's verse superbly expressed the beliefs about life's origins that prevailed throughout the Dark Ages:

> *The Earth obey'd and straight*
> *Op'ning her fertile womb, teem'd at a birth*
> *Innumerous living creatures, perfect forms,*
> *Limb'd and full grown.*

But by the beginning of the eighteenth century the idea that the variety of life upon the earth might have arisen from the same beginnings was once more abroad.

An extraordinary English physician, Dr. Erasmus Darwin, sensed it keenly. He was a Dickensian figure, a huge man with a "plum pudding face," with wide-ranging interests, and with friendships that included the great of his day. He was accounted one of the outstanding physicians of England.

As he made his medical rounds in his sulky—an equipage

fitted out with holds for books, paper, and ink and a skylight—
he devoted himself to poetry:

> *Soon shall thy arm*
> *Unconquer'd steam! Afar*
> *Drag the slow barge or drive the rapid car,*
> *Or on wide-waving wings expanded bear*
> *The flying chariot through the fields of air.*

His masterpiece, a long poem called *Zoonomia*, was de-
signed to serve not only as a medical textbook that would un-
ravel the theory of disease, but as an explanation of life itself.
"Would it be too bold to imagine that in the great length of
time since the earth began to exist, perhaps millions of years
ago, would it be too bold to imagine that all warm-blooded animals have arisen from one living filament?" he asked. The
world listened, for the *Zoonomia* ran into three editions in
seven years and was translated into French, German, and Italian. The physician had felt the great truth of evolution and
predicted it in much the same sense that he forecast the coming
of the automobile and the airplane.

But the amazing Dr. Darwin was to be remembered principally for another reason. He was the grandfather of Charles
Darwin.

The growing awareness of the idea of evolution and the
deeply felt need for a scientific explanation of life's development extensively influenced the men and literature of the early
nineteenth century. The idea of evolution was in the minds of
many, and yet, like Dr. Darwin's prognostications, it was often
more of a feeling, a hope, or an ungrounded reflection than a
scientific theory. Then suddenly in the middle of the nineteenth
century all was changed. A whole new prospect opened. Men's
minds and the thinking of centuries were challenged. Men's
thought about the origin of life and of man took its first great
leap forward.

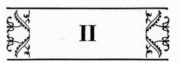

II

CHARLES DARWIN

LIFE: LIKENESSES AND DIFFERENCES

ON THE 27TH OF DECEMBER 1831 His Majesty's Ship *Beagle,* a ten-ton brig, sailed from Devonport. She was under orders to complete a survey of Patagonia and Tierra del Fuego and to carry a chain of chronometrical measurements around the world.

This she did.

But the five-year voyage of the *Beagle* round South America, across the South Seas, round the Cape of Good Hope, and back to England was to accomplish a far greater mission than the charting of unknown waters. This voyage was to chart a new and world-upsetting answer to one of the most elemental of all unknowns: how did man and all the teeming kinds of life around him originate?

On board the *Beagle* was a young naturalist, twenty-two years old, named Charles Darwin. He was a born collector suddenly presented with the whole world in which to collect. More than this, he had an amazingly discerning eye not only for detail, but for the total meanings, which elude most men.

As the *Beagle* slowly made her way around the world, he was struck by the curious likenesses and the curious dissimilarities of the plants, the animals, the insects, the fish, the shells, the fossils, and the geological specimens he omnivorously gathered. The same puzzling relationships were there whether they came from the depths of the Brazilian forest, from the bleak plains of Patagonia, from the high slopes of the Andes, from continental shores, or from tiny mid-ocean islands.

If each species had been separately created, as he and virtually the entire world then thought, why, he asked himself, should the unique giant tortoises of the Galapagos Islands still vaguely resemble those of the South American mainland? Why should some upland species of ducks which were never near water have webbed feet? Why did living things vary as they did?

Early in the voyage a daring explanation began to shape up in Darwin's mind. If each species of man, or whale, or rat, or beetle had not been separately created, but had evolved from an earlier form of life, the unexplainable could be explained. And if the lands and waters had risen and fallen and changed position as he saw they had, it was possible to see why living things were distributed about the earth as they were. A thousand new questions—many thousands—were immediately raised. Proof would have to be supplied, for these were strange and unanticipated relatives who were being introduced. And yet if this was the pattern, proof should be obtainable.

The young scientist to whom these revolutionary ideas came was deeply, painfully modest. He was no intellectual rebel; no man ever was more mentally cautious.

He did not hasten to record his developing theory in the notebooks and journal that he kept throughout the voyage. Darwin lacked the words and the presumption to write, as did Keats: "Then felt I like some watcher of the skies when a new planet swims into his ken." It is probable that at first he did not consciously admit even to himself that he was forming a new and dangerously challenging concept of life's origins.

But from an early stage in the voyage every act indicated that the major points in his famous theory clearly were in his mind. Was the odd little fish he caught in the net he towed behind the *Beagle* unique? How did it differ? Had the upthrusting of a mountain range halted the movements of animals, and had new species developed behind the barriers? His questions and his observations all were within this framework.

For the rest of the voyage, and the rest of his life, all his thoughts and work were pointed toward proving—or disproving, Darwin would have said—that life had descended

THE ROUTE OF THE "BEAGLE"

from common parents and had spread from one place upon the earth to all others. His underlying belief in this principle was unwavering, though he was eager to submit every point to every test. It soon became the core of his being—his whole life testifies to this.

The young man who boarded the *Beagle* on October 24, 1831, showed no obvious promise of becoming one of those few geniuses who explain to men a part of the world that lies around them. He was, in fact, considered something of a problem. His father, Dr. Robert W. Darwin, a distinguished physician, and the son of the even more noted Dr. Erasmus Darwin, had hoped that his two sons, Erasmus and Charles Robert, would enter the medical profession. Both dutifully enrolled in the medical courses of the University of Edinburgh.

Charles said many years later in his autobiography that the courses, some of them beginning at eight o'clock on a cold winter's morning, both bored and disgusted him. His aversion to the operating amphitheater was even stronger. He went twice to watch operations. In those days before chloroform, the sight was gruesome. He rushed from the room both times, only to be haunted for the rest of his life by the memories. At about this time Charles became convinced "from various small circumstances" that he would inherit enough property from his father to keep him comfortably all his life. That put an end to any strenuous efforts to study medicine.

Charles had two real interests: collecting—shells, bugs, birds, minerals, some marine specimens that he found trawling with Scottish fishermen—and shooting. To his father, the first seemed of no consequence; the second was a source of grave worry. Charles took so avidly to the partridge shooting each fall at Maer, the beautiful and hospitable home of his uncle Josiah Wedgwood, that his father seriously feared he would "turn into an idle sporting man."

Josiah Wedgwood was the son of the famed Josiah Wedgwood who founded the noted Wedgwood potteries. The first Josiah and Erasmus Darwin, the grandfather of Charles, had been lifelong friends. The close ties between the two families were drawn all the closer when Robert Darwin, the son of Erasmus, married Susannah Wedgwood, the daughter of Josiah. Robert and Susannah became the parents of Charles. The two families constantly visited each other, and the children were almost as much at home in one household as in the other.[1]

Dr. Robert Darwin looked with no favor on a playboy career. He suggested with characteristic forcefulness that his medically disinclined son become a clergyman. Charles could not or would not resist his father. After thinking it over, he decided that he liked the idea of being a "country" clergyman and that he could accept the creed of the Church of England. That settled the matter.

He was sent to Cambridge in 1828 to take the degree he would need. During three happy years there he rather off-handedly did what studying was required, moved with the shooting crowd, ardently collected beetles, and out of a common interest in nature and natural science formed a close, warm friendship with the Reverend John Steven Henslow, Cambridge professor of botany. He became known as "the man who walks with Henslow."

In his last year at Cambridge he read Alexander von Humboldt's *Personal Narrative of Travels to the Equinoctial Regions of America during the years 1799–1804,* and Sir John Herschel's *Introduction to the Study of Natural Philosophy.* Humboldt fired him with an intense wish to see the Americas and particularly the island of Tenerife. Herschel, Darwin wrote later, stirred in him "a burning zeal to add even the most humble contribution to the noble structure of Natural Science." In this frame of mind, he willingly accepted Henslow's suggestion that he begin the study of geology.

During the late summer of 1831, after he had taken his de-

---

[1] This long and satisfying relationship later was carried over into the third generation by the marriage of Charles and his first cousin, Emma Wedgwood, the daughter of his uncle Josiah.

As the Wedgwood pottery and dinnerware became famed around the world, the Wedgwood fortune flourished. The inheritances of Charles's mother and his wife contributed substantially to the comfortable fortune that made it possible for Charles Darwin to pursue a scientific career without worry about finances.

gree, he joined his geology professor, Adam Sedgwick, on a walking trip through the Midland counties. Along the way, Charles came upon a tropical shell that had been found embedded in a gravel pit. The fledgling geologist was excited by his discovery until Sedgwick dryly told him that if the shell actually had been embedded in the pit, it would be a great misfortune to geology, for it would overthrow all that was known about the superficial deposits of the Welsh border counties. Suddenly Darwin realized that science "consists of grouping facts, so that general laws and conclusions may be drawn from them."

Darwin hurried home from this expedition, in order to go on to Maer for the opening of the fall shooting. At home—the Mount, his father's fine house overlooking the Severn—a letter was waiting for him which completely changed and determined the course of his life. It was from Henslow.

The Cambridge professor had been asked by Captain Robert Fitzroy of the Royal Navy to recommend a young man to go with him, without pay, as a naturalist on the *Beagle's* forthcoming voyage around the world. During an earlier survey Fitzroy had decided that if the Admiralty should authorize the completion of his work, he wanted to take with him "a scientific person qualified to examine the land." Henslow recommended Darwin.

Charles was swept with excitement. It was everything he wanted. Dr. Darwin took a different view. He did not want another change of profession and considered it a "wild scheme" that would contribute nothing to the character of a clergyman.

Dejected, but again yielding to his father's decision, Charles went to Maer. His uncle and the family there were as enthusiastic about the proposal as Dr. Darwin had been cold. Mr. Wedgwood drew up a letter to the doctor, answering his principal objections—the pursuit of natural history was suitable to a clergyman; the voyage was not likely to make Charles more "unsteady and unable to settle"; if Charles were absorbed in professional studies, as he was not, it might not be advisable to interrupt them, but his present pursuit of knowledge was in the same track as he would have to follow on the expedition. Mr. Wedgwood then made a special trip with Charles to present this document to the redoubtable doctor. Dr. Darwin gracefully gave in. He generously agreed to finance the trip. And so, a few months later, Charles Darwin set sail in the *Beagle.*

When the *Beagle* made her first lengthy stop at Bahia, in Brazil, Darwin already was hard at work, examining everything, collecting everything. He tried to collect every living creature he could catch and as many plants and geological specimens as possible. They overflowed the tight little decks of the *Beagle.* From the base at Bahia he made many expeditions into the Brazilian forest. Its luxuriance, its intense greenness, its loftiness and quiet were to Darwin one of the memorable experiences of his life.

One day in the forest he found a curious fungus. Darwin knew a similar English fungus and knew how it attracted beetles by its odious smell. As he walked along, turning it over in his hand, a beetle alighted on it. Darwin marveled. The two fungi belonged to different species. The beetles were of different species. And yet there in the tropics and in distant England a similar relationship had developed between plants and insects of the same families. To see, to understand, that the beetle's attraction was not by chance was to touch upon basic questions. Why, if the English and Brazilian beetles and fungi had been separately created, had the same link developed between them?

The same incredible fitting together of plants, animals, and environment struck Darwin over and over again. In the Río Negro district of Argentina he went to visit a salt lake, or salina. During the winter it was a shallow pool of brine; in the summer, a field of snow-white salt. It seemed to the young naturalist that nothing could live in the brine, but in the salt-caked mud along the edges worms crawled about among crystals of soda and lime.

In the summer, before the lake dried up, flamingos came there to breed and ate the worms. The worms in their turn probably fed upon the tiny organisms that colored the lake's froth green and upon the infusoria that gave the water a reddish cast when it was seen from a distance. And wherever Darwin came upon lakes of brine, in Patagonia, in northern Chile, or in the Galapagos Islands, he saw the same type of flamingos, worms, and minute organisms. He read too that in Siberian salt lakes there was the same chain of life. There was a little living world within itself, adapted to these inland lakes of brine.

If life could flourish in this inhospitable, salty environment, Darwin thought: "Well may we affirm that every part of the world is habitable! Whether lakes of brine, or those subterranean ones hidden beneath volcanic mountains—warm mineral springs—the wide expanse and depths of the ocean—the upper regions of the atmosphere, and even the surface of perpetual snow—all support organic beings."

The *Beagle* pushed on south.

Darwin rode with the gauchos and admiringly watched them hurl their bolas overhead and let go. Down would come an ostrich or steer, the ball-tipped thongs wrapped tight around its legs. But above all he watched every change in the country. Closely allied plants and animals replaced one another as he went southward, just as they, he realized, must have moved southward in ages past.

Across the Salado the coarse high grass of the pampas changed into a "fine green verdure." At first Darwin thought the change was due to some alteration in the nature of the soil. This proved not to be so. The introduction of cattle had disturbed the old order. Their grazing and manure had made the difference. Darwin pondered whether the fine new grasses resulted from the introduction of new species, from the altered growth of species already there, or from the grasses having obtained a new and favorable edge.

Part of the change, at least, he thought came from new species carried in by the cattle. The manured lands, Darwin noted in his journal, served "as channels of communication across wide districts."

On the undulating plains of the Banda Oriental, a European invader had shown what a newcomer could do. The prickly cardoon, a relative of the artichoke, had taken over hundreds of square miles and with its inpenetrable mass had made the land impassable to man or beast. Everything else had been choked out. Darwin thought it the most striking record he had seen of an "invasion on so great a scale."

The young scientist was beginning to grasp the significance of the struggle going on in nature. A change—the cattle and the importation of the cardoon—had changed the balance. The old had succumbed; the established had lost out to the new in the struggle for living-space.

This critical point became clearer as the *Beagle* worked her way up and down the coast. In some red mud capping the gravel plain above Port Julian, in Patagonia, Darwin found the fossil bones of a remarkable animal. It was as large as a camel, and it had the elongated neck of the camel and that animal's South American relative, the llama. But it also had the ponderous unmistakable build of the rhinoceros and the tapir.

Here, undoubtedly, was an ancient ancestor of the llama, whose friendly and curious attention Darwin had attracted by lying on his back and kicking his heels in the air. Here was a link between ancient and living species. Darwin sensed the full significance of his find. He wrote in his journal: "This wonderful relationship in the same continent between the dead and the living, will, I do not doubt, hereafter throw more light on the appearance of organic beings on our earth and their disappearance from it, than any other class of facts."

Such strange monsters of the past must once have swarmed

upon the continent; the pampas seemed almost to be one vast sepulcher. They had become extinct, and yet since they had lived, no great change had occurred in the land.

THE PRICKLY CARDOON. THIS EUROPEAN INVADER TOOK OVER HUNDREDS OF SQUARE MILES IN SOUTH AMERICA.

What had extinguished so many species and even whole genera? Darwin ruled out a great natural catastrophe. He himself had found fossils throughout the length of South America, and others had discovered them as far north as Bering Strait. Any moment calamitous enough to have wiped out all of them surely would have shaken the framework of the globe. Besides, Darwin already had seen enough to convince him that the changes that had altered the shape and elevation of the continent were immeasurably slow.

Darwin felt there must be some other explanation. He saw

not only what it might be, but why, "out of our great ignorance of the condition of existence of animals," the scientific world might have missed it.

Some species laid eggs by the thousands, and countless seeds wafted their way through the air from countless parent plants. Any one race would overrun the world in a short time if some check did not intervene. That a check did intervene was obvious, for even such sturdy invaders as the cardoon came to a halt, and long-established species remained fairly constant in numbers. And yet even the closest observers were seldom able to tell when the check was applied or precisely what it was.

Studying this problem, Darwin noticed that species first became rare and then extinct. In this rarity, he reasoned to himself, was the plainest evidence that less favorable conditions led to extinction. Why, then, marvel when any species ceased to exist, or assume that some calamity must account for its demise? You might as well, said Darwin, admit that sickness is a prelude to death and feel no surprise at it; and yet when death comes to the sick man insist that he died through some violence.

Other fossil finds opened other vistas—Darwin's shipmates groaned that he had brought in enough old bones to start a menagerie. Near Buenos Aires he came upon a fossil treasure; the teeth of a toxodon and of a mastodon, a fossil armadillo covered with armor like that of the existing animals, and the tooth of a fossil horse.

The last set Darwin to poring over his books and to comparing the fossil horses found in North America. The ancient animals were more nearly alike than their living descendants! "The more I reflect on this case, the more interesting it appears," Darwin wrote in his notebook. "I know of no other instance where one can almost mark the period and the manner of the splitting up of one great region into two well-characterized zoological provinces."

With his growing knowledge of geology Darwin could understand how the elevation of the Mexican plateau and the subsidence of the Caribbean area might physically have divided the continents and opened the way for the zoological divergence. At every point on the voyage the young naturalist had been studying "the vast oscillations which have affected the earth's crust within late periods." From the Río de la Plata to Tierra del Fuego, a distance of twelve hundred miles, he had determined by his own measurements that the land had been raised in mass, in Patagonia to a height of between three hundred and four hundred feet. The movement had been interrupted by eight periods of rest, while the relentless sea ate deep into the land.

At Tierra del Fuego, that storm-lashed somber land at the tip of the continent, Darwin caught a new insight into the work of ice in altering the earth—and into the differences in men. As the *Beagle* penetrated into the passages around the cape, she came upon gigantic icebergs, many "as tall as a cathedral," and riding upon some of the floating mountains of ice, great blocks of rock borne far away from their original site. Darwin also understood that the "erratic" boulders he saw lying near the lofty mountains of this strange land had been carried there by ice.

Although Darwin never forgot this wild, desolate country or its awful storms, which sent the sea spray flying over a cliff two hundred feet high, the experience etched most deeply into his thinking then and later was his meeting with the "savage" Fuegians.

The *Beagle* had come safely to anchor in Good Success Bay, a harbor sheltered from the gales and squalls. A group of Fuegians had followed the ship in. They would emerge from the dense gloomy forest that came down to the water's edge, utter a few wild cries, and dodge back into their cover. The next morning the captain sent Darwin and a party ashore to treat with them.

"It was without exception the most curious and interesting spectacle I ever beheld," Darwin wrote in his notes. "I could not have believed how wide was the difference between savage and civilized man."

The Fuegians were naked; their only protection against the cold and ice was a guanaco skin, which they tossed over their shoulders, "leaving their persons as often exposed as covered." The face of one leader was crossed by two transverse bars: one, which stretched from ear to ear and included the upper lip, a bright red, and the other which extended above and parallel to the first in such a way that even the eyelids were colored, a chalk white. They immediately tied around their necks the red cloth which the *Beagle* party presented to them.

On the first voyage of the *Beagle*, Captain Fitzroy had seized three Fuegians as hostages for a boat that had been stolen. He had taken them, and a child he had purchased for a pearl button, back to England to be educated and "instructed in religion."

One of the objects of the second voyage of the *Beagle* was to return the Fuegians to their native land. One of the men had died of smallpox, but the others, Jemmy Button (whose name identifies him), York Minster, and Fuegia Basket, went back much changed. Jemmy Button was a favorite—cheerful, smart, fond of his kid gloves and highly polished shoes. Fuegia Basket had shown a decided gift for languages, and on the voyage had picked up more than a smattering of Spanish and Portuguese to add to her English.

And yet, when the *Beagle* put into another harbor, and another party of Fuegians came out to meet the ship, they did not have even the guanaco skins for protection, and one woman, nursing a newly born child, stood for hours gazing at the *Beagle* "whilst the sleet fell and thawed on her naked bosom and the skin of her naked baby." The Fuegians slept at night on the wet ground coiled up like animals, and principally lived on shellfish or small fish they caught on hookless lines.

"Whilst beholding these savages, one asks, whence have they come?" Darwin asked. "What would have tempted a tribe of men to travel down the Cordillera or backbone of America . . . to one of the most inhospitable countries within the limits of the globe?

"Although such reflections must at first seize on the mind, yet we may feel sure they are partly erroneous. There is no reason to believe the Fuegians decrease in number. . . . Nature has fitted the Fuegian to the climate and the productions of his miserable country."

After the *Beagle* rounded Cape Horn and was sailing up the west coast of South America, Darwin was to get a first-hand view of nature in the production of more of the geologic changes he had glimpsed on the east coast. The *Beagle* was lying off the island of Chiloé when the great earthquake of February 20, 1835 shook the land. Those aboard the ship heard the explosion. Black water boiled up around them and a great tide swept across the sea.

Shortly afterward the *Beagle* entered the harbor of devastated Concepción. Darwin discovered that the land around the bay had been upraised two to three feet. At an island thirty miles away Captain Fitzroy found beds of still putrid mussels adhering to rocks ten feet above the high-water mark.

A climax to which the tremendous workings of nature had risen lay magnificently before their eyes—the Andes. Darwin made an unforgettable crossing of these great walled mountains. Returning through a 7,000-foot pass, he saw a bare slope with some snow-white projecting columns. They proved to be petrified trees. The stumps projected several feet above the ground and measured from three to five feet in circumference.

Darwin could interpret "the marvellous story which this scene at once unfolded," though he was at first so astonished he "could scarcely believe the evidence."

The trees had grown on the shores of the Atlantic at a time

when that ocean—then seven hundred miles distant—rolled
over the plains and up to the foot of the Andes. Later the trees
and the shore on which they stood sank below the still on-
coming tides. Sand drifted down upon them. In one of the
frequent upheavals of this perpetually uneasy area, a mass of
lava, at places one thousand feet thick, flowed over them. Five
times this story was repeated; sand and lava, and sand and lava
again.

Although the ocean must have been profoundly deep to
receive such masses, the majestic subterranean forces exerted
themselves again. The bed of the ocean was upthrust into a
towering range of mountains.

The wind and weather then began their work. Valleys were
cut, and in time the petrified trunks of the trees that once
waved their branches above the Atlantic were bared on the
gaunt mountain slope.

"Vast and scarcely comprehensible as such changes must
appear, yet they have occurred within a period, recent when
compared to the history of the Cordillera, and the Cordillera
itself is absolutely modern compared with the many fossiliferous strata of Europe and America," mused Darwin. His sense
of the vastness of time was taking on a vividness seldom to be
realized from books or geological time scales.

Another piece of Darwin's puzzle fitted in. The Andes were
a barrier as formidable as an ocean. He was no longer surprised, then, that the thirteen species of mice he had collected
on the Atlantic coast differed completely from the five species
obtained on the Pacific side of the mountains. The traditional
theory, which Darwin still nominally accepted, would have explained that the mice were different because they were separately created. Different kinds had been set down on different
sides of the mountains.

A passage from Darwin reveals, however, how his mind was
running. He wrote, after stating the traditional view: "otherwise the difference in the species of the two regions might be

considered as superinduced during a length of time." Obviously
Darwin was on the side of the "otherwise."

These gathering doubts about the separate creation of each
species were given dramatic new impetus when the *Beagle*

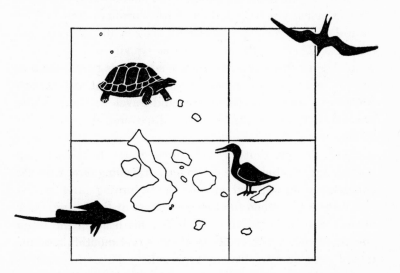

THE GALAPAGOS ARCHIPELAGO AND FOUR OF ITS STRANGE "ABO-
RIGINAL CREATURES."

reached the ten lonely islands of the Galapagos archipelago.
Among the craters, the slag, and the "cyclopean" landscape of
these remote volcanic islands crawled giant tortoises, huge
black lizards which hunted for their food in the surf, and other
weird "aboriginal creatures." And yet these rare island inhabitants revealed a certain resemblance to the similar species
on the South American mainland, a good five hundred miles
away by open ocean.

As Darwin climbed about among the gaping pits and craters
of Chatham Island, one of the first he visited, he was startled to
come upon two of the huge tortoises. One of them, which he

estimated to weigh about two hundred pounds, was calmly eating a piece of cactus. It stared at the unexpected visitor and slowly walked away. The other merely gave a deep hiss and drew in its head. They were no more alarmed and disturbed by the intruding man than were the dull-colored birds.

The monster reptiles in their setting of black lava, leafless shrubs, and large cacti seemed to Darwin like antediluvian creatures. Their habits struck him as equally strange. Broad, well-beaten paths interlaced the island, running from the seacoast to springs in the higher central section. At first Darwin could not imagine what animal would travel "so methodically along well-chosen tracks." He soon discovered that it was the tortoise.

"Near the springs it was a curious spectacle to behold many of the huge creatures, one set eagerly travelling onwards with outstretched necks, and another set returning after having drunk their fill. When the tortoise arrives at the spring, quite regardless of any spectator, he buries his head in the water above his eyes and greedily swallows great mouthfuls, at the rate of ten a minute," Darwin reported.

Later Darwin sometimes amused himself by climbing on the back of a tortoise and giving a few raps on the hind part of the shell. At this signal, almost like a horse responding to the rein, it would rise up and walk away. Darwin added that he found it difficult to keep his balance on his unusual steed.

As he studied the tortoises closely, Darwin was convinced that they were aboriginal productions, though there were certain haunting resemblances to the tortoises of the Americas.

Lizards were so abundant that Darwin found it difficult to walk without stepping into their burrows, but he could find no frogs. He suspected the reason. It was conceivable that in times past a few lizard eggs in their calcareous shells might have drifted in from South America. The slimy spawn of frogs, on the other hand, could not have survived the salt and the mauling of the sea over any such distances.

Darwin bagged twenty-six kinds of land birds. All were peculiar and were found nowhere else, except one far-ranging larklike finch. There was a hawk, curiously intermediate between a buzzard and the American group of carrion-feeding Polybori. "It might be fancied," Darwin wrote, "that a bird originally a buzzard had been induced here to undertake the office of the carrion-feeding Polybori of the American continent." Two owls, a wren, three tyrant flycatchers, and a dove were all distinct from American species and yet analogous to them.

The shells were equally revealing. Fifteen of the 16 kinds of land shells Darwin collected were peculiar to the archipelago. Out of 90 sea shells that had been found earlier, 47 were unknown elsewhere, "a wonderful fact considering how widely distributed sea shells are." Of the 43 shells that could be found in other parts of the world, 25 were from creatures inhabiting the west coast of America. The others bore the stamp of the Pacific islands.

"The fact of shells from the central part of the Pacific occurring here deserves notice," Darwin wrote, "for not a single sea shell is known to be common to the islands of that ocean and to the west coast of America. The space of open seas running north and south off the west coast separates two distinct conchological provinces, but at the Galapagos Archipelago we have a halting place, where many new forms have been created and whither two great conchological provinces have each sent several colonists."

The flowers and plants fitted into the same pattern.

"This archipelago though standing in the Pacific Ocean is zoologically part of America," Darwin decided. "If this character were merely owing to immigrants there would be little remarkable in it; but we see that a vast majority of all land animals and that more than half of the flowering plants are aboriginal productions.

"It was most striking to be surrounded by new birds, new

reptiles, new shells, new insects, new plants and yet by innumerable trifling details of structure and even by the tones of voice and plumage of the birds to have the temperate plains of Patagonia or the hot deserts of Chile brought vividly before my eyes."

A vice-governor of the islands casually told Darwin that the big lazy tortoises differed so much that he could tell from which of the islands any one of them came. The remark almost slipped by the young scientist. He did not dream that islands only fifty or sixty miles apart, with the same climate, and made of the same twisted basaltic rock, could be differently tenanted. But they were.

Darwin discovered "the truly wonderful fact" that of the 38 distinctive Galapagian plants, 30 lived only on James Island.

As Darwin delved excitedly into the best natural laboratory of evolution the world provided, he caught the clearest sight he had yet had of how all species might have originated and spread throughout the world.

Between the islands ran strong currents. Their direction was such that it was most unlikely that any egg or seed or bit of life would be carried from one to the other. The archipelago was also free of high winds. There were no gales to blow lighter birds and insects or seeds from one to the other. And finally the profound depth of the ocean between the islands and their volcanic origin indicated that they never had been united.

Very, very few migrant plants and animals or their seeds or eggs had been able to reach the isolated Galapagos; and once there, they had not been able to move to other islands in the group. Shut away from the world and from each other, the few successful immigrants had developed in their separate ways until in the end new species had been formed.

Awed at this insight, Darwin felt he had been brought near to that "great fact, the mystery of mysteries—the first appearances of new beings on earth."

The *Beagle* sailed on across the Pacific, 3,200 miles west to Tahiti. As dawn broke on the ship's arrival, the storied beauty of the islands was not visible. Great rolling clouds obscured Tahiti's green shores and revealed only the wild, precipitous peaks at the center of the island. When the clouds lifted, however, Darwin was as completely charmed as visitors have been from time immemorial. Within the reef that broke the rush of the sea stretched the smooth lagoon and beaches of coral sand covered with "the most beautiful productions of the intertropical regions."

Bananas, oranges, coconuts, breadfruit, yams, sugarcane, pineapples—even the brushwood bore a fruit, the guava. Darwin was particularly impressed with the breadfruit tree, which grew in groves and "sent forth its branches with the vigour of an English oak," and yet was loaded with large and nutritious fruit.

Darwin climbed one of the nearest slopes. The luxuriance of the beach level gave way to dwarf ferns and grasses that reminded him of Wales, for this zone was relatively dry. In the damp, cloudy upper zone Darwin was delighted with the tree ferns. But beautiful as he considered these woods, he explained scrupulously, they could not equal the "splendor" of the forests of Brazil.

And then one of those points which were later to be important in the development of his theory of evolution flashed into his mind: "The vast number of productions which characterize a continent cannot be expected to occur in an island."

Darwin succumbed completely to Tahiti when native guides took him on a climb of several days up the central peaks. They made their way along narrow paths that skirted precipices, and climbed along the edges of a double cascade that poured in falls of several hundred feet into the valley below. One night they camped on a ledge near the waterfall. In ten minutes the skillful Tahitians had heated stones and wrapped pieces of fish, beef, ripe and unripe bananas, and wild arum into leaf parcels. The green parcels were placed between the hot stones. In a quarter of an hour the food was "deliciously cooked." It was spread out on a cloth of banana leaves, and "with a cocoanut shell we drank the cool water of the running stream and thus enjoyed our rustic meal," Darwin recalled. "From our position almost suspended on the mountainside there were glimpses into the depths of the valleys, and the lofty mountains towering up within 60 degrees of the zenith, hid half the evening sky. Thus seated it was a sublime spectacle to watch the shades of night gradually obscuring the last and highest pinnacles."

New Zealand and Australia, with their English settlers extending their hold on these raw lands, caused Darwin to note that the varieties of men seemed to act on one another in much the same way as different species of animals: the stronger always extirpated the weaker.

The process was not a pleasant one to see. Darwin was shocked by the filth and degradation in which some of the natives lived. The English settlements stood in crude contrast to his nostalgic dreams of home. He was glad to leave both countries, and yet he left with this salute to Australia: "Australia! you are a rising child, and doubtless some day will reign a great princess in the South, but you are too great and ambitious for affection, and yet not great enough for respect."

Then on into the Indian Ocean and the coral atolls of the Cocos Islands. As the *Beagle* entered a still lagoon, the scene that lay before Darwin seemed a curious one to him. Its beauty, he felt, lay entirely in the brilliancy of its color.

The shallow clear water of the lagoon turned a vivid green when it "was illumined by the rays of the vertical sun." On one side, this emerald expanse was set off from the deep blue of the sea by a line of snow-white breakers. Along the remainder of its circling perimeter it was separated from the blue vault of the sky by the green tops of the coconut trees. A few white clouds flecked the azure sky in much the same way that a few bands of living coral streaked the green water of the lagoon.

Darwin sat beneath the palms his first night there and watched the moon shimmering on the spray of the reef. He had already formed a theory about that reef. It had come to him while he was studying the rise and subsidence of the coastal regions in South America.

The next day he waded out to the "living mounds of coral" on which the swell of the sea was breaking. What he saw confirmed what he thought, and it ran counter to what most observers of the time believed.

The prevailing theory was that either the reefs were built upon submerged volcanic craters, or the coral polypi had built their structures from the bottom. Darwin's gift for going to the facts demolished both ideas. No craters could have been so large or shaped as were many of the coral atolls. Suadiva was 44 miles in diameter in one direction and four miles in another; Rimsky was 54 miles wide. Bow stretched 30 miles one way and only 6 the other.

As for being built up from the ocean depths, Darwin saw that corals could live only within twenty to thirty fathoms of the sea's surface. Depth was the key. Darwin reasoned that the atolls could be built only on a base no more than twenty to thirty fathoms down.

As he saw it, mountains that once had thrust their peaks above the sea had slowly subsided. As they sank, bases were afforded for the growth of the corals. The endlessly persistent little animals built their branching, indestructible reefs wherever there were bases within their reach and water temperatures favorable to them.

"We see in each barrier reef a proof that the land there has subsided and in each atoll a monument over an island now lost," Darwin wrote in his journal. "We may thus gain some insight into the great system by which the surface of the globe has been broken up and the land and water interchanged."

After briefly touching again at South America, the *Beagle*

returned to England. Five years and a world had passed by since she had left her harbor there on a gray day in 1831. The fledgling young naturalist who had sailed with her had become a seasoned scientist. Some portions of his journal, sent home

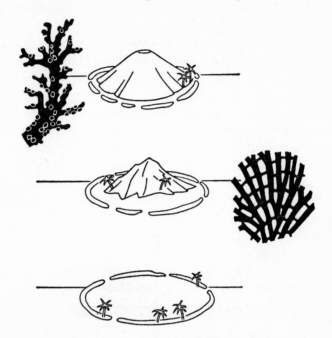

EVOLUTION OF A CORAL ATOLL. A VOLCANIC CONE THRUSTS HIGH ABOVE THE SEA "LIKE A CASTLE SITUATED ON THE SUMMIT OF A LOFTY SUBMARINE MOUNTAIN." USING THE SUBMERGED SLOPES AS A BASE, CORAL POLYPI BUILD THEIR REEF.

THE PEAK BEGINS TO WEATHER AWAY. THE PEAK HAS DISAPPEARED BENEATH THE WAVES. ONLY THE LIVING CORAL REEF REMAINS, "A MONUMENT OVER AN ISLAND NOW LOST."

ahead of him, had been read before the Philosophical Society. The reports had created so much interest that the society printed them in a 31-page pamphlet for distribution to its members.

The fossils and other specimens that Darwin also had shipped back at intervals—partly because the *Beagle* could not possibly have held them all—had also excited the scientists who saw them. Sedgwick, Darwin's professor of geology at Cambridge, called on Dr. Darwin and told him his son would take a place "among leading scientific men."

But it was the comparisons Darwin had made and the generalizations he was drawing from them that were to rank the voyage of the *Beagle* among the great voyages of all time. By the time Darwin returned, he was keenly aware that the differences and similarities of life were not matters of chance or of a Creator's whim. The inhabitants of the earth were alike, he was beginning to see, because they had descended from common ancestors.

But on October 2, 1836, when the *Beagle* docked at Falmouth, all of this was only in the mind of a very homesick young man.

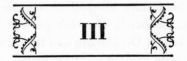

III

CHARLES DARWIN

ORIGINS

Proof of the great natural laws often is not found until long after their discovery. The evidence to support the earlier-born theory of the undulation of light and the belief that the earth revolved on its own axis was not brought forth until Darwin's day.

Darwin, however, not only stated the theory of evolution; at the same time he assembled the monumental evidence to support it. In this dual achievement lay his greatest genius and his enduring fame.

This approach was part of his nature, an inherent thing. His extreme humility and caution would not permit him to advance any belief until he had backed it with every possible fact. And even then he was not satisfied. He liked to think that he worked on pure Baconian principles, collecting facts on a massive scale, without any preconceived theory about them.

It is true that this man, venturing into fields untouched, kept a remarkably open mind. He sought counterarguments, weighed them, took them into the fullest account, and willingly yielded if the facts fell on the other side. Nevertheless, it is doubtful if any worker in science ever directed a search more persistently or pointedly to one end.

The idea of species that the voyage of the *Beagle* had awakened in him stayed constantly in his mind, though he spent the first two years after his return putting his collections in order and preparing his journal of the voyage for publication. To his genuine surprise and pleasure the *Journal* sold well when it came out in 1839. The second edition went to 10,000 copies. The book also did well in the United States, where it was called *The Voyage of the Beagle.*

Not until July 1837, however, did Darwin begin his first formal notebook on the origin of species. He modestly hoped, by collecting all the facts that bore in any way on the variation of animals and plants, to "throw some light on the whole subject."

It was June 1842, Darwin wrote later in his autobiography, "before I first allowed myself the satisfaction of writing a brief abstract of my theory in pencil in 35 pages." This was enlarged during the summer of 1844 into a 230-page statement, which he copied out and showed to a few close associates.

A letter written about this time to Sir Joseph Dalton Hooker, his close friend and a fellow scientist, tells us: "I have been ever since my return engaged in a very presumptuous work and I know no one individual who would not say a very foolish one. . . .

"I was so struck with the distribution of the Galapagos organisms etc. etc. and with the character of the American fossil mammifers etc. etc. that I determined to collect blindly every sort of fact which could bear in any way on what are species. I have read heaps of agricultural and horticultural books and have never ceased collecting facts. At last gleams of light have come, and I am almost convinced (quite contrary to the opinion I started with) that species are not (it is like confessing a murder) immutable."

For twenty years Darwin continued collecting his facts. He experimented. He read, underlining, abstracting, cutting books in two if that was the easiest way to keep them. He corresponded regularly with Hooker, the director of Kew Gardens, with Asa Gray, the American botanist, and with other scientists. And he planned a definitive book. Although his friends were urging him to hurry with the writing, he still felt he was not ready. Perhaps he never would have been truly ready, for his subject, life itself, was infinite.

Then came one of those classic coincidences of science, unexpected, improbable, strange beyond imagination.

In June 1858, when Darwin had been at work for more than twenty years on his enormous project, a letter arrived from Alfred Russel Wallace, a naturalist then working in Malaya. It contained an essay "On the Tendency of Varieties to Depart Indefinitely from the Original Type." There, in the slender manuscript that had dropped out of the mails, was Darwin's theory; all of it was there, set forth clearly and ably. Wallace had independently arrived at the same conclusions. Darwin was stunned.

To his friend and adviser, the noted geologist Sir Charles Lyell, he poured out his shock:

"Your words have come true with a vengeance—that I should be forestalled.

"I never saw a more striking coincidence; if Wallace had my MS sketch written out in 1842 he could not have made a better short abstract!

"Even his terms now stand as heads of my chapters.

"So all my originality, whatever it may amount to will be smashed, though my book, if it will ever have any value will not be deteriorated; as all the labour consists in the application of the theory."

Wallace had asked Darwin, if he thought well of his essay, to send it to Lyell. This Darwin did, with the same letter from which the above words are taken.

Even at this first jarring moment, Darwin decided immediately and characteristically that he would offer to send Wallace's manuscript to one of the scientific journals. He also wrote Lyell that he hoped he would approve Wallace's sketch and give him permission to tell Wallace of Lyell's approval. Darwin also wrote to Lyell: "I would far rather burn my whole book than that he (Wallace) or any other man should think I had behaved in a paltry spirit."

Lyell and Hooker, who also had been informed at once of what had happened, were intensely disturbed. They quickly proposed a joint presentation before the Linnean Society of Wallace's essay and of Darwin's 1844 abstract, plus a letter that Darwin had written to Asa Gray on September 5, 1857, outlining the cardinal points in the theory.

In their letter to the society submitting these materials, Lyell and Hooker said that they had approved Darwin's plan to publish Wallace's essay "provided Mr. Darwin did not withhold from the public, as he was strongly inclined to do (in favour of Mr. Wallace) the memoir which he himself had written on the subject, and which as before stated, one of us had perused in 1844, and the contents of which we had both of us been privy to for many years." The two scientists explained that they were not "solely considering the relative claims to priority of Darwin and Wallace," but the "interests of science generally."

The Linnean Society met on July 1, 1858, and the work of both men was read by the secretary. Neither was present. When the reading ended, silence fell. There was no discussion.

Some of those present realized they had lived through a historic moment, though they could not have known that the words they had just heard would thereafter radically change the thought of the scientific and lay worlds. Hooker said that under the silence lay sharp excitement.

The overwhelmed members of the society had come together to hear a paper by George Bentham, asserting the fixity of species. To be told that the exact opposite was true was so novel and ominous, Hooker reported, that "the old school" did not dare "to enter the lists before armouring." Nevertheless, the effect was so startling that Bentham at once withdrew his own paper, not because he agreed with what had been said, but because he instantly recognized that the whole basis had changed.

At Lyell and Hooker's urgent advice, Darwin began at once to prepare an abstract of his work for publication in a scientific journal. As he worked, he soon saw he could not condense even an abstract into the size of a journal article. It grew into a book. By unremitting effort, despite constant ill health, Darwin finished his book-size abstract in thirteen months and ten days.

It was *The Origin of Species*. Darwin's original title for it had been *An Abstract of an Essay on the Origin of Species and Varieties through Natural Selection or the Preservation of Favoured Races in the Struggle for Life.*

The 1,250 copies printed were snatched up instantly and the publisher called for a second edition. And from this point on, the storm gathered. British men of science lined up on one side or the other. The reviews poured in, some favorable, some scathing. The *Times* gave *The Origin* an extraordinary, favorable three-and-a-half column article, brilliantly analyzing the whole theory. It had been written by T. H. Huxley.

The opening furore came to a head at a meeting of the British Association for the Advancement of Science in Oxford in June 1860. After a mild beginning, Samuel Wilberforce, Bishop of Oxford, tore into the doctrine. He ridiculed Darwin's "proofs," and, turning to Huxley, who sat on the platform, asked in tones icy with sarcasm whether it was through his grandmother or grandfather that he claimed descent from a monkey.

Huxley whispered: "The Lord hath delivered him into my hands." He lashed into the bishop's arguments; working up to his climax, he shouted that he would prefer an ape to the bishop as an ancestor.

At this direct insult to the clergy, the jammed room was thrown into confusion. Lady Brewster fainted. Admiral Robert Fitzroy, the extremely devout and excitable former captain of the *Beagle*, waved a Bible aloft and screamed over the tumult that it, not the viper he once had harbored in his ship, was the unimpeachable authority.

In all of *The Origin* there had been no discussion of the origin of man. In a sole sentence in his conclusion Darwin had said that his theory of species might throw light on the origin of man and his history. But the argument was on. It was to rage unabated from that time forward.

The Origin of Species, as Julian Huxley, grandson of T. H. Huxley, Darwin's fiery defender, has shown, is based on three observable groups of fact and two deductions drawn from them.

Darwin's first great fact is the tendency of all organisms to increase in geometrical ratio.

Even slow-breeding man, Darwin saw in his day, had doubled his numbers in twenty-five years. Linnæus had calculated that if an annual plant produced only two seeds—and no plant is so unproductive—and if the chain continued in this way, there would be a million plants in existence in twenty years.

Darwin pointed out that even the slowest breeder of them all, the elephant, would soon overrun the world if unchecked. He estimated that if a pair of elephants brought forth six young and if their descendants continued to breed at the same rate, 19,000,000 elephants would be crashing about the world in 750 years.

Darwin did not have to rely on calculations alone to prove his point. He had seen how the prickly cardoon ran riot when it suddenly found new and favorable conditions in South America. "Lighten any check, mitigate the destruction ever so little, and the number of the species will almost instantaneously increase to any amount," Darwin warned in *The Origin*.

This led to Darwin's second great fact. In spite of the tendency to multiply, the numbers of a given species remain more or less constant. Even the runaways sooner or later came to a halt. The established species tended to remain fairly constant.

From these two major facts Darwin drew his first essential deduction: there is a struggle for existence, a universal struggle for life.

By these words Darwin was presupposing not only a tooth-and-claw battle. He meant far more: he meant the dependence of one being on another; he meant, beyond the struggle of the individual to survive, his success in leaving progeny. In this sense a plant on the edge of the desert could be said to be in a struggle for life against drought.

Darwin cleared a plot of ground three feet long by two feet wide and counted all the native weeds that came up. Exactly 357 reared their heads, and out of this number 295 were destroyed, principally by birds and slugs. The weed's struggle was arduous.

In Surrey there was an old heath where cattle had roamed from time immemorial. And above the heath on the hilltops were a few clumps of Scotch fir. In Darwin's time a part of the heath was enclosed and the cattle shut out.

At once Scotch firs sprang up by the million. After making sure they had not been planted, Darwin began to investigate. Looking closely between the stems of the heather, he found a multitude of seedlings and little firs whose tops formerly had been nibbled off by the cattle. In one square yard he counted thirty-one. The cattle had kept them down in the struggle for existence; as soon as the cattle were gone, up they came.

On the open part of the heath where the cattle still browsed, Darwin could not find one young fir tree.

"What a play of forces, determining the kind and proportion of each plant in a square yard of turf," he wrote to Hooker.

"Battle within battle must be continually recurring," Darwin said in *The Origin*. And yet in the long run, he noted, forces are so nicely balanced that the face of nature remains uniform for long periods.

By experiment, Darwin learned that the visits of bees were

necessary for the fertilization of some kinds of clover. When he shut the bees away, the clover produced not a seed. He saw also that only bumblebees visited one kind of red clover. Without them it would have disappeared. And the number of bumblebees depended on how many of their nests were destroyed by field mice. And the number of mice depended on the number of cats round about. Near villages where many cats were kept, the red clover flourished. There it had an edge in the battle.

The battle, however, was keenest between individuals and varieties of the same species. An imported bee, Darwin had seen, drove out the stingless native Australian bee. The Asiatic cockroach defeated the Russian variety.

Thus Darwin came to his third great fact: all living things vary. Few disputed the point; it was obvious to all with eyes to see, and even more evident to the scientist who compared closely. Darwin, comparing rigorously, found that every part varied to some slight degree in every species.

Can we doubt (remembering that more individuals are born than can possibly survive), can we doubt, asked Darwin, that individuals with some advantage, however slight, have the best chance of surviving and procreating their kind? Or that those with injurious variations will be destroyed?

This was Darwin's second major deduction. He called it natural selection, or the survival of the fittest.

The leaf-eating insect whose green most perfectly matched that of the leaf on which it lived had the best chance of living and producing offspring. And so it was with bark-feeders colored and patterned like the tree trunks and branches; with alpine ptarmigans protected by a winter coat of white; and with the red grouse in the heather. They were best sheltered. They had the best chance of escaping birds and beasts of prey.

And natural selection worked in far more complex ways to adapt living things to one another and to their environment. A friend sent Darwin an orchid, preserved in spirits of wine, that demonstrated to what extraordinarily fine lengths adaptation can be carried. The lower lip of the orchid Coryanthes forms a great bucket that is kept half filled with pure water from two secreting horns that stand above it. In another hollow chamber are some curious fleshy ridges. "The most ingenious man, if he had not witnessed what takes place, could never have imagined what purpose all these parts serve," marveled Darwin.

Darwin's specimen showed. Crowds of bees visit the huge flower of the orchid not only to suck its nectar but to gnaw off the fleshy ridges in the chamber above the bucket. In the competition for the delicacy, some of the bees are pushed into the bucket of water. With their wings wet, they cannot fly away, but are compelled to crawl through a passage in such a way that they rub against the viscid stigma and the viscid glands of the pollen masses. The pollen masses are thus glued to the back of the bees and carried away, ultimately to fertilize other orchids.

Darwin's friend saw a "continual procession" of bees crawling out of their involuntary bath, and in the orchid he sent to Darwin was one of them, killed with the pollen mass still fastened to its back.

The laden bees then fall into another orchid bucket, and as they again crawl out, the viscid stigma catches the pollen on their back and the flower is fertilized.

"Now at last we see the full use of every part of the flower, of the water-secreting horns, of the bucket half full of water which prevents the bees from flying away and forces them to crawl through the spout and rub against the properly placed viscid pollen masses and the viscid stigma," Darwin said. In time, through such processes, living things became almost perfectly modified and adapted to each other and "to the wondrous and exquisitely beautiful contingencies to which every living being is exposed."

Charles Darwin at the age of seventy-two. He is wearing the soft black hat and short cloak that he always used for cool days in his garden at Down House.

PLATE I

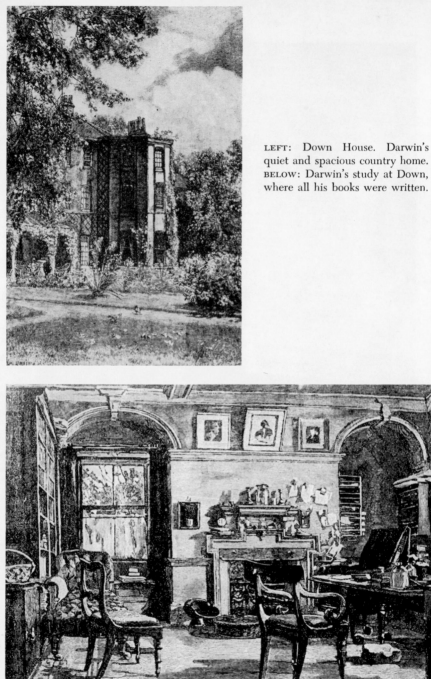

LEFT: Down House. Darwin's quiet and spacious country home. BELOW: Darwin's study at Down, where all his books were written.

PLATE II

Sir Arthur Keith, noted anthropologist who later lived on the Darwin estate, standing by the "old oak" at the entrance to Darwin's well-loved "sand-walk."

PLATE III

Cope's own field sketch of *Elasmosaurus platyurus Cope*. This prehistoric Kansas monster coul[d] raise its snakelike body above the water and sway its head in a circle with a twenty-foot radiu[s]

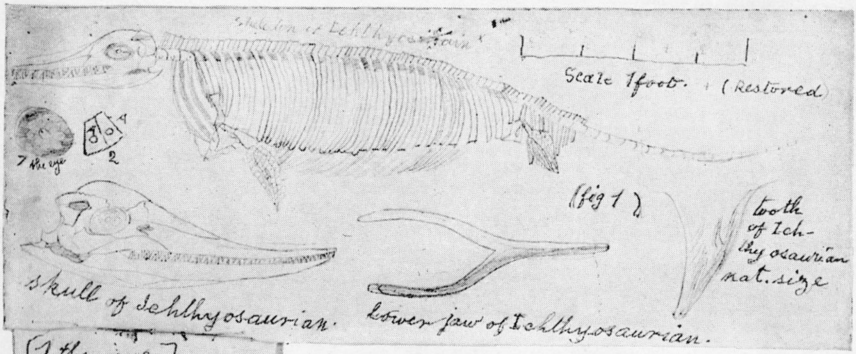

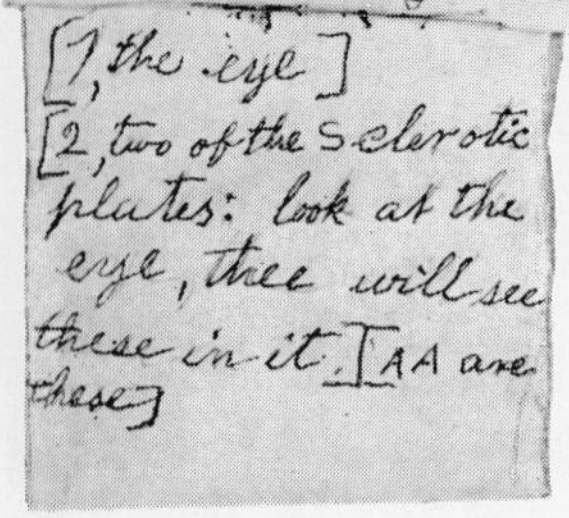

At the age of ten, Cope sketched Ichthyosaurus in the Philadelphia Museum of Natural History.

PLATE IV

The Horned Lizard
ad th..... siduestris(...)
£5 X 15 feet. Forest and .....

The horned lizard as Cope thought it had looked.

Cope's notebook sketch of the fin-back lizard.

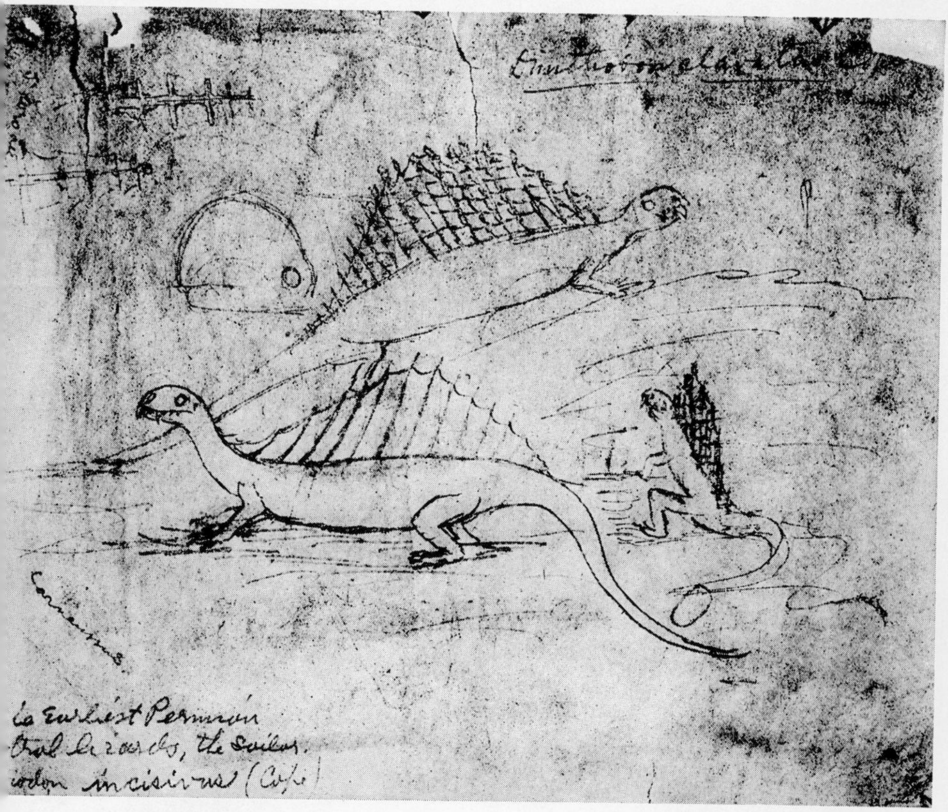

...e Earliest Permian
...bal lizards, the Sailor,
...odon incisivus (Cope)

PLATE V

Diplodocus Marsh. A restoration drawing of one of the fantastic creatures found by Cope's great rival, Professor Marsh.

A restoration painting of Cope's fin-back lizard, later found to be incorrect in some details.

PLATE VI

The domed nest of the South American village bird, which helps the brightly colored female to survive.

One of the great sea serpents that Cope dug from the Kansas limestone. A restoration.

PLATE VII

Alfred Russel Wallace. He arrived independently at the principles of evolution.

Lamarck. He insisted that acquired characteristics may be inherited.

Hugo de Vries. The Dutch botanist who showed that changes may occur by mutation.

Edward Drinker Cope. A master naturalist who unearthed fossil wealth in the West.

PLATE VIII

By the piling up of such variations in one direction, Darwin reasoned, new species ultimately would be produced.

Simple as this thesis sounds, it was beset with many knotty problems. Why did plants and animals descended from common stock tend to diverge in character as they became modified?

For years Darwin wrestled with this important question. Then, one day while he was out driving in his carriage, the solution flashed into his mind—he always remembered the exact spot in the road.

The brilliant answer was essentially simple. The more diversified a species became, the more likely its members were to be able to seize upon any new area or opening in nature. And thus they were the ones able to increase.

Among the carnivorous quadrupeds, for example, the species that increased were those which varied so that they were able to feed on new kinds of prey, or to inhabit colder or warmer lands, or to climb trees or live in the water. In nature it paid to be different. The different survived and spread. Inevitably the descendants differed from their ancestors.

In the long run, the big groups producing the most variations—such as the fish, the reptiles, and man—predominated on the earth. As another accurate observer of nature remarked many years later: "Them as has, gets."

By the same token, the smaller groups, which did not produce enough variations to let them take over new homes and new food, lost out. They became rare and disappeared.

"It is a truly wonderful fact," Darwin wrote in *The Origin,* "the wonder of which we are apt to overlook with familiarity—that all animals and all plants throughout all time should be related to each other in groups and sub-groups."

A myriad of additional problems surrounded these facts and major deductions. Why did all living things vary? How were the variations accumulated?

The laws of genetics were not known in Darwin's time. Over and over again Darwin was forced to say: "Our ignorance of the laws of variation is profound. Not in one case out of a hundred can we pretend to assign any reason why this or that part has varied."

He was impressed during his long studies of selection and the breeding of domestic plants and animals with the fact that the breeder could "never act by selection, except on variations which are first given him in some slight degree by nature."

At the same time Darwin was fairly well convinced that the conditions of life also affect inheritance. Certainly the fur of animals living in the north is thicker. Shells are pinker in the south, and insects smaller in the mountains.

"Who can tell," he asked, "how much of the difference may be due to the warmest-clad individuals having been favoured and preserved during many generations and how much to the action of the severe climate, for it would appear the climate has some direct action on the hair of our domestic quadrupeds."

Darwin was also puzzled by the winglessness of many of the beetles on the wind-swept Madeira Islands. When the wind blew, they hid—or they would have been blown out to sea. In any event, they did not use their wings, and many of them lost them. Perhaps disuse was a factor in their disappearance.

Darwin was inclined to attribute the winglessness of the beetles to a combination of natural selection and disuse. Yet, as he continued his work, he often wavered by placing a preponderant emphasis upon disuse as a factor in inheritance.

The rediscovery in 1900 that heredity is contained in the germ cells alone dealt a death-blow to the theory of use and disuse.[1] For a while Darwin's whole theory was to be severely discredited because of its grave weakness on this point.

Darwin's solution of some of the other technical problems involved in his theory of the origin of species was more successful. If living things originated from a single beginning at

[1] See Chapter ix, on Mendel.

a single point on the earth, how had they spread around the world, over the oceans, mountains, and other barriers?

Geologists in the middle of the nineteenth century imagined the continents rising and falling almost like so many banks of elevators. Although this notion would have made it easy for Darwin to get plants and animals from one continent to another, he rejected it. He insisted upon the infinite slowness of the movements that had connected and disconnected continents. But he did maintain that far, far in the past, land bridges had existed over which dry-land animals might have migrated dry-shod.

Some of Darwin's most ingenious experiments were devised to test how plants and animals might have reached the oceanic islands, the islands that could never have been connected to the continents.

Could seeds have floated in, as he suspected? Darwin soaked some in a tank of snow-water. They began to smell and emitted so much mucus, he playfully wrote Hooker, that he expected them to turn into tadpoles. But cress and lettuce seed germinated after twenty-one days' immersion. In a sea current traveling a mile an hour, these seeds could have traveled 168 miles in a week, and lived to grow!

Or perhaps seeds were carried to such remote islands as the Galapagos by fish and birds. To test the theory Darwin fed some water-soaked seeds to fish in tanks at the always co-operative Zoological Society.

"In my imagination," he wryly wrote Hooker, "they had been swallowed, fish and all, by a heron, had been carried a hundred miles, been voided on the banks of some lake and germinated splendidly, when behold, the fish ejected vehemently, and with a disgust equal to my own, all the seeds from their mouths."

Later the experiment succeeded. Darwin fed aquatic grass seed to fish and fed the fish to a stork. In due time the seeds were voided, and they germinated. From a ball of mud taken

from a bird's plumage, Darwin raised eighty-two plants belonging to five separate species!

The routes of travel of many of the oceanic migrants were
thus mapped.

Nearly all of Darwin's colossal work was done at Down,
the quiet country house he purchased soon after his marriage
in 1842 to his cousin Emma Wedgwood. Although it was only
sixteen miles from London, it was so out of the way that visitors
had a difficult time reaching it. Its remoteness and the placid
Surrey countryside suited the kind of life Darwin then knew he
would have to live.

Not long after his return from the voyage, his health had
broken. For the rest of his life he suffered extreme fatigue,
headaches, and a nausea that became acute with the least excitement. Work, or mere existence, was often a severe ordeal,
though there was no clear medical explanation of his illness.

Partly through this circumstance and partly because of the
unusual character of Darwin's work and disposition, life at
Down had the quality of a Victorian pastoral, a rare evenness,
a warm formality, an other-century gentleness.

Darwin usually awoke early and went out into the garden
for an early walk. He liked to tell his children how once or
twice he had met foxes trotting home at dawn.

After breakfasting alone, at seven forty-five he went immediately to work. The period between eight and half past
nine was one of his most productive working times. At nine
thirty he went down to the drawing-room for his mail, rejoicing, his son Sir Francis Darwin said, if the post was a light
one and worrying if it was not. While he lay on a sofa, Emma,
or in later years one of the seven children, read aloud family
letters or a novel until half past ten. At that time he went back
to work and remained at it until shortly after noon. By that
time he felt that the most important part of the day's work was
done.

He then went for his midday walk. Generally it began with

a call at the greenhouse, where he always had experiments under way, and continued with a turn around the "sand-walk." The sand-walk was actually a gravel one bordering an acre-and-a-half stretch of lawn. To one side was a small wood, and beyond the low quickset hedge on the other side there was a small valley in which grew hazel and larch. The charm and peacefulness of this valley view had originally drawn Darwin to Down, and he never tired of it.

As he strolled, often accompanied by Polly, his terrier, he played with the children and inspected the gardens. He took no personal part in the management of the garden, but knew every flower and could not help personalizing them. "The little beggars are doing just what I don't want them to," he would remark half admiringly.

After luncheon there was another period of rest in the drawing-room and more reading aloud. Then Darwin would take his place in a hugh horsehair chair by the fire to read the newspapers and work on his correspondence.

Another rest in his bedroom, another hour and a half of work, dinner, two games of backgammon with his wife, and more reading aloud completed the placid routine of his day. Frequently this careful schedule was interrupted by severe illness, but only rarely by a trip to London or to a water cure, or by visitors.

Darwin ably managed the sizable property he inherited from his father, keeping his accounts with great care and balancing them at the end of the year, almost like a merchant, his son said. By the standards of the day he was a rich man and had to give no thought to earning a living.

He was wonderfully liberal with his children. His son Sir Francis recalled that when his father settled some college debts of his, he "almost made it seem a virtue in me to have told him of them." In his own youth, particularly when he was on the voyage of the *Beagle,* Darwin always was deeply apologetic when he called on his father for funds. "Tell father," he wrote

to his sister in 1834, "I have kept my promise of being extrava-
gant in Chile. I have drawn a bill for £100. £50 goes to the
captain for the ensuing year, and £30 I take to sea for the
small ports; so that bona fide I have not spent £180 these last
four months. I hope not to draw another bill for six months."

And again just before the *Beagle* sailed out across the Pacific: "In September we will leave the coast of America; and
my Father will believe I *will* not draw money in crossing the
Pacific, because I *cannot*. My travelling expenses are nothing;
but when I reach a point as Coquimbo, whilst my horses are
resting, I hear of something very wonderful 100 miles off.

"A muleteer offers to take me for so many dollars, and I
cannot, or rather never have, resisted the Temptation. My
father's patience must be exhausted."

Actually Dr. Darwin made no objection to meeting his son's
expenses.

Darwin was about six feet tall. When he stretched his ham-
mock in the small cabin of the *Beagle,* he had to remove some
books from a shelf to make room for his feet, and in later years
he always was looking for high-seated chairs. He sometimes
built up a chair to suit him by putting a footstool on it.

His eyes were bluish gray under deep overhanging brows
and thick eyebrows. Despite his illness his face was smooth and
ruddy, and he once wrote to Hooker: "Everyone tells me that
I look quite blooming and beautiful, and most think I am
shamming, but you have never been one of those." This
thoughtful, gentle face was made more severe in later years
by a full, almost untrimmed beard.

In the excitement of pleasant talk Darwin's manner was
bright and animated. His hands frequently were in use to explain a point—perhaps how a flower is fertilized, or perhaps
some animals he had seen on the voyage of the *Beagle*.

The brooding mood shown in the famous photograph of
him on his veranda did not seem typical to those who knew him
well. But the cape in which he was wrapped in that picture

was the one he wore habitually in the garden. He had one other idiosyncrasy of dress. In the house he nearly always wore a shawl over his shoulders and big, loose fur-lined cloth boots that he could slip on over his indoor shoes.

During the twenty years he piled up material for *The Origin of Species* Darwin also worked for a solid eight years on a study of barnacles. An odd little barnacle he found burrowing in a shell on the coast of Chile—instead of merely clinging as all good barnacles should have done—got him into this labor.

The Chile barnacle was so unusual that he set out to dissect and compare it with other forms. Darwin was no more able to let go than one of his barnacles, and continued until he had described all known species in two thick volumes. He was fond of saying to his children: "It's dogged does it," but the barnacle study stretched to such lengths that Darwin knew Sir E. Lytton Bulwer had him in mind when the novelist caricatured a Professor Long who had written two huge volumes on limpets.

Following the publication of *The Origin,* Darwin wrote another book on variations in plants and animals under domestication, and did studies of orchids and climbing plants.

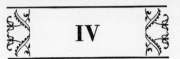

IV

CHARLES DARWIN
UP AT LAST TO MAN

ONE MAJOR and inevitable work remained.

Back in the 1830's, when Darwin had become convinced that species are mutable, he "could not avoid" the thought that man must come under the same law. For his own satisfaction, he told himself, he collected notes on the origin and descent of man—in some of the big portfolios into which he always slipped reserve materials.

He did not use this evidence in *The Origin* because he thought it unfair to parade his views without giving all the material to support them. And time did not permit that. But Darwin also was fearful of the prejudices he knew would be aroused by any out-and-out statement that man had descended from lower animals.

When he was in the midst of writing *The Origin of Species,* Wallace asked him in a letter if he would discuss man. Darwin's answer was: "I think I shall avoid the whole subject, as so surrounded with prejudices; though I fully admit that it is the highest and most interesting problem for the naturalist." Nevertheless, his scrupulous regard for the whole truth made him feel that he could not conceal his views.

Many years later, in his autobiography, Darwin explained the famous sentence with which he resolved his conflict: "Although in *The Origin of Species* the derivation of any particular species is never discussed, yet I thought it best, in order that no honorable man should accuse me of concealing my views, to add that by the work 'light would be thrown on the origin of man and his history.'"

The one statement, and of course the inescapable implications of the whole book, bestirred the furore Darwin had dreaded. Passions and prejudices were unleashed as fully as though he had spelled out word by word his argument that man is not a special creation.

But the acceptance that *The Origin of Species* met from the scientists whose opinion he most valued changed Darwin's mind in the end. Ten years later he decided it would be advisable "to work up such notes as I possessed and publish a special treatise on the origin of man." Darwin also wanted to discuss sexual selection, a subject that greatly interested him and on which he had collected voluminous material.

He was then free to use all his data and did not have to suffer, as he did in writing *The Origin,* from the thought that he could present only an abstract. The work thus took three years. Out of it came, in 1871, *The Descent of Man, and Selection in Relation to Sex.*

Its one great conclusion is that man is descended from an earlier form of life, ultimately from that filament of which his grandfather, Dr. Erasmus Darwin, had written.

"He who wishes to decide whether man is the modified descendant of some pre-existing form would probably first enquire whether man varies, however slightly in bodily structures and in mental faculties; and if it is so, whether the variations are transmitted to his offspring in accordance with the laws which prevail with the lower animals," Darwin began.

He further defined his problem: Are the variations the result, "as far as our ignorance permits us to judge," of the same causes? Does man give rise to varieties and sub-races? Does man increase at a rate so rapid as to lead to occasional severe struggles for existence?

Darwin turned first, however, to the bodily structure of man. Did it show traces, more or less plain, of his descent from other forms?

He found the similarity striking. All the bones of the skeleton could be compared with the corresponding bones in a "monkey, bat or seal." The muscles, the nerves, the blood vessels, the viscera, were similar. So too was the brain, even to the pattern of its convolutions.

Darwin thought some less obvious points equally revealing. Man could contract hydrophobia, cholera, and other diseases from animals and transmit some of his own ills to them. To Darwin this spoke more plainly of the close similarity of blood and tissues "than any comparison under the microscope or by the aid of the best chemical analysis." Even the same parasites, internal and external, plagued both, and evolved with their hosts.

Furthermore, the wounds of both were repaired by the same process of healing, and the reproduction of the species was essentially the same in all mammals "from the first act of courtship by the male to the birth and nurturing of the young."

There was another proof, uncanny, mysterious, and recurrent. Each animal in its own embryonic development accurately, though briefly, relived the history of its race. Almost as in the beginning of life, man developed from a single cell, from an ovule one 125th of an inch in diameter, a cell that differed in no respect from the ovules of other animals.

Darwin felt certain that most of his readers would never have seen a drawing of a human embryo. He had one reproduced just above another scale drawing of the embryo of a dog at the same stage, and point by point indicated how each testifies to their joint immemorial descent from older and simpler ancestors.

In the necks of both were gill-like slits, strange and transient reminders that all life began in the seas. And there was the heart, no more than a simple pulsating vessel in both. In the human embryo the os coccyx extended, like a true tail, well beyond the rudimentary legs.

Darwin felt that he could do no better than quote Huxley, who, after asking if man originates differently from the dog, bird, frog, or fish, gave this answer: "The reply is not doubtful for a moment; without question, the mode of origin and the early stage of development of man are identical with those of the animals immediately below him in the scale."

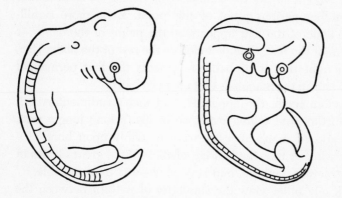

EMBRYO OF MAN (LEFT) AND DOG (RIGHT). AT THIS STAGE THE TWO ARE VERY MUCH ALIKE. IN THE NECKS OF BOTH ARE GILL-LIKE SLITS, TRANSIENT REMINDERS THAT THEIR ANCESTORS ONCE LIVED IN THE SEA. THE HUMAN OS COCCYX PROJECTS LIKE A TRUE TAIL, WELL BEYOND THE RUDIMENTARY LEGS.

The gills would close and the tail disappear well before birth, but, Darwin emphasized, every man and animal would carry with him throughout life a number of structures, useless to his present life, but once perhaps essential to some remote ancestor. These were the leftovers, the rudiments, explainable only if living things had descended from other living creatures. Darwin cited an interesting list of them: unused remnants of the muscles with which horses and many other animals twitch their skin; rudiments of the muscles with which ancestral animals once cocked and turned their ears. Sometimes the latter were scarcely rudimentary. Darwin had seen a man who could move his ears forward, and he collected reports of others who could move them upward and even backward.

"There can be little doubt," he continued, "that the hairs scattered over the body are the rudiments of the uniform hairy coat of the lower animals." The fine wool-like hair, called the lanugo, which covers the human fetus during its sixth month was another curious proof of this point. Even more significantly, none of the hair appears on the palms of the hands or the soles of the feet, though it clothes the rest of the body. Darwin thought that it probably represents the first permanent coat of hair in the mammals that are born hairy.

Wisdom teeth, the appendix, and man's rudimentary tail were further and telling evidence of man's long jungle past. The marks of man's ancestry were indelibly upon him.

Darwin felt that the bearing of these three great classes of fact—structure, embryo, and rudiments—was unmistakable.

"On any other view the similarity of pattern between the hand of a man or monkey, the foot of a horse, the flipper of a seal, the wing of a bat etc., is utterly inexplicable," he wrote. "It is no scientific explanation to assert that all have been formed on the same ideal plan.

"No other explanation has ever been given of the marvellous fact that the embryos of a man, dog, seal, bat, reptile etc. can at first hardly be distinguished from each other." Consequently, Darwin argued, "we ought frankly to admit" our community of descent. It seemed to him only prejudice and arrogance for men to insist upon their descent from demigods.

But could natural selection, perhaps abetted by other means, account for man's development from some primate ancestor? Without any fossil remains to show him what had happened, Darwin was forced to struggle with this crucial problem as best he could.

If "some ancient member" of the great order of primates had become less arboreal, he theorized, its whole manner of moving about would have changed. Did not baboons that had learned to live upon the ground in hilly and rocky districts acquire "almost the gait of a dog"? "Man alone has become a biped, and we can, I think, partly see how he has come to assume his erect attitude," said Darwin.

The story, as Darwin reconstructed it, went something like this:

Man could not have attained his present "dominant position" in the world without the use of his hands. But the hands could not have become "perfect enough" to have made weapons or hurled stones or spears with true aim as long as they had to be habitually used for locomotion. Thus it would have been a tremendous advantage to become a biped.

To gain this decisive advantage, the feet would have to become flatter, better adapted to support and walking. Once this had happened and man had gained the pre-eminent advantage of having his hands and arms free, it undoubtedly would become advantageous for him to grow more erect and more bipedal. And those who varied more in this direction would be the ones most likely to survive and leave progeny. Darwin pointed out that the gorilla with its sidewise shambling gait and the Hylobates, which can walk upright with "tolerable quickness," are living proof that a gait somewhere in between that of the quadruped and man is possible.

As the manner of walking changed, Darwin saw that other bodily changes would be necessary. He pointed out that the pelvis would have to be broadened, the spine curved "peculiarly," and the head carried in a new position.

Although not an expert anatomist, he was remarkably aware that one change often brings others in its train. Whether it was through natural selection or "the inherited effects of the increased use of certain parts," Darwin was not sure. But he noted: "The free use of the hands and arms, partly the cause and partly the result of man's erect position, appears to have led in an indirect manner to other modifications of structure."

He caught sight of another fact only recently established

by the newest experimental anthropology—a change in the powerful jaw muscle can affect the shape of the skull. It is the pull of heavy jaw muscles that produces the heavy ridges and protuberances in the skulls of the apes, and thus accounts for their "truly frightful physiognomy," Darwin wrote.

As man's ancestors took more and more to the use of weapons and relied less and less on fighting with their teeth, it was likely, he thought, that the teeth and jaws became reduced in size and the skull thus came to resemble that of existing man.

Darwin also saw that an increase in "mental powers" would lead to a higher, larger skull.

Out beyond the sand-walk in the garden, Darwin nearly always kept some hutches of rabbits. By studying them he had been impressed with how easily the shape of the skull can be changed. Even so trifling a thing as the "lopping forward" of one ear of a long-eared rabbit pulled forward all the bones on that side of the skull. No longer did they correspond to the bones on the other side.

Some of the rabbits he raised also grew very large—much larger than the wild rabbits that came into the garden to nibble at his flowers. At first Darwin was greatly surprised to discover that the skulls of the domestic rabbits had become longer than those of the wild, 4.3 inches as compared with 3.15.

"One of the most marked distinctions in different races of men is that the skull in some is elongated and in others rounded," he wrote. "Here the explanation suggested by the case of the rabbits may hold good. Short men . . . incline more toward rounded heads and tall men may be compared with the larger and longer bodied rabbits, all of which have elongated skulls."

By such evidence and logic Darwin was convinced that the most distinctive characteristics of man were in all probability acquired through the action of natural selection.

But Darwin was under strong attack for his claim in the first edition of *The Origin of Species* that natural selection could account for all change. His critics pounded at him, insisting that he explain, if he could, how structures of no survival value could have arisen. How could natural selection have produced the gorgeous colors in a peacock's tail, when color certainly could not have increased the peacock's fitness to survive?

On the defensive, Darwin wrote in *The Descent of Man:* "I am convinced . . . that many structures which now appear to us useless, will hereafter be proved to be useful and will therefore come within the range of natural selection. Nevertheless I did not formerly consider sufficiently the existence of structures, which as far as we can at present judge, are neither beneficial nor injurious, and this I believe to be one of the greatest oversights yet detected in my work."

Darwin then granted that the inherited effects of use and disuse might strongly affect the struggle for existence. He said too that "it appears" that various "unimportant characters" were acquired through sexual selection.

With his great gift of acknowledging the facts regardless of how contrary they might seem, he added further: "An unexplained residuum of change must be left to the assumed uniform action of those unknown agencies, which occasionally induce strongly marked and abrupt deviations of structure."

The four together—natural selection, use and disuse, sexual selection, and the strange spontaneous variations—he believed could account for the bodily development of man.

Darwin felt a deep obligation, almost a compulsion, to answer all the arguments and objections raised to his theory. He once explained that he tried to follow a "golden rule." Whenever he came upon a statement or a fact or a thought opposed to his general results, he at once made a memorandum of it. "For," he said with that impeccable fairness of his, "I had found by experience that such facts and thoughts were far more apt to escape from the memory than favorable ones."

It was not surprising, then, that Darwin should think it absolutely necessary to deal with the most basic objection raised to his theory: that though evolution might account for the bodily structure of man, it could not explain his mental or spiritual powers. Critics argued then—as they do now—that there is an unbridgeable difference in kind between man and ape, and not merely one of degree.

Darwin conceded immediately that the difference between even the most highly organized ape and the "lowest savage" is tremendous. The distance is also vast, he pointed out, between such a savage "who has no words to express any number higher than four and who uses hardly any abstract terms" and the mind of a Newton or a Shakspere.

Darwin, however, had seen with his own eyes that one of these gaps was not so infinite as it appeared. He remembered the Fuegians who came down to their wild and broken shores to meet the *Beagle*. They were naked, painted, wild, startled, scarcely human. He remembered too, the three who had spent three years in England and who were returned to their home by the *Beagle*. And he remembered his "continual surprise" at how the latter "resembled us in disposition and in most of our mental faculties."

"If no organic being except man had possessed any mental power, or if his powers had been of a wholly different nature from those of the lower animals, then we should never have been able to convince ourselves that our high faculties had been gradually developed," Darwin argued.

"But it can be shewn that there is no fundamental difference of this kind. We must also admit there is a much wider interval in mental power between one of the lowest fishes, as a lamprey or lancelet, and one of the higher apes; yet this interval is filled up by numberless gradations.

"My object is to shew that there is no fundamental difference between man and the higher mammals in their mental faculties."

Darwin's proofs sometimes have a naïve sound. Often they are homely rather than scientific in the usual sense of the word, and yet they frequently carry the conviction that goes with the homely and the simple.

He pointed out first that the lower animals feel pleasure, pain, happiness, and misery like man, and react physically to these emotions, just as man does. In terror, the muscles tremble, the heart palpitates, the hair stands on end.

Maternal affection also was very much the same. A female baboon regularly stole and affectionately raised young dogs and cats. When one of her adopted kittens scratched her, she immediately examined its feet and promptly nipped off the points of its claws.

Despite his lifelong study of animals, Darwin was surprised one day to be told that monkeys, which instinctively dread snakes, still could not "desist from occasionally satiating their horror" by lifting up the lid and looking into a box where snakes were kept. He decided to test the story.

With full permission, he carried a stuffed snake into the monkey house of the Zoological Gardens. At first some of the monkeys were panic-stricken. A few others acted as though they were not interested. Then Darwin put the stuffed snake down on the floor. In a short time all the monkeys, the panicky and the indifferent alike, were gathered around it in a large circle, staring intently.

When Darwin tried them with a dead fish, a mouse, and a living turtle, the monkeys behaved very differently. They were frightened at first, but soon approached and were handling all three.

Then he placed a small live snake in a paper bag with the mouth loosely closed. One monkey approached cautiously, peeked in, and dashed away. The others were not deterred. One by one they sidled up, took a momentary look at the dreadful object in the bag, and fled precipitately.

Darwin's point was that animals as well as man also experience the more "intellectual" emotions, such as wonder and curiosity.

Darwin maintained that they also have excellent memories. He had an interesting experience of his own with a dog's memory.

When he returned from the voyage of the *Beagle,* having been gone exactly five years and two days, he went out to the stable where his dog lived, and shouted to him in his old manner. The dog showed no excitement, but instantly followed him out for a walk and obeyed "exactly as if I had parted with him only half an hour before."

Darwin maintained stanchly that animals can learn, and thus ran headlong into the insistence of Archbishop Sumner that man alone is capable of progressive improvement. Darwin piled up case after case to support his point. There was the American monkey taught to open hard palm nuts by cracking them with a stone. Thereafter it used stones to open all kinds of nuts and boxes. And there were the baboons that rolled stones down a mountainside to rout an enemy.

Darwin admitted that it is difficult to determine whether the lower animals have any ability to deal with abstract ideas. But there was his own terrier. When he said in an eager voice: "Hi, Hi, where is it?" she at once understood something was to be hunted. She rushed to the nearest thicket to scent for game. If she found nothing, she would look up the trees for a squirrel. Perhaps it was the dog-lover, perhaps it was the scientist in Darwin that asked: "Now do not these actions clearly shew that she had in her mind a general idea or concept that some animal is to be discovered and hunted?"

In Darwin's lifetime, as today, opponents of evolution cite language as the final insurmountable proof that man and ape could not be of the same kind. "The habitual use of articulate language is peculiar to man," Darwin readily conceded, "but he uses in common with the lower animals, inarticulate cries to express his meaning, aided by gestures and movements of the muscles of the face."

He noted that man is not distinguished by the understanding of articulate words, for dogs understand words and many sentences; nor by mere articulation itself, for parrots and other birds also possess this power. As Darwin saw the language problem, the sole difference lay in man's infinitely greater power to associate the most diversified sounds and ideas. This he felt could be attributed solely to man's greater mental ability.

That apes cannot put together a simple declarative sentence Darwin insisted is due to the fact that their intellect has not developed as has man's. He noted parenthetically that language itself has undergone an evolution closely similar to that of species.

Darwin braved public wrath even further by maintaining that man's moral sense and conscience developed out of the urge that many animals show to help one another.

In Abyssinia a troop of baboons was set upon by dogs as it was crossing a valley. Some of the older males already had reached the safety of the opposite mountain when the others were attacked. Without waiting, the males rushed down to the rescue, roaring so loudly and threateningly that the dogs withdrew. Under this diversion, all the baboons escaped except one frightened young one, which crawled up on a rock and stayed there. The dogs again rushed in to attack it. In this crisis one of the largest of the baboons again came down from the mountain, went to the young one, coaxed him off his rock, and led him to safety. The dogs watched, seemingly too astonished or fearful to attack again.

Darwin told another story to illustrate how animals overcome their own fear to aid one another. A little American monkey, a warm friend of his keeper, lived in constant fear of a baboon that shared his compartment. Nevertheless, one day when the baboon attacked the keeper, the monkey jumped on his dreaded enemy. His biting and shrieking enabled the keeper to escape.

"Besides love and sympathy, animals exhibit other qualities

connected with the social instincts which in us would be called moral," said Darwin. He concluded that the difference in mind between man and the higher animals, great as it is, is "certainly one of degree and not of kind."

Darwin wondered that many persons would deny any possibility of the evolution of human intelligence and moral sense when "we daily see these faculties developing in every infant."

Two other cases seemed to him to clinch the point. It is possible to find every grade of intelligence, from the mind of an idiot "lower in the scale than many an animal," to the mind of a Newton. And was there not the same complete gradation from the barbarous tribe to the most highly civilized nation?

At the time at which Darwin wrote, the latter order of progress was by no means taken for granted. The Duke of Argyll and Archbishop Whately both had argued heatedly and publicly that man came into the world as a civilized being. Savages, to this school, were men who had undergone "degradation."

To support his insistence that the record was exactly the opposite, that all civilized nations once were barbarous, Darwin used a favorite technique. He pointed out that there are many clear traces of a "former low condition" in still-existing customs and languages. For example, the carrying over of the count of ten—for ten fingers—into the decimal system, and the survival of ancient superstitions. To believe that man originally was civilized and then suffered "utter degradation" seemed to Darwin to take "a pitiably low view of human nature."

If man was descended from some lower form, as he maintained, Darwin had to face both the serious question of what form and the deriding allegation that he was declaring apes to be man's direct ancestors.

There also was the taunting inquiry: "Where are the connecting links?"

Unlike some of those who came after him, Darwin always opposed the view that man had descended from the living anthropoid apes. His position, backed by many facts, was that man is a co-descendant with other mammals from "some unknown and lower form." He emphasized that man had undergone an extraordinary amount of modification, "chiefly in consequence of his brain and erect position." "We must not fall into the error of supposing that the early progenitors of the whole Simian stock, including man, were identical with or even closely resembled any existing ape or monkey," he cautioned.

That there were no fossil remains to bridge the great gap between the Simian stock and man did not alarm Darwin. He calmly noted that the discovery of fossils had been a slow and fortuitous process, and that the regions most likely to afford remains connecting man with some extinct apelike creature "have not as yet been searched by geologists."

By the process of reason, which so often and so remarkably led him to correct conclusions, Darwin arrived at the opinion that Africa might have been the birthplace of man.

Since man's ancestors had diverged from Old World Simian stock, they must have lived in the Old World. In each region of the world the living mammals are closely related to the extinct species of the same region. It is therefore probable that Africa formerly was inhabited by extinct apes allied to the gorilla and the chimpanzee. And since the two species now are man's closest relatives, it is "somewhat more probable" that man's early forerunners inhabited the African continent. Thus Darwin reasoned it out.

Darwin briefly drew man's genealogy. From some primordial cell, he carried life upward through the fish, the amphibians, the mammals, the New World and Old World monkeys, and, at some remote period in the past, up at last to "Man, the wonder and glory of the Universe." A little sadly Darwin admitted that the pedigree he had given man was not of "noble quality." Neither did he feel the human race had any need to feel ashamed of it.

"The most humble organism is something much higher than the inorganic dust, and no one with an unbiased mind can study any living creature, however humble, without being struck with enthusiasm at its marvellous structure and properties," he wrote with characteristic sincerity and awe.

In Darwin's day nothing was known of the effect of the glands of internal secretion on the secondary sexual characteristics—the special organs of the female for caring for her young, and "the greater size, strength, and pugnacity of the male, his weapons of offence and defence against rivals, his gaudy colouring, his power of song, and other such characters." Darwin believed that he must attempt to account for these characteristics by inheritance and selection. Why were they transmitted to one sex and not to the other?

In writing *The Descent of Man,* Darwin also was under the necessity of explaining how the secondary sexual characteristics could have developed, if they did not affect the success of the individual in the life-and-death struggle for survival. "It is clear," he wrote, "that these characters are the result of sexual and not of ordinary selection, since unarmed, unornamented, or unattractive males would succeed equally well in the battle for life and leaving a numerous progeny, but for the presence of better endowed males."

Darwin collected a tremendous volume of material on the special structures and the sexual behavior—the battles and the dances—of mammals, birds, fishes, insects, and even crustaceans. He was well aware that his carefully worked out interpretations were inadequate, for knowledge was lacking at many points, and yet he was almost convinced.

"It seems to me almost certain that if the individuals of one sex were during a long series of generations to prefer pairing with certain individuals of the other sex . . . the offspring would slowly but surely become modified in the same manner."

Publication of *The Descent of Man* only added new fuel to the controversy started by *The Origin of Species*. The dispute became more strident.

And yet with all the argument and clangor, there grew a cosmic change in the world's thinking. By the late 1870's it was a different battle that was being fought. Even the opposition had shifted ground.

In one of the last revisions of *The Origin of Species*, Darwin himself noted: "Now things are wholly changed, and almost every naturalist admits the great principle of evolution."

Some, however, admitted it only partially. In the late 1870's several "eminent naturalists" published their belief that though the multitude of species might have arisen by evolution, the few real species from which the multitude had sprung had been independently created. "They admit that a multitude of forms, which until lately they themselves thought were special creations . . . have been produced by variation, but they refuse to extend the same view to other slightly different forms," Darwin wrote.

And in *The Origin* he put a series of highly embarrassing questions to this group. Did they believe that the elemental atoms had been commanded suddenly to flash into living tissues? Did they believe that at each supposed act of creation one individual or many were produced? Were all the infinitely numerous kinds of plants and animals created as seeds, or eggs, or as fully grown beings?

"As a record of the former state of things, I have retained in the foregoing paragraphs, and elsewhere, several sentences which imply that naturalists believe in the separate creation of each species; and I have been much censured for having thus expressed myself," Darwin added. "But undoubtedly this was the belief when the first edition of the present work appeared."

Never before *The Origin Of Species* appeared, Darwin felt, had he encountered sympathetic agreement. Any who did believe in evolution, he further recalled, either were silent or spoke so ambiguously that their meaning could not be understood.

And so the opposition—and it was strong—fought on a new base. The scientific world, for its part, almost universally accepted the fact of evolution if not all of the doctrines, and went on to build on the new foundation that Darwin had provided. The world at large sensed that Darwin had brought about one of those redirecting changes in thought that come only a few times in many centuries.

Darwin himself felt that the greatest part of his work was done. Not long after publication of *The Descent of Man* he decided that he would undertake no more theorizing about fundamental problems, and especially not on "so difficult a subject as Evolution." He believed that some of his friends had lapsed into rash speculation in their later years. "No man can tell when his intellectual powers begin to fade," he gently explained.

Many of the earlier tensions were gone. Consciously and unconsciously Darwin was able to relax, and when he did, his precarious health improved considerably. He went more often to London and received more visitors at Down House.

Late in November 1877 he traveled to Cambridge to receive an LL.D. degree from his beloved university. Wearing a flowing scarlet gown, he walked beside the master of Christ's into the Senate House, where he was greeted with a great cheer from the students and guests.

Darwin stood the excitement of the ceremony and the elaborate lunch that followed, but he did not remain for the "resplendent" dinner given that night by the Philosophical Club. Huxley was the principal speaker at the dinner. After lightly chiding the university for waiting until it was "safe and superfluous" to award Darwin an honorary degree, he declared that from "Aristotle's great summary of the biological knowledge of his time down to the present day there is nothing comparable to *The Origin of Species* as a connected survey of the phenomena of life permeated and vivified by a central idea."

Although Darwin had given up further attempts to grapple with the major problems of evolution, he was far from idle. He worked steadily and productively at experiments and writing. In 1876 he published *The Effects of Cross Fertilization in the Vegetable Kingdom,* in 1877 *The Different Forms of Flowers on Plants of the Same Species.* He said in his autobiography, on which he was also working off and on during these years, that no other discovery of his ever gave him so much pleasure as "making out the meaning" of the heterostyled flowers.

And, Darwin added: "The results of crossing such flowers in an illegitimate manner, I believe to be very important, as bearing on the sterility of hybrids; although these results have been noticed by only a few persons."

In 1880, with the assistance of his son Frank (Francis), he published *The Power of Movement in Plants,* and in the following year *The Formation of Vegetable Mould through the Action of Worms.* The latter was a rounding out of a paper he had presented almost forty years earlier before the Geological Society. He was very doubtful that it would interest many readers, but this account of how the humble worm had remade the soil and buried ancient civilizations appealed warmly to many persons.

Despite the improvement of his health, Darwin had aged in appearance. At sixty his long beard and shaggy eyebrows were white. He stooped markedly as he walked in the garden in his full black cape and wide-brimmed black hat. In these days too he nearly always carried a long pointed staff and occasionally would stop to lean upon it.

Life was moving at its smooth routine when Darwin suffered a slight heart attack in December 1881. He seemed to recover, but in thanking a friend for congratulations sent to him on his seventy-third birthday, February 12, 1882, he calmly forecast: "My course is nearly run." Death came quietly at Down on April 19 of the same year.

The *Times* in its eulogy undoubtedly expressed the feeling of the great majority when it spoke of him as "beyond rivalry among the men of today, and side by side with two or three great discoverers of the past."

Only burial in Westminster Abbey could do him justice and the country honor. The great congregation that gathered for his funeral included "leaders of men and leaders of thought, political opponents, scientific workers, eminent discoverers, and practitioners of the arts." Scientific societies of France, Germany, Italy, Spain, Russia, and the United States as well as of Great Britain sent official representatives.

In this august setting and company, the words of the first anthem rang out: "Happy is the man that findeth wisdom, and the man that getteth understanding." And as Charles Darwin was laid to rest in a grave beside that of the great Newton, the choir sang: "Let his body be buried in peace, his name liveth evermore."

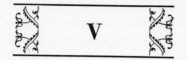

LAMARCK

THE SCIENTIFIC OPPOSITION

D ARWIN'S DEATH did not still the controversy over the theory that he had thrust upon a largely unwilling, though partly welcoming world. The battle raged on, often ferociously.

The attack upon "Darwinism" came principally from two directions: from religious groups and from scientists. The religious forces, continuing to find a spokesman in the Bishop of Oxford, did not neglect any of the arguments against the theories of Darwin. In the end, though, the overriding objection was stated by the bishop: "Evolution is a denial that man was created in the image of God." On this plane the issue largely was unarguable.

The scientific opposition, on the other hand, could fight in the same arena. Questions could be asked and proof demanded.

After the 1860's few scientists differed with Darwin's basic ideas—that species are the product of evolution rather than of a special act of creation, and that in the great struggle for life the fittest survive. Nearly all of the outstanding scientists of the time were with him, certainly to that extent—Wallace, Spencer, Huxley, Lyell, Hooker, Henry Walter Bates; the Germans, Ernst Heinrich Haeckel and Karl Semper; the Americans, Asa Gray and Joseph Leidy, and many others.

The scientific opposition arose on other grounds.

In explaining how evolution occurs—in contrast with the fact that it does occur—Darwin's facts undoubtedly were fewer

and his proofs weak. He had shown convincingly that the fittest
survive; he had not, as one of his more perceptive opponents
pointed out, demonstrated how "the fittest originate." *The
Origin of Species* had been misnamed!

Darwin had never pretended that he understood why all
living things vary as they do. He readily and wisely wrote in
The Origin of Species: "I have sometimes spoken as if variations . . . were due to chance. This, of course, is a wholly incorrect expression, but it serves to acknowledge plainly our
ignorance of the cause of each particular variation."

At times, however, Darwin leaned rather heavily toward the
theory that climate and other external factors, such as "use and
disuse," bring about inheritable changes. Unfortunately the discoveries in heredity that largely would have settled the issue
did not become known for many years.

So it was that during the last decades of the nineteenth
century a noisy, often angry fight seethed around the question
of how differences and species originate. The logical French
were among the most insistent in demanding that any theory
of evolution account for this basic point.

The French made their challenge in 1888. The amphitheater
of the old Sorbonne—the famous court where the great of
French science had lectured in their day—was filled early. It
could not hold the crowd of students and scientists who had
come from all sections of France, for this was a notable day
for French science.

Alfred Giard, brilliant young biologist, would soon step to
the lectern to give France's first course in evolution.

Almost three decades had passed since Darwin had published *The Origin of Species,* and evolutionary ideas had swept
the world outside France. France, however, remained officially
and actually a bastion of the ebbing belief in special creation.

Lacaze-Duthiers, the leading figure of French biology, refused even to acknowledge the work of Darwin. In order that
he might identify any who should dare to dabble with such

heinous doctrines, he sent a spy to the Giard lectures to make a
list of all who might attend.

It had been a highly significant event when the Paris municipal council called for a course in evolution and appointed a
young professor—then forty-two and only recently come up
from Lille—to present it. It marked the opening of a new era
of biology in France and of a new scientific defiance of Darwinism.

When he stepped before that expectant Sorbonne audience,
Giard traced the big steps in the history of evolution—the
contributions of Buffon, Lamarck, Goethe, Darwin, *"les hon-
neurs de trois grands peuples."* But as the course continued, it
was to Lamarck that Giard gave first place. This was not an
unpopular emphasis, since Lamarck had preceded Darwin, and
evolution could thereby be called a French science.

Giard devoted the whole first year of the course to Lamarck,
and this, more than eighty years after Lamarck's death, was his
first real hearing before the French people and the world.

The French scientist whose work was so belatedly unearthed,
but whose ideas then became the rallying-point of the scientific
opposition to Darwinism, was born Jean-Baptiste-Pierre-Antoine de Monet, Chevalier de Lamarck.

His birthplace was in Picardy, in northern France, and the
year was 1744. As the eleventh and youngest child in a noble
though impoverished family, he early was consigned to the
church. But the religious life had little appeal for Lamarck.
Soon after the death of his father he fled the Jesuit seminary in
which he had been forced to study. Mounted on a nag reput-
edly as bony as d'Artagnan's, the seventeen-year-old Lamarck,
like many another young gentleman from the provinces, set
out to seek fame and fortune. Lamarck headed straight for the
army.

The French were then deep in the Seven Years' War and
were campaigning in Germany. On the day after Lamarck

reached the fighting forces and enlisted, the French armies under Marshal de Broglie and the Prince de Soubise attacked the army of Prince Ferdinand of Brunswick near the small town of Fissinghausen. The battle went against the French. As the Germans pressed their advantage, German guns caught Lamarck's company in a direct line of fire, and all the commissioned and noncommissioned officers were killed or wounded. Lamarck, with his one day's experience, collected the survivors and held the company's post until help arrived. For this intrepid deed he was awarded a lieutenant's commission.

Lamarck's hopes for a brilliant career in the army soared. But his life was never to run in expected channels or smoothly. Every fine promising climax was to be followed by a series of long, dreary, unpredictable anticlimaxes.

The newly commissioned lieutenant was sent to Toulon on garrison duty. Since he was without money or influence, his bright prospects of a military career soon began to dim, and when his neck was injured in a playful wrestling bout, he resigned from the army.

With only a few francs in his pocket, Lamarck this time headed for Paris. In approved romantic style he lived in a garret in the Latin Quarter and eked out a living doing literary hackwork while he studied medicine, music, and science.

In some of his rambles through the Parisian countryside, Lamarck met Jean-Jacques Rousseau. The details of their acquaintance are sketchy, but thereafter he seems frequently to have accompanied the great French philosopher on his "herborizations." Whether or not it was this association that channeled Lamarck's scientific interests into botany is not certain. Nevertheless, for almost ten years he made a close study of the French flora.

In 1778, when he was thirty-four years old, Lamarck completed the writing of his *Flore française*. It was a masterful job. At a time when botany was a fashionable science, it established his reputation in scientific circles and even brought him to the attention of the court. Once again he was a man of mark. George Buffon, then the first man of French science and keeper of the Jardin du Roi, obtained Lamarck's admittance to the Académie Française.

FLORE
FRANÇAISE,
ou
DESCRIPTIONS SUCCINCTES
DE TOUTES LES PLANTES

TITLE PAGE OF LAMARCK'S "FLORE FRANÇAISE." THE FLORE OF-
FERED "SUCCINCT DESCRIPTIONS OF ALL THE PLANTS GROWING NAT-
URALLY IN FRANCE."

Buffon also employed Lamarck to travel about Europe as a companion to his son and as a collector for the royal gardens. But on his return the best post that could be found for the brilliant botanist was that of keeper of the herbarium at the minute salary of one thousand francs a year. Lamarck was desperately pressed for money, for he had made the first of his four marriages, and the first of his seven children had been born.

Nevertheless he made a strikingly handsome appearance in the high stock and laurel-embroidered coat of an Academy member. His nose was long and straight, his lips sensitively curved. Deep lines cut into his cheeks.

And his mind ranged over the universe. Not only was he systematizing French botany; he was forming theories on the nature of chemistry, on the origin of the globe and its atmosphere, and on the other great scientific problems of the day. Some of these he presented to the startled Academy. All the while he seemed unable to advance beyond his lowly post at the gardens.

Then there came the French Revolution. The name Jardin du Roi promised to be fatal to this old institution; revolutionary extremists were demanding its suppression as an annex of the King's palace. In this crisis friends of the garden persuaded the government to accept a suggestion of Lamarck's—that the name be changed to Jardin des Plantes and the research program be greatly enlarged. The guillotine was doing its deadly work only a short distance away. But Lamarck's renaming of the garden, combined with his humble position and absorption in his studies, enabled him to ride through the Revolution without difficulties.

Then in 1793, on the eve of the Reign of Terror, the National Convention, in a transport of reform, changed the botanical gardens into the Musée National d'Histoire Naturelle, and established a number of new professorships, including two in zoology.

Since revolutionary France had no zoologists, one of the places was offered to Lamarck, and the other to Geoffroy Saint-Hilaire, twenty-two years old, whose specialty was mineralogy. The two newly created zoologists decided to divide the field between them, Geoffroy taking the vertebrates and Lamarck the invertebrates.

Lamarck's full title and status were set out in a museum publication of 1794: "Lamarck—50 years old; married for the second time; wife enceinte; professor of zoology, of insects, or worms, and microscopic animals." At an age when most men are settled in their careers, Lamarck began a new one in a science new to him. Undismayed at having to make a fresh start in a field comprising nine tenths of the animal kingdom, he plunged into research.

Lamarck was not long in deciding where he was going. Linnæus, the great Swedish classifier, had divided all animals below the vertebrates into two classes: insects and worms. The result, from the standpoint of study, was chaos; and Lamarck quickly decided to produce some logical order in the vast disorderly hodgepodge. It was his idea that the innumerable invertebrates should be classified on the basis of their fundamental organs of respiration and circulation and on the form of their nervous systems.

He bent over his microscope for endless hours, until his eyes were strained and painful. The galleries of the museum were loaded with zoological specimens, and more were constantly being brought in by the expeditions the revolutionary government began sending to Egypt, Africa, and other parts of the world.

Lamarck's new status had not relieved his financial difficulties. When the Republic, in 1794, set up a fund to be paid to citizens eminent in literature and art, Lamarck hastened to apply for a grant. He received one, and the next year applied again. He explained in his application that a small pension he had received from the Academy of Sciences had been canceled, and added: "The loss of my pension . . . and the enormous increase in the price of articles of subsistence have placed me and my numerous family in a state of distress that leaves me neither the time nor the freedom from care to cultivate science in a useful way."

Despite his worries and the immensity of his task, Lamarck pushed ahead. In 1801, less than eight years after he had jumped into his monumental job of classification, he succeeded in publishing the first volume of his *Système des animaux sans vertèbres*. With some exceptions, the classifications Lamarck established then hold good today. It was an extraordinary achievement.

As he compared and classified, Lamarck was impressed with the graduated differences he saw in the animal kingdom. He decided that they could not be random and began to shape a theory of life.

All the major groups of animals could be fitted into a stair-step series, a "veritable chain," a progression extending from the simplest little polyp on one end to man at the other. Or when he started with man and looked back, Lamarck was struck with the "astonishing" gradual stepping down in the major organs. He called it a *"dégradation."*

With remarkable prescience, Lamarck concluded that the simple forms at the lower end of the scale were the material with which Nature began and out of which with the aid of limitless time and favorable circumstances she had formed all the others.

The theory was startling, revolutionary. Lamarck knew that he would have to support it with all the facts he could muster. And that he proceeded to do.

It would have been logical for him to present his proofs by starting with the simplest forms and working upward "in the order nature appeared to have followed." But because the mammals were better known than the miniscule bits of life at the other end of the scale, Lamarck began at the top and moved downward. He chose to go from the known to the un-known.

At the top Lamarck unhesitatingly placed the mammals. They were the most intelligent and they had more faculties than any of the others. They had backbones, a head that could be moved around, eyes with eyelids, a diaphragm, a heart with two ventricles, and warm blood.

One step down were the birds. Lamarck noted that they also are intelligent, have a number of faculties, a two-ventricle heart, and warm blood. But they were egg-layers; they did not have the mammalian organs of reproduction, and neither did any of the other animals.

The reptiles, one more step down, had a single-compartment heart. Instead of the warm blood of the mammals and birds, the blood of the reptiles was cold, like that of all the animals below them. Their lungs were simpler too, and in some

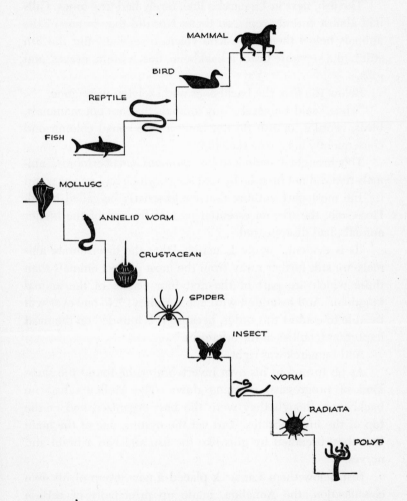

LAMARCK'S GREAT PROGRESSION OF LIFE. FROM MAN AND THE OTHER MAMMALS AT THE TOP THERE WAS A GRADUAL STEPPING DOWN TO THE SIMPLE LITTLE POLYP AT THE OTHER END.

species had been replaced by gills of a kind never found in more advanced animals. Furthermore, their legs had nearly disappeared. But the reptiles still had a spinal column, a brain, nerves, and that cold blood.

The fish, next in Lamarck's line, rarely had true lungs. Gills had almost entirely replaced them. Nor did they or any of the animals below them have true voices or eyelids. But the fish still had a separate head, a backbone, fins, a brain, nerves, and gills.

Below the fish, the backbones and skeleton were gone.

"Thus," said Lamarck, "any animals that are not mammals, birds, reptiles, or fish do not have a true spinal column and consequently not a true skeleton."

This brought Lamarck to his *"animaux sans vertèbres,"* animals that did not breathe by real lungs, which had no voice and for the most part nothing that could strictly be called blood. Here, too, the iris, an essential part of the eye of the higher animals, had disappeared.

"It is evident," wrote Lamarck, "that the invertebrate animals are still farther away from the most perfect animals than those which are part of the first four classes of the animal kingdom." And he added with fine certainty: "No one ever will be able to contest this order, because it is founded on the most important faculties of the organism."

And Lamarck was right.

As he turned to his own invertebrates, he found the same kind of progressive stepping down. The Mollusca had no backbones, though they were the best organized and at the top of the invertebrates. And yet the oysters, one of the main branches, breathed by gills like the fish and had a brain and nerves.

Just below them Lamarck placed a new group of his own classification, the Annelida, made up principally of certain marine worms. Lamarck gave them a special standing because he considered that they breathed through gills, even though the gills might be hidden under the pores of the skin.

Still another step down were the crustaceans. The race of the crabs had hearts, arteries, and veins, and they breathed through gills, too.

Below the crustaceans no other animals possessed hearts. "One finds nothing similar [to the heart] in the animals below, whatever may be the methods of movement of the fluids of the body," Lamarck pointed out.

The spiders, next down the scale, were the first animals with a respiratory organ inferior to gills. They also lacked a heart and had no arteries, no veins. Although they were close to the insects, Lamarck insisted on giving them a higher classification because they did not go through changing stages and had feet and eyes in a primitive state of development.

After the spiders Lamarck ranked the insects, that immense series of animals, the most numerous of them all. And they were the lowest group in which sexual reproduction was still to be found. In all lower groups sexual reproduction was replaced by division.

The worms, in the next lower rank, were a group in which for the first time there were no organs of sight or of hearing, and no tongues.

Down on the eleventh rung, in the next to last place, were the Radiata, a group marked by radial symmetry. They had no sense organs, though there were traces of respiratory trachea. All their parts were regenerative—if one was cut off, another would grow in its place—and they had no head, no feet, no circulatory organs.

At the very bottom, at the border line where the distinction between animal and vegetable grows sketchy and uncertain, Lamarck put the polyps. They were the simplest of all, and, Lamarck felt sure, the first formed by nature.

These little blobs of matter had no special organs of feeling, breathing, circulation, or reproduction. All their viscera were reduced to a single alimentary canal. Any part of the body could absorb nourishment. They were little more than cor-puscles of gelatine; they were the beginnings, the almost form-less beginnings.

All living animals were there; all were accounted for in this system. Once Lamarck had pointed it out, it was clear that there was a progressive simplification, a degradation, a dimin-ishing in the number of faculties. "Citizens," said Lamarck, "go from the simplest to the most complex and you will have the true thread that connects all the productions of nature; you will have an accurate idea of her progression; you will be convinced that the simplest of living things have given rise to all the others."

Lamarck was never a man to stop short of ultimate conclu-sions. He saw clearly where his materials led. In 1802, seven years before Darwin was born and fifty-seven years before *The Origin of Species* was written, Lamarck made public a carefully thought-out, scientific theory of evolution. He argued on grounds that he supported with evidence from his *Système* that the multitude of living species had developed over a vast period of time from simple undifferentiated bits of living mat-ter.

More than this, Lamarck had a complete explanation of how and why this climb from jelly globule to man had oc-curred, and of how species had developed.

His theory was set forth in a slender little book: *Recherches sur l'organisation des corps vivans.* It was a summary of his opening lecture that year at the museum. He had no expecta-tion that it would set the world aflame. In his introduction he wrote: "I have no thought of producing a work of any im-portance, but only of publishing my lecture in leaflet form for distribution to those who might be interested in my observa-tions."

Thus in the very opening years of the nineteenth century

the world was presented with a theory of evolution which could have upset the old order as thoroughly as did Darwin's half a century later. The world at that time, however, was oblivious and unheeding.

Georges Cuvier, the leading figure of the day in French science, was disdainful, though undisturbed. He dismissed Lamarck's theory as the naturalist's "new piece of madness." No one else was perturbed or excited, or fearful that the foundations of thought and faith were being rocked. There were no outraged protests from the church, though some complained that Lamarck made no allusions to the Deity. Even in the turbulent, scientifically aware years of the early Republic, Lamarck's theory was the tree falling in the forest with no one to hear.

Not until Lamarck was rediscovered by Giard and his contemporaries of the 1880's did the scientific and lay worlds begin to appreciate how remarkable his work had been. Only then was it seen that Lamarck, rather than Darwin, might possibly have been entitled to the honor of being the first scientific evolutionist.

But Lamarck, expecting nothing, was not disappointed. He went right on with his inquiry into why evolution had occurred. He was sure "environment" was the answer. Climate, temperature, altitude, place, all the great diversity of nature had acted upon living matter to change it and shape it.

"It is not the organs—that is, the character and form of the animal's bodily parts—that have given rise to its habits and particular structures," he announced. "It is the habits and manner of life and the conditions in which its ancestors lived that have in the course of time fashioned its bodily form, its organs and qualities."

Living animals and the animals in the collections of museums demonstrated the truth of this, Lamarck believed. An animal that lived high in the mountains, in a cold climate and with only limited food to eat, differed, Lamarck saw, in size, form, color, proportions, agility, industry, and length of life from an animal that lived in a warm, lush climate at the base of that mountain. The circumstances of life forced an animal to exercise certain parts of its body, and thus to develop them and bring them to their peak. Or if the environment offered no challenge, perhaps certain organs were not used. Not being exercised, they weakened and disappeared. This in essence was Lamarck's famous doctrine of use and disuse.

Or, as he put it in his own words: "The more frequent and longer sustained use of an organ gradually strengthens this organ, develops it, enlarges it, and gives it a power proportionate to the length of time it has been used. On the other hand, the constant lack of use of an organ insensibly weakens it, causes it to deteriorate, progressively diminishes its faculties, and tends to make it waste away."

Lamarck here was stating a fact upon which the world always had acted. By exercise the athlete built up his muscles and endurance. The dog that spent the winter in the open developed a thicker coat than one kept in the house.

But Lamarck carried his reasoning and, he thought, his observations one step farther. He insisted that the bigger muscles and the thicker coat were inherited by the offspring. Thus acquired changes were passed along and gradually, over a vast period of time, transformed the simple organism into a complex one. In short, acquired characteristics were inherited. If there were any questions about this doctrine, Lamarck insisted that they could easily be answered by experiment.

It is notable, however, that Lamarck did not undertake those experiments, though he did propose a hypothetical one. He was a man who believed in reason rather than the test-tube.

Suppose, Lamarck said, that the left eyes of two infants were masked when they were born and that they never were permitted to use the masked eye. If they were mated and their offspring also were deprived of the use of the left eye, and if this were continued over enough generations, the left eye undoubtedly, said Lamarck, would gradually be eliminated. In the end, he felt certain, the right eye would strengthen to offset the loss of the left, and a one-eyed breed of men would be produced.

Lamarck, a kindly man with no sadistic inclinations toward the human race, felt no need to perform the experiment. Was there not abundant proof in nature of exactly the same process?

It was well known that the mole's eyes were tiny and almost out of sight because "they had been exercised so little." And the aspalax of Olivier, a mole-like rodent that lived even more deeply in the dark, had totally lost its sight. Not only were the eyes gone, but even the vestiges of them were hidden under the skin in such a way that all light was kept away from them. Furthermore, this same little animal, relying as it did on its ears, had developed greatly enlarged organs of hearing.

Or take the teeth. Animals that did not use them lost them.

Thus it could be seen, said Lamarck, that lack of use of an organ modifies it, impoverishes it, and finally eliminates it.

Lamarck also considered that nature offered copious proof that use of an organ would strengthen it, extend it, enlarge it, and if there was need, even create it. It was all there to be seen.

Birds that had to alight on the water to find their food had to stretch their toes constantly, both in landing and in propelling themselves. In time the membranes between the toes stretched and their webbed feet developed. And did not this same principle explain too how membranes had developed between the toes of frogs, sea tortoises, and other animals? Examples were everywhere.

Birds that lived on the riverbank and wanted to fish in the shallow water were forced to extend their legs in order to keep their bodies dry. And this, said Lamarck, was how the waders got their stilt-like naked legs. And if swans and geese did not acquire such long legs, it was because they could plunge their heads into the water to catch aquatic larvæ. Their necks grew long and graceful.

"Wants, always occasioned by circumstances and followed by sustained efforts to satisfy them, are not limited in results," wrote Lamarck. "The fishes that habitually swim in large bodies of water and have need of seeing laterally have their eyes placed on the side of the head."

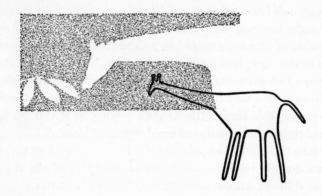

THE GIRAFFE, "THAT TALLEST OF MAMMALS, LIVING IN ARID LOCALITIES, IS OBLIGED TO BROWSE ON THE FOLIAGE OF TREES."

Even more remarkable results of habit could be observed in the herbivorous animals, Lamarck maintained. There were the elephant, the rhinoceros, the ox, and the buffalo, which, "from daily consuming great amounts of food and moving little," acquired thick, massive, heavy bodies. And the animals that found safety in flight and therefore developed slender bodies and delicate legs. The giraffe was another noteworthy case.

"We know," Lamarck pointed out, "that this tallest of mammals living in arid localities, is obliged to browse on the foliage of trees. It has resulted from this habit, maintained over a long period of time, that in all individuals of the race the forelegs have become longer than the hinder ones, and that the neck is so elongated that it raises the head almost six meters (20 feet) in height."

And were not claws the same story all over again? Furthermore, if the claws proved hindrances in moving about, had not the cats, the tigers, and the lions learned to retract them?

These environmentally induced changes, Lamarck wrote in his *Recherches,* are passed along to the offspring, who, living under the same circumstances, do not have to acquire them by the same process that created them.

So it was that Lamarck explained all the variety of life. His theory was satisfyingly complete; there were no gaps in it. The heat, the cold, the heights, the depths, the inexhaustible variety of nature shaped and developed all the characteristic organs of living things and thus gave rise to modern species. Oddly enough, Lamarck, the great student of the essential organs of all animals, drew none of his illustrations from the material he knew so well.

Many years later Darwin was to make it clear that the giraffe got its long neck, not by stretching up to browse on the high-hanging leaves, but because only those giraffes with necks long enough to reach the leaves survived and left offspring. The difference was profound. Still later, modern science completely upheld Darwin. Lamarck's fine, logical theory was wrong because he had failed to distinguish between the changeable aspect of the individual—the hair, the muscles, and other features that are affected by climate, food, and environmental conditions—and the individual's very stable genetic pattern. Modern geneticists call the first the phenotype and the second the genotype, and regard the individual's appearance as a by-product of his genes, rather than vice versa, as Lamarck believed.

But, in a subtle sense unsuspected by Lamarck, it was conceded that the environment does affect the individual's inheritable make-up. An animal whose genes make it possible to develop thicker fur in a cold climate is the one that stays

alive and leaves progeny. Thus the climate—the environment—
ultimately has a decisive effect, though in a very different way
from what Lamarck thought.

Lamarck was dramatically wrong about the inheritance of
acquired characteristics. Nevertheless, it took more than a century to reveal his error, and traces of the old Lamarckian beliefs still are abroad in the world today.[1]

The French naturalist's fame has grown for another reason.
Historians point out that his sensing that evolution has a direction was one of the great jumps forward in modern thought.
Earlier Newton, Buffon, and others had proved that the earth's
surface and environment are changing. Matter is in motion, not
fixed, as the belief always had been. Lamarck saw that the
same principle of graduated change applied to organic life
and that the change had been progressive. This daring, original
insight alone promises to place him among the great men of all
time.

Lamarck, however, was busying himself with ever grander
schemes. The over-all theory, the all-encompassing project,
had an irresistible appeal for him. He cherished the idea of
preparing an eight-volume *Système de la nature* that would
bring together all the knowledge of natural production up to
his day. The naturalist appealed to the National Convention
for funds "to put this beautiful project into execution." With
the payment of a lump sum of twenty thousand francs,
Lamarck wrote to the Convention, he would endeavor in seven
years to produce the new and French equivalent of Linnæus's
Systema naturæ.

Somehow the money was never forthcoming. Lamarck had
to content himself with lesser undertakings. He was growing
old; his hair was long and white and straggly and his eyes were
becoming weak. But his keenness never flagged and some of

---

[1] Lysenko in Russia still takes what is essentially a Lamarckian
position.

the ideas at which he worked in his offices at the museum were immeasurably ahead of his time.

He repeatedly emphasized the element of time in evolution, great stretches of time. As the first of his four laws of evolution, Lamarck set down: "All the organic bodies of our globe are veritable productions of nature, which she has created in succession at the end of much time." And again: "Time and favorable circumstances are the two principal means that Nature employs to give existence to all her productions; we know that, for her, time has no limits and that consequently it is ever at her disposal."

Lamarck's fertile, sensitive mind also caught more than a glimpse of Darwin's "struggle for existence." "The multiplication of small species is so considerable, and the renewals of their generations are so prompt, that these small species would render the earth uninhabitable to others if nature had not set a limit to their prodigious multiplications," he wrote.

The preying of other animals and the rigors of the environment kept down the excess, Lamarck explained. The large animals "killed one another off," and man, who with his intelligence had put himself in a position to dominate all the others, was held in check by his own passions and weaknesses.

In these observations Lamarck was almost within touch of the theory of natural selection. At the critical moment, however, he veered away, and it was left to Darwin to show how the struggle for life shapes life.

Lamarck saw, though, that the sea must have been the mother of life and its cradle. Only in the waters of the seas or in other humid places, he wrote, does nature form—and, he added, continue to form—those mysterious first organisms which are so slightly over the line separating the living from the non-living. And Lamarck put in for good measure: "from which have been derived all other animals."

The next to evolve, the polyps building their coral reefs,

and the sponges, lived only in the water. The worms too seldom ventured far from a damp ancestral environment. Lamarck
suspected also that the early forerunners of the great tribe of
the crabs were the first to venture ashore.

From the aquatic worms, floating deep in the sea and never
exposing themselves to the outer air, came the barnacles and
mollusks, Lamarck thought. He went on with his progression:
from the mollusks, after a hiatus, the fish, and from the fish the
reptiles; from one branch of the reptiles the birds and from
another the amphibious mammals, "which have in their turn
given origin to all the other mammals. . . . I therefore believe
myself authorized to think that the terrestrial mammals originally descended from those aquatic mammals which we call
Amphibia."

Lamarck was speculating, and yet his speculations were
uncannily sagacious. His guess that the birds and mammals had
arisen from the reptiles was confirmed a century later by paleontologists and morphologists.

Lamarck had spoken of life as a chain, a series, a succession of steps, though in using these figures of speech he was
only trying to explain that there had been a progression. He
understood, more clearly than any of those who had gone before, that life had not developed along an incline. Rather, it
had grown like a tree. Just as the mammals and birds had
branched out from the reptiles, so had other groups branched
out from other species. Lamarck probably was the first to compare life to a tree, and to use the tree as a means of demon-
strating the relationships of animals.

These potent, logical, far-ranging ideas and arguments
might well have convinced the eighteenth-century world of the
great fact of evolution. That they did not was probably the result of circumstances—circumstances that, like Lamarck's environment, molded the facts.

Lamarck was a lesser figure in a brilliant period of French
science. He was recognized as a fine systematist, but withal

only a small struggling professor well down the line. The leaders of the day, Cuvier and Bichat, still were firm believers in the special creation of species. Their opposition discredited Lamarck's theories before they could impress themselves on science at large.

There were other balances against Lamarck. His theory essentially was materialistic—environment molding life, life reacting—at a time when thought was moving in the opposite direction. Lamarck seemed to hark back to earlier ideas of the then despised seventeenth century.

Part of the difficulty also lay in Lamarck himself. He had not been trained as a scientist, and without limiting himself to the sometimes restrictive facts, he let his mind range far and wide. His speculations often far outran his observations. One of his early works had the remarkable title: *Mémoires de physique et d'histoire naturelle, établis sur des bases de raisonnement indépendants de toute théorie.* Reason alone was an odd base for a collection of essays on meteorology and geology.

Before devoting himself wholly to zoology, Lamarck had dabbled in some of the profounder problems of the other physical sciences. In the *Mémoires* he arrived at the startling conclusion that oxygen could not be an essential part of air and water; no chemist had ever seen it; no one had been able to prove its existence. "It is not compatible with reason, and therefore is impossible," he proclaimed.

With equal sureness Lamarck denied that air conveys sound. Was a cannon-shot not heard better at a distance with an ear to the ground?

Even in zoology Lamarck's most brilliant concepts were often found side by side with theories that sound to the world today, as they did to his own, like the sheerest fantasy. Underneath and pervading all life was an ethereal fire, a peculiar fluid related to heat and electricity. And Lamarck also insisted that the spontaneous generation of life goes on inces-

santly under the influence of this mysterious, all-pervading substance.

A literal reading of his words can easily give the impression that even the essential organs of breathing and reproduction, as well as the lesser ones, could be willed into existence.
It was this seeming flight that provoked the ordinarily mild
Darwin to burst forth in a letter to Hooker: "Heaven defend
me from Lamarck's nonsense of a 'tendency to progression,'
adaptations from the slow willing of animals etc. Lamarck's
work appears to me to be extremely poor; I got no fact or idea
from it. But the conclusions I am led to are not widely different
from his; though the means of change are wholly so."

Lowell satirized this same "willing" idea in his *Biglow
Papers:*

> *Some filosifers think that a fakkilty's granted
> The minnit it's felt to be thoroughly wanted.*
>
> *That the fears of a monkey whose holt
>   chanced to fail
> Drawed the vertibry out to a prehensile tail.*

A less literal interpretation of Lamarck's words puts some of
his fanciest contentions in a better light. By willing, it can well
be argued, he implied only a response to the heat or cold or
other conditions of life. But such an interpretation was not the
common one. Lamarck seemed convicted of scientific extrava-
gance. Probably for this reason, besides his other handicaps, his
original and almost inspired theories of evolution failed completely to awaken his own time. Lamarck showed no sense of
bitterness at this lack of recognition. On the contrary, he
seemed, despite the boldness of his writing, to have little ex-
pectation of fame or acceptance. He worked because work was
part of him, and not for the reward.

During the last ten years of his life his eyesight, which
long had been strained by intensive work with the microscope,

failed. Lamarck became blind. He continued nonetheless to attend meetings of the museum staff and to carry on as much of his work as possible. He also dictated to his two daughters, who lived with him and devoted their lives to him, the last volumes of his famous *Animaux sans vertèbres.*

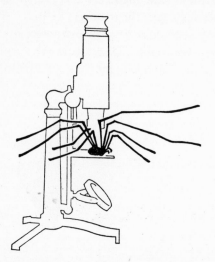

LAMARCK STUDIED HIS INVERTEBRATES UNDER SUCH A MICROSCOPE AS THIS.

Little is known of his final illness, though the records indicate that he died on December 28, 1829, at the age of eighty-five.

He was buried in the cemetery of Montparnasse. Geoffroy Saint-Hilaire pronounced the eulogy in the name of and on behalf of his colleagues at the museum. Cuvier, Lamarck's great critic, was to prepare another eulogy. Significantly enough, it was not read before the Académie Française until almost two years later; and, in the form in which it appears in the records, it has as lukewarm a tone as such a document well can have.

And this apparently was all the ceremony there was. The grave in which Lamarck was laid was not one chosen by the nation to do honor to its great men. It was, on the contrary, a grave reserved for those who could afford no other. Although even a clear record is lacking, it appears that Lamarck was buried in a trench at one side of the cemetery, a trench from which the bones were frequently removed to make way for the remains of others who were poor or unknown.

The world's recognition was never Lamarck's in life; nor at death. It was to come only belatedly.

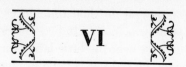

VI

GIARD

SHRIMPS AND NEW EVIDENCE

THE RISING SUN burnished a path across the waves beating on the Calais coast. In the gathering light of the pleasant French dawn, a bearded, solidly built man and several younger men picked their way across the rocky points of the cape—Cape Gris-Nez.

They stopped frequently. Often they turned over rocks and peered beneath them. They poked into crevices wet with the surf. Every now and then they would drop some specimen of the marine life they were collecting into the containers they carried.

The leader of the little group was Alfred Giard, professor of zoology at the University of Lille. The younger men were his students. They were on one of their regular early morning specimen-hunting expeditions.

But the diatoms, the algæ, the worms, and other organisms they picked up on the rocks and those that they collected on the sandy beaches that stretched toward Ambleteuse or on the tidal flats meant more to Giard than material for his students to dissect. The remarkable similarities of the countless little sea creatures were convincing Giard that Darwin had been correct in maintaining that all life had evolved from earlier and simpler forms. The relatedness of all living things seemed undeniable.

At the same time, Giard was struck by the differences he saw. As he studied the perfect adaptation of the tiny organisms to the waves on which they floated, to the rocks to which they clung, or to the moist sand in which they burrowed, he became

convinced that it was their environment that made them what
they were and accounted for their differences.

Although Giard principally studied the marine life that
abounded on the coast near the little laboratory he had established at Wimereux, he did not believe in ignoring the life of •
the land. He and his students often took a land route. As they
walked along the northern French roads or through the woods
and fields, Giard would demonstrate his points. He would pull
off a rosette of leaves.

LEAVES, BEAKER, FOSSIL FISH

Note, he would tell his students, how the leaves have turned
to the sun; how this plant has adapted itself to its environment.
Or he would pick up a leaf that had rolled itself into a tube. In
this way, he would explain, the leaf resists the drought.

At a place where the road lay open to the sea winds, Giard
always stopped to point out how the trees and shrubs had
spread out their roots. By that adaptation they saved themselves from being uprooted by the force of the wind.

Such differences, Giard began to believe, could not have
been produced by natural selection alone. His logical French
mind was keenly aware that Darwin had not truly explained
how species had originated, for had the great English naturalist
not failed to explain how individual living things came to be
different?

In his search for support of this thesis that was forming in his mind, Giard turned to an earlier French scientist, to a man whose work had almost been forgotten—to Lamarck.

Lamarck, Giard joyfully discovered, had explained all. He had demonstrated that environment shapes all living things; that the endless differences in the environment make all living things different.

Giard delved deeper into Lamarck. He turned back to Lamarck's first lectures at the museum as well as to his *Philosophie zoologique* and his *Histoire des animaux sans vertèbres*. So little attention had been given to the early work of Lamarck that Giard had difficulty in finding a copy of his first lectures.

The Lille professor began to discuss Lamarck's conclusions and his own observations, which seemed to confirm them. His reputation as an evolutionist spread.

In anti-evolutionist France much of the attention Giard began to attract was unfavorable. Academic advancement might have become difficult for the young professor if the criticism had not been blunted in large part by the high regard in which he was held personally and as a teacher and citizen.

Giard had been born at Valenciennes, a city only a short distance from Lille, on August 8, 1846. His special interests and talents soon were in clear evidence. When he was scarcely out of the nursery, he could identify the animals, the birds, and the flowers of his native soil. And despite his intense love of the out-of-doors, Giard also was good in school. At the age of fifteen he could read Greek fluently and quote at length from the French poets.

In 1867 he went to Paris to study natural science at the École Supérieure. Again he was outstanding, and after he received his degree, in 1872, Lacaze-Duthiers, professor of natural history at the Sorbonne, selected him for his assistant. The following year Giard was appointed to the faculty of the University of Lille. Seven years later he was made full professor of zoology.

While he taught and carried on his studies at his Wimereux laboratory, Giard also continued his interest in his native district. In working with an industrial institute at Lille he made a number of studies of the resources of the section.

The latter work increased his already wide acquaintance with the people of Lille. It was not surprising that he was chosen as a representative to the National Assembly. With his gift for getting along with people, Giard might easily have continued in politics. Many of the political leaders with whom he served in his several years at the Palais Bourbon remained his friends throughout his life.

But his devotion to natural science was even deeper. In 1887 when Giard was offered a post as *maître de conferences* (lecturer) at his alma mater, the École Supérieure, he quickly accepted. He reached Paris at just the right time.

Evolution was gaining ground in France despite the opposition of the leaders in science. In 1888 the Paris municipal council called for a course in evolution at the Sorbonne. The newly arrived professor from Lille was the logical man to present it, and thus it was that Giard stepped into that crowded court of the old Sorbonne to open a new era of science in France.

One of the students who attended the first year's course, which dealt principally with Lamarck, recalled even after many years that Giard spoke with "marvelous clarity." As Giard saw it, Lamarck had hit upon the primary, the major factors in evolution, and Darwin only upon the secondary.

In his view, the influence of environment and the inheritance of the changes it brought about were the true stuff of evolution. Natural selection only eliminated or preserved the changes produced.

In his first lectures, Giard discussed these primary factors: heat, climate, light, electricity, the saltiness of the sea, the humidity of the air, the movement and circulation of water, and nutrition. These were the elements, he believed, which had molded living creatures.

To support his contention, Giard cited the newer experimental evidence. He pointed to the experiments of Brown-Séquard, who thought—mistakenly, as it turned out—that by interfering with the nervous system of guinea pigs he had induced an epilepsy-like disease that was inherited by their young.

The Sorbonne's first professor of evolution was on stronger ground when he insisted that natural selection alone could not explain the origin of species. He listed the many phenomena that could not be accounted for by natural selection. On the other hand, he did not deny the existence of selection; he only relegated it to second place. The whole world of life, Giard was fond of saying, cannot be boiled down into any one simple formula.

Giard also explained his own position with the remark: "In the tradition of Lamarck, I try to pick up the land of promise revealed by Darwin." To Giard, it was the meaning of facts that was important; he considered it the function of the scientist to generalize, to organize his facts into the most comprehensive picture possible. He told his pupils: "The facts that I lay before you matter little. I could add many others to them. All that counts are the interpretations drawn from these facts." Nevertheless, Giard was first of all a scientist looking for the facts that made the theories. To be fruitful, he believed, science had first to be pragmatic.[1]

Giard acted upon this belief at his laboratory at Wimereux. Until 1900 it was a tiny three-room house. Tables loaded with collections filled it to the door, and the scientist and his students worked elbow to elbow. At night they swung up ham-

---

[1] Giard wrote: "Detailed and conscientious observation of facts that may seem unimportant in their extreme minutiæ can awaken in an alert mind theories of the highest scientific import. The examples of Étienne Geoffroy Saint-Hilaire and Darwin are instructive in this regard."

mocks. There was no running water and no aquarium, despite the fact that Wimereux was a marine laboratory. Professor and students carried water up from the sea and kept their specimens alive in glass jars. But equipment did not matter. Without it, Giard and his pupils were able to set up a demonstration that stage by stage showed the complete development of the sole and the turbot. At the time no other laboratory had been able to record so completely the life cycle of these fish.

Unlike Lamarck, Giard always was surrounded by devoted students and warm friends and was able to attract support for his work. In 1900 a rich donor built a fine new laboratory for him on the dunes, close to the point where the Wimereux empties into the sea. In accordance with Giard's wishes, the new laboratory consisted mainly of one big workroom, well lighted, with huge bay windows. Everyone had his own little section for working, and Giard's was like all the rest.

The professor spent hours there, bent over his microscope, from time to time calling some student to him to look at a larva, a parasite, or a diatom that he thought of interest. Sometimes he would answer questions without lifting his eyes from the microscope. Again, he would go over to sit beside a student to help him with his observations and research. At a time when many laboratory directors worked in their own private sanctums and a strict laboratory hierarchy prevailed, Giard's democracy was all the more remarkable. He must have been a very great teacher.

At the opening of the new laboratory, he announced that there was only one rule that never was to be broken: "The laboratory that we are organizing will not be a show aquarium, nor one of those laboratories where one can enter only by surrendering a part of his own personality. We shall take for our inspiration the fine words of the immortal Savigny: 'Dictatorial requirements paralyze the mind; they seem to alter the will itself. If good observations are the fruit of patience, they are also the fruit of full and entire freedom.'"

It was understandable that the students should have been wholly devoted to this warm, democratic, considerate, and inspiring man. George Bohn, one of those who became a biologist under the ægis of Giard, recalled in a biography of his teacher: "Liberty and respect for individual interests were encouraged. This was the means Giard used to leave to science a large number of workers, fascinated by his genius as a naturalist, but each with his own specialty."

Primarily it was the material that he gathered on his daily expeditions and studied under his microscope that convinced Giard that Lamarck had been right. Lamarck's proofs often had been farfetched. By the 1880's and '90's no zoologist could seriously subscribe to Lamarck's account of how the serpent lost its legs or of how the giraffe acquired its long neck. Such fancies had moved over into the realm of fable.

In addition to his general observations, Giard found support for the basic Lamarckian thesis on careful scientific grounds. His measurements, comparisons, and tests indicated that environment profoundly affected living organisms, and Giard thought that the changes thus produced could be inherited.

Along the coast near Wimereux were many crabs. Examining some of them that were infested with parasites, Giard made an "absolutely disconcerting discovery." Under the influence of the parasite and certain other circumstances, a crab could successively develop two different sexes.

Giard was astonished and fascinated. He realized at once that he had stumbled on something important and eagerly began a study of the strange phenomenon. That meant finding more such crabs. To obtain enough to confirm this almost unbelievable transformation, Giard and his students had to capture and cut open more than ten thousand of the squirmy, pinching creatures. To make the search worse, the parasite for which they were looking was all but invisible to the naked eye. Hence every crab had to be held close and examined with a magnifying glass. It is hard to imagine a more onerous piece of research.

Persistence, and probably innumerable pinched fingers, paid in the end. Giard learned that if the parasite had for any reason been sexually modified, the host that harbored it was also modified profoundly. Could such a change be produced experimentally? This was the inevitable next question.

With that scientific patience and exactitude which always defy lay understanding, Giard castrated some of the parasites and returned them to their hosts. The results again were astonishing. The big pincers of the male crab began to grow smaller, and his tail enlarged as that of the female does for sheltering eggs. In this case the enlargement was not to shelter eggs, but the parasite.

Giard tried the same experiment with oysters. Some of those so treated began to manifest the maternal instinct. The parasite was treated with whatever care would normally have been given to offspring.

Giard found equally striking changes in secondary sexual characteristics when he altered the parasites infesting certain birds. A female bird would take on the plumage of the male, become bellicose, and utter male cries.

Another test was made with bees. Normally the female bee has large brushes for collecting pollen from the flowers. When a male parasite attached itself to the bee the brushes became larger; when a female, they grew smaller and were no longer used to carry pollen. The bee harboring a female parasite would go to the flowers only to feed itself and not to carry nectar back to the hive. Further research revealed the same phenomenon in worms, insects, and a long list of animals, and also in flowers and vegetables. It seemed without question that the parasite—an external influence—could deeply change its host. To Giard this meant that Lamarck was right, that there was verifiable support for his contention that living things are modified by their environment.

"From all this it becomes apparent that external circumstances exert a considerable and important influence not only on the organs they directly affect, but, by a correlation of whose mechanism we are ignorant, upon other organs, particularly on the glands and reproductive functions," said Giard.

"This is what Darwin meant when he called attention to the special sensibility of the reproductive organs to external influences. If sexual organs thus modified are able to reproduce— and nothing forces us to deny that in certain cases they can— any offspring must be modified more or less profoundly in its structure and constitution.

"The facts revealed by the study of parasitic castration seem to me to constitute an important argument in favor of the possibility of the hereditary transmission of certain acquired characteristics."

Unfortunately for this complex and ingenious theory, no detailed reports were made by Giard of any changed offspring thus produced. The experiment, careful as it was in its initial phases, was not carried through to substantiate the latter part of Giard's conclusions—that the offspring would be different.

Giard was concerned with another problem, one that also led him to Lamarckian conclusions. This was the mystifying resemblances of certain very different species—mimicry. "It is a remarkable fact," Giard wrote, "that some well-separated phylogenetic types, thanks to certain biological influences, become so similar in their external appearance that not only is the inexperienced eye led into error, but biologists may inexactly appreciate their real affinities."

One case that particularly impressed Giard, oriented as he was to the sea, was the resemblance of certain crustacean parasites to other organisms that float on the surface of the waves. He also happened upon one marine mollusk that had taken on the most varied colors "in a marvelous adaptation to the objects in its environment." In these protective resemblances, Giard felt that Darwin's explanations were not sufficient. He could not see how selection alone could explain them. In the early stages, would a slight resemblance have any value in preserving the copycat animal?

Giard was convinced that an appeal also had to be made to a Lamarckian explanation. He argued that it was the same environment that was making two different groups alike. But he conceded that both natural selection and environmental change might be involved. On the other hand, there were equally perplexing differences between those that should have looked alike.

One day Giard gave a luncheon for his students at which he served some very fine shrimp. They seemed to be the same excellent shrimp that they frequently enjoyed from the Wimereux estuary. Then Giard sprang his little surprise. The shrimps on the table were of the same family as the familiar ones from the Wimereux, but they came from fresh water, from Naples.

Fresh water or salt water, they seemed at first glance to be the same. The species quite evidently had adapted itself to varying degrees of salinity. There was, however, an important difference. Those whose ancestors had left the salt of the sea produced only about 25 rather large eggs. Those which remained in their ancient habitat produced about 300, all of them small. Here was a striking difference between creatures of the same family, even of the same species, when they lived in the salty water of the sea or in the fresh water of the land.

To Giard it seemed that this significant difference had to be attributed to the difference in environment, and that it undoubtedly had been inherited. The salt or the lack of salt in the waters in which they spent their life had changed the shrimps and their descendants so effectively that they were no longer alike in their reproductive functions. Giard granted, however, that selection might have had a secondary effect in producing the change. Again he warned his students that both influences might have been at work.

In the meanwhile a German biologist, August Weismann,

was becoming increasingly irritated by such fine-drawn arguments. If changes produced by the environment could be inherited, he defied the Lamarckians to perform a few simple experiments to prove their point.

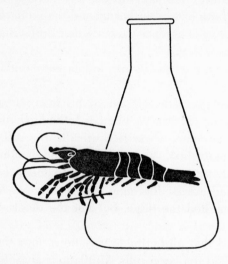

SHRIMP AND A LABORATORY BOTTLE

When no one took up his challenge, Weismann testily went to work on his own. One day in 1887 he cut off the tails of twelve white mice, seven of them females and five males. Within fourteen months 333 young were born to the twelve tailless mice. Every single one of the offspring had a tail of the normal eleven- or twelve-millimeter length.

Weismann knew that his opponents might argue that the effect of a mutilation might not show up for several generations. He moved fifteen of the first-generation offspring to another cage. As soon as they were able to see, he cut off their tails. In a little more than a year, the 15 produced 237 young. And every one of this generation possessed a normal tail. The German scientist performed the same experiment with some of the third, fourth, and fifth generations. The mice born to the fifth generation, though they came from five sets of tailless ancestors, all had full-length tails. Not even a single rudimentary tail had appeared.

Weismann's experiment startled both the scientific and lay worlds. An article of faith had been shaken, and the Lamarckians went to great lengths to produce evidence that the German biologist somehow was wrong.

With considerable publicity a German father and daughter were brought to Weismann. The father's left ear had been cut in dueling at a university. The left ear of his five-year-old daughter had a ridge almost exactly like her father's, though there was no scar. Weismann, it was felt, was disproved. But the scientist was not perturbed. When the father and daughter came to him, he gently turned the little girl around and looked at her right ear. It had exactly the same kind of ridge as did her left. She had inherited the ridge, but not the deformity from dueling.

Weismann insisted that all heritable variations have their origin in what he called the germ cells. Mutilations and other changes produced by the environment, he argued, are never passed along to offspring.

Giard was compelled to face this challenge. He did not think it a particularly serious one. He was quite willing to concede that a wooden leg was not inherited, but held that "general modifications" are. "Weismann seems to have taken a lot of trouble for a meager result in cutting off the tails of five successive generations of white mice," said Giard. "This proves only that the section of the tail of a mouse does not involve any profound modification."

As a conscientious scientist and not a doctrinaire, Giard in the end somewhat shifted his position. He held that environment might produce its effects by modifying the germ cells. Perhaps this was why animals taken to mountainous Kashmir developed heavy coats, and hairy animals taken to the tropics lost theirs. And if man did not show similar changes when he made similar moves, did it not prove only that the effect of climate is not immediate or absolute? And did not all of this prove that the genes can be influenced and that, after all, Lamarck's principles applied, Giard asked.

This uncommon ability to form strong views of his own and yet to keep an open-minded appreciation of the work of others was typical of him. He was a man of calmness, poise, and great though gentle strength. An artist sketching him as he sat at his desk would probably have used a series of curves. The bald dome of his head rounded into the broad curve of his back. His forehead was low and the outlines of his face softened by a mustache, beard, and sideburns. His eyes were deepset behind small, gold-rimmed glasses that had cut deeply into the ridge of his large and somewhat pointed nose. The nose was the one break in the curved Giard line. The velvet jacket that he wore also seemed in character.

When he was not at Wimereux, the biologist lived in a comfortable apartment in Paris, which he had transformed into a second laboratory, library, and headquarters from which he kept in touch with scientists in all parts of the world, and particularly with those who followed his Lamarckian beliefs.

On an ordinary day it was not unusual for twenty letters to go out to other scientists. Some of them went to Russia, some to England, and some to the United States, and nearly always they were written in the language of the recipient. Giard's early gift for languages had matured. He had mastered all the major ones.

His work also was aided by his phenomenal memory. He not only could immediately recall all the details of his huge correspondence, but never forgot names, dates, or the place where he had met someone. He knew the titles of the books that filled his shelves and spilled over onto tables and even the floor, and often could cite the exact page where some reference might be found.

Despite his early clash with the forces that wanted to keep evolution out of France and his later brush with Weismann, Giard was held in high and affectionate regard by most of his fellow scientists. In 1900 he was elected to the Académie des Sciences and in 1904 was chosen president of the Société de Biologie, the highest honor that could be conferred by biologists.

Giard's long and even career ended when he died on August 8, 1908. Shortly after his death a group of his former students and friends met to decide how best they could honor his memory. His loss had been a deep personal grief to them. They decided to have a medal struck, but they also chose another way of honoring him, one that took time, effort, and devotion. They brought together in a single volume the outstanding writings of Giard. The dedication of that book is one of the proudest that could be given to any man, and particularly to a teacher: "Alfred Giard—Works, collected and republished by a group of his students and friends."

Giard had won the scientific battle for evolution in France and had taught France and the world the greatness and originality of Lamarck. In doing so he raised one of the major issues that have confronted evolution.

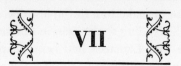

VII

COPE

FOSSILS AND LAMARCKISM

Liberté, égalité, fraternité"—these sounding cymbals of the French Revolution stood boldly at the head of an unusual letter that arived at the Philadelphia Museum of Natural History late in 1796. It was from Paris—from the Musée National d'Histoire Naturelle—and it was signed in the unadorned, prescribed style of that day: Lamarck—Geoffroy.

The two French naturalists, after expressing their pleasure at the possibility of opening relations and exchanging collections with the American museum, continued in more scientifically interesting than grammatical English:

"Give us leave, Sir, to call your attention to the subjects which we desire to receive first. Those enormous bones which are found in great quantity on the borders of the Ohio the exact knowledge of those objects is more important toward the theory of the earth, than is generally thought of. . . ."

Lamarck and Geoffroy were accurate prophets. The "enormous bones"—fossils, of course—were to be highly important not only to the history of the earth, but to the history of the life that evolved upon the earth. They were the preserved record of the past.

But great quantities of the "objects" were not to be found for many years, and then not on the borders of the Ohio. When they were eventually unearthed in such numbers, the principal finder, by one of those strange yet recurrent coincidences of science, was a Philadelphian closely associated with the Museum of Natural History.

Furthermore, the conclusions the Philadelphian drew from those fossils were to make him in the last decades of the nineteenth century the leading spokesman in America for the evolutionary doctrine that Lamarck had been shaping at the very time he wrote to the museum in the last decade of the eighteenth century.

This great fossil-finder and Lamarckian was Edward Drinker Cope.

Cope was born at Fairfield, his father's large and substantial house on the York Road near Philadelphia, on July 28, 1840. The family was a prominent Quaker one.

The signs that he probably would become a naturalist, and probably a fossil-hunter and a systematic scientist, appeared early. At the age of six he began to record his doings, observations, and impressions in letters, drawings, and his "Journal." At this same ripe age he wrote to his grandmother: "I have been to the museum and I saw Hydrarchas [1] and Mammoth, does thee know what that is? It is a great skeleton of a serpent. It was so long it had to be put through three rooms. . . ."

From his ninth to his twelfth year Edward attended a Quaker day school in Philadelphia and continued to haunt the museum, generally keeping a notebook of his sketches and jottings. He also was a contributor of a sort, for he brought in for identification a large assortment of toads, snakes, salamanders, and other Philadelphia fauna captured in the vicinity of Fairfield.

His museum drawings showed rare powers of observation as well as the skill of a natural artist. At the age of ten he sketched the ichthyosaurus to scale. In small detail drawings, arranged in nearly professional style around his main drawing, were the separate bones of the skull and the plates surrounding the eyes. Each was numbered, and his key at the bottom of the page announced: "(1) The eye; (2) two of the sclerotic plates; look at the eye, thee will see these in it; AA are these."

[1] Hydrarchas, a primitive whale or zeuglodon.

When he was twelve, Edward was sent to the Friends' Boarding School at Westtown. He did well, but as he was small for his age, his father decided to have him spend the summer on a farm. Cope hoped that it would both build up his son's muscles and arouse his interest in becoming a farmer. In any event, the farm gave Edward muscles that were to withstand the most rugged kind of exploring, and the experiment was repeated for the next four summers. At eighteen Edward was presented by his father with a fine farm, which with his lifelong flair for imposing names, he immediately called McShag's Pinnacle.

What really interested the young Cope, though, was the animal life around the farm.

During his first summer in the country, when he was fourteen, he took with him Ruschenberger's *Entomology,* and wrote his father for an ornithology, herpetology, and ichthyology in the same series. "I should very much like to have them so that I might know something about the birds and snakes and fishes that abound here—that is, if thee thinks right or if it is convenient or proper."

The books arrived, and soon after Edward caught a large water snake, or water wampum, and brought it home. It was about the length of his leg, and protruded with a frog it had swallowed. His hosts, quite evidently appalled, apparently tried to separate him from his find by warning him that it would bite and that the wampum was poisonous.

"The way it struck at me scared me a little," Edward wrote to his father, "but I soon convinced myself it was not by examining its mouth which wanted fangs and as all nonvenemous have, IT had four rows of small teeth in its upper and two rows in its lower jaws, and two rows of scales under the tail."

Certainly this was a scientific way of ascertaining a pertinent fact!

In the 1850's, none of the colleges, with the possible excep-

tion of Harvard, offered the kind of scientific training that
would have appealed to Cope. After finishing at Westtown he
went to his farm. His great complaint was that the press of farm
work did not leave him enough time for his observations and
studies. His interest in farming never increased.

"Tho the cultivation of corn is a very necessary thing," he
wrote his father, "yet the time spent in cultivating it in the
present manner seems almost wasted to me."

In September 1860 he suggested that he would like to attend the lectures in anatomy offered at the University of Pennsylvania by Dr. Joseph Leidy, one of the great figures of American biology. His father readily consented and he enrolled. The
following two winters he studied at the Smithsonian Institution
in Washington.

These were the years in which the world was shaken by two
different and unrelated events, both of which carried old controversies to the point of no return and opened the way to a
changed future.

One was the publication of *The Origin of Species* in 1859.
Cope, who had avidly read Darwin's *Voyage of the Beagle,*
quickly got a copy of the *Origin.* It collided headlong with the
strict religious views of creation to which he had been brought
up, and for a while left him confused and unhappy. He could
not know then that *The Origin* would completely alter the
framework of the rest of his life.

The other event, of course, was the Civil War. From the
close vantage point of the Smithsonian in Washington, Cope
watched the North and South plunge into war and, unper-
turbed, listened to the talk of creating a "metropolitan police
force" to defend the capital.

He was for the union, it went without saying; but in a
young way he was critical of the administration. He wrote to
his sister on January 4, 1863: "One hears nothing but anathemas
against Lincoln Stanton Halleck & Co., even from administration men. As father often says the president's fault is his want

of judgment in selecting men." A plaint with a highly familiar ring!

Probably to prevent Cope's being drafted or enlisting in violation of his Quaker principles, his father sent him abroad for the next two years.

The letters Cope carried with him to the leading scientists of Europe brought him not only introductions, but many opportunities to talk at length with these men, to visit their laboratories and attend their societies. Thus the young scientist completed his unorthodox but excellent education. Upon his return, in 1864, he was a finished naturalist and comparative anatomist.

He immediately was appointed professor of zoology at Haverford College, and soon afterward married Annie Pim, a distant cousin, who like himself had been educated in Quaker schools and brought up in the peaceful, devout atmosphere of a Quaker home. The marriage was a very happy one.

When not in the classroom, Cope began to scout for vertebrate fossils. A few finds, and the fever rose in him. Teaching, with its restrictions, interfered, just as farming had done, with the things that mattered to Cope; so he resigned his post. His next step was to sell McShag's Pinnacle to raise funds for what he knew would be an expensive career. Then he was ready for his life work.

The West, Cope was sure, was a fossil-collector's treasure house, almost untouched, in which was hidden an unknown segment of the world's history. Great shallow seas, in the distant reaches of the past, had washed over the whole central basin of this country, and the bones and shells of countless animals had drifted down to the bottom of those ancient waters. Many of them and their casts—even the casts of delicate leaves and flowers—had been preserved in the thick sediments and sands.

And in time the seas had receded. The land had risen, bringing up with it, entombed in the stone that the sediments had

become, the bony remains. As the elements then began to wear
down the stone, streams cut through the newly risen lands,
ponds formed, beaches were washed up on rocky shores. In the
quicksands of the river beds, in the soft mud of the ponds, in
the impressionable sand of the beaches, more and different
myriads of animals left their bones and prints.

Again the covering seas moved in, and again the land rose
from their shallow embrace. As this history was repeated over
endless eons of time, the last and most modern withdrawals of
the sea had left many of those ancient beds high and dry and
exposed.

The hunters, the fur-traders, the pioneers, the men who
were seeking gold, and all the others who opened the West
had passed them by with only an occasional puzzled glance.
Some tales had come back about the "enormous bones," and
some specimens had been sent to museums. The general opinion was that the queer things probably were the bones of animals drowned in the Great Flood—Noah's flood.

All of this was waiting for a Cope and other scientists like
him. Not since the first settlers stepped ashore on this continent
had such an unlimited prospect opened before a special group
of men.

Three men, Leidy, Cope's former professor, F. V. Hayden,
head of a government geological survey, and one other had
preceded Cope into the field and had done enough work to
show what incredible fossil riches the West held.

The other man was Othniel Charles Marsh, professor of
paleontology at Yale University. He was a wealthy, imperious
man who let nothing stand in his way. A colleague of Marsh's,
Professor Arnold Guyot, of Princeton, once had arranged to
purchase an unusual fossil. It was crated and at the station
awaiting shipment when Marsh heard of it. He at once wired
the collector an offer of double the money Guyot was paying;
and to make certain that he should get it, he hired a special

train to go after it. Guyot, a man whose purse did not permit such competition, simply withdrew from fossil-collecting.

Marsh had done some highly rewarding fossil-hunting in Kansas in 1870, and therefore considered the territory his exclusively. When Cope, the following year, decided upon an expedition to the same field, Marsh automatically became his enemy. To Marsh, Cope was a poacher. Cope for his part was also a man of determination and not one to back down. He went to Kansas.

The West was pioneer land in those days. Not far beyond Topeka a herd of buffalo cantered along beside Cope's train, and some of the bulls caused a minor crisis by trying to cross in front of the engine. Farther along, the scattered herds multiplied into thousands, and the right-of-way along the tracks gleamed white with their bones. Travelers had amused themselves as they rode along by shooting down the great shaggy beasts.

Cope made Fort Wallace his base. With seven men, two large wagons, and fourteen mules he struck out for the shallow canyon country of western Kansas. Thick layers of yellow limestone capped the bluffs that bounded the canyons; below lay a shaly blue limestone. Near the upper line of the blue beds were the fossils.

Cope scarcely could believe the sight revealed to his dazzled eyes. From a bank above a dry creek projected the head bones of a huge fossil serpent. He and his men began to dig excitedly, chopping with their picks, scraping the dirt away with their hands, brushing it gently off the bones it had held for so many centuries. In the bank was the skull and nearly all the other important parts of this fabulous animal, though it was so long, much like Hydrarchas in the Philadelphia museum, that it extended all the way through the bank. Cope found the tail bones on the other side. He estimated its length at seventy-five feet.

That night around his campfire, and accompanied by the howling of wolves and the barking of coyotes, Cope named this giant reptile *Liodon Dyspelor Cope*.

Cope explored in the other directions across the flat Kansas prairies. In an affectionate letter to his five-year-old daughter, Julia, he vividly described the country: "This country is as level as our parlor and is covered with grass and has no trees in it. Nobody lives here except the Indians and a few soldiers and the men I go to find fossil bones with are soldiers." [2]

The going generally was hard. There was no water, and the party was often thirsty. Sandstorms were frequent. One of them struck while Cope was digging out another of the elongated sea serpents. The wind hit the bluff and was deflected upward, filling the air with driving particles of sand and dust. Cope pierced two minute holes in his hankerchief for vision, tied it completely over his face, and stubbornly went on working. He was rewarded with a "fine relic."

The fantastic sea creatures Cope was unearthing in this flat land of drought and sandstorms had lived during the Cretaceous period, an age when reptiles dominated the earth, dated traditionally at about 60 to 130 million years ago. *Liodon Dyspelor Cope* had been one of the larger serpents swimming through the primordial Kansas seas. It pursued big prey, switching its elongated, powerful body through the waters with flippers something like those of a seal. Its habit of swallowing "large bodies," Cope pointed out, in Lamarckian explanation, "had necessitated the prolongation of the mouth of the gullet. Its neck apparently had been as loose and baggy as a pelican's.

---

[2] Cope's descriptions of the prairie animals in other letters to Julia are delightful: "The antelope is a very pretty animal, as large as a little pony, that runs all over the country in little herds. It has feet like a cow and is brown on its back, with a large white spot at the end of its back. The father antelope has black horns, the mother none. They have thin legs and run so fast nothing can catch them except a bullet out of a gun. When they are frightened they make all the hair in the white spot on their back end stand up, so that they seem to be carrying a great white cushion to sit down upon."

Elasmosaurus platyurus Cope—another important Kansas find—had a huge snakelike body, which it raised above the water while it swayed its arrow-shaped head in a circle of twenty-foot radius. Or, without altering its position, it could sink to the depths forty feet below. And there were flying reptiles with a wingspread of twenty-five feet, and a fish with a head larger than that of a fully grown grizzly bear. Cope also found their bones in some Kansas chalk.

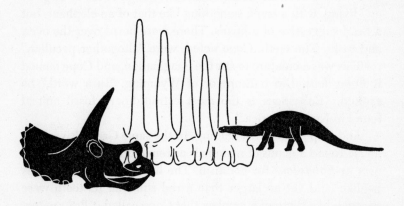

WEIRD DENIZENS OF A LONG-GONE WEIRD WORLD WRITHED THROUGH THE NIGHTMARES THAT OFTEN SEIZED COPE AFTER AN EXHAUSTING DAY IN THE FIELD. HERE, A "TERRIBLE HORNED" PRE-HISTORIC MONSTER, A BACKBONE, A DINOSAUR.

All of these and the great tortoises, the bony marauding fish, and the other creatures that swarmed in the ancient seas—during the 1870's more than thirty-seven species were discovered—were horrendous, nightmarish creatures. And these weird denizens of a long-gone weird world writhed through the all too real nightmares that often seized Cope after an exhausting day in the field.

The next summer Cope proposed to move on to the Bridger fields in Wyoming. Marsh had been there also with a Yale expedition, and once again considered the territory his own. He put every obstacle in Cope's way, and their enmity grew.

The difficulties were great, but Cope went into the butte country, over into the Green River Valley, and into the Washakie territory.

Near his camp on the Green River, Cope discovered a skull of monstrous size—more than three feet long. He pulled out his pencil and sketched this creature as it must have looked—as bulky and ponderous as a rhinoceros, though twice as large as any living, with a trunk something like that of an elephant, but a head suggestive of a boar's. There were horns over the eyes, and tusks. The teeth, Cope noted, were "altogether peculiar."

This was a creature to stir the imagination, and Cope named it *Eobasileus,* Dawn Emperor of Wyoming. "In a word," he exulted, "Eobasileus is the most extraordinary fossil animal found in North America."

And Cope's luck was holding. In the same Green River Valley he found a genus of mammals as remarkable for its minuteness as *Eobasileus* for giantism. The little hoofed animal was hoglike, and yet no larger than a red squirrel. Its teeth were so much like those of a monkey that Cope called it *Pithecodon.*

Nothing like these creatures had ever been seen by man. The great quadrupeds went back to the Eocene, a period from which no fossils had been found up to that time. This was a new world, or rather a new old, old world, that Cope had uncovered. It was of the utmost importance in his growing war with Marsh for Cope to stake out his claim to priority in the discoveries.

The country was difficult, the water, even in the springs, was charged with alkali, the days were hot, the nights were cold, and Cope suffered a bad attack of "mountain fever." But he worked late into the night, speeding off reports.

Telegram after telegram went to the secretary of the American Philosophical Society. "I have discovered in southern Wyoming the following species," Cope wired, "Lefalophodon

Cope; incisor one tusk, canine none, premolars four," and so on. In this particular telegram Cope had written *Loxolophodon;* A telegraph operator, understandably enough, had garbled it to *Lefalophodon.*

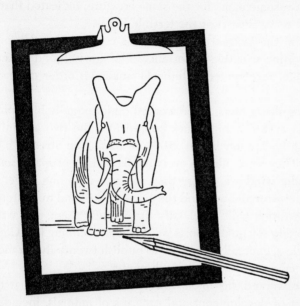

COPE'S OWN SKETCH OF "EOBASILEUS," THE DAWN EMPEROR OF WYOMING. COPE CONSIDERED THE EMPEROR ONE OF THE MOST RE-MARKABLE FOSSILS EVER FOUND.

Two days after this message reached the Philosophical Society, Marsh filed a claim for a similar animal, which he named *Tinoceras Marsh.* Because of the mistake in spelling, Cope's animal was listed under Marsh's heading. Cope was mistakenly given second place.

This kind of error was not unusual in the war between the two men. The rush for priority of publication and of names led to many situations bordering on the absurd. Each was determined to make the fancy Greek names he coined for the helpless prehistoric creatures he was extracting from the earth, *the* names.

Loxolophodon, which caused so much trouble, meant simply "beast of the crested tooth." *Tinoceras,* Marsh's almost equally awesome name for the same creature, indicated that it belonged to the beasts of the terrible horns.

Despite the farcical aspects of this competition, the finds were of prime scientific importance. The newly found Eocene quadrupeds represented a hitherto unknown order of mammals.

During the winters, Cope worked under equally high pressure. The crates of big bones poured into the two adjoining houses he had purchased at 2100 and 2102 Pine Street, Philadelphia. They were piled in every available inch of space, some even in the windows, where they were an unfailing target of attraction for small boys; and the overflow still had to be stored in an exposition hall. To classify them, study them, and write the necessary scientific reports was an overwhelming job. Cope, nevertheless, generally managed to publish twenty-five or more full-fledged scientific reports each winter.

As he worked, his main object was always "to get at the principles of development and progress of animals, including man." He was a thoroughgoing evolutionist by this time, and had written an article on "Methods of Creation of Organic Forms" in 1871. When Cope was recommended for a newly endowed chair in natural history at Princeton, some of the faculty objected because of his views on evolution. "Those views are much condemned at Princeton," Cope commented in a letter to a friend.

Cope was so swamped, however, with merely reporting his finds that he had little time during these years for theoretical books or articles. And he could not bring himself to stay out of the field during the summers.

Marsh, on the other hand, withdrew from exploration for

several years in the mid-seventies and published material announcing to the world that his Odontornithes—birds with teeth
—were the conclusive links between birds and reptiles. He also
made a very clear presentation of the descent of the horse.
Interest in both theories was intense all over the world, and
Marsh's reputation was enhanced. He seemed to be outdis-
tancing his busier rival.

Cope was concerned about this situation, and also about
the unfavorable reaction their competition was provoking in
scientific circles. When he was invited to Great Britain to become a member of the British Association for the Advancement
of Science, in 1878, he wondered what his welcome would be.
He was honored, however, and cordially received wherever he
went in Europe. The feeling that many leading scientists understood his side of the rivalry heartened him.

While he was in Paris, a superlative collection of fossils
from the Argentine pampas was offered for sale. These fossils—
many of them similar to those which had awakened Darwin's
interest during the voyage of the *Beagle*—had been brought to
France for the Paris Exposition of 1878. Cope's huge outlays
for his expeditions and for the collectors he had working for
him all over the West already were straining the comfortable
fortune he had inherited from his father. Nevertheless, he
could not resist the Argentine Pampean collection. He bought
it and had it shipped to the United States. In the rush of the
years ahead many of the boxes were not opened, and Cope
never knew in full how rich and rare was this collection which
he had captured for his country.

During the next decade there were more expeditions to the
West—to New Mexico, old Mexico, again to Wyoming, to California, and to Washington and Oregon. Tremendous dinosaurs
were found, and other monsters from half a dozen different
ages. Although he never managed to catch up with what was
collected, Cope turned out a prodigious number of reports.

By this time Cope was in serious financial trouble. In an effort to recoup he invested heavily in Western mining stocks, which went the way of many mining stocks of the time.

Some earlier support from the government, particularly in the publication of his work, also failed. The four separate government geological surveys, with one of which Cope had worked, had been consolidated into the United States Geological Survey. The new agency did not carry out a promise of one of its predecessor agencies to publish Cope's work.

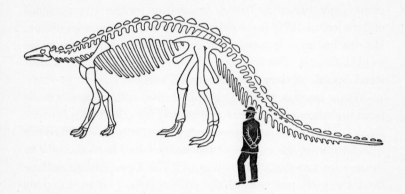

HUGE DINOSAURS WERE UNEARTHED IN THE WEST.

The trouble here again, Cope believed, was Marsh. The Yale professor had obtained an appointment as paleontologist of the new survey. He not only blocked any further assistance to Cope but, Cope was sure, circumvented his efforts to get special publication funds from Congress. Everything seemed to turn against the Philadelphia scientist; the eighties were a troublous decade.

In 1889, however, the outlook brightened. Cope was offered a professorship of geology and mineralogy at the University of Pennsylvania. He also sold his unmatched and unmatchable collection of North American mammals to the American Museum of Natural History, in New York, for $32,149. Although this was only a fraction of what it had cost him to collect the fossils, it relieved his financial plight.

The collection contained 10,000 specimens, representing 463 species! All the major species in many of the great geologic periods were there. It was a parade of life from which the life of today had sprung; and it will remain one of the nation's priceless scientific possessions.

During the long years of the war with Marsh, Cope had been piling up evidence against his adversary. Whenever he came upon an error or evidence of any action he considered less than ethical he dropped a note about it into a capacious drawer in the big desk-table where he did much of his work.

A letter from the Secretary of Interior, which Cope interpreted as a new act of aggression, finally brought his notes out of the drawer. The Secretary wrote instructing Cope to turn over to the United States National Museum all his Cretaceous and Tertiary fossils. The Secretary's assumption was that they were public property. They had been collected in co-operation with the government surveys, but Cope had paid all his own expenses, and his only compensation was to have been the publication of his work—the publication that did not materialize. At the Secretary's action, in which he was sure he saw Marsh's hand, Cope's rage boiled over.

Cope showed some of his long-stored ammunition against Marsh to William Hosea Ballou, a reporter for the *New York Herald*. The stories broke with a smash: "Scientists wage bitter warfare. . . . Prof. Cope of the University of Pennsylvania brings serious charges against Director Powell and Prof. Marsh of the Geological Survey. . . . Learned men come to the Pennsylvanian's support with allegations of ignorance, plagiarism, and incompetence against accused officials. The Academy of Science, of which Prof. Marsh is president, is charged with being packed in the interests of the Survey."

The survey, it was implied, was a scientific-political machine. Cope specifically charged that Marsh's work on the horse duplicated a genealogy made in Europe previously, that his work on the toothed serpents, the Odontornithes, was written by one of his assistants, and that much of his other work was done by assistants without credit being given. With his biting wit, Cope added: "The charges as to the authorship of Prof. Marsh's books and essays have been abundantly proven by the men who wrote the books. . . . I have been fully prepared to hear the opinion that it is legitimate to buy the brains of other men and also the assertion 'We all do it.' "

Marsh's answer was carefully documented—indicating long preparation, too. It was dignified, and had a tone of hurt. After insisting that he was being unjustifiably attacked, he slammed back with a list of Cope's scientific errors. The most telling: Cope's mistake in placing the head of the Elasmosaurus on its tail.

By this time, most men of science were lined up on one side or the other. Few personal feuds have so completely split American science. Two strong, aggressive men had collided, and it was like a battle of two of their "terrible-horned" prehistoric monsters.

Cope gave no quarter when he fought, although away from the arena he could laugh about the "war"; and he did not let it affect his normally cheerful, pleasant disposition.

As Ballou pointed out in his articles, Cope was a man of distinguished appearance, with deepset, alert eyes under heavy brows, thick light-brown hair, a Vandyke type of beard. He was slender, moved with quick assurance, and, when compelled to sit for his portrait, gave the impression of a wire under tension.

In the field he was indefatigable. Even after an illness that left him weak and shaky, he seemed to pick up strength the moment he reached the open country. He could endure any hardship if there was a fossil at the end of it, or a promise of fossils. Without hesitation Cope spent his personal fortune to make the most complete collection possible of American fossils, and to do it first—or in any event not second.

And yet in his relations with his wife, daughter, and friends he was easy, affectionate, even gay.

His scholarship was unquestioned, despite a number of "wrong-end foremost" errors that were inevitable under the speed with which he worked. His life made impossible the kind of checking and rechecking reserved for a library pedant or for a man with a large staff.

Crowded as his life was, Cope managed to arrange his materials to fill in some of the gaps of human and animal ancestry. Through his masterly knowledge of anatomy he was able to connect ancient species with their modern descendants. He traced the mammals back to the mammal-reptiles of the Permian epoch, the reptiles back to the Amphibia, the Amphibia to the lobe-finned fishes, and these last to the sharks. Moreover, he had the fossils to demonstrate his points. His work in this field was brilliant, though he was fond of his own theories, and laughingly told a friend when a fossil refused to fit: "I'd like to throw that bone out the window."

With his analytical mind and insistence on thinking for himself, Cope differed early with Darwin.

He was only thirty-one when he invented the phrase under which the Lamarckians—or Neo-Lamarckians as they called themselves—made their most damaging attack: Darwin's failure to explain the "origin of the fittest."

Cope used the phrase first in his Walker Prize essay of 1871, in which he also set forth the evolutionary views he supported for the rest of his life:

"The influences and forces which have operated to produce the type structures of the animal kingdom have been plainly of two kinds: 1. Originative; 2. Directive. The prime importance of the former is obvious; that the latter is only secondary in the order of time or succession, is evident from the fact that it controls the preservation or destruction of the results or creations of the first.

"Wallace and Darwin have propounded as the cause of modification in descent their law of natural selection. This law has been epitomized by Spencer as the 'survival of the fittest.' This neat expression no doubt covers the case, but it leaves the origin of the fittest entirely untouched. Darwin assumes a 'tendency to variation' in nature and it is plainly necessary to do this, in order that materials for the exercise of a selection should exist. Darwin and Wallace's law is, then, only restrictive, directive, conservative or destructive of something already created. I propose then to seek for the originative laws by which these subjects are furnished—in other words, for the causes of the origin of the fittest."

It was a bold objective, and it led Cope straight to Lamarck, for the French naturalist had demonstrated how the variations arose.

Cope's gift for going first soon made him the accepted leader of the Neo-Lamarckian school in America. In co-operation with a number of scientists he brought together a series of twenty-one essays under the title: *The Origin of the Fittest.*

Natural selection, the essays repeated, does not originate anything; it acts only upon variations that exist—a point Darwin had made himself. Cope also derided the idea that variations stem from inheritance. What, he asked, is inheritance but a repetition of characters possessed by some ancestor? The question was where and how the ancestor obtained the peculiarity.

In 1896 Cope took a leading part in the publication of a second collaborative volume, *Primary Factors of Organic Evolution.* It reviewed and reaffirmed the Neo-Lamarckian point of view.

Even before it appeared, August Weismann had begun to supply conclusive evidence that acquired characters cannot be inherited. Weismann traced inheritance to the germ cell and to the germ cell alone.

Cope only fought all the harder for Lamarckism. He insisted upon the inheritance not only of direct changes produced by the environment, but of the indirect as well. This went even beyond Lamarck. To Cope the changes that he saw in his fossils were an undeniable demonstration of the effect of environment. As conditions had changed, so had the animals living in the varying environments.

In animals, such as man, which used the hind legs for walking, the hind legs became elongated. If both front and hind legs were used, as in the case of the elephant, both developed. And in the animals that used the forelegs for climbing, the forelegs grew long. "Those elements which receive the principal impact in progression are those which increase in length," Cope declared in his *Primary Factors of Organic Evolution,* Part II.

Much in the manner of Lamarck, Cope went on to cite the effect of environment on plants, on mollusks, on the color of butterflies, on the eyes of cave animals. Always he drew upon experiments and observations that were not his own. Henry Fairfield Osborn in his excellent full-length biography of Cope, *Cope, Master Naturalist,* pointed out that Cope ceased to be an observer, much less an experimentalist.

To explain how acquired characters might be inherited, Cope postulated various forces that he endowed with names as esoteric as those he had given to his prehistoric fossil animals. Thus there were coined *bathmogenesis, ergogenesis, emphytogenesis, statogenesis,* and finally the most staggering of them all, *mnemogenesis.* The explanations were as involved as the names, but at bottom they were the old Lamarckian forces in a slightly changed guise.

The evolutionists were hopelessly divided on natural selection versus inheritance of acquired characters as an explanation of evolution. Experiment after experiment was made to settle the issue, but always there was something on the other side, and new doubt. The two sides came no closer together.

Nevertheless, appreciation of Cope's great contributions to

American science was growing. In 1895 he was elected president of the American Association for the Advancement of Science.

Shortly after this high point of his life, Cope became ill. He made a slight recovery, and life in the fossil-crowded house on Pine Street returned to its usual hectic pace. Then suddenly Cope's illness took a turn for the worse. It was not considered wise to move him, and on April 27, 1897 Cope died on his office cot—a cot surrounded by huge bones and great stacks of fossil-filled paper boxes, one stack topped by a cranium of Erypos.

His close friends gathered in the Pine Street house for the simple Quaker services. As they sat in silence, there was no sound except that of Cope's Florida tortoise crawling about.

When Osborn could bear the silence no longer, he rose and read the following verses from Job: "Where wast thou when I laid the foundations of the earth? Declare, if thou hast understanding." "These are the problems to which our friend devoted his life," he said.

How superb a collector Cope had been became evident when his collections were sold. In addition to his mammal collection of ten thousand specimens, which had gone to the American Museum earlier, the naturalist had three other vast collections: that of North American fish, amphibians, and reptiles; the South American collection from the pampas; and his European collections. His executors estimated that these collections with their 23,245 specimens had cost Cope about $50,-000. They were sold to the American Museum for $28,550.

When the curator of the museum went to Philadelphia to supervise their packing, he was moved to comment: "I got there a good line on Cope's methods of study and character. Perhaps the most important was a deep appreciation of the fundamental scientific honesty of the man, together with an intellectual brilliancy that enabled him to interpret scanty and fragmentary evidence with an almost uncanny insight."

Cope's lifetime friend Henry Fairfield Osborn did not hesitate to give him the title of "master naturalist." It was one that he was willing to accord only to such great men as Aristotle, Agassiz, Leidy, and a few others. "Cope covered with giant strides the great branches of natural science, and was one of the few capable of embracing the whole realm of life," said Osborn.

If Cope was wrong in some interpretations, he was one of the great discoverers.

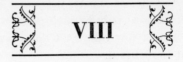

VIII

DE VRIES

PRIMROSES AND MUTATIONS

The origin of species is a natural phenomenon.
—LAMARCK
The origin of species is an object of inquiry.
—DARWIN
The origin of species is an object of experimental investigation.
—DE VRIES [1]

A DEEPLY TROUBLESOME PROBLEM kept turning over and over in the mind of a young Dutch botanist. He was full of respect, even veneration, for "the unsurpassed genius" of Darwin. In his judgment there was no doubt whatsoever that Darwin was right in his main thesis that "descent with modification is the main law of nature in the organic world."

But how did the modification come about? Exclusively through the action of natural selection on an infinitude of small changes, as the Darwinians of his day insisted?

To the Dutch botanist this seemed to contradict what he saw about him. Plant-breeders were able to make only small improvements by selecting the sweetest sugar beets, the fullest ears of corn, the blackest tulips; they could not produce new species in this way. New species were developed only when some new and different character cropped up in nature to give the breeders fresh material with which to work.

The young botanist suspected that such new material origi-nated in certain sudden changes, in "sports," or mutations, as

[1] Quoted on the flyleaf of De Vries's book *Species and Varieties*.

he preferred to call them; and that the truly new was born full-blown.

But this botanist was an unusual person for his day, a scientist who believed first in experiment and close observation rather than in philosophizing. If sudden changes and not small variations were the stuff out of which new species were fashioned, it should be possible to find the evidence in nature and to study it in the experimental garden.

In that spirit of inquiry he set out to look for the changes, a quest that was to make his name famous—for he was Hugo de Vries. He was then, in 1886, a thirty-eight-year-old professor of botany at the University of Amsterdam.

He had been born at Haarlem in 1848, and he seemed to love flowers almost from the day of his birth. After a thorough training in botany at Leyden, Heidelberg, and Würzburg he was appointed a lecturer at the University of Amsterdam. That was 1877. The following year he was made a full professor.

Then and throughout his life, de Vries was handsome in a special kind of way, with the handsomeness that comes from an aliveness in every line. The thinness of his face was emphasized by his pointed beard and mustache. He was the Dutchman of Rembrandt's physicians rather than of the heavy-jowled, hearty burghers of Frans Hals.

In the garden he was patience itself, and always the flower-lover as well as the scientist. He did not quail before the job of counting the dozens of florets on thousands of marigolds or collecting and meticulously labeling the seed from thousands of plants. To his students he insisted that experimental work on heredity required principally "assiduity and exactitude."

His research forced him to destroy hundreds of seedlings that did not bear upon the experiment he was conducting, but he always did it with an underfeeling of regret. He would speak of having "ruthlessly" to weed out the unneeded plants, and he found it difficult in referring to a flower or a plant not to precede its name with the adjective "beautiful."

Having decided to look for the birth of new forms, de Vries began to search the countryside around Amsterdam. He was on the alert first for any peculiarities or monstrosities among the members of a group of plants. That, he thought, would indicate a tendency toward change that would bear watching.

He examined minutely more than one hundred species, some of which he carried home to plant in his garden at the university. But except for small individual variations, each went on producing others just like itself. Gertrude Stein had not yet come along to observe that "a rose is a rose is a rose," but the point was impressed on de Vries with discouraging regularity.

Or that was his experience until he came one day to an abandoned potato field near Hilversum.

In 1870 the owner of the field, Dr. Juris Six, had ordered a new canal built along the southern boundary. Since canals already shut it off on two other sides and no road led into the field from the fourth side, it became so inaccessible that no one would rent it. From then on it lay fallow. The sudden surcease from man's grubbing opened a rich opportunity to the wild plants of the vicinity. They quickly seized upon this new free space and spread out in the quiet, undisturbed field.

One of the later plants to enter the field was the great evening primrose, *Œnothera lamarckiana*. It had escaped from a small cultivated bed in an adjoining park, but had long since run wild. When de Vries came upon the field, the primrose plants formed a dense jungle, as high as a man's head, in the corner of the field nearest the park.

Even from a distance, as he first saw the golden mass of the flowers in the warm light of the Dutch afternoon, de Vries was impressed. As their name indicated, they opened only toward evening. To the botanist's appreciative eye they seemed to pick up the brilliance the sun was relinquishing for the day.

On closer sight, de Vries was struck by the "stately beauty" of the plants. Their tall, densely leaved stems were crowned with the yellow flowers, and as the flowers succeeded one another they left behind long spikes of young fruit. Bumble-bees and moths flocked to them, and it was thus that they were pollinated.

Almost at once de Vries sensed that the whole setting was promising. Obviously there had been a rapid multiplication of the Œnothera and other plants in a short space of time. And new conditions and expansion always had been considered the most favorable circumstances for the appearance of change in any living thing.

De Vries returned to the field and began what was to be one of the most thorough flower studies ever made. To his intense excitement, he saw that the rampant primrose exhibited a high degree of variability, in the form of the leaves, the height of the stem, the mode of branching—in fact, in all the organs and characters. Furthermore, though most of the plants were biennials, many were annuals, and a few lived for three years.

It was exactly the kind of situation de Vries thought might reveal Nature at her creative work. "Here was a wonderful opportunity of getting an insight into the phenomenon of variation as exhibited by a plant that was multiplying rapidly," he recalled later.

De Vries spent the summers of 1886, '87, and '88 at a house only a few minutes' walk from the field. For hours at a time, every week and often every day, he was at the field studying his evening primrose.

His patience and devotion were richly rewarded during the second summer—1887. In one corner of the field, far removed from any other oenotheras, de Vries found ten specimens that he immediately recognized as a new type. Their petals were smaller and oval in contrast to the heart-shaped petals of the lamarckianas. Their leaves were smoother, and, de Vries thought, produced a "much prettier foliage."

Five of the plants formed the nucleus of a little group of

about one hundred individuals. In the previous year on this spot de Vries had seen some first-year rosettes, but no flowering plants. A short distance away grew five other new-type plants. They also were isolated from the crowd of œnotheras.

Without any intermediate steps, without any transition, the new primrose had sprung into blossom. De Vries named it *Œnothera lævifolia*, for it was a new species. Almost under his eyes a fresh species had been created by mutation!

For many years afterward the plants with the smooth leaves and the oval-shaped petals continued to grow in their original corner of the field. The bees and the moths undoubtedly brought them pollen from the lamarckianas, and in time the group became mixed with both types. But the fact that the new form continued to maintain itself even when allowed to cross freely with the other plants indicated to de Vries "the operation of a definite hereditary process."

During the same memorable summer of 1887 de Vries found a second primrose that had mutated. It differed so markedly from the lamarckiana that he named it, too, a new species, *Œnothera brevistylis*. It grew quite close to the park bed from which all the primroses had spread, but it continued to maintain its own different identity.

With the consent of the field's owner, de Vries had transplanted some rosettes to his experimental garden. He also collected seed from the lævifolia.

While he laid his plans during the winter for a thorough test of the plants under the most rigid observation and record-keeping, de Vries delved into the history of his primrose. It was an American plant, an import from the New World. Old records indicated that one species was taken from Virginia to Europe in 1614. Two other species were imported in 1788 and 1789, though de Vries was unable to find any record of the arrival of the lamarckiana.

The species whose yellow brilliance had attracted his attention at Hilversum was first heard of in Europe growing in

the garden of the Musée d'Histoire Naturelle at Paris during
the early years of the eighteenth century. There it caught the
eye of another skilled botanist—Lamarck. The great French
scientist immediately recognized it as an undescribed species.
Not long after Lamarck described the evening primrose, one of
his colleagues formally named it for him: the lamarckiana.

The description written by Lamarck and his type specimens
still were preserved in the herbarium of the museum when
de Vries visited it to compare them with his Hilversum species.
De Vries savored the coincidence. With obvious pleasure he
wrote: "So Lamarck unconsciously discovered and described
the plant that after a century was to become the means of an
empiricial demonstration of his far-reaching views on the common origin of all living beings."

But the two new forms were not to be found in the herbaria
of Leyden, Paris, or Kew, nor could de Vries discover that they
had been described in any other localities. He thought it very
likely that they had arisen for the first time in his or rather the
Six field. He felt so sure of this that his hopes were high of
witnessing the origin of other species from the same stock—and
his hopes soon were to be fulfilled.

The nine lamarckiana rosettes that de Vries had transplanted to his own garden in the fall of 1886 flowered the next
year. The botanist carefully harvested their seed.

The next generation was sown in 1888, and from it, in
1889, grew more than fifteen thousand plants. To examine each
one of the seedlings, to watch the leaves, the stems, and all the
organs for the slightest deviation, was a colossal job. Somehow
de Vries and his gardeners managed it, and ten of the fifteen
thousand showed diverging characters. Five were of a new
type that de Vries called *O. lata*—they were solely female—and
five were a new drawf type, which he named *O. nannella*. The
ten were jealously protected.

When they flowered the next year, their distinctiveness was
obvious. There were no intermediates between them and their

parents, and there had been no indication of their appearance in that of their parents.

"They came into existence at once, fully equipped, without preparation or intermediate steps," wrote de Vries. "No series of generations, no selection, no struggle for existence was needed. It was a sudden leap into a new type, a sport in the

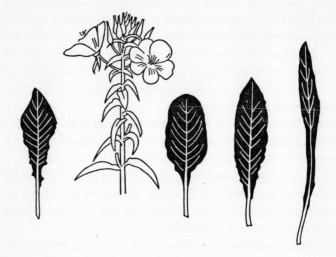

THE GREAT EVENING PRIMROSE. NEW FORMS OF THIS GOLDEN PLANT SUDDENLY CAME INTO EXISTENCE—MUTATIONS. FROM LEFT TO RIGHT, GIGAS, THE PRIMROSE PLANT, LATA, LAMARCKIANA, MURICATA.

best accepted tradition of the word. It fulfilled my hopes and at once gave proof of the possibility of direct observation of the origin of species and of the experimental control thereof."

The story of de Vries's work with this plant is a record of the unsparing attention to minutiæ and of the persistence and patience that were to characterize much of the new era of experimental science which it helped to usher in.

The third generation in de Vries's garden was in the main a repetition of the second. De Vries raised some ten thousand seedlings and out of this host found three lata and three nannella, or nearly the same proportion as in the previous year.

But in addition there was one other seedling of a very different stripe, another new type, another mutation. When it flowered in the following year, de Vries named it *O. rubrinervis,* for its veins were red, and red streaks marked the fruit. The red tint also seemed to have deepened the yellow of the petals. It was a tall plant, with almost silvery white leaves.

The appearance of three mutations in so short a time suggested the stimulating possibility that lamarckiana might have still others in store. The problem was how they might be found. To continue as he had been doing was impossible; the work was overwhelming and de Vries feared that even the closest field examination might miss some new, almost imperceptible twist or turn. He saw that he would have to better his methods of cultivation and examination. For three years he called off the main part of the work—though he continued with the *O. lævifolia* family—while he experimented on a large scale with cultivation, manuring, and artificial fertilization.

He learned that when the young plants were given more room, enough to develop the full rosette the primrose produces in its first year, differences became apparent sooner. Mutations were detectable even in youth. Therefore de Vries began to examine his seedlings early. Those which displayed any deviation were taken out, planted in pots in well-manured soil, and kept under glass.

Out of the 14,000 seedlings with which in 1895 he resumed the main line of his work, 334 young plants were exceptional enough to merit pots of their own. Among them were 60 nannella, 73 lata, and 8 rubrinervis.

But the most curious fact of that year was the appearance of *O. oblonga.* It was a weak whitish form, which de Vries was convinced had probably appeared before, but had escaped attention until the plants were raised separately. Spindling though it might be, it proved as uniform and constant as its three predecessors. De Vries prized it because he felt that the close examination it had been given to identify it in its early stages would certainly have revealed any intermediate stages if there had been any. But no connecting links were found.

PRIMROSE ROSETTE AND SEEDBOX

Albida, another weak form, also was born. Both it and oblonga needed special protection and would not have survived long in an open field.

The great event of the year, though, was the appearance of two other new forms, new types as strong as the other two were weak. *Scintillans* was a brilliantly colored plant, and *gigas* a giant form.

Gigas escaped destruction only by chance. In the seedling state it showed no remarkable qualities and it should have been uprooted. Somehow it was overlooked, and produced a vigorous, sturdy rosette. Again it probably would not have been preserved except that de Vries wanted a few strong rosettes to carry over the winter as future seed plants.

Having survived two such narrow chances, the rosettes were set out in the garden the next year. They looked like any other lamarckianas then until the first flowers opened. One had a much larger crown of bright blossoms.

De Vries watched it closely, and when some of the flowers faded and the young fruits grew, he felt certain that another new type was showing itself. On that indication he removed all the already fertilized flowers and young fruits, and protected the remaining buds from the visits of insects. Thus the isolated flowers were fertilized only with their own pollen, and the purity of the seed was assured.

The seeds from the beautifully flowered plant were sown again the next spring. From them sprang a uniform crop of nearly three hundred young plants. Their stems were almost twice as thick as those of the lamarckiana, their foliage was denser and greener, the flowers were not only brighter but larger, and the fruits broader. Here was a giant among primroses, and so it was named *O. gigas*.

De Vries was again nearly overwhelmed by the abundance of his garden. In 1896 he reduced his general plantings of lamarckiana in order to make a closer study of the repeated production of the new forms. In the fifth generation, 8,000 seedlings were raised. Among them were 377 deviates. All of the forms that had appeared before cropped up again with the sole exception of gigas. Most of the deviates, however, were the weak oblonga and lata. No additional new types came forth.

De Vries suspected that the capacity of his original strain was about exhausted. This conclusion was confirmed by the plantings of the next three generations. They yielded only the mutants commonly seen in former years.

His point had been made; de Vries could summarize his findings. In eight gererations he had raised 53,509 plants.

Among them had been eight new types, all of which appeared in considerable numbers except gigas, which reared its handsome head only once, and scintillans, which occurred only eight times.

Studying this prodigious experiment—selecting the plants and keeping records alone were a formidable undertaking—de Vries felt that he could discern the laws of mutability that had governed the production of new forms in the evening primrose, and that they would hold as true for other plants.

The rules, as he saw them, were these:

1. New elementary species appear suddenly without intermediate steps.

All the attributes that make the new types different from their ancestors are in full display at once. No series of generations, no selection, no struggle is necessary. Afterward, too, the new types remain true, without showing any return to ancestral forms. Occasionally the ancestral forms may reappear in a planting, but they are themselves, while the deviates are clearly deviates. There are no in-betweens, there is no blurring.

2. New forms spring laterally from the main stem.

At the time de Vries began his work, it was generally thought that the older species gradually changed into the newer ones. It was assumed that most individuals were affected in the same degree and in the same direction. By intercrossing, the whole group was believed to move along together.

The evening primrose, it seemed to de Vries, flatly contradicted that prevailing idea. There was neither a slow nor a sudden change in all individuals. On the contrary, the majority remained unchanged; the lamarckianas in the garden and field went on repeating themselves during all the years de Vries kept them under observation. Nor did the strain die out.

"If our gigas and rubrinervis were growing in equal numbers with the lamarckiana in the native field, would it be possible to decide which of them was the progenitor?" asked de Vries.

To one who had not watched and recorded the appearance of the new types, the origin and relation of the three would have been as much a mystery as the origin and relationship of three species of violets, or probably of three species of cats, or three races of humans.

3. New elementary species attain their full constancy at once.

From the first, most of the new primroses were constant. When they were artificially self-fertilized, all the children were just like the parents.

4. Some of the new strains are evidently elementary species, while others are to be considered retrograde varieties.

De Vries noted that gigas, rubrinervis, oblonga, and albida differed from their lamarckiana forebears not in one or two characters, but in several. Each was definitely different, though it might be only in a small degree. De Vries could tell them apart almost from the moment the first shoots appeared above the ground. Their foliage was different and perhaps, along with it, the stature, the flowers, the seeds. De Vries felt that all the changes must somehow be related, but why each type varied as it did he could not then explain.

5. The same new species are produced in a large number of individuals.

It seemed a curious point to de Vries that a number of the same mutations should appear in the same year, and again in other years. He puzzled over the problem and decided that the capacity to mutate must somehow lie latent in the parent.

Certainly such repeated mutations would be more important in the formation of a new species than would a single one. The chances of a single different plant surviving the struggle for space, for food, for air, might be scanty. Any weakness might cause the single deviate to lose out in the race for life and reproduction.

6. The ordinary differences that exist between individuals have nothing to do with mutations.

Some individuals are taller, some are shorter, but all such variations, de Vries pointed out, are grouped around a mean. The shortest lamarckiana, he found, was never as small as even the tallest *O. nannella* dwarf. There always was a gap.

Nor could the dwarf nannella be created by "accumulating" the shortness of the shortest lamarckianas. Although the shortest plants were selected for any number of generations, de Vries was convinced, it would be impossible to create a true dwarf race. Only a mutation could take that step, he said. The great Dutch botanist thus denied again that natural selection molds new species and that "varieties are incipient species."

7. Mutations take place in nearly all directions.

Darwin had assumed all kinds of changes, some favorable, some detrimental, many without significance. He was including both individual variations and the "sports" that he felt were a factor in evolution, though one he did not clearly define.

Some of Darwin's followers, on the other hand, insisted that variations were not random, but directed. Had life not advanced from the simplest beginnings up to man? Did that not indicate direction in the changes?

On this critical point de Vries took his stand squarely with Darwin. He saw no directing pattern in mutations. On the contrary, some of his new primroses were stronger than the parent stock, and some were weaker, some had broader leaves, some narrower; some flaunted brighter blossoms, some paler; some were heavy with seed, others produced none. The mutations occurred in every direction, and de Vries, like Darwin, saw that a change that might be of no importance in the Hilversum field could save the species if it were suddenly transported into a different climate.

In his book *The Mutation Theory,* de Vries added: "Nature does not confine herself to procuring just what is wanted; her creative power seems to be almost unlimited. She furnishes every possibility, so to speak, and leaves it to the environment to choose what suits it."

The publication of de Vries's findings aroused the scientific world. More clearly than ever before, science understood the importance of the abrupt changes in nature. The old doctrine of *"Natura non facit saltus"* fell once and for all. Nature did take sudden leaps.

In a very real sense de Vries also produced a mutation in scientific research. Whole new possibilities of investigation were opened, and science moved forward on a new tack. He himself considered this one of the most important outgrowths of his work. Workers all around the world began to study mutations not only in plants, but in animals. Some made their start by checking the work of de Vries himself.

Soon disquieting reports were heard. Others maintained that de Vries's beautiful yellow primrose had not been the pure species that he thought. It might, not too far back in its development, have been a hybrid, and some of the mutations that de Vries watched with such gratification seemed to have been only recombinations of characters already present in the plant.

But most of the principles of mutation that de Vries had drawn from his work were proved over and over again. There were mutations and they occurred almost as de Vries had said.

The final verdict on de Vries's meticulous study of the evening primrose and the substantiation of the principle of mutation took a number of years. De Vries in the meanwhile was pushing into another phase of his work, almost as important as the first.

As he watched the mutations in the Œnothera, de Vries was impressed by the fact that no mutating plant changed as an inseparable whole, according to the prevailing theory of the day. De Vries saw that only the shape of the leaf might change, or more likely a group of characters. Along with the shift in the leaf might come a change in the color of the blossom or the shape of the fruit. "When new species or varieties originate, it is not the whole nature of the organism that is changed; on the contrary, everything remains in a state of rest except at one or two points, and it is only to the changes at these points that all the improvement is due," he explained.

His keen observation and his willingness to test old rules led de Vries to a deeply significant conclusion: each character is the product of a separate hereditary unit. Each could change independently.

"Attributes of organisms consist of distinct, separate, and independent units," de Vries continued. "These units can be associated in groups and we find in allied species the same units and groups of units. Transitions such as we so frequently meet with in the external form both of animals and of plants are as completely absent from between these units as they are between two molecules."

A mutation, then, was a change in one of the hereditary units now known as genes.

The idea was basic, precedent-breaking. Upon it was to rest the whole foundation of modern heredity research. But another man, whose work was then unknown to de Vries and to the scientific world, had previously made the same discovery. The credit for carrying the science of evolution forward in the greatest jump since Darwin wrote *The Origin of Species* was in the end to go only in a lesser degree to de Vries.

When the Dutch scientist began to think along these lines, he launched into a search for background, for antecedents in the literature of the subject. In a work by a German investigator, W. O. Focke, *Die Pflanzenmischlinge*, was an intriguing reference to some findings by an unknown Austrian monk: "Mendel believed he had found constant numerical ratios among the types produced by hybridization." De Vries tracked down the reference. In a thirty-four-year-old publication by the Brünn Society for the Study of Natural History he found two monographs by Gregor Johann Mendel, abbot of Brünn.

The two papers not only set forth the idea of unit characters, but, with a brilliance and scientific precision seldom equaled, outlined the laws according to which the units were combined and recombined to make all living things what they are. It was one of the great scientific demonstrations of all times.

During the very years when Darwin had been struggling to explain how and why living things vary, the work that would have supplied the answer was being carried on in a remote monastery garden. And he knew nothing of it. The report of Mendel's findings lay buried until 1900. The world did not know that the whole concept of heredity had been radically changed. The very few who were aware of what had been done at Brünn failed completely to realize its significance.

But in the intervening years science had been moving closer and closer to the unknown findings of Mendel. By 1900 what Mendel had done could be understood and appreciated.

De Vries repeated Mendel's experiment with corn and found the Mendelian laws accurate, as did all the others who tested them.

But de Vries's great interest was elsewhere, in the phenomenon of mutation. He felt that a fuller view must be had of nature at work creating new species. "We must try to arrange things so as to be present at the time when nature produces another of these rare changes," he said.

He continued his work with his lifelong favorite, the evening primrose, but sowed and worked with and studied other plants, too. In this way he managed to be present when the toadflax produced a rare five-spurred flower. He pollinated and nursed it and its offspring for eight years until suddenly there appeared a plant that had only five-spurred flowers. Another new species had been created before his eyes. He had witnessed another of those rare jumps in nature, and again there were no intermediate forms.

How frequently might such mutations occur? De Vries sowed ten cubic centimeters of seed from the parents of the plant that had produced the mutation. He obtained 1,750 flowering plants, and among them were 16 that bore only the five-spurred flowers. The mutation rate in this case was about one per cent.

With the same methods, de Vries obtained a double-flowered marigold. He began by isolating blossoms with twelve rays. This meant counting the ray-florets on the flowers on fifteen hundred plants, not in the laboratory, where they could be pulled apart, but in the garden. And they had to be handled so gently that none would be injured.

De Vries persisted, counting endlessly but exactly, watching always for a flower with more rays. He found it, and soon among the plants that deviated the most he found one that had a secondary head with one more ray than any of the others. After four years of following the descendants of this unusual plant, he went into the garden one day to find a double marigold, big, bright, a delight to the scientist and to the gardener both. And this double race remained constant.

De Vries was equally lucky with his clovers. By watching for the plant that was different, he succeeded in the end in raising three-, four-, five-, and seven-leaved clovers on the same plant.

Always de Vries continued to visit his field at Hilversum. After a few years the owner decided to plant some of it with trees. This ended the undisputed sway of the golden primrose, but it continued to flourish. A number of new forms, the same as those in de Vries's garden, appeared in the field, though there most of the newcomers perished. The weaker mutants could not survive in the rough of competition.

De Vries's fame was growing almost like the generations of his plants. In 1904 he was invited to give a long series of lectures on "Species and Varieties—Their Origin by Mutation" at the University of California. They were later published in this country.

While he was in California, de Vries met Luther Burbank, the great American plant-grower and originator of new varieties. His interest in the marvels Burbank was producing was so keen that he later wrote a book on the subject. Texas and the Grand Canyon and the flowers of each aroused de Vries's admiration, and he also made use of his visit to the United States to search for some of the American ancestors of his "beautiful evening primrose."

CLOVERS WITH THREE, FOUR, FIVE, SIX AND SEVEN LEAVES GREW ON THE SAME PLANT. DEVRIES SAW THIS COME ABOUT THROUGH MUTATION.

As the work with mutations continued, the debate about their occurrence dwindled away. No one could seriously question any longer that a new type might appear when any young plant pushed through the ground or a young animal was born. The big question was whether mutations are the principal means of evolution or slow, gradual changes play the largest part.

De Vries's answer was firm: species have not arisen gradually through the operation of selection. They have arisen only by sudden, though often small changes—by mutation. "The doctrine of mutation lays stress on sudden or discontinuous changes and regards only these as active in the formation of species," de Vries wrote.

In support of his position, the distinguished Dutch botanist returned time and again to his own experience and to that of the breeders. Only mutations produced new constant types. Try as he would, de Vries could obtain no permanent changes in species through selection. He succeeded through selection in creating an ear of corn with many extra rows of kernels. But as soon as he stopped crossing the multiple-rowed with the multiple-rowed, "the excellence of the race at once disappeared." In two or three seasons the corn was back to its average number of rows. But, de Vries argued, if a larger number of rows had appeared through mutation, the multiple-rowed corn would have continued to breed true. That was his point of difference.

Only after a species is created does natural selection come into play, he repeated. As in the days when the evening primrose was first performing its miracle of transformation for him, de Vries said again and again: "Natural selection creates nothing; it only sifts."

In 1918, at the age of seventy, famous and respected, de Vries retired from his post at the university. To honor the occasion his friends brought out a six-volume collected edition of his work. It testified to how far his facts and theories had reached. In it were many articles he had published in Holland, Germany, France, Great Britain, and the United States.

During the remainder of his life de Vries lived at Lunteren. There, surrounded by his beloved flowers, he continued producing new plant forms until the time of his death, on May 21, 1935.

The undeniable fact of mutation and the brilliance of de Vries's logic convinced a large part of the scientific world that Darwin's theory of evolution by natural selection had been disproved and supplanted by the theory of evolution by mutation. Well into the second decade of the twentieth century, and perhaps later, evolutionists split along this new dividing line. There seemed to be no ground for compromise. The books and the papers poured forth. Evolution, they sought to prove, had to be the result either of natural selection or of mutation. The conflict was bitter.

When the great dispute finally was resolved by the development of the modern theory of evolution, the older quarrel was found to be without foundation. The theory of mutation related to a different level of the evolutionary process from that on which natural selection operates. The two theories were not alternatives. Both were right.

De Vries's discovery of the origin of hereditary variation through mutation accounted for the presence of the material upon which selection works. And the greatest difficulty in Darwin's theory was thereby removed.

The flower-loving Dutch botanist with his scrupulous regard for science had caught an important part of the truth. In addition he had demonstrated that the great changes in nature can be studied experimentally. His work was the principal milestone in the transition from the old ideas to the modern theory of heredity. De Vries's top place in history was secure.

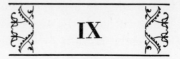

IX

MENDEL

THE DISCOVERY OF HEREDITY

LYING JUST OUTSIDE the white walls of the stately Augustinian monastery of Altbrünn in Austria is a little strip of garden, no more than twenty feet wide and one hundred and twenty feet long. A path and a hedge set it apart from the fields beyond. During the 1850's and '60's, it was filled each spring with masses of flowers and with hundreds of pea plants, some of them clinging to staves, some fastened to the branches of trees, some growing along stretched strings.

Moving about among the flowering plants was a young, vigorous, decidedly stout monk. With fine forceps and a skillful hand he opened the white and violet blossoms of the peas, removed the keel and carefully detached the anthers. Taking a camel's-hair brush he then dusted the stigma with pollen from another pea plant. That done, he wrapped the treated blossom in a little bag of paper or calico, to prevent any bee or pea-weevil from carrying in other pollen.

The monk was Gregor Johann Mendel, and the work he was so lovingly and indefatigably doing was eventually to show the world how all characteristics are passed along from parent to offspring. In that quiet, sheltered garden Mendel discovered the laws of heredity.

But Mendel was a man ahead of his time. For many years the laws he worked out with an amazing precision and perception were to lie buried in the *Proceedings* of the Brünn Society for the Study of Natural Science. Not until 1900 were they discovered.

The man whose brilliant experiments were to carry evolution forward in its second great leap was born on July 22, 1822 in Heinzendorf, a tiny village in the extreme northeastern corner of Moravia where the borders of Germany, Poland, and Czechoslovakia so uneasily adjoin. His parents were peasants who only two generations before had risen from the status of cotter. When Johann was born, his father, Anton held "peasant holding No. 58," comprising a house, a garden, and "thirty yoke" of rolling plowlands and meadows. In addition to tending his own land, Anton had to work, under the *corvée*, three days a week for the lord of the manor. He had little spare time, and yet he always managed some margin for working with his fruit trees, which he grafted with improved varieties supplied him by the village priest from the gardens of the Countess Waldburg, the lady of the manor. At a very early age young Johann began to help his father in the orchard. He also learned more about fruit-growing and beekeeping at the village school, where such training had been added at the specific request of the countess.

Johann did so well in the village school that the master urged he be sent on to the higher school in Leipnik, thirteen miles away. The story was repeated there. Because of his excellent record the earnest, broad-shouldered youngster was recommended for the still higher school at Troppau. The Mendels found it impossible to pay the full fees, and Johann was entered on "half rations." To fill out his meager fare, the Mendels sent him bread and butter whenever the carrier made the twenty-mile trip from Heinzendorf to Troppau.

When Johann was about sixteen, heavy expenses at home cut off even the thin trickle of support. To continue his studies, which he knew meant everything to him, Johann assumed a heavy schedule of tutoring; but the strain was great, and in 1838 he became ill and had to go home. He returned to school the following year and by a constant struggle, interspersed with illness, finished his studies at the Troppau school and enrolled in the Olmütz Philosophical Institute. Again the going was hard, and Mendel often was ill.

By the time he finished the two-year philosophical course, in 1843, as he wrote later in a third-person autobiographical note, he had decided that "it had become impossible for him to continue such strenuous exertions. It was incumbent on him to enter a profession in which he would be spared perpetual anxiety about a means of livelihood. His private circumstances determined his choice of profession."

An Olmütz professor who had been asked to recommend promising young men as candidates for the Augustinian monastery at Brünn was happy to recommend Mendel. He wrote the monks that Mendel during his two-year course had almost invariably "the most exceptional reports and is a young man of very solid character." And so it was that on October 9, 1843 Mendel was admitted to the monastery as a novice and assumed the name of Gregor.

By becoming an Augustinian, Mendel's autobiography notes: "His material position had been completely transformed. Now that he had been relieved of anxiety about the physical basis of existence, which is so detrimental to study, the respectful undersigned acquired fresh courage and energy, so that it is with pleasure and love that he undertook the course of classical studies prescribed for the years of probation. In his free time he occupied himself with the small botanical and mineralogical collection available at the monastery. His fondness for natural science grew with every fresh opportunity for making himself acquainted with it.

"Although he had no oral guidance in this undertaking (and perhaps there is no other department of knowledge in which the self-taught student has such difficulties to face and moves so slowly toward his goal), he has ever since been so much addicted to the study of nature that he would shrink from no exertions that might help him, by further diligence on his own

part and by the advice of men who had had practical experience, to fill the gaps in his information."

Mendel did not begin his prescribed four-year theological
course until 1845. By the end of his third year, however, the
prelate of the monastery applied to the bishop, asking that
Mendel, "who has lived blamelessly, piously, and religiously,"
be given the higher orders *"dispensando."* Consent was
granted, and on his twenty-fifth birthday Mendel was ordained
subdeacon; two days later, priest.

From the outset, however, Mendel found the regular duties
of a priest impossible to one of his disposition. The sight of
suffering and death affected him so strongly that he became ill
himself. The prelate, who was aware of the young priest's solid
worth in other fields, wisely assigned him to teaching.

Although Mendel had no training other than his tutoring
experience, he also took to teaching with "pleasure and love,"
and tried to present mathematics and the other subjects he
taught "in a way the pupils would find it easy to understand."
The pupils responded to this approach and became deeply
attached to him.

The school authorities felt so confident of Mendel's abilities
that they urged him to take the state examination for high-
school teachers. Mendel wrote the necessary essays and studied
hard; but somehow he failed, partly, it seemed, because he
lacked the formal knowledge expected, and partly because
some of his views ran contrary to those of the examiners.

In 1851 the monastery decided to send Mendel to the University of Vienna for "higher scientific training." Hugo Iltis, a
fellow townsman who devoted a lifetime to assembling the
little-known facts about Mendel's life, was unable to learn
much about these years except that Mendel spent four terms
at the university.[1] At the end of this time he returned to Brünn
and resumed teaching in the Brünn Modern School. Again he

[1] Iltis: *Life of Mendel.*

was highly successful as a teacher, a friend to his pupils rather than the stern master so common at the time.

For years afterward his pupils remembered him—a man of medium height, broad-shouldered and already a little corpulent, with a big head and high forehead, and blue eyes that gazed earnestly, though often smilingly, through gold-rimmed glasses. Almost always he was dressed, not in a priest's robe, but in the plain clothes considered proper for a member of the Augustinian order acting as a schoolmaster—tall hat, frock coat, usually rather too big for him, short trousers tucked into top boots.

His pupils also remembered his fondness for animals. Occasionally he would show them the gray and white mice with which he undoubtedly had begun hybridization experiments— experiments regarded with disfavor by the ecclesiastical authorities, and never mentioned by Mendel in any of his known monographs or letters.

Or Mendel would invite his pupils to the monastery, where he would walk with them through the gardens, showing them his bees, the pineapples growing in the forcing-house, and the experimental work with the peas—though he did not indicate that he was the investigator whose handiwork they were admiring. He used plain words to describe matters of sex, and if this produced a titter, he would say: "Don't be stupid. These are natural things." For a priest in the middle of the nineteenth century this was a remarkably liberal attitude.

The school authorities reported their complete satisfaction with Mendel's teaching and spoke of his "zealous and successful endeavors." But when he went to Vienna to take another examination for a teacher's certificate, he again seems to have failed. Nevertheless, he continued as a not fully accredited teacher.

All during these happy, tranquil years of teaching Mendel was carrying on his famous experiments. His own explanation of how he happened to start is a simple one. In trying to produce new color varieties in the flowers he loved, he noticed the remarkable regularity with which the same hybrid forms continually recurred when fertilization took place between the same species. Mendel said that he decided to follow up the development of the hybrids in their offspring.

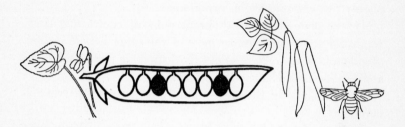

EACH SPRING THE NARROW LITTLE STRIP OF GARDEN BENEATH THE WALLS OF THE AUGUSTINIAN MONASTERY AT ALTBRÜNN, AUSTRIA WAS FILLED WITH MASSES OF FLOWERS AND WITH PEA AND BEAN PLANTS.

This was in 1854. *The Origin of Species* had not yet been published, and it seems unlikely that Mendel was planning to delve into the problem of evolution, though evolution was in the air and many were asking how the great multiplicity of species could be explained. Mendel's immediate concern was heredity. Nevertheless, he was well aware of its evolutionary implications.

"One who surveys the work done in this field will come to the conclusion that, among the numerous experiments, not one has been carried out comprehensively enough to determine the number of different forms under which the offspring of hybrids appear, or to arrange these forms with certainty according to their separate generations, or definitely to ascertain their statistical relations," he wrote in the introduction to the first of his monographs. "Some courage is, indeed, needed to undertake such far-reaching labors. Still, that would seem to be the only right way of ultimately achieving the solution of a problem that is of enormous importance in its bearing upon the evolutionary history of organic forms."

Mendel chose the pea, the ordinary edible pea, with which to work. After collecting thirty-four varieties and testing them for two years to make certain they ran true to form, he selected twenty-two varieties for his experiment.

He singled out seven different pairs of contrasting characters for study, and unlike most of the other experimenters, Mendel chose characters so clearly distinctive that to tell them apart called for no hairline decisions:

1. The shape of the seed—round in some plants, wrinkled in others.

2. The colors of the peas (cotyledons)—some yellow, some green.

3. The tint of the seed coat—white, gray, grayish brown, buff with violet spots.

4. The shape of the ripe pods—simple curved (inflated) or constricted between the peas.

5. The tint of the unripe pods—green or yellow.

6. The position of the flower—axial or terminal.

7. The stature of the plant—tall or dwarf.

In the lovely Austrian spring of 1856 the peas in Mendel's overcrowded little garden were ready to blossom. Using his careful technique, Mendel deposited the pollen from a plant that always had produced round peas on the stigma of a wrinkle-seeded plant. And he made the same kind of crosses of each of his other pairs. Then Mendel hovered anxiously over his "children," watching carefully while he waited for the peas to ripen.

When that exciting day came, he found that all the peas formed from his first cross were round! There was no sign of the wrinkling of the other parent. Evidently roundness was a "dominant" character, and the wrinkling a "recessive" one. When the two came together, the dominant roundness prevailed over the recessive wrinkling. And it was the same with all of his other pairs. One character was dominant and one recessive, and all the peas formed from the first cross were like the dominant parent.

Mendel strongly suspected, however, that this was only the beginning.

The next spring when the vines again blossomed, Mendel dusted the pollen from one hybrid on the flowers of another. Again there was that tantalizing waiting. But this time when the peas formed, there was a very different situation, a highly enlightening one. Three peas out of every four were round; the other was wrinkled. The wrinkling of the grandparent was appearing again; it had not been lost! And the same steady 3:1 ratio appeared in all the hybrid crosses.

The next spring Mendel eagerly resumed his work. But this year he let each pea plant reproduce itself by self-fertilization, in the normal, usual way of peas. The ripening of the peas brought another astonishing result. The peas formed on wrinkle-seeded plants were all wrinkled. Evidently when the recessive wrinkled were crossed with wrinkled they gave only wrinkled. The wrinkled character of the great-grandparent plant had separated out again in pure form. And it remained pure as long as Mendel crossed wrinkled with wrinkled.

But there were 565 plants that had been grown from round seeds. Here there was a sharp division. Out of this group, 193 plants produced only peas with round seeds. But 372 bore round and wrinkled seeds in the ratio of 3:1.

Exactly the same ratios appeared in all Mendel's other pairs, and though he continued the experiment through six or seven generations in all cases, the same patterns always emerged from the same kind of crosses.

Mendel saw that when two hybrids were crossed, one fourth of the offspring were pure dominants: as long as they were crossed with their own kind, they would produce only dominants—in this case, only round peas.

Two fourths looked to all appearances like the dominants—they had round seeds, too. But when they were allowed to reproduce, they brought forth one pure recessive. Thus two of the hybrid offspring were mixtures. And if the ostensibly round, yet actually mixed peas were allowed to reproduce, their offspring would separate once more into the 3:1 ratio, or actually into a 1:2:1 ratio if their true nature rather than their appearance was taken into account.

And the final one fourth were pure recessives; their seeds were wrinkled and had no other hereditary factor in them.

Mendel, with a fine simplicity that all geneticists since have followed, designated the dominants with capital A and the recessives with a small a.

That made it easy to chart the pea generations and to see exactly what had happened:

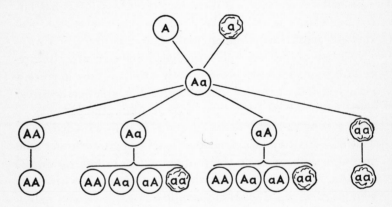

THE CROSSING OF THE ROUND AND WRINKLED PEA

By concentrating on simple contrasting characteristics, instead of looking at the plant as a whole, Mendel could trace inheritance from parent to offspring.

But what would happen if the parents differed in two contrasted pairs of characters? Once again Mendel proceeded directly and simply to find out.

He crossed peas with round yellow seeds with those bearing wrinkled green seeds. Since roundness and yellowness were dominant, Mendel expected all the peas to be round and yellow. And so they were!

The following year, when spring came again to the monastery garden, he crossed the round yellow hybrids with other round yellow hybrid pollen. The fifteen plants thus treated bore 556 seeds. The seeds were of four different kinds, and frequently the four were found side by side in the same pod. There were 315 round and yellow peas, 101 wrinkled and yellow, 108 round and green, and 32 wrinkled and green.

Mendel saw that when two pairs of contrasted characters were crossed, the separation no longer took place according to the 3:1 ratio, but was approximately 300:100:100:33, or 9:3:3:1.

Mendel designated the dominant characters round and yellow with the capital letters A and B, and the recessives, wrinkled and green, with the small letters a and b.

The monk working so tenderly and laboriously in his garden was also an excellent mathematician. He understood quickly that he had obtained every possible combination that could be made from the two original series A 2Aa a, and B 2Bb b. Among the sixteen forms were nine that differed inwardly in their hereditary factors, whereas when there was only one pair of contrasted characters, there were only three differing forms.

What would be the result if three contrasting characters were crossed? Mendel went on to find out. He crossed plants with round yellow seeds and a tinted seed coat (ABC) with pollen from wrinkled green peas with a white seed coat (abc). The work was tedious and difficult, but it yielded 27 different forms, or all the combinations that could be obtained by putting together three series, A 2Aa a; B 2Bb b; C 2Cc c.

It was easy to see how it went. With one pair, 3 different forms; with two pairs, 9; with three pairs, 27. The different forms would rapidly pile up, 3 times 3 times 3.

Darwin and other experimenters had also worked with peas, and Darwin had noted the uniformity of the first generation and the separation of characters in the second generation. He had even obtained peas in the Mendelian ratios. All the isolated facts that would have explained how inheritance goes were in his hands, but the logical mathematical tie and the significance of the combinations eluded him.

Mendel not only grasped the mathematical basis and the inevitability of the combinations; he went straight to the biological principles that underlay the phenomenon demonstrated by the peas climbing toward the sun in his monastery garden.

From his work he formulated three laws of inheritance:

1. Any living thing is a complex of a number of independent heritable units, and each unit is independent of the others. (This was the conclusion to which de Vries and others came many years later.)

2. Each pair of contrasted characters undergoes its own hereditary separation. And thus all possible combinations can be produced by hybridization.

3. The hereditary factors are unaltered and unaffected by their long association in each individual.

In a letter Mendel explained: "The course of development consists simply in this, that in each successive generation the two primal characters issue distinct and unaltered out of the hybridized form, there being nothing whatever to show that either of them has inherited or taken over anything from the other."

This was Mendel's doctrine of the purity of the gametes, or the reproductive cells.

To test the correctness of this theory and to make no unproved assertions, Mendel, the meticulous investigator, fertilized the hybrid AaBb, a plant with round yellow seeds, with pollen from the parent form AB, which also had round yellow seeds. Outwardly the two looked alike.

If his doctrine of the purity of the gametes was correct, the hybrid should have four kinds of reproductive cells, AB, Ab, aB, ab. And crossed with AB, four hybrids should result: AB, ABb, AaB, AaBb. And since each pair contained both a dominant A and B, all should have round yellow seeds.

The young plants grew tall on their staves and strings, and when the peas matured, there were ninety-eight. Each single pea was round and yellow!

Still wanting to check in every possible way, Mendel fertilized the hybrid AaBb with pollen from a plant with wrinkled green seeds, ab. According to his law, this "back cross with the recessive parent" should have produced hybrid forms AaBb (round and yellow), Aab (round and green), aBb (wrinkled and yellow), and ab (wrinkled and green), and in equal numbers.

Mendel once again had to wait for the rain and sun to mature the peas in their pods. When the day came, he found in the pods hanging on the vines 31 round yellow peas, 28 round and green, 27 wrinkled and yellow, and 26 wrinkled and green. If enough plants had been raised, the slight variations would have disappeared; the ratio was as Mendel had expected 1:1:1:1.

To predict and to have the peas form in their pods in exactly the kinds and proportions predicted could only mean that his theories were correct. They were the laws of nature.

Mendel decided to wait no longer. All during the fall and winter of 1864 he checked and re-checked his findings and in his fine copperplate script wrote the paper that eventually was to explain the phenomenon of inheritance to the world.

The February 1865 meeting of the Brünn Society for the Study of Natural Science was held at the Modern School. The night was cold and clear, and most of the members came out to hear Mendel report on the work he had so long had under way. The several other botanists who belonged to the society and the other members—a geologist, an astronomer, a chemist, and an authority on cryptograms—listened with amazement to Mendel's account of the seemingly invariable ratios in which roundness and greenness and other characters had appeared among his hybrid peas. Mendel spoke for about an hour. When he finished, he said that at the next meeting he would explain why the peculiar and regular segregation of the characters took place.

The next month, when Mendel began his mathematical deductions, attention seemed to wander. It was a strange, unheard-of combination of mathematics and botany that he was expounding. And the general idea that lay behind it, that each living thing is a mosaic of hereditary characters, was so at variance with the prevailing thought that it probably was incomprehensible. The minutes show no questions and no discussion.

It was the custom of the society to collect all the papers read during a year and to publish them in the following year. Mendel was asked to put his paper in order for publication. Although it had provoked no comment at the meeting, members and friends had talked to him about it afterward.

"I encountered various views," Mendel later wrote, "but so far as I know, no one undertook a repetition of the experiment. When I was asked to publish the lecture in the *Proceedings* of the society, I agreed to do so after I had once more looked through my notes relating to the various years of the experiment without being able to discover any sort of mistake."

The printed version of Mendel's work—*Versuche über Pflanzenhybriden*—appeared in 1866. According to the society's custom, copies of the *Proceedings* were sent to Vienna, Berlin, Rome, St. Petersburg, and Uppsala. But the slim monograph, which could have upset the world's ideas of heredity and brought about a drastic revision in the theory of evolution while Darwin still was alive, attracted no attention whatever. It stood unnoticed on a few library shelves and for many years was heard of no more.

Mendel was disappointed that his work, the significance of which he clearly understood, had failed to arouse any shadow of interest. On New Year's Eve 1866 he wrote a long, carefully planned letter to a man from whom he hoped for understanding, Karl von Nägeli, one of the leading botanists of the day. "Your well-known services in the detection and classification of plant hybrids growing in the wild state make it my agreeable duty to bring to your kindly knowledge the description of a few experiments concerning the artificial fertilization of plants," Mendel modestly began his letter.

Mendel enclosed a copy of his monograph and diffidently suggested that Nägeli might care to check his results. He also indicated that he was thinking about carrying on experiments with the hawkweed, a plant with which Nägeli had extensively experimented, and added: "I hope you will not refuse me your esteemed participation when, in any instance, I need advice."

Several months later Nägeli replied. The tone of his letter was condescending. The only comment on Mendel's experiments was that "far from being finished," they were "only beginning." He asked for some of the hybrid seeds Mendel had offered, and encouraged Mendel to work with his hawkweed.

Mendel had raised more than 10,000 plants, had made 355 artificial fertilizations on peas alone, and had recorded his observations on 12,980 hybrid specimens, but he showed no resentment at Nägeli's remark that he was only beginning. On the contrary, he was delighted to have heard from the great botanist, and promptly sent Nägeli 140 packets of his seeds. A correspondence began that ran on for almost eight years.

Largely as a result of it, Mendel began to work with hawkweed (hieracium), a plant that proved difficult and unsuited for his purposes. Even to collect the dandelion-like material was a hardship, for by that time Mendel had become so stout that the necessary expeditions to the hills proved very taxing.

The flowers were small, and the tube through which the

pistil passes so tiny that Mendel had to make use of "an illuminating device"—a mirror and lens—to operate on it with a needle. Since the sun struck the mirror, Mendel's eyes became badly strained, and for more than six months his work was seriously hampered.

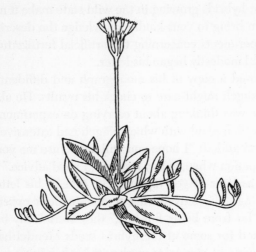

THE HIERACIUM OR HAWKWEED. WORK WITH THIS PLANT HAMPERED MENDEL'S INVESTIGATIONS.

Mendel obtained a number of hybrids, but the results were puzzling. Some of the hybrids resembled the mother plant; some seemed to be in between the two parents. Nothing was known at the time about apogamy—a process in which a seed is formed without fertilization—but this was the unusual situation into which Mendel had stumbled. In effect, the hybrids that resembled the mother plant were nothing more than shoots. Although his results were disappointing to him, Mendel reported them in a second monograph before the Brünn society.

Nothing is said in either of these two tightly written papers about Mendel's work with other plants. Although he was concentrating his efforts on the hawkweed, he experimented with many others—the snapdragon, stock, the violet, the bean, the four-o'clock, and maize.

The hybrids of the four-o'clock and maize behaved like those of peas, Mendel reported in a letter to Nägeli; but odd things happened when he crossed a bean with white flowers and white seed coat with another that had scarlet flowers and a peach-colored seed coat spotted with black. Instead of being either white or scarlet, the flowers blossomed in a range of shades from scarlet to pale violet, and only one plant among thirty-one had white flowers. The seed coats also ran through a wide range of colors. And yet the shape of the plant followed exactly the laws of inheritance he had seen in the pea.

Mendel thought long about this seeming anomaly. If, he reasoned, the red flower tint was not determined by a single hereditary factor but by two factors, A_1 and A_2, each of which, acting by itself, could produce a particular shade of red, the irregularity could be explained. In that case, as in the dihybrid (that is, a hybrid whose parents differ in two characters), there would be nine different types of color among every sixteen individuals, and only one would be a pure recessive white.

Many years later, research was to demonstrate that this was exactly the factor that governed the in-betweenness not only of the bean but of many human and plant traits. Mendel was thus on the verge of working out another of the major laws of heredity. He clearly glimpsed the principle.

But the unexplainable behavior of the hawkweeds and the deviation from the expected ratios in the beans, and also in stock, smothered Mendel's hope that the laws of heredity he had worked out with his peas would be universally valid. Mendel thought—mistakenly—that he had failed in this final objective.

Even so, he might have pushed on with his investigations if his fellow monks had not elected him abbot of the monastery. On April 1, 1868, when he was forty-six, Mendel was chosen head of the wealthy, important monastery of Altbrünn.

To give up his pupils and teaching was difficult, for he was deeply attached to both, but he hoped that his election would make possible increased research. As abbot he could have all the space he might want in the big monastery gardens; his work would no longer have to be crowded into the little strip of garden beneath the walls.

To the great loss of science, the hope proved illusive. Duties and honors immediately began to press in upon the new prelate. The Moravian Diet, for example, appointed him a member of the administrative council of the Moravian Mortgage bank.

His experimental work soon suffered. Mendel, however, improved and extended the monastery gardens and orchards, and many of the fruit trees bore the little lead seal initialed G.M. that he attached to all his grafts. He also gave a considerable part of his spare time to his bees. He had always kept them in hives to which were attached slates showing when the queen had been installed, out of which crossing she had sprung, the dates of the nuptial flight and the slaughter of the drones. After he became abbot, Mendel had a special fertilization cage built to limit fertilization to one kind of drone.

Mendel also continued his lifelong interest in meteorology, and the regular observations he made for the Central Institute for Meteorology. When a tornado struck in Brünn in 1870, Mendel made typically precise observations—even of the piece of tile that sailed through his room: "Since there are double windows and the projectiles went through both strata, the relative position of the opening in the outer and inner panes shows their trajectory. But according to the before mentioned law of circular storms, the missiles ought to have come from the NNE, NE, and ENE." In this good-humored report, Mendel even had a little fun with the towns-people, who attributed some of the freaks of the storm to the doings of the devil.

Neither in this nor in Mendel's other writing is there any clerical flavor or any of the religious allusions so common at that day. And the library of the monastery contained all of Darwin's books, many of them with notations in Mendel's hand, and numerous other books which showed that the liberal-minded priest paid little attention to the Index Librorum Prohibitorum.

Nevertheless, Mendel, the scientist and the open-minded priest, soon was completely engulfed in a bitter clerical struggle. In 1874 the German-Liberal Party, to which Mendel belonged, passed a law taxing the monasteries for the support of other activities of the Catholic church. Mendel regarded it as a violation of the ancient rights of the monastery—rights he had sworn to protect. He refused to pay.

Friendly high officials who had no wish to quarrel with the powerful abbot tried in every way to persuade him to comply, and hinted that there were means by which he could get around the law. Mendel refused flatly. Since a principle was at stake, he would not accept a victory by evasion. All conciliatory tactics having failed, the state was forced in the end to sequester the property of the monastery. Mendel fought all the harder.

The struggle continued for fourteen years, taking more and more of Mendel's time and attention. It brought all his experimental work to an end and finally began to undermine his health. Mendel had grown increasingly corpulent with the years and ultimately developed dropsy. After an illness of many months he quietly died in the monastery on January 6, 1884.

A great crowd of mourners attended the funeral services—clergy, professors, teachers, the Protestant pastor, and the Jewish rabbi of Brünn, representatives of the scientific societies to which Mendel had belonged, and many a man and woman whom Mendel had quietly aided and befriended. There was genuine grief at the passing of a priest and prelate so gentle and so modest and yet so unrelenting in his fight for what he believed to be the right. Ironically, probably not one person in the large funeral assemblage knew that a great scientist had gone or even sensed that a man whose reputation would become imperishable was being laid to rest.

Mendel's unique research seemed to be as completely buried as his bones. His papers and scientific notes were burned, for no one had recognized their importance.

And yet a few fragile tendrils of his ideas still were abroad in the world. Scientists in many countries, investigating the baffling problem of heredity, began to pile up information on sexual reproduction and cell division, and this brought them closer to Mendel's experiments.

W. O. Focke, one of those working on the heredity problem, somehow came upon a reference to Mendel's work. He told Iltis, Mendel's biographer, that he could not recall what publication had drawn his attention to it; nevertheless, he was sufficiently interested to look up Mendel's monographs and, without recognizing their full significance, still was enough impressed to refer to them in his own book on hybrids.

The one reference proved enough, brief and transient though it was. Suddenly in 1900 not only de Vries but two other scientists independently came upon it, and through it discovered Mendel's great accomplishment. The joint discovery after the many years of oblivion was another of those explainable—for the time at last was ripe—and yet always astonishing coincidences of science.

De Vries was the first to startle the world with a report of what Mendel had done. In a paper read before the German Botanical Society on March 24, 1900, the Dutch scientist told of the series of events that had led him to Mendel: "My experiments have led me to formulate the two following propositions:

"1. Of the two antagonistic qualities, the hybrid always exhibits one only, and that in full development.

"2. During the formation of the pollen cells and ovules the two antagonistic qualities separate each from the other.

"These two propositions were, in essentials, formulated long ago by Mendel for a special case. They fell into oblivion, however, and were misunderstood. According to my own experiments, they are generally valid for true hybrids. . . . This important monograph [of Mendel's] is so rarely quoted that I myself did not become acquainted with it until I had concluded most of my experiments and had independently deduced the above propositions."

One month later, on April 24, before the same German Botanical Society, Karl Correns, a German scientist, reported that in his experiments with peas and maize he had come to the same conclusions:

"In noting the regular succession of phenomena and in finding an explanation for them I believed myself, as de Vries obviously believed himself, to be an innovator," he wrote. "Subsequently, however, I found that in Brünn, during the sixties, Abbot Gregor Mendel, devoting many years to the most extensive experiments on peas, not only had obtained the same results as de Vries and myself, but had actually given the same explanation, so far as this was possible in the year 1866. . . . This paper of Mendel's to which Focke refers (though without doing full justice to its importance) is among the best works ever written on the subject of hybrids."

And the coincidence stretched even farther. Two months later, on June 24, in the *Reports* of the same German Botanical Society, the Viennese botanist Erich Tschermak told how in 1898 he had decided to carry on Darwin's work on the hybridization of the pea. In the first hybrid generation all the peas took on the character of the dominant parent. In the second hybrid generation they split 3:1.

In a postscript Tschermak added: "Correns's recent report shows that his experiments, like mine, confirm the Mendelian doctrine. The simultaneous discovery of Mendel by Correns, de Vries, and myself seems to me particularly gratifying. I too, as late as the second year of my experiment, believed that I had happened upon something entirely new."

The three men—the Dutchman, the German, and the Austrian—had missed the immortality that might have been theirs, and yet with no smallness of spirit they gave full credit to Mendel. The dramatic triple rediscovery of the long-forgotten work of the Austrian monk thoroughly awakened the world to its significance.

Mendel's brief monographs were reissued, and biology thereby was revolutionized. Science could set out on a new and highly fruitful path in its unending search for truth.

To the quiet little town of Brünn the abrupt acclaim of the former abbot came as an almost inconceivable surprise. The people responded slowly to an appeal to erect a monument. In the end, however, the funds were raised and a fine, calm statue of Mendel, standing against a background of his pea and bean vines, was unveiled and dedicated in 1911. Its inscription read simply: "To the Investigator P. Gregor Mendel, 1822–1884.

In 1922, the one hundredth anniversary of Mendel's birth, there was a world-wide observance and in Brünn a centenary festival was held. Only four years before, World War I had drawn to a bitter close, and the broken ties between the German and the Allied scientific worlds had not been restored; but so much did Mendel belong to science as a whole that all united to honor him. Speeches in German, Czech, English, and French were delivered before the Mendel monument in Brünn. In respect to the man who at last had discovered how heredity passes from parent to child, the enmities of a great world struggle were dropped.

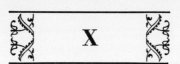

HALDANE

TWO CAMPS INTO ONE

INHERITANCE, then, had been shown to be a precise, an exact, a mathematical process. It could be studied and predicted, though its complexities and the almost limitless play of circumstances outran even the long reach of most mathematics.

But by studying heredity in much the way that a life-insurance company studies the rates of life and death, three scientists, J. B. S. Haldane and Ronald Aylmer Fisher in England and Sewall Wright in the United States, saw and proved that both Darwin and the mutationists were right. Complex formulas, stretching out over pages, demonstrated that natural selection was the primary shaping agent that Darwin had believed it to be. On the other hand, the analyses by these three men made clear that mutations supplied the raw material upon which selection acts. The theories were not alternatives; both were right, both were essential; they related to different levels of the evolutionary process. Out of this insight the two theories were brought together and welded into the modern theory of evolution.

Haldane started at the venturesome age of four upon the scientific career that was to make him an evolutionist. He made such an unusually early beginning because he had a distinguished scientist for a father. Dr. J. S. Haldane was a physiologist who believed fervently in experiment.

At about the time his son John Burdon Sanderson Haldane was born, in 1892, Dr. Haldane had become interested in the problem of bad air. What made air bad? Why was it dangerous to breathe?

The doctor's first problem was to collect bad air to study. Loaded down with bottles for collecting specimens, he went down into the sewers, into reeking alleys, and into other places of ill odor. Often these excursions were made between midnight and dawn to avoid the interference and curiosity of an uncomprehending public.

But the air he collected with such pains proved nothing. Tests showed nothing unusual in its composition. The doctor saw he would have to develop another method of study. He then built an air-tight wooden chamber and took turns shutting himself and a fellow worker in it. They learned the hard way, when they collapsed, that it was the accumulation of carbon dioxide that made bad air dangerous. Unless the excess CO_2 was removed a man could not stay alive in a confined space. The announcement of this conclusion was greeted with ridicule by some of the leading scientists of England.

To prove his accusations against carbon dioxide, Dr. Haldane built a test apparatus that he could carry into mines. His young son had started working with him on the project about the time he could hand his father a piece of apparatus. Later, Haldane explained, he became chief bottle-washer and calculator. By the time the portable mine apparatus was ready, Haldane was a schoolboy, and it went without saying that he accompanied his father and the test party on some of the mine expeditions.

The little group climbed into an old-style mine bucket, dropped deep into an abandoned pit, and crawled through tunnels until they reached a place where a man could stand. One of the men lighted his safety lamp. It filled with a blue flame and went out with a pop—an open flame would have caused an explosion. The air at the top of the tunnel was full of methane, a gas with a high but not immediately fatal percentage of CO_2.

To demonstrate the effect of the gas, Dr. Haldane had his son stand and begin to recite Mark Antony's speech beginning: "Friends, Romans, countrymen." The boy soon began to pant. By the time he reached "the noble Brutus," his legs gave way and he collapsed on the floor. The better air there soon revived him. There was sufficient methane or firedamp to cause difficulty in breathing, but since it was lighter than air, it stayed at the top of the tunnel, where a man could escape it.

In time the Haldanes also proved that the blackdamp which accumulates at the bottom of shafts and in holes is extremely dangerous. In it oxygen has been wholly or largely replaced by carbon dioxide. They also convinced English mine authorities that the carbon monoxide produced by an explosion often causes more deaths than the force of the explosion.

Having proved that excessive carbon dioxide makes air bad, Dr. Haldane went on to study a more profound problem: "Why do we breathe?" He knew that the physiological purpose of breathing was to absorb oxygen and rid the body of carbon dioxide. He still did not know what made people breathe or why the brain sent messages to the breathing-muscles about twenty times a minute.

The doctor built a coffin-like box that would enable him to make exact measurements of breathing. Haldane, who had continued to work with his father during his school days at Eton and his college years at Oxford, spent a considerable time in this apparatus. He lay in the "coffin" with his head projecting into the open through a rubber collar and with instruments recording the changes in air pressure in the cylinder as he breathed. Through these experiments the doctor and his son gradually learned that a little carbon dioxide added to the air increases the depth of breathing. It seemed clear to them that breathing was governed by carbon dioxide rather than by oxygen.

Again the father and son went out into the field to test their laboratory conclusions. They climbed with their instruments to the top of some of the highest mountains and descended into the depth of some of the deepest mines. Their reactions convinced them that carbon dioxide stimulated the brain to send the message to the breathing-muscles. But did it do so because it made the blood more acid, or for some other reason?

Haldane took over this problem. One way to test the point was to make the blood more acid by drinking hydrochloric acid. But even in diluted form Haldane could take only the smallest amount of this burning, searing poison. To smuggle it into his system, so to speak, he drank a solution of ammonium chloride, which in small quantities causes vomiting and in larger ones death. By staying just under the danger line Haldane was able to swallow enough of it to make himself very short of breath. Evidently it was an acid reaction that affected breathing. The finding later proved of use in saving the lives of babies who were subject to a certain kind of fit because their blood was too alkaline.

"If we want an answer from nature, we must put our questions in acts, not words," said Haldane in an essay, "Some Adventures of a Biologist." "And the acts may take us to curious places. Some questions were answered in the laboratory, others in mines, others in a hospital where a surgeon pushed tubes in my arteries to get blood samples, others on top of Pike's Peak in the Rocky Mountains, or in a diving dress on the bottom of the sea. That is one of the things I like about scientific research. You never know where it will take you next."

There was never much question about Haldane's choice of a career. He had grown up to be a scientist, and by the time he was graduated from Oxford he had decided that biochemistry would be his particular field.

Before he could make a start, World War I broke out. Haldane went into the Black Watch regiment and saw service in France, Egypt, and Iraq. At the war's end he was a captain.

Haldane returned as soon as possible to science. From 1922

to 1932 he was Fullerian professor of physiology at the Royal Institution, in London, and then he went to the University of London, where he has served as professor of biometry since 1937.

As a professor, Haldane saw no reason to limit his interests. He wrote, and wrote well, a number of books on science, and he did not hesitate to venture into popular discussions of such subjects as what is life, what is death?

One of the curious places into which his liking for experiment led him was the Communist Party. From 1940 to 1949 he was chairman of the editorial board of the London *Daily Worker*, the English Communist newspaper.

A man of quick, irascible temper, as well as wit and erudition, Haldane has been photographed glaring over his black-rimmed glasses at a world that sometimes has put him in the spotlight when he did not want to be there. His bushy, toothbrush type of mustache seems on such occasions to bristle with indignation. Nevertheless, the well-known Haldane name, his scientific and political exploits, and his involvement in two divorce actions—once as corespondent and once as defendant—inevitably made him top newspaper news.

In 1939 the submarine *Thetis* sank with a loss of ninety-nine lives. Haldane, the expert on air and breathing, was asked to head an official investigation. After the submarine was raised, he and four assistants spent fourteen and one half hours in one of the sealed chambers to study what had caused the fearful death toll. They were gasping for breath and felt that they were dying before Haldane signaled for their release. For science Haldane would take the greatest risk.

His work in the field of evolution was quieter and less sensational. Nevertheless, in writing generally on this problem as well as on others, he occasionally did not fear to drop scientific guardedness. He even dared to be playful at times. For the layman there is no more enlightening or pleasant summing up of the respective parts natural selection and mutation play in evolution than Haldane's. If there were some selector wise enough, he said, it might be possible, using the genes now present in the human race, to produce an average intellect equal to that of a Shakspere, and an average physique like that of Primo Carnera.

But he added, with obvious enjoyment, there would be no chance of creating a race of angels. For the moral character or for the wings, the selector would have to wait for or produce suitable mutations.

This was Haldane's apt way of saying that though natural selection might accomplish the incredible and even the stupendous, it still could not do everything. For something truly new and not now existing in the human constitution, such as a seraphic disposition and home-grown wings, only a mutation would suffice.

Despite Haldane's lightness of touch, his analogy was backed by solid scientific study and experiment. By the 1930's the knowledge of how and why living things vary had gone considerably beyond Mendel and de Vries. The independent, self-reproducing units conceived by de Vries had been identified as molecules, or aggregates of molecules, called genes. Since the same genes were transmitted from generation to generation, it was certain that cats would produce cats and not rats. The genes were the carriers of heredity.

But how did they produce their effects? Haldane worked at this problem and also drew upon the work of a good many other investigators. It seemed clear, first of all, that some characteristics are produced by a single gene. When that gene is present, a certain predictable character appears.

Chinese primrose plants coming from a long line of ancestors with roundish leaves were crossed with plants whose ancestors had a fern type of leaf. All of the first generation burst forth with roundish leaves. Only the one characteristic was affected; hence it must have been produced by a single gene.

Frequently, though, inheritance is not so clear-cut a matter. In the nucleus of each cell are thousands of genes, and several of them may affect one characteristic.

This problem also was studied with the Chinese primrose. Hundreds of plants were raised. As they were crossed and recrossed, the experimenters discovered that no less than eight genes affect the color of the plant's stem.

It was nothing for a mathematician of Haldane's skill to calculate that the eight could combine in enough different ways to produce 384 different stem colors. If a gardener of genius could grow all of them, he predicted that there would be a complete gradation of all the shades from green to purple—a natural color continuum much more finely graded than the color spectrums on cards distributed by paint companies.

A fellow worker of Haldane's undertook the experiment in part. She crossed and recrossed green- and purple-stemmed plants until she obtained 48 different shades of stem color. It was not necessary to continue. Once again a mathematical prediction had been proved in nature.

Although such fine-drawn experiments made it possible to plot the behavior of genes in the primrose, the same techniques obviously could not be applied to studying human characteristics, such as height, which seemed to be of the same continuously variable kind. But work with animals could supply some closer information.

A race of fowls weighing an average of 1,300 grams was crossed with a race of bantams whose weight averaged about 750 grams. The offspring ranged in between. The hybrids were neither so heavy as one parent nor so light as the other. But when the hybrids were crossed, there was a "wild outburst" of variation. Some of the birds were lighter than the bantam grandparents and some were heavier than the cocks, weighing up to 1,700 grams.

Again Haldane turned to his mathematics. If ten genes affected weight, they could combine in enough different ways to produce 59,049 different weights. The variations within this range, for all practical purposes, would be continuous. It was possible to say, tentatively at least, that the weight of fowl probably is determined by a number of genes.

At the time Haldane was working on this problem of height and weight, huge masses of material had been assembled about human weight and stature. Schools and armies had weighed and measured thousands of men and women. Most often their height and weight was not that of either of the parents.

Even before the animal experiments had indicated that this was what might have been expected, Fisher had shown mathematically that man's hereditary height would vary widely if it were determined by a number of genes. The final proof was not in, but it looked very much as though the answer to the puzzling question of why living things come in a wide range of heights and weights lay in the controlling influence of a number of genes.

But the variation that came from this normal, Mendelian remixing of the old was not the whole story. As de Vries had shown, new and utterly different characteristics can appear. This had indicated that the gene itself undergoes change, that it mutates, or changes its nature, probably through a chemical process. In such a case, the characteristic it produces is of course altered.

And such changes are not rare. Haldane called attention to the work of Lewis Stadler, an American geneticist (1930). In a study of 1,500,000 wheat seeds, Stadler found that seven of the eight wheat genes mutated at least once and that one gene changed with great frequency. The changes gave us some of the best new wheats.

Another study of 200,000 Chinese primrose plants disclosed one visible mutation of one kind or another in every 20,000 plants. Further investigation revealed still other types of mutation.

Under the microscope it is easy to see that the heredity-carrying genes are strung together in little threadlike strands. The strands are called chromosomes. Although the comparison is not accurate, the genes look to the layman like disk-shaped beads on a string. The gene arrangement in a chromosome also has been compared to a stack of coins in a money-changer.

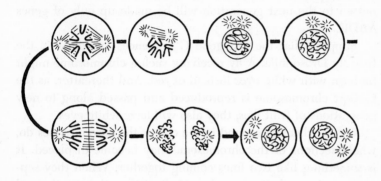

TWO CELLS FROM ONE—CELL DIVISION.

BEGINNING AT THE UPPER RIGHT: A CELL AT REST.

THE CHROMATIN MATERIAL IN THE NUCLEUS FORMS INTO LONG SLENDER THREADS—CHROMOSOMES. THE CENTRIOLES AT THE TOP OF THE NUCLEUS BEGIN TO MOVE APART. A GELATINOUS "SPINDLE" FORMS.

THE CHROMOSOMES DIVIDE AND MOVE TOWARD THE TWO POLES OF THE SPINDLE.

THE CELL BEGINS TO DIVIDE.

TWO COMPLETE AND SEPARATE DAUGHTER CELLS RESULT.

When a cell is fertilized, the chromosomes produce replicas of themselves. And a complete set of replicas passes into each new cell formed by the division of the parent cell. If all goes well, each new cell therefore has the same hereditary units as its parent cells. The same genes are transmitted from generation to generation, and life preserves its continuity.

Occasionally, however, there are some slip-ups in this complex and wonderful process. As the threadlike chromosomes move around in the cell and realign themselves just before the parent cell divides, one or several of the genes in the strand may become lost. If the original chromosome carries genes ABCDE and gene C somehow is lost, the chromosome transmitted to the next generation will be made up only of genes ABDE.

Suppose that the lost gene C influences eye color in the fruit fly Drosophila. A fly receiving such a chromosome might be born with white eyes instead of red. And thereafter, as the C-short chromosome is reproduced and passed along to new generations of fruit flies, they also will have white eyes.

Or, in wheeling around in the cell as the chromosomes do, whole sections of the chromosome may become displaced. It is something like two lines coming together. When they separate again, each line may have half of the other, or the end of one line may have joined the other.

In the first case, imagine that chromosomes ABCDE and FGHIJ temporarily come together. When they separate, the line-up might be ABCHIJ and FGDE. Each would be a new type of chromosome and would produce different characteristics, which thereafter probably would be handed on intact to future generations. In the second case, Haldane pointed out: "It is as though the end section of the chromosome with all its genes had been removed and stuck on in the opposite order in the other."

Still another kind of structural change in the tiny strands that carry the gene-determiners of heredity often produces striking, inheritable changes in living things. Occasionally a plant appears with larger leaves or flowers than usual. Science gradually learned that in these cases there may be no basic chemical change in the gene nor any change in the arrangement of genes or chromosomes, but rather an increase in the number of chromosomes. Instead of producing a single replica of itself, a chromosome may give rise to several sets. The new chromosomes are exactly like the parents, but a plant may thus acquire three or four sets. A new whole has been added.

A plant that normally has two sets of chromosomes and thus gains an extra pair is known as a triploid; or if it picks up two extra sets, as a tetraploid. Such a plant possesses all the genes that are present in its ancestors and no different ones. It simply has more of them. It may, however, be so changed as to form a separate species.

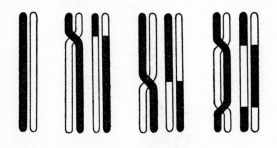

TWO CHROMOSOMES. IN THE PROCESS OF CELL DIVISION THEY MAY "CROSS OVER" IN MANY DIFFERENT WAYS. HERE ARE THREE TYPES OF CROSSING OVER.

Haldane pointed out that such cases are fairly common. He cited the tomato. If tomato plants are cut back and new shoots pruned until the plant is almost exhausted, about six out of one hundred plants will suddenly produce a branch with larger leaves. It is a tetraploid. If the flowers of these branches are cross-fertilized, the seedling also will have four sets of chromosomes. They can quite easily be distinguished from ordinary plants. Some of the most important crop plants—wheat, oats, cotton, tobacco, potatoes, bananas, sugarcane, and coffee—are polyploids. These suddenly born plants, with their larger leaves and flowers and general differentness, are actual cases of the origin of a new species.

In the broader sense all of these structural changes in the genes and chromosomes, as well as actual chemical changes in the gene itself, can be considered mutations.

"The fundamental importance of mutation for any account of evolution is clear," Haldane wrote in his *Causes of Evolution*. "It enables us to escape from the impasse of the pure line.

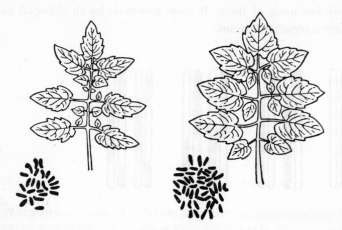

A NORMAL TOMATO PLANT AND ITS TWENTY-FOUR CHROMOSOMES. THROUGH ONE TYPE OF MUTATION THE NUMBER OF CHROMO-SOMES IS DOUBLED. THE NEW FORTY-EIGHT CHROMOSOME PLANT HAS LARGER LEAVES.

Selection within a pure line will be ineffective until a mutation arises. Among a few million individuals a mutation of the desired type is not unlikely. Among a few thousand it is most improbable."

A few shifts, a few hereditary accidents, and there were changed plants and animals. From new combinations of the same hereditary building blocks—the genes—came a wide variety of forms. But could the variations produced by the Mendelian shuffling of the genes and by mutation account for the rise of varieties and species? This remained, as in Darwin's day, the leading question.

Haldane faced it and brought some new techniques to bear in trying to answer it. If Darwin had been right in thinking that species arose from the accumulation of minute, gradual changes, it should have been difficult to distinguish recently formed groups. And yet the differences generally were clear-cut from the first.

To analyze the differences between two varieties of one species—say, two varieties of *Felis domestica,* a Manx short-tailed cat and a long-tailed blue—geneticists mate them, and then mate the offspring. This particular experiment revealed, Haldane noted, that the differences stemmed from four dominant genes, one causing short tails, one short hair, one banded hairs in certain areas, and one dense pigmentation. Varieties are different, then, because they differ in a few genes—four in this case.

Generally speaking, it is not possible to analyze differences in species in the same way, for, with some exceptions, members of two different species cannot be mated, or if they can, the offspring, like the mule, is likely to be sterile.

But there are a few exceptions. They could be studied and they afforded a clue. When species with an even number of chromosomes, like the tetraploids, were mated and produced fertile offspring, scientists saw that the differences between species were similar to those between varieties.

"Inter-specific differences [differences between species] are of the same nature as inter-varietal differences," Haldane summed it up. "But the latter generally are due to a few genes with relatively large effects, and rarely to differences involving whole chromosomes or large parts of them. The reverse is true of differences between species. The number of genes involved is often great, and cytologically observable differences common. It is largely these latter which are the causes of inter-specific sterility."

Thus Haldane made the highly important point that the genetic differences between species are only wider and sharper than those between varieties. And yet how did every living plant and animal become so perfectly adjusted to its environment?

Haldane unquestionably put natural selection in first place as the maker of the world's variety. His re-examination of the principle in the light of what had been learned about genetics only strengthened the original view of Darwin that natural selection was the great shaping agent.

The struggle for life and the victories of the fittest were going on everywhere, and yet Haldane was almost as hard put to it as Darwin to find illustrations that could be pinned down and proved.

An Italian scientist, di Cesnola, devised one ingenious test. In a small plot of green grass he tied 20 green and 45 brown specimens of the praying mantis, *Mantis religiosa*. Nineteen days later, 35 of the brown insects had been eaten by birds; all the green ones had survived. Then the procedure was reversed. In a plot of brown grass the scientist tethered 20 brown mantises and 25 green. All of the green were dead in eleven days, five having been killed by ants. All of the browns, which matched their background, were alive at the end of nineteen days.

Haldane considered some work with bacteria even more convincing. Normal bacteria, when grown on agar, produce enough hydrogen peroxide to kill themselves, or in any event to slow down their rate of growth. When they invade the cells of some unhappy human or animal, however, they are protected by a peroxide-destroying material produced by their host. Thus after a few weeks of culture on agar, only the glossy and nonvirulent types survive. The others have been killed. On the other hand when a little peroxide-destroying material is added to the agar, the virulent grow as well as the nonvirulent.

One vital change in the environment means life or death, and natural selection moves fast.

Since the bacteria divide every half hour and the experiment ran thirty-nine days, some two thousand bacteria generations occurred. In human evolution this would equal fifty thousand years. So great was the promise of this work with the small, rapidly reproducing bacteria that it was carried on by a number of workers.

Another later and significant experiment dealt with the colon bacteria, *Escherichia coli*. Like the other bacteria it is attacked by bacteriophages. Within a few minutes, in some cases, the phage will destroy nearly all of the bacterial cells. Sometimes, however, a few cells survive and form colonies that thereafter are resistant to the bacteriophage.

Luria and Delbruck showed that this resistant strain arises by mutation, regardless of the presence or absence of the bacteriophage. The bacteria-killer thus does not produce resistant strains. It acts only as a selective agent that destroys all nonmutant cells. In the presence of the bacteriophage only the mutants can survive and reproduce.

But the mutant strain that is resistant to one bacteriophage will probably not be resistant to another. Demerec and Fano found in one strain of *Escherichia coli* at least eight different kinds of mutants, each resistant to one or more of seven bacteriophage strains.

And then it was learned that the phage mutates. New forms were able to attack bacteria that had become resistant to the original phage.

Since the resistant type of bacteria arises regardless of exposure to the bacteriophage, it might seem that in the end only resistant bacteria would be left, that they would be the winners in the struggle. Except in the presence of the phage, though, the resistant bacteria are not so well adapted to the ordinary form of life. To grow properly they require an extra substance not needed by the susceptible bacteria. Thus it is that selection keeps down the number of the resistant strains, though there always are some few of them, and on these few the survival of the species depends if a bacteriophage comes along.

A Yorkshire wood provided Haldane with another example of natural selection at work, much as the heath and the Scotch firs had done for Darwin. In 1800 a mixed wood of pine, birch, and alder that grew on Eston Moore in Yorkshire was separated into two parts by half a mile of heather. Eighty-five years later the pines had been replaced by birch in the southern section. In contrast, in the northern half the pines predominated and the birches and alders became rare. In less than a century, the two woods that had once been similar had become different.

The moths that lived in the two woods told another story of natural selection at its amazing work. In the northern pine wood almost 96 per cent of the moths belonged to a dark species, and only 4 per cent to a light one. An observer looking around the woods could see why. The owls, nightjars, and bats that fed on the moths ate only the bodies and let the wings flutter to the ground. Most of the wings lying on the ground were light, though there were few light moths. In the pine woods it was estimated that the light moth was thirty times as likely to be caught as the dark variety. Not many were left.

Seemingly the light moths did much better in the southern birchwood, though the reason was not clear. Perhaps it was because fewer birds and bats lived there.

There was also the case of the peppered moth. A black form of this moth spread rapidly through the industrial sections of Germany and England during several decades of the nineteenth century. Within fifty years the black form became more frequent than the original paler moth and in the end supplanted it. Experiment revealed that the dark form differed from its paler relatives in a single dominant gene.

It was believed that the dark form is more vital, but that it had been at a disadvantage until smoke darkened the landscape. When the grime of the cities offered protection, its superior viability reasserted itself and it rapidly spread.

Natural selection was always at work, shaping, forming, adapting. But no new characters, no new trees, no different moths could be seen emerging from the process. In answer to critics who dwelt upon this point, Haldane admitted that novelty is brought about by selection only when previously rare characters are combined.

THE PEPPERED MOTH SPREAD RAPIDLY THROUGH THE INDUSTRIAL DISTRICTS OF ENGLAND AND GERMANY AFTER SMOKE HAD DARKENED THE LANDSCAPE AND AFFORDED IT A PROTECTIVE ADVANTAGE.

He could back his observation with mathematics. If any fifteen different characters were found in one per cent of the population, all fifteen would come together in only one person in a quintillion. But, Haldane continued, suppose natural selection acts on the fifteen characters until they are found in 99 per cent of the population. The combination of the fifteen then would occur in 86 per cent of the population. "No one has ever observed this happening in nature," Haldane explained. "Because of the slowness of natural selection it would probably require 10,000 years of observation. But as Darwin realized, it has been happening as the result of natural selection."

The domesticated pig was taken by Haldane as typical of animals that might have evolved in this way. It differs from the wild boar in some thirty or forty ways. Some of the variations are believed due to the action of the same gene on different organs; others may require the action of several genes. Many of the genes, however, may have been harbored as rarities in the wild species. Others may have appeared after domestication, though they also probably occurred previously in the wild species. As the favored genes appeared more and more frequently, the new domestic type of pig arose.

Haldane argued—and carried modern science along with him—that neither natural selection nor mutation alone can furnish the basis for prolonged evolution. Selection by itself, he wrote, may produce considerable changes in a highly mixed population. But the material upon which it acts must be supplied by mutation.

Haldane felt there had been a failure on the part of both the Darwinians and the mutationists to appreciate the extraordinary subtlety of natural selection. At first even the scientist sees only the claws that are so obviously right for grabbing and holding the available prey, or the brown color that so perfectly matches the background. Upon closer analysis, the high water-imbibing power of the colloids or the low freezing-point of the cell content of plants that defy the cold are seen to be the incredibly perfect workings of natural selection.

But why, asked Haldane, do the very characteristics that enable the scientist to distinguish one species from another often show no adaptive value?

The scientist proposed two possible answers to his own question. Often when one part of the anatomy changes, other parts change along with it. Darwin was well aware of this, and modern genetics looks upon these related changes as the multiple effects of a single gene.

Does not one gene in the Chinese primrose incise the petals, double the number of sepals, break up the number of bracts, and, when certain other genes are present, increase the crimping of the leaves? And in Drosophila does not one gene modify both wings and bristles? And in order to be hairy must not a stock have colored flowers?

Haldane also suggested that differences invisible under the microscope may have an effect on selection.

A staphylococcal infection that killed a group of Japanese waltzing mice had no effect on European mice or on first-generation hybrids. The European breed seemed to owe its immunity to a dominant gene.

Perhaps some seemingly unimportant gene may have been vital to survival at some remote period in the past, or perhaps life and death might depend upon it at some unforeseeable time in the future.

Haldane cited certain sponges. Normally the sponges that live on rocks between the tide marks have elaborate systems for ejecting water great distances. In the domain of the pounding surf, this ability has no use or value. But about once in a century a violent rainstorm or a great heat at a low spring tide kills off all the sponges in a wide area. Only sponges living in caves or in other sheltered spots survive, and they survive the loss of the clean-scouring rush of water only because their own internal canal system can move the stagnant water of their sheltered cove. The implication was clear in Haldane's opinion. Some seemingly valueless character might mean the difference between life and death in some future day of change or stress.

Many of the means plants use to spread to new areas are also subtle and not easily visible to man. The pollen of the tropical tree Shorea ordinarily is spread by a fruit fly with a range of about one hundred yards. Since the tree takes thirty years to grow to maturity, it might presumably require five hundred years to spread one mile. And yet a single seed carried on the wings of a typhoon or in the fur of an animal could upset this calculation completely.

Another subtle influence lies in the struggle of plants to

pollinate their fellows. As Haldane noted, there always are far more pollen grains on a flower after fertilization than are needed to fertilize all the ovules.

Clouds of pollen fill the air, and the plant that constantly has pollen available will be more heavily represented in the next generation than one whose production is niggardly. The bane of the hay-fever sufferer is the plant's boon. From this it follows that a gene that accelerates pollen growth will spread throughout the species.

Natural selection is affected, too, by the extent of a species. Widely distributed species are less likely to break up and change than are smaller groups. To illustrate the point Haldane chose the prickly buckler fern, a rare fern of which four varieties are found in England. Because of its rarity, each variety had a good chance of evolving along its own path without being swamped by close-pressing relatives.

"If we come to the conclusion that natural selection is probably the major cause of change," he wrote, "we certainly need not go back completely to Darwin's view. In the first place we have every reason to believe that new species may arise quite suddenly, perhaps by hybridization, sometimes perhaps by other means. Such species do not arise as Darwin thought by natural selection. When they have arisen they must justify their existence before the tribunal of natural selection, but that is a very different matter.

"Natural selection can act only on the variations available and these are not as Darwin thought in every direction. Most mutations lead to a loss of complexity, as in the substitution of leaves for tendrils in the pea and reduction in the size of the wings in Drosophila. Also mutations seem to occur along certain lines."

The cow, Haldane pointed out, has a great capacity for variation in the direction of increased milk yield. Yet, according to Herodotus, the Scythians lived largely on the milk of mares. If mares had shown the same capacity for producing milk, they presumably might have been selected, just as well as cows, for the world's milk-producers. But, Haldane added, "we no more breed milch mares than we do racing bulls." He remarked that it probably would be possible to produce a race of horned horses, but that he was very doubtful, despite the example of Pegasus, that horses possess the capacity of producing feathers.

"To sum it up," said Haldane, "it would seem that natural selection is the main cause of evolutionary change in the species as a whole. But the actual steps by which individuals come to differ from their parents are due to causes other than natural selection, and in consequence evolution can only follow certain paths.

"These paths are determined by factors which we can only dimly conjecture. Only a thoroughgoing study of variation will lighten our darkness. Although we have found reason to differ from Darwin on many points, it appears that he was commonly right when he thought for himself, but often wrong when he took the prevailing views of his time, on heredity, for example."

Haldane was particularly well equipped to extract the strengths of two major theories and weld them into one. The tradition of looking at a scientific problem without preformed conclusions was bred in him. So too was the ability to cut through to the main question. This, combined with his skill at mathematics, made him one of the three leading synthesizers of what has been called the modern theory of evolution. There is little responsible disagreement with this verdict.

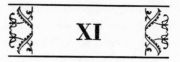

FISHER

NATURAL SELECTION AND CHANCE

A SINGLE visible bubble of gas may contain several billion molecules, all in constant tumult and flux. And yet that bubble, that uneasy assemblage of turbulent particles, will obey the laws of gases. Its behavior can be predicted with great certainty.

Charles Darwin was the first to see clearly that another assemblage of billions of shifting, moving, unruly individuals, human, animal, and plant, also might obey certain laws. The laws were those of natural selection. Darwin set them forth with great clarity and backed them with an amazing collection of proof from nature. It remained, however, for three mathematical biologists of the twentieth century to demonstrate that the laws of natural selection and of evolution function with all the precision and certainty of physical laws. Not all of the limitless movement of life could be encompassed within their formulas. What could be, proved predictable and orderly.

One of the three who subjected evolution to this test was Sir Ronald Aylmer Fisher, professor of genetics at Cambridge University.

Fisher was another natural mathematician. That was apparent early in his school days at Harrow, and at Gonville and Caius College, Cambridge University. Immediately after his graduation he became a statistician for an investment company. He later spent four years in teaching and fourteen years in scientific research before he went to University College, London, as Galton professor of eugenics. He remained there for ten years until in 1943 he was named professor of genetics at Cambridge. As befits a geneticist, he is the father of eight children, two sons and six daughters. He was knighted in 1952.

At London and Cambridge, Fisher turned to the basic problem of evolution: Is there a provable, certain relation between progress in fitness and survival? Working at this point on which the theory of natural selection hinges, Fisher arrived at a theorem, which I quote more with the thought that such an awesome calculation should be seen than with the hope that it may be enlightening for the non-mathematical majority:

$$\frac{d}{dt} \log \left(\frac{p}{q} \right) = a$$

which may be written: $\frac{1}{p} + \frac{1}{q} dp = adt$
whence it follows that

$$adp = pqa\alpha dt$$

and, taking all factors into consideration, the total increase in fitness, $\Sigma(\alpha dp) = \Sigma(pqa\alpha)dt = Wdt$.

Fisher stated it in the following form: "The rate of increase in fitness of an organism at any time is equal to its genetic variance in fitness at that time."

The regularity in rate of progress disclosed by the theorem was guaranteed, Fisher pointed out, by the same circumstances that make the particles in a gas bubble obey the laws of gases without appreciable deviation.

Fisher's fundamental theorem, in fact, bears many remarkable resemblances to the second law of thermodynamics. Both describe the properties of populations or aggregations. Both hold true irrespective of the nature of the units that compose them. Each requires the increase of a measurable quantity —in one case, of a physical system, and in the other, of a population.

Eddington, the great English physicist, once remarked: "The law that entropy [1] always increases—the second law of

[1] The tendency to run down.

thermodynamics—holds, I thing, the supreme position among the laws of nature." Even so conservative a scientist as Fisher felt free to say on the basis of his theorem: "It is not a little instructive that so similar a law should hold the supreme position among biological sciences."

The working-out of proof that there is regularity and order in the intricate course of evolution put Fisher in a fortunate position to comment on the often heard charge that natural selection is nothing more than a succession of favorable chances. With a touch of humor that occasionally breaks through even in such an austere and formidable book as his *Genetical Theory of Natural Selection,* Fisher noted that it all depends upon what the critic means by chance.

"The income derived from a casino by its proprietor may, in one sense, be said to depend upon a succession of favorable chances, although the phrase contains a suggestion of improbability more appropriate to the hopes of the patrons of his establishment.

"It is easy without any profound logical analysis to perceive the difference between a succession of favorable deviations from the laws of chance, and on the other hand, the continuous and cumulative action of these laws. It is on the latter that the principle of natural selection relies."

In Fisher's opinion, natural selection definitely belongs in the proprietor's order of chance, and not in the patron's. Essentially this has become the modern position—the outcome of the struggle for existence seems sure, given sufficient time and population.

Although it long has been granted that all living things constantly are adapting themselves to their surroundings, the world always has marveled at the incredible fineness of the adjustment. The bee, as Darwin pointed out, is the right size to enter the flower, and the pollen is so placed that it will brush off upon the visitor, even though this means leading the bee along a circuitous floral route.

Fisher again made use of mathematics and statistics to show how such a seeming natural miracle might come about. His calculations indicated that two organisms can conform to one another in such intricate, different ways only if the fitting is accomplished by minute steps.

The importance of small steps is understandable if it is recognized that most living things already are closely and amazingly well adapted to both the internal and external world in which they live. They are round pegs in round holes or their species would not be alive. Obviously, any big change in either the peg or the hole is likely to make matters worse. A small rounding or polishing or adjusting, on the other hand, may bring about an improvement in fit.

Fisher suggested the better comparison of the microscope. If the microscope is reasonably well focused, any big movements of the lenses, or abrupt changes in the refractive index, or other rough alterations certainly will not improve the adjustment. With small delicate changes, there would be a chance of improvement.

This, however, is not a stationary, fixed, and finished universe. Few things in nature stand still for long in the flow of time. The fine adaptations established over the endless centuries constantly are menaced by change both in the organism and in the environment. A large mutation may upset the "within" balance for the individual, and force drastic changes. Probably it is for this reason that most mutations that have been observed have been deleterious in their effects. Not infrequently they are lethal.

The environment is even more changeable. Climate is always becoming warmer or colder or moister or drier; mountains rise and erode away; barriers are created and removed. And for most species these changes are harmful, for they upset an arrangement that is working fairly well.

As even more important than climatic changes Fisher placed evolutionary changes in associated organisms, in other animals and plants. A fleeter enemy, it is apparent, requires new speed in the hunted.

Thus the action of natural selection in steadily increasing the fitness of every creature is to a very considerable extent offset by deterioration of the organic and inorganic environment. If the improvement exceeds the deterioration, the race will thrive and multiply. If the obstacles outrank the gains in fitness, the end must be shrinkage and ultimately oblivion.

But even for the winners the victory is limited and beset by difficulties. The race that multiplies prodigiously will prove to be its own worst enemy, for its own increase impairs its environment as effectively as would an increase in the numbers or efficiency of its enemies. As its numbers grow, food becomes a little scarcer and life a little harder for each individual. In the end, there must be a slowdown.

Fisher put this natural warning to the overly prolific and successful into a differential equation, which is not for the mathematical kindergartner, but is interesting:

$$\frac{dM}{dt} + \frac{M}{C} = W - D$$

"M is the mean of the Malthusian parameter. C is a constant expressing the relation between fitness and population increase, and defined as the increase in the natural logarithm of the population, supposed stationary at each stage, produced by unit increase in the value of M. W is the rate of actual increase in fitness determined by natural selection and D is the rate of loss due to the deterioration of the environment.

"If C, W, and D are constant the equation has the solution:

$$M = \frac{W - D}{C} + Ae^{-t/c}$$

"In this equation A is an arbitrary constant, dependent upon the initial conditions. C has the physical dimensions of time and may therefore be reckoned in years or generations, and the equation shows that if C, W, and D remain constant for any length of time much greater than C, the value of M will approach to the constant value given by

$$M = \frac{W - D}{C}$$

"In this steady state the whole of the organism's advantage or disadvantage will be compensated by change in population, and not at all by change in the value of M." [2]

Fisher's studies of the fate suffered by rapidly increasing populations led him to challenge one of the most commonly held beliefs about population changes. Malthus had worried the world and strongly influenced the thinking of Darwin and Wallace by his insistence that if it were not for certain checks, populations would increase geometrically. On the basis of this point, many attributed the "struggle for existence" to an excessive production of offspring: since too many were born, many had to be eliminated.

Fisher's approach was from the opposite direction. He pointed out that if a species is to maintain itself, each adult must produce more than two young, for some of the young certainly will be killed off by predators, parasites, disease, and other hazards. Therefore, he argued, if mortality is heavy in the young, as it is in many species, "the ratio of excess" must be large.

But only in an ideal, imaginary world, he added, would there be a geometric increase. And with a bit of irony: "a high geometric rate of increase can be attained only by abolishing a real death rate while retaining a real rate of reproduction.

A cod may spawn a million eggs, but to say that its offspring are subject to natural selection for this reason is, according to

[2] Only a part of Fisher's equation is quoted. I shall not attempt to explain it other than to say that the whole equation shows that a race which multiplies too fast will outrun its food supply. It is included only to give the non-mathematical a glimpse of what such mathematics looks like, and in the hope that it may be interesting in much the same way as a picture of some undecipherable hieroglyphics.

this logic, putting the cart before the horse, or, perhaps it should be said, selection before the eggs.

"The historical fact that both Darwin and Wallace were led through reading Malthus' essay on population to appreciate the efficacy of selection, should no longer constrain us to confuse the consequences of that principle with its foundation," Fisher wrote.

The work of Fisher, along with that of Haldane and Sewall Wright, piled up convincing evidence that selection is the guiding agent of evolution. Mutations were assigned quite another role.

Fisher put it differently from the occasionally irreverent Haldane. Where Haldane suggested that mutation would be required to supply anything so utterly lacking now in the human make-up as wings and an angelic disposition, Fisher soberly said: "The function of mutation is to maintain the stock of genetic variance at a high level."

The mathematical biologists were depriving mutation of the star part in the great evolutionary drama, the all-important part claimed for it by de Vries and others. But the place they gave mutation in the modern theory was still highly significant. Without the new variations brought in by mutation, they emphasized, life might sink into a rut, unready to cope with any changes that might be sprung by ever moving nature.

According to this theory, the most harmful mutations—and they greatly predominate—are weeded out by natural selection. The others, often too small to be perceived by ordinary human measurement, mix into the genetic stock and spread, thereby greatly enriching the potentialities of the species.

One troublesome point in any such theory is this question: how can a single change, no matter how beneficial, spread throughout the race? Would it not be lost if the individual should be killed or fail to produce any offspring? And might it not be lost in the course of a few generations in the ordinary shuffling and reshuffling of genes?

Fisher supplied a convincing answer by means of mathematics. He assumed a mutation that might give its possessor a mere one-per-cent advantage over his fellows. Perhaps in the deer mouse this might be a shade just perceptibly closer in color to the sand on which the species lives.

Fisher's figures showed that the chances are slim that the single one-per-cent mutation—the more concealing color—will be passed along to descendants. There is only one chance in fifty that the new gene that produces the tiny improvement will establish itself and sweep through the entire species.

And yet in the long procession of time that one chance can matter mightily. The one new favorable type could take over the entire species in 250 generations and might do so in 10.

Of the mutant genes that ultimately pervade the species, a large proportion are derived from that one individual mutation which first has the good fortune to establish itself in appreciable numbers, Fisher pointed out. If that one history-making mutant gene appears in a species that is rapidly increasing in numbers, its spread can be fast and far.

And this circumstance leads to a fact of prime importance not only for the human race but for the other mammals, for the birds, for the reptiles, and for the other large groups that largely have inherited the earth. For it means that the big groups grow more variable, and the small, declining families less variable.

With their greater variability, their readiness to withstand new climates and modes of life, the big groups can spread into new territories, conquer new enemies and further establish themselves. It is the explanation of why a relatively few big populations occupy what may seem like a disproportionate share of the surface of the globe, its waters, and the air above it.

"The great contrast between abundant and rare species lies in the number of individuals available in each generation as possible mutants," Fisher wrote.

Fisher was not worried, however, that the human race, or any of the other bigs, might be caught short of enough variability to meet almost any new conditions that might arise. If each species differs only in 100 factors, he figured, the number of combinations that might be formed from them would total 2 to the 100th power, which would require 31 figures in the decimal notation. Even if the population grew to a billion individuals, only a small fraction of the possible combinations would be exhibited.

Fisher's point was that, over and above all the combinations that do appear in individuals, there is a great unexplored region of combinations, none of which may ever occur unless the system of gene ratios is modified in the right direction. And, according to Fisher, there are literally millions of directions that such modification might take.

In his careful scientific way Fisher was saying that even with the present gene equipment, living creatures might develop along tangents now scarcely conceivable.

He added: "It has often been remarked, and truly, that without mutation, evolutionary progress, whatever direction it might take, will ultimately come to a standstill for lack of further improvements.

"It has not so often been realized how very far most species must be from such a state of stagnation or how easily with no more than 100 factors a species may be modified to a condition considerably outside the range of its previous variation, and this in a large number of different characteristics."

Mutations or no, the scientist's reassuring conclusion was that living creatures are pretty well ready for come what may in the way of worldly change.

In studying how and why living things vary, Darwin delved into plant-breeders' records on various well-marked varieties. His second chapter in *The Origin of Species* summarizes his findings. Although Hooker persuaded him not to publish his tabulations, this check of actual plant records also showed that "wide ranging, much diffused and common species vary most."

Darwin also was convinced from these studies, that in any "limited country" the species with the largest number of individuals "oftenest give rise to varieties sufficiently well marked to have been recorded in botanical works."

Fisher had an unusual opportunity to check this theory in nature. He was presented a collection of more than five thousand night-flying moths. Their beautifully marked and patterned wings were visible diagrams of the ways in which they varied.

It was just as Darwin and his own statistical work had predicted. The twelve species of moths classed as "abundant" or "very common" varied between seventy and eighty per cent more than the thirteen species that were relatively rare. The twelve "common" species were in between.

Darwin was again confirmed when it turned out that the moths with the widest geographical range displayed more variation than species living in a narrower territory. The significance of the point in the theory of evolution had already been indicated by Darwin—abundant species will make the most rapid evolutionary progress and will tend to supplant less abundant groups with which they may come into competition.

Fisher emphasized several further inferences: although many smaller species are decreasing and a few large species are increasing, the number of species remains about the same, for the more abundant groups are always dividing. Furthermore, the disappearance of the rarer species—like the much lamented dodo of Mauritius and the moa of New Zealand—prevents too great and unsafe a specialization.

But how does a big, booming, closely linked group break into separate species?

Since Darwin had visited the Galapagos and seen how new species developed from the few migrants that reached those remote oceanic islands, there had been little doubt that a group of animals geographically isolated from its fellows would take a separate evolutionary course. Or that any two separated groups, evolving in almost complete independence and in different habitats, would in time differ enough to be classified as separate species. This was one origin of species.

Fisher pointed out that there were other ways in which a group could be shut away enough to evolve differently.

THE LATE LAMENTED DODO AND THE ISLAND OF MAURITIUS WHERE IT FLOURISHED AND DIED.

Geographic distance is one. In some cases it may be almost as divisive as the fastnesses and isolation of an island. A species spread across a great interior basin like that of the Mississippi finds such extremes as the cold of Minnesota and the heat of Louisiana at the outer edges of its domain. Genes favored at the one extreme, and with the tendency to increase there, may prove disadvantageous at the other. If conditions remain constant and outweigh the mingling of populations through migration or mating, the groups at the outer fringes will tend to become more and more different, until ultimately they may be recognized as distinct species. In such cases division comes through stretching rather than rupture.

Or certain heritable instincts may be the agency to divide a species. A fish adapted to life in water of low salinity sometimes swims up the fresh-water rivers to avoid being carried farther out into the salt of the sea. Such river migrants mingle less with the deep-ocean and coastal members of their species. Each begins to go its own way; and the two main groups evolve to what may finally be complete independence. In this case, however, there long may be intermediate groups between the two separatists.

According to some authorities this ancient and always active process of dividing and separating explains the blindness of cave animals. A fish or any other animal living in the deep gloom of caverns, will grope its way toward the light if it can see or sense the brightness outside. Whether it perishes or survives in the unaccustomed sun, it is removed from the body of cave denizens. The cave creatures that remain are those with little sensitivity to visual stimuli. They are the blind and they beget the blind.

In the close walls of the cave or in any other habitat so restricted, selection may be very intense and produce rapid evolutionary effects. In a very short time, as time is measured, the cavern-dwellers are blind—as they are the world around.

It may be one single venturesome pair that reaches the remote island, or one single animal better adapted to life at the edges of the continent that starts the new species. Such are the founders, the ancestors.

The smallness of the distinctive ancestral group was impressed upon Fisher as he mathematically traced back the ancestry of some currently flourishing species. A mere one hundred generations back he discovered, in some cases, the ancestors not only were few but embraced nearly all whose differentness or superiority made their descendants what they typically are.

The Cambridge geneticist went back 200, 1,000, 10,000 generations, still only in the infancy of some species. Always the ancestral lines narrowed down to the few who were different or who climbed over the highest mountain or drifted to the distant island.

Fisher then gave another interesting turn to his studies of the remote and small ancestry of most species. How much, he asked, how much of the genetic variance of any individual is due to the hereditary differences of his parents and how much to the remixing of their genes—a process called genetic segregation?

The non-scientist long has pondered the same problem, though in other terms. The baby, it is said, has its mother's eyes and its father's nose. It owes this assortment of features to the hereditary differences of its parents. On the other hand, full brothers and sisters, all of whom have the same ancestral background, frequently are strikingly different. Their unlikeness comes from what Fisher calls genetic segregation, from the particular lot of genes they happened to receive, from their deal of the genetic cards.

Fisher decided from his survey of human statistics that the hereditary differences of the parents account for about three fifths of the distinctive characteristics of each individual, and genetic segregation for the other two fifths.

But the hereditary differences of the parents in their turn had stemmed partly from segregation and partly from the hereditary differences of the grandparents.

Going farther and farther back, Fisher held that the proportion of any individual's characteristics that might be credited to ancestry rapidly becomes smaller and smaller. Ancestors ten generations back, by his figuring, account for only one part in 160 in the current individual. Those 30 generations distant for less than one part in 4,000,000! Fisher gave up the quest at this stage, sparing the ancestor-worshipper any further shocks about the thinness of his inheritance.

But he had another unsettling observation for those whose pride might lie in race rather than family tree.

"It is only the geographic and other barriers to sexual intercourse between different races . . . which prevent the whole of mankind from having had, apart from the last 1,000 years, a practically identical ancestry," he wrote.

"The ancestry of members of the same nation can differ little beyond the last 500 years. At 2,000 years the only differences that would seem to remain would be those between distinct ethnographic races. These, or at least some of the elements of these, may indeed be extremely ancient, but this could only be the case if for long ages the diffusion of blood between the separated groups was almost non-existent."

Two other aspects of evolution particularly engaged the attention of the distinguished red-bearded Cambridge professor of genetics. Both were problems Darwin had studied. Later research had illumined both and brought the necessity for re-evaluation.

One of Darwin's great difficulties was to account for the evolution of secondary sexual characteristics.

Darwin concluded that the selection of sires which resulted from the grim battles some animals fought for the female could explain the development of such special weapons as the great antlers of the elk and the exaggerated pugnacity of certain breeds during the mating season.

Darwin, of course, knew nothing of the action of the sex hormones on such features, for those discoveries were not to come for many years afterward. When hormone research did show that genetic modification of the whole species could be manifest in one sex only, "the only difficulty that might have been felt about Darwin's theory" was removed, Fisher wrote.

Darwin had proposed an even bolder theory to explain a second class of secondary sexual characteristics—for example, the brilliant plumage of the male pheasant and other birds. Could it not be accounted for, Darwin queried, by the preference of the female and her choice of the most dramatically colored males?

Other naturalists disagreed. Wallace was one who could not bring himself to imagine that female preference could affect evolution. This battle raged with a pugnacity worthy of the elks.

Fisher was of the opinion that here, as in the larger fight between mutation and natural selection, much of the trouble came because each side found its own explanations so satisfactory that it had no inclination to look farther. He tried to bring the two together by setting up some "impartial principles of interpretation." To show how such an approach might be applied, Fisher chose a case that had been argued long and loud.

Whenever a female bird is as brilliantly and conspicuously colored as the male, the nest generally is concealed, perhaps in a hole in a tree or in the ground, perhaps under a dome of mud out in the open.

Wallace argued that it is because of the hidden nest that the female bird does not need to have drab-colored feathers to hide her as she sits brooding. She can be as gaudy as the male. The Duke of Argyll answered that a large domed nest would be as conspicuous in its way as brilliant plumage. Darwin was inclined to agree with the duke. He thought either the concealed nest or the domed one would be easily found by "tree-haunting" enemies. Wallace replied that as a matter of fact the domed nest must serve as protection, since hawks and crows do not pluck it to pieces.

Fisher suggested that the whole dispute was on the wrong track. The issue he said, is not whether the domed nest is advantageous or disadvantageous, but whether it affects selection. From such a point of view, it quite obviously does. Without the nest to conceal her, the brilliantly colored brooding female might be a shining target for her enemies. In very short order few richly plumaged females would be left to produce another generation. Only females whose colors might protectively merge with their surroundings during the brooding season would be likely to survive.

Two fundamental conditions must be fulfilled if evolutionary change is to be ascribed to sexual selection, Fisher said. The two are the existence of sexual preference in at least one sex, and conditions in which such preference confers a reproductive advantage. Under these terms such a showy ornament as the peacock's tail, which serves no useful purpose and is at its most brilliant during the mating season, would be considered to have evolutionary significance.

Fisher thought Darwin mistaken in the example he chose to show sexual preference in birds. Darwin had pointed out that when one bird of a pair is killed, it is almost immediately replaced by another bird of the same sex. From this he drew the deduction that there must be many unpaired birds, and that such birds remain single because they can find no mate to please them. If birds were so discriminating, Fisher maintained, few would be mated. He also cited later bird studies, establishing that birds are unpaired only because they are not in possession of a territory where they can nest unmolested. When a vacancy occurs, they move in fast.

The Cambridge professor's general conclusion on the whole question of sexual selection in evolution was summed up simply: whenever sexual preference confers an advantage in the struggle for life, it can become established in a species. Darwin once again had been found substantially right in the light of modern investigations.

Few things in nature seem so strange and uncanny as the mimicry with which many species copy others.

The Oriental *Danaida tytia* butterfly is a lovely thing, its grayish upper wings marked with a delicate tracery of black, and its lower wings as exquisitely etched in brown. In some of the districts where it abounds there is a swallowtail butterfly, called *Papilio agestor,* which mimics it with astounding fidelity. The black tracery on the upper wings follows almost the same pattern, and so it is too with the brown markings on the lower wing.

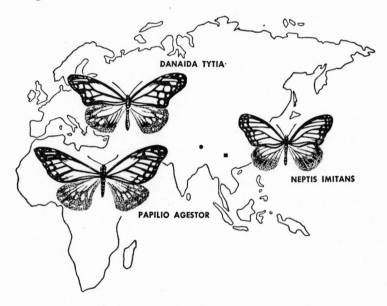

THE LOVELY BUT TOUGH DANAIDA TYTIA BUTTERFLY AND THE TWO
MIMICS WHOSE RESEMBLANCE TO TYTIA DECEIVES THE BIRDS INTO
LETTING THEM ALONE TOO. TYTIA AND AGESTOR ARE FOUND IN THE
SAME AREA OF INDIA; TYTIA AND IMITANS LIVE IN SOUTHWEST
CHINA.

In southwest China, tytia has another mimic almost as exact. *Neptis imitans* is slightly smaller, but flaunts the same characteristic gray and black patterns, the same concentration of color at the edges of the wings. A casual observer—as well as the birds—can easily mistake either of the two for its tytia model.

Observers long had noticed that the mimics, such as *Papilio agestor* and *Neptis imitans,* are much sought by the birds. Evidently they are delicate, tender morsels. On the other hand, the fragile-appearing tytia is in actuality a flexible, rubbery creature, so tough that it has been seen to survive unharmed after being seized and distastefully spit out by a bird. The birds avoid it. Thus the more the mimics can look like tytia, the greater their chance of escaping their natural enemies.

During the 1890's and after the rediscovery of Mendelian principles in 1900, mimicry was a major field of study. It was generally considered as presenting an undeniable example of "discontinous origin," or of what could be done by mutation. The mimics were believed to be mutations that just happened to hit it off.

Fisher argued, on the contrary, that mimicry is an outstanding example of natural selection. In the first place, such complete resemblances cannot be simple. Successful mimicry involves color, pattern, form, posture, movement, and sometimes also sound. Fisher emphasized that natural selection is the only means known to biology by which such complex adaptations of structure to function can be brought about.

The biologist made these additional points: the variety of means the mimics use to gain their ends is a further characteristic of natural selection. One investigator has reported four distinct ways used by different species in imitating the superficial appearance of an ant! In a single mimicry group five different methods have been developed to give an appearance of transparency to the wings of moths and butterflies.

"Systematic affinity" as an explanation of mimicry was quickly dismissed by Fisher. There were too many cases of mimicry between different classes of animals for such an argument to hold water. A mite, for example, is known to fool a certain class of blind ants by using its hind legs to mimic the movement of their antennæ. Since the ants use antenna signals to obtain food from one another, the imitative mite manages to cut himself in on a free food supply.

Furthermore, mimics look no more like their model than necessary. There are no similarities that do not aid in strengthening the superficial likeness.

Mimicry occurs between species inhabiting the same region, appearing at the same seasons and hours, and frequently captured flying together. Such close association would be unlikely if the mimics were the creation of mutations that had just happened to hit it off, Fisher noted. No, said Fisher, only natural selection could produce such extraordinary, fine adaptations.

Wherever he looked, Fisher saw evidence of the discriminatory hand of natural selection. Chance, so called, seemed to him to have little effect on evolution. Natural selection by favoring any variation for the better, molded the individual to the environment. Mutations supplied much of the raw material, and yet the combination and recombination of genes in the mating of individuals could alone produce a vast range of variation upon which selection could act. Natural selection could explain the spread and multiplication of the big species, like man, mice, and fish, and the shrinkage of the small ones. It could account for the formation of new species.

In short, Fisher maintained, natural selection explains not only adaptation but evolution. It is the driving force. "Evolution is progressive adaptation and consists of nothing else," he declared.

And modern science went a long way with him in giving natural selection the predominant part in the endless panorama of evolution and change.

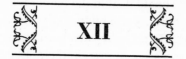

WRIGHT

DIVERSITY AND DRIFT

ALL ABOUT US, wherever we look or turn, is limitless diversity. No two human beings, except identical twins, are the same. Each of the more than two billion people on this globe is different—different from his parents, from his brothers and sisters, from his relatives, from his countrymen, from others of the same race; in short, from every other individual who lives or ever lived.

On the other hand, the living world is not a mass of random individuals. All of the almost limitless number of individuals are gathered together in an array of families, races, species, and other groups.

How can such diversity be? And how do all of these sharply different individuals happen to be clustered together in groups of various sizes and kinds?

Scholars long have puzzled over these basic problems, but not until recently did a scientific answer become possible. Only as genetics began to learn about the nature of difference and as mathematics was applied to the matter of populations was the way opened for a clearer understanding of why we are both different and alike.

An erudite professor at the University of Chicago has given one of the most enlightening explanations of why each individual is unique and yet a member of a group. His name is Sewall Wright. His investigations brought him close to the starting-point of the modern theory of evolution, which he, along with Haldane and Fisher, has had an important hand in shaping.

That Wright should deal in the higher realms of difference, similarity, possibility, probability, order, change, and chance is not surprising. He probably was born to such concerns. The Chicago professor's great-grandfather, Elizur Wright, was known not only as a leader in the antislavery movement, but as the "father of insurance." He took what was essentially a gamble and, by mathematically working out its probabilities and possibilities, turned it into an exact and certain business.

Wright's father was a professor of mathematics, and one brother, Theodore P. Wright, is a vice-president of Cornell University in charge of research programs. Another brother, Quincy Wright, is a member of the faculty of the University of Chicago and a distinguished authority on international relations.

Sewall Wright was born at Melrose, Massachusetts, on December 21, 1889. Soon afterward his father was appointed to the faculty of Lombard College, at Galesburg, Illinois, and the family moved to the Middle West. When young Wright in due course entered Lombard as an undergraduate, it did not offer much of an array of science courses. Nevertheless, he took all of them he could, as well as all the available courses in mathematics. He was thinking of becoming either a chemist or an engineer.

But chemistry in a small college in the first decades of the 1900's tended to be a fixed and final subject. It was assumed that almost everything that needed to be known was known, and the student was "fed a lot of cookbook stuff." That did not long hold a young student who could juggle higher equations in his head.

Biology was another matter. A gifted teacher, Wilhelmine E. Key, talked of the tremendous work still to be done. That struck a responsive note in Wright, who thereupon decided to be a biologist and went to the University of Illinois to take a master's degree in the field. During the year he was there, W. E. Castle, pioneer geneticist of Harvard, came to Illinois to lecture. When he talked about how the new Mendelian principles were being applied to further studies of heredity, Wright was fascinated. He inquired about the possibility of obtaining a research assistantship to work with Castle, and got it.

At about the time Wright went to Harvard his attention was caught by a report by J. T. Gulick on differences in the snails of the Hawaiian Islands. The snails did not differ in the way they should have. They lived in the green valleys which radiated out from the volcanic cones that tower over most of the islands. One valley was very much like another and the plants on which the snails lived were closely alike. Since the snails were subjected to the same climate, the same food, and the same selective influences in general, they should have been very much alike. Or if they differed at all, those in adjacent valleys should have differed less than those in more remote valleys.

But this was not the way it was. Some of the snails were small and stout and some were longer and more slender. And these two extreme types sometimes were found in adjoining valleys. Wright began to wonder. Obviously the snails, with their low mobility, seldom crawled out of their ancestral valleys. Could their isolation have sent them off on a different tack even when their environment was the same?

Castle had put his young assistant to work on a genetics problem that involved the inbreeding and crossbreeding of guinea pigs. Wright decided to watch at the same time for any non-selective differences that might develop in the animals.

A few years later the Department of Agriculture launched an experiment to improve the breed of livestock. The question was the extent to which hogs, chickens, sheep, and cattle could be made better by inbreeding and crossbreeding. Since the genetic problems were too complex to be worked out on paper, the best possibility seemed to be to study them with laboratory animals, and in this case with the guinea pig.

Wright's experience marked him as the man for the job. Because the place offered him an opportunity for large-scale investigation of problems in which he had already become interested, he accepted. For ten years he served as a "senior animal husbandman" in the Department of Agriculture. Twenty-four lines of guinea pigs were started. To test the effects of inbreeding, brothers and sisters, and in some cases parents and offspring, were mated.

The guinea pigs lived in the same laboratory and the same kind of cages, and their genetic background could not have been closer, but Wright soon saw that the different lines were drifting apart. Each line was becoming a little different from the others. It looked more and more as though some factor other than selection was at work. Wright had a clue that was to occupy him from then on.

In 1926 he went to the University of Chicago and took some of the guinea pigs with him. Away from the Department he could study them not for what they might show about the improvement of livestock, but for the evolutionary consequences of that strange drift he saw in them.

There have been few days since when Wright had not been in his laboratory in "guinea-pig house" on the Chicago campus, working with the descendants of the original guinea pigs, and sometimes fretting "because they're so slow." There were guinea pigs and guinea pigs and guinea pigs. With that incredible patience of scientists, Wright kept his lines going. Some of them were inbred for more than forty generations, the equivalent of ten human centuries.

All the while the differences between the lines became more marked. Wright had no difficulty distinguishing them as he watched the guinea pigs on the laboratory floor. Strain 13 had a somewhat Roman nose, in contrast with the pointed nose of strain 2. The eyes of strain 35 bugged out; those of 13 were sunken. Strain 39 was sway-backed. Some strains were a third heavier than others. Some were longer, some were shorter. Some even redeveloped the extra toe that the species as a whole had long since lost.

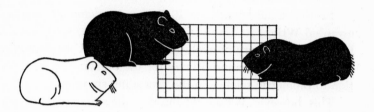

SOME OF THE LONG INBRED LINES OF GUINEA PIGS WERE SWAY-BACKED. SOME WERE HEAVIER THAN OTHERS. ONE STRAIN HAD A ROMAN NOSE.

They also differed in disposition. Strain 35 was nervous and squirmed when handled. The animals of 13 were phlegmatic and could be picked up like so many sacks of meal.

Here was the phenomenon of the snails happening all over again in the controlled precincts of the laboratory. Wright suspected that the chance differences the lines had developed might well supply rich material for later evolution. He reasoned that if an occasional local strain should prove successful, so successful that it would have an edge in the struggle for life, it would increase and spread beyond the narrow limits of its point of origin. If it then mingled with other different groups, still further new combinations might result.

Wright did not use the illustration, but he might have supposed that a painter had by chance produced a new shade of blue on one part of his palette and a new yellow on another. If the two should mix, suddenly there would be a new green, a green that would not have been possible without the particular new blue and yellow.

This was a theory that could be studied and tested mathematically. If one thing happened, the probabilities of another following could be calculated. Mathematics as well as guinea pigs and snails led Wright to the evolutionary conclusions that were to win him national and international honors.

In the same month in 1947 the Academy of Sciences awarded Wright its Daniel Giraud Elliot medal for his contribution to the theory of evolution, and Oxford University gave him its Weldon Memorial Prize for the outstanding contribution to biometric science in the preceding six years.

This, however, is running ahead of the story. Years of work went into the development of his theories before these honors came to Wright. In his austere office in the biology building, with no rugs, no curtains, he marshaled the most formidable mathematics to establish his points.

Even his colleagues on the faculty stood in awe of the difficulty of the work he was doing. One fellow professor is reputed to have said after listening to a Wright paper: "I didn't understand twenty per cent of it, but I know it is one of the most important papers in the field that I've ever heard."

Students also find the Wright theories far from easy. They sometimes audit a course for a semester before officially enrolling, for they feel the need of a preliminary once-over in order to grasp the profundities and to pass. To explain one equation, Wright is likely to scribble out another.

The fact is that the professor's mind works in a mathematical upper stratosphere. If communications are not good between him and the non-mathematical majority, it is because there is something of a gap between the two types of mind.

Wright certainly is not intentionally highbrow or obscure. He is a kindly, extremely quiet man who looks the college professor he is. His hair is a thick gray lightly mixed with brown; his blue eyes behind rimless glasses are shy. His manner seems a little old-fashioned, a little formal, a little stiff, not because he tries for or wants such an effect, but because he is preoccupied with other matters.

Wright's contributions to the theory of evolution are set forth in a series of publications, nearly all of which are brief, distilled, imposing, and, for the layman, nearly impenetrable. And yet the problems with which he deals must have tantalizingly crossed the mind of almost every human being.

Each of us must always have been aware from a very early age that he is different, and when Wright began his work it also was agreed that these differences of all living things have their origin in the gene, that submicroscopic carrier of heredity.

In a few cases a single gene produces a single characteristic; for example, the blood group A, B, or O. More frequently a number of genes act together to determine such characteristics as the height, the color of the hair, or the shape of the mouth. Despite the fact that many genes have been identified by their action, no one knows how many there are in the human cells, or in the cells of many other species. But certainly the number runs into the thousands.

Wright calculated that if there were only one hundred sets of human genes, instead of the thousands there are, and if each set had only four alternative forms, the number of combinations that could be formed from them would be staggering. The number has no name; it can be written only as 10 to the 100th power, or as 10,000,000,000,000,000,000,000,000,000,000,000,-000,000,000,000,000,000,000,000,000,000,000,000,000,000,-000,000,000,000,000,000,000.

The number of possible gene combinations is almost beyond comprehension. It makes the billions that sometimes are tossed around shrink into insignificance. It dwarfs almost every other figure. In fact, Wright pointed out, it vastly exceeds the total number of electrons in the visible universe. The electrons could be counted by writing the figure ten followed by fewer than one hundred zeros.

To bring the idea of what can be done by combining numbers down to terms that can be grasped, think of the number of combinations that can be made by shuffling and reshuffling even so small a field as a deck of cards. Select any one combination, say four aces. See how many times the fifty-two cards will have to be dealt to obtain that one simple little foursome.

10,000,000,000,000,000,000,000,000,000,000,000,000,000,000,000,000,000,000,000,000,000,000,000,000,000,000,000,000,000,000,000,000,000,000,000,000,000

NO TWO HUMAN BEINGS EXCEPT IDENTICAL TWINS ARE EVER LIKELY TO BE THE SAME. AN INFINITE NUMBER OF GENE COMBINATIONS, AND HENCE OF DIFFERENT INDIVIDUALS, IS POSSIBLE.

In fact, however, only a part of the vast potential number of gene combinations is easily available in an ordinary interbreeding population. Not every individual is a potential mate for a given individual. So the number of individuals among whom any particular individual is likely to find a mate probably is somewhat limited. This is true even with such mobile creatures as birds. They show an extraordinary tendency always to return to the same locality for breeding.

There is another reason why the number of possible gene combinations is not unlimited. As eons have succeeded eons, certain groups of genes have come to be prevalent in large groups of people; that is why there are race, national, and family similarities.

The field thus is relatively narrowed. Suppose, however, that the same genes should appear in 95 per cent of the members of one group and that only 5 per cent of the genes in each individual were different. In other words, assume that in a card game everyone held 95 black and 5 red cards. In the genetic game, the average individual in such a 95-to-5 group still would differ in fifty respects.

If the deck were stacked in this 95-to-5 way, obviously not so many combinations could result as if it were half red and half black. The population would be confined to an infinitesimal portion of the field of possible gene combinations.

And yet even under such circumstances, the possible number of gene combinations would be so great that there would be no chance that any two sexually produced individuals would have exactly the same genetic constitution in a species of millions upon millions of individuals persisting over millions of generations. Each individual would be unique not only in his own generation, but as far back as it is possible to go. "There is no difficulty accounting for the probable genetic uniqueness of each individual human being or other organism which is the product of bi-parental reproduction," said Wright.

But there was that other fact too—that the living world is not a mass of random combining genes, or of random individuals. It is rather a multitude of families or clusters of individuals with common characteristics, or, in genetic terms, related gene combinations.

According to some of the best estimates, there are at least 1,500,000 such clusters or species of animals and plants. Each of them, like the lion, for example, has a distinctive structure, organs, and behavior and with this equipment is able to find food for itself and its young and generally to get along in its habitat.

And each of these groups is different from all of the others. There is discontinuity, a gap between even the closest of the clusters. A young animal immediately can be identified as belonging to the species of lions, *Felis leo,* or to the species of house cats, *Felis domestica.* No one has ever had any difficulty deciding which.

Wright hit upon a brilliant way of visualizing and studying this complex grouping of all living things. He imagined a vast mountainous country whose inhabitants live only on the innumerable peaks that stud the ranges and mountain systems. Each species is clustered on its own peak. A shallow though unoccupied valley separates it from near-by peaks on which other species live.

On the more adjacent peaks the species are related. Near the peak that the lion occupies are other peaks inhabited by the tiger, the puma, the leopard. A little farther away are those held by the wolf, the coyote, and the jackal. The feline adaptive peaks, however, form a group quite different from the group of canine peaks.

Together, the feline, canine, ursine, musteline, and some other groups of peaks make up the adaptive "range" of the carnivores, a great range separated by a deep valley from the ranges of the rodents, ungulates, primates, and others. In turn the mountains of the mammals are separated from the huge systems held by the birds and reptiles.[1]

Wright began to explore the extremely interesting question of why the inhabitants of this world—for it is the living world—dwell only on the peaks. Why are there no in-between species in the valleys?

And how does a group make its way to a new and higher peak? Obviously new peaks have been captured, for in the beginning only a few elevations would have been tenanted. And some of the peaks are much higher than others, with man's towering above all the rest. How did man reach his heights?

Wright assumed first that one particular group of genes affecting one particular characteristic provides the maximum adaptation. In a hot tropical climate it might be a gene combination that produces a skin capable of resisting the burning rays of the sun.

[1] I am indebted to Theodosius Dobzhansky for this grouping. See *Genetics and the Origin of Species*, third edition, Columbia University Press.

If this is true, Wright demonstrated mathematically, the selective value of the other gene combinations affecting the same characteristic will fall off more or less regularly according to the degree by which they are removed from the best gene combination. In non-mathematical terms and using the same example, individuals born with a skin not so well adapted to withstanding the sun will be less likely to survive and leave descendants.

In this way a species that is clustered about some combination other than the best will tend inevitably to move up toward a peak. Eventually nearly all members of the group would have skins sufficiently pigmented to protect them from the sun.

And so each of the species—lions, larks, and man—have moved up to the adaptive peaks they occupy. Those which did not failed to survive and the valleys became empty.

Each species in its climb also moved farther away from its relatives on near-by peaks. And thus the groups became sharply separated.

If it is not a question of a single characteristic, such as the pigmentation of the skin or a blood group, but of the fitness of the organism as a whole, the whole problem becomes much more complicated. As he worked in his laboratory and with his mathematics, Wright saw more and more clearly that there might be a number of different combinations of characteristics that could be harmonious and adapted to external conditions. Hence there might be a number of satisfactory solutions to the problem of getting along well in nature.

To continue the analogy, groups might find other means than pigmentation of the skin for accommodating themselves to the tropic heat. As Fisher noted, different groups of insects found four different ways of imitating the appearance of an ant and thus gaining protection.

But how then could a species ever find its way from a point where it was doing well to the best adaptation? How would it get off of a high but suitable peak and make its way to a higher pinnacle? The question is, in effect, under what conditions will there be evolutionary progress?

Wright pondered this difficult problem and again undertook a mathematical examination. If the species is large and interbreeds freely, and if there is no decided change in the condi-

LARKS, LIONS, AND MAN. EACH OCCUPIES A PEAK SHARPLY SEPARATED FROM THE PEAKS HELD BY ALL OTHER SPECIES.

tions under which it lives, his figures indicated that it would not evolve much farther. It would remain on the peak it occupies.

And this checked with the evidence of the eyes. Men, who are just such a species, are showing no tendency to evolve into supermen. Individuals, of course, will vary. But Wright's calculations indicated that a large, freely interbreeding group would as a whole reach an equilibrium, unless—and there generally must be an unless—conditions should change or a new and distinctly favorable mutation should occur.

Fortunately for progress, environmental conditions seldom remain the same. As all the evolutionists have emphasized, the environment, living and non-living, is in continuous change. An ice age comes and the glaciers pushing down from the north turn a once tropical land into a frozen tundra. Or the seas rise and inundate a great inland valley. Or an irresistible enemy appears. Or a prickly cardoon, the plant that Darwin saw taking over whole territories in South America, is introduced and runs wild.

Mathematical prediction of what will happen in the face of an extreme change is not difficult. Darwin has long since pointed out what occurs in nature. If a species that has been well adapted to a lush, warm climate is not able to adapt to a new cold climate, it becomes extinct. Its peak stands empty. The species becomes the victim, as many have, of having fitted too well into conditions that no longer exist.

But if the cold is more moderate and if selection is not so severe, perhaps some slightly different individuals or groups within the species will do quite well. Perhaps some mutant variation that was of little importance in the old environment will be exactly what is needed for the new.

While Wright was picturing this process mathematically, many experiments and experiences underlined it. A group of scientists put a population of "wild type" (winged) Drosophila into a cage with a population of "vestigial" flies (with short wings, incapable of flight). Under normal conditions the winged flies soon predominated. They reached a peak. But when conditions changed, when the cages were kept in a place open to wind, the winglessness that had been a disadvantage under normal conditions became a marked advantage. The wingless flies soon outnumbered the winged.

This same ability of living organisms to go off on a new tack when conditions change seriously damaged California citrus crops. The citrus-growers long had used hydrocyanic gas to kill the scale insects (Coccidæ) which attacked their trees. It was highly effective. About 1914, however, reports began to come in that the gas was no longer controlling the red scale.

Many years later a genetic study disclosed the presence of two distinct strains of red scale, one nonresistant, and the other relatively resistant to the gas. They differed only in a single incompletely dominant gene. To the sorrow of the citrus-growers, this gene enabled the species to survive when its environment was filled with the gas that almost eliminated the older form.

Under such circumstances there is a very good chance that the newly favored form will move immediately to a new peak. In getting along with a new climate, new foods, new enemies, the successful part of a species may advance rapidly. It will make evolutionary progress.

"There we undoubtedly have an evolutionary process of major importance," said Wright. "It is essentially that which Darwin and Wallace put first. It is also that to which most attention has been devoted by Haldane and Fisher in their studies of the evolutionary implications of statistical genetics."

By general agreement, this is the process primarily responsible for carrying life from the water to the land, from the reptiles to the mammals, and from the mammals to man. By adapting themselves to new conditions and new opportunities, variable groups rose higher in the evolutionary line, or, in Wright's analogy, to high peaks in the mountain ranges of adaptation.

But Wright became convinced, largely by the changes he saw in his guinea pigs, that this was not the whole story of life's great climb. Even though there were no change in the environment or no favorable mutations, he saw another way in which a species might make its way to a new and higher peak.

Man himself had used this route, Wright believed. Back in his earlier days, man was much more sharply divided into local groups than he is in this era of roads, trains, and planes. Each little community was more or less independent, and there was not much mixing. For generations the people of one section married others from the same vicinity. As a result there was a considerable degree of inbreeding.

By the random, chance shuffling and reshuffling of the limited number of genes represented in the group, Wright maintained, each community, like the guinea pigs and snails, tended to become a little different. There was a "drifting apart" that was not due purely to selection and to the survival of the fittest, but to the interaction of chance and selection.

How chance shuffling can bring about changes in a limited group can be demonstrated in an oversimplified way with cards. Take five red and five black cards, shuffle them well, and deal them out into two groups of five.

Probably one group will contain three blacks and two reds and the other three reds and two blacks. Assume that one group represents Locality One and the other Locality Two. Thus this will be your line-up:

Locality One   *Locality Two*

To keep the experiment going, duplicate each group. In genetic terms, mate each with another individual of the same kind.

Thus:

Shuffle the cards of Locality One, and again deal them out in fives. On one sample run in Locality One, four new deals all came out three blacks and two reds. But on the next shuffle there was a change. The cards fell in this way:

To the four blacks and one red another four blacks and one red were added. The cards were shuffled. For the next four deals the same assortment turned up, four blacks and one red. But on the next deal there was another change. One hand was all black and the other held three blacks and two reds:

In the other original hand, Locality Two, the three reds and two blacks were duplicated and dealt. On the first deal this was the distribution:

The four reds and the one black were matched or inbred with another four reds and one black. For the next two deals they came out in the same arrangement, four to one. But on the next deal there was a shift. The cards fell:

By the reshuffling of this limited number of genes (cards) a decided change had come about. A few of the inhabitants of Locality One in this illustration had become all black and a fairly high degree of blackness ran through all the others.

On the other hand, some of the dwellers in Locality Two had become all red, and others showed a decided red influence. In this random way, the populations of two localities, originally identical, had drifted apart; they had become different by a process that was not affected, in this case, by natural selection.

But—and this is Wright's major point—the differentness that developed by chance may become highly important thereafter in evolution. "Such a race," said Wright, "will expand in numbers and by cross breeding with other races, as well as by actual displacement of others, will pull the species as a whole toward a new position. Fine sub-division into partially isolated populations provides a most effective mechanism for trial and error in the field of gene combinations and thus for evolutionary advance by inter-group selection."

An analogous process in cultural evolution pulled ancient Greece to the great heights it reached, Wright thinks. The people of Athens, after developing a distinctive and superior civilization under considerable local isolation, carried this to other parts of Greece. The people of Sparta, who had arrived at another distinctive and favorable way of life, did the same. Athenians and Spartans met, mixed, and influenced each other, and out of the intermingling came new and better combinations.

Wright is convinced that the unparalleled evolutionary progress of ancient Greece can be explained by the fact that the Greek cities and their people were distinctively different. In contrast, uniformity was imposed in the Persian Empire. There was no opportunity there for the development of the rich differences that might have contributed to new and superior patterns, and the Persians did not reach the heights scaled by the Greeks.

In more recent times in Europe, but when the barriers of language and distance still counted more heavily that they do now, the French, the Germans, the Italians, and other groups each developed its own genius. As intergroup selection came into play, the whole of Europe rose to a new and higher position. Wright scarcely needed to point out how much the people of Europe have changed over four hundred to five hundred years.

The idea that chance, or a random drift of gene frequencies, could have evolutionary significance became known as the "Sewall Wright effect." Wright, modesty aside, is not particularly fond of the designation. Too often, he fears, people think it applies only to the phenomenon of drift and do not realize that the intergroup selection, which grows out of favorable chance combinations, is the point he considers critical to evolution.

Fisher was willing to concede that chance is involved in the mutation of the individual gene. Beyond that he would not go. The English authority and Wright clashed. One of those sharp and continuing controversies which often spring up in science was under way. Charges and rebuttals, principally in the form of highly scientific pamphlets, began to fly back and forth. With the scientific equivalent of the sounding of trumpets, Fisher and E. B. Ford announced in 1947 that they had data "fatal" to the "Wright effect."

In the vicinity of Oxford is a moth called *Panaxia dominula*. Its numbers are small and it is strictly isolated (in something of the manner of Wright's guinea pigs and the snails). For more than twenty years English scientists had noticed that some of the moths bore a color not found anywhere else. It is called *medionigra*.

Before 1929, only 1.2 per cent of the moths were medionigra-colored. By 1939 the frequency of the rare color reached 9.2 per cent, and in 1940 it climbed to 11.1 per cent. After that, fewer medionigra moths were counted, and the occurrence of the color dropped to between 4.3 and 6.5 per cent.

By statistical analysis, Fisher and Ford reported, they had proved that such fluctuations could not have arisen from accidents in sampling. Only natural selection, they said, could account for the change in the appearance of medionigra. Thus Wright was wrong! His theory that there is "a special evolutionary advantage to small isolated communities" was demolished. The two English scientists said so in no uncertain terms.

Wright did not in the least agree. In a pamphlet called *Fisher and Ford on the "Sewall Wright Effect,"* he shot right back. In the first place, Wright said, he did not hold the views attributed to him. He had not claimed, he emphasized, that there is an evolutionary advantage to small isolated communities, but rather that random variation in a number of small isolated populations can provide the material for an evolutionary advance if the local populations begin to spill over and crossbreed with others. That was a different matter.

The continuing dispute simmers down in the end to the old and long-debated question: how much chance is there in evolution? Do "time and chance happen to them all"? [2]

To many who came along much before Fisher, the idea of any chance at all in evolution seemed unthinkable. It appeared impossible that the incredibly fine adjustments of the leaf to the tree and the bee to the orchid could have been achieved if any degree of chance figured in it.

Lamarck was one of the first to reach this belief. The astute French scientist ruled out chance; the action of the environment and the inheritance of the changes it produced explained all. Others eliminated chance by the proposal that all evolution is an unfolding of innate possibilities, in much the way that a child grows into a man. Evolution, in this view, follows a set, a fixed, a predetermined course. Some of Darwin's followers, rather than Darwin himself, argued that natural selec-

---

[2] "I returned, and saw under the sun that the race is not to the swift, nor the battle to the strong, neither yet bread to the wise, nor yet riches to men of understanding, nor yet favor to men of skill; but time and chance happeneth to them all." (Ecclesiastes ix, 11.)

tion alone, with no element of chance in it, can explain the complexity of nature and the development of species.

At the opposite extreme were those who held that the "whole character complex" of a species might spring from a single chance event—a mutation. De Vries, the outstanding spokesman for this school, traced all evolutionary progress to change through mutation, and thus, basically, through chance.

Haldane, Fisher, and Wright settled part of this long and perplexing controversy by sorting out the issues. Their work generally convinced science that mutation is not the force that controls and guides evolution. Mutation, they demonstrated, has the job of keeping life out of a rut by furnishing it with a stock of variability. They also convinced the scientific world that natural selection is the great shaping force; that it is natural selection that adjusts and leads life onward.

Wright, however, gave chance a significant part at two levels in the majestic process—in the mutation of the gene and in the small interbreeding population. Fisher conceded it only at the first level. Only time, and perhaps chance, will settle the issue.

Aside from this dispute, the three have made the following points basic in the modern theory of evolution. As Wright stated them:

1. Evolutionary transformation consists almost wholly in changes in the frequencies of the genes.

2. The course of such transformation is largely controlled by selection.

3. Mutations merely furnish random raw material for evolution, and rarely if ever determine the course of the process.

Thus the old quarrel of mutation versus natural selection was settled. And men could see more clearly than ever before why they are different and why at the same time they are members of various groups essential to their lives. Or rather, men could see, provided that the story told by these erudite men reached them.

Part II

MAN'S BURIED RECORD

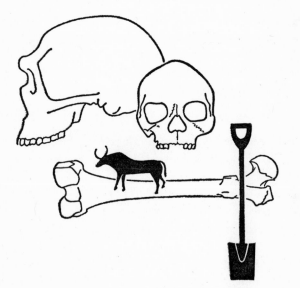

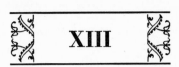

XIII

DUBOIS AND VON KOENIGSWALD
JAVA: PITHECANTHROPUS AND GIANTS

> *Was the oldest Homo sapiens Pliocene or*
> *Miocene? In still older strata do the fos-*
> *silized bones of an ape, more anthropoid, or*
> *a man, more pithecoid than any yet known*
> *await the researches of some unborn pale-*
> *ontologist?*
>
> —T. H. HUXLEY:
> *Man's Place in Nature* (1863)

IF MANKIND evolved from some form of apelike ancestor, where was the evidence? Why were there no bones to testify to the stages through which man had passed on his upward climb? Why were there missing links?

These questions were hurled at Darwin, and there was no effective answer he could give. He could reply only that the geological record was incomplete, that very little of the earth's surface had been searched for the remains of early man and his forebears.

It was true that strange bones occasionally had been found. Men had looked at them and wondered. But in the end they were dismissed as the relics of animals or of some kind of freak. Cuvier, the great French scientist, Lamarck's contemporary and opponent, was completely sure that man could not have

evolved from forms differing from man in his own time.
"*L'homme fossile n'existe pas*," he declared.[1]

Then in 1856 a particularly disturbing skull was uncovered
near Düsseldorf, Germany. It was a large one, with great bony
ridges over the eyes, and with thick cranial bones.

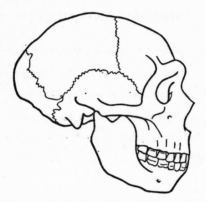

THE NEANDERTHAL SKULL. ITS HEAVY BONES AND KNOBBY RIDGES
PUZZLED THE SCIENTISTS OF THE NINETEENTH CENTURY AND MADE
LATER ONES DOUBT THAT NEANDERTHAL MAN WAS IN MAN'S DI-
RECT ANCESTRAL LINE.

When a description of it was published, excitement ran
high, and scientists hurried forward with a variety of explanations. Rudolf Virchow, the leading pathologist of the nineteenth
century, held that the skull was a pathological specimen. A
physician learnedly proved that the creature from which it
came was affected by "hypertrophic deformation." Another described it as that of "an individual affected with idiocy and

---

[1] "Fossil man does not exist." Or, less literally, Cuvier's dictum
might be translated: "There is no such thing as fossil man."

rickets." A prominent French anthropologist contributed the theory that it was the skull of "a powerfully organized Celt, somewhat resembling the skull of a modern Irishman with low mental organization." Equally remarkable was the opinion of a German authority; the remains, he argued, were those of "one of the Cossacks who came from Russia in 1814."

Huxley gave a long account of this "Neanderthal" skull in his *Man's Place in Nature,* published in 1863. "Under whatever aspect we view this cranium," he wrote, "whether we regard its vertical depression, the enormous thickness of the super-ciliary ridges, its sloping occiput, or its long straight squamosal suture, we meet with ape-like characters, stamping it as the most pithecoid cranium yet discovered." And yet at another point in his book Huxley cautioned: "In no sense can the Neanderthal bones be regarded as the remains of a human being intermediate between men and apes."

Darwin in his *Descent of Man* made only a brief reference to the Neanderthal skull and ventured no judgment upon it.

The opinions and counter-opinions about the Neanderthal skull and other odd skulls, jaws, and bones that turned up in Europe kept science and the keenly interested lay public in something of an uproar for many years.

One important outgrowth of the loud conflict was its effect upon a young Dutchman, Eugène Dubois. Dubois was born in 1858, only two years after the finding of the Neanderthal skull. As he grew up and began the study of medicine at the University of Amsterdam, his imagination was caught by the continuing debate about the meaning of the primitive unexplainable skull. In 1886 Dubois was appointed a lecturer in anatomy at the university, but his dreams were of the origin of man. He was fired by the urge to search for other remains that might throw new light on man's shadowy beginnings.

The young Dutch physician reasoned that man must have originated either in Africa, where the gorilla and chimpanzee still live, or in the Indo-Malayan region, where the orangutan survives.[2] Since Java and Sumatra had escaped the destruction of the glaciers during the ice age, he decided that these islands would be particularly favorable places to search. Dubois succeeded in obtaining an appointment as a surgeon in the Royal Dutch Army, and sailed for Padang, Sumatra, in November 1887, determined to discover the first man.

As soon as he could get some time from his hospital duties, Dubois began to search the caves of Sumatra. His only interesting finds were some teeth of the orangutan, then extinct in Sumatra.

About this time word reached him of the finding of a human skull near Wadjak, on the southern coast of central Java. Dubois had his lead. He persuaded the government to send him to Java specifically to look for "fossil vertebra fauna."

Like the neighboring great islands of Borneo and Sumatra, Java once had been joined to the Asiatic mainland. Living things could have moved down into this tropical land freely and dry-shod. Later the land connection was broken by vast earth movements, and the sea swept in to submerge all except the highest points of the old continent. It was these peaks, standing free above the waters, that formed the islands.

At Wadjak Dubois quickly discovered another skull. It did not seem old enough, however, so he said nothing about it and pressed on inland.

Near the hamlet of Trinil, the Solo River was lazily cutting its way through thick beds of the volcanic tuff that had spewed from the volcanoes in the neighboring hills. At places the tuff, and the sand and clay that had accumulated upon it, were 350 feet thick.

The natives long had known that there were ancient bones in some of the deposits. The huge fossilized bones of some ex-

---

[2] The Malayans regard the orangutan as a kind of man. Their name for this large ape—orangutan, meaning "forest man"—has been taken over by the world.

;or Mendel. The Austrian monk who dis-
red the laws of inheritance.

Sewall Wright. A geneticist who threw new
light on differences and likenesses.

)avidson Black. The discoverer of Peking

Dr. Robert Broom. The Scottish discoverer of
the South African ape-men.

PLATE IX

On the far bank of this sleepy Java river, the Solo, Dubois found *Pithecanthropus erectus*.

G. H. R. von Koenigswald holds up a fragment of the skull of *Pithecanthropus II*, found a the same Solo River.

PLATE X

The collectors crept up the hillside looking for every fragment of the bones of another Pithecanthropus.

The Java site where a third Pithecanthropus skull was discovered in 1938.

PLATE XI

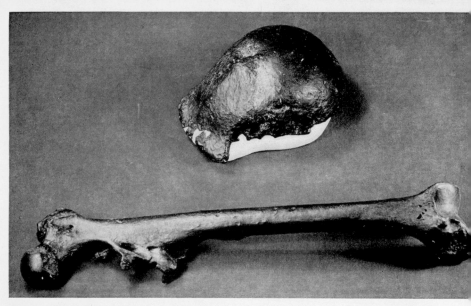

The apelike skull and the human leg bone of Pithecanthropus.

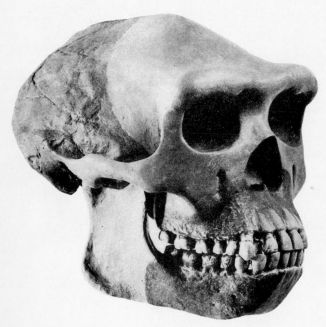

The skull of Pithecanthropus as restored by Weidenreich.

PLATE XII

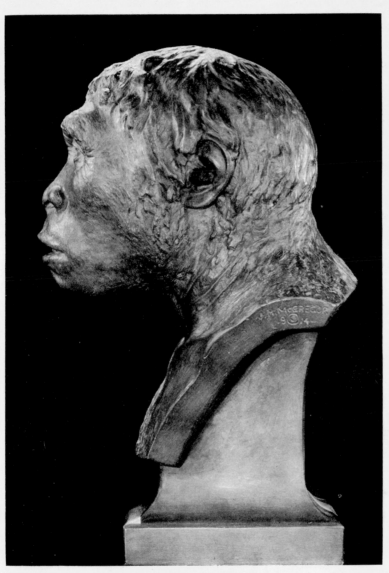

Pithecanthropus as he probably looked in life. This very early man stood erect and walked upright. His brain had reached 900 cubic centimeters, well above the 650 cubic centimeters of the ape, but well below the 1,300 to 1,500 cubic centimeters of man.

PLATE XIII

Teeth tell one story of the evolution of man. From LEFT to RIGHT: Third lower molar of Gigantopithecus, a giant early ancestor of man, found in a Chinese drugstore dealing in "dragon teeth." Third lower molar of a gorilla. Second lower molar of Peking man. First lower molar of modern man.

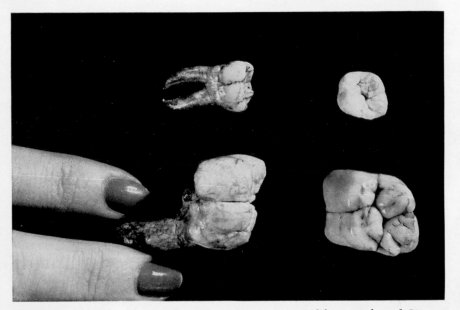

Giant teeth and the teeth of modern man. BELOW: upper and lower molars of Gigantopithecus. ABOVE: the same teeth in modern man.

PLATE XIV

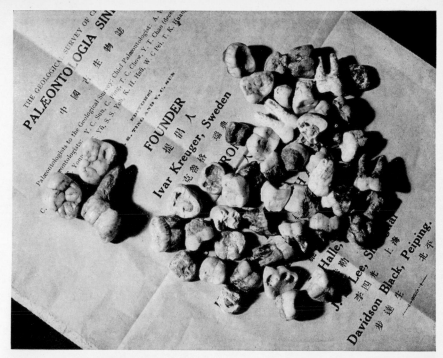

"Dragon teeth" from Hongkong and Canton, collected by von Koenigswald in drug-stores. LEFT: three giant molars. RIGHT: teeth of an extinct orangutan.

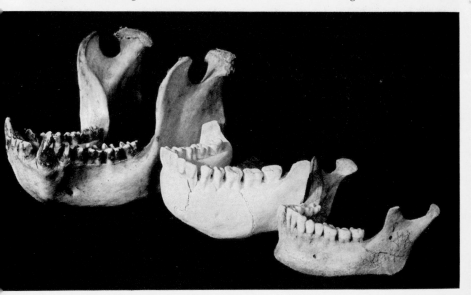

...e changing jaw. LEFT: gorilla. CENTER: *Meganthropus paleojavanicus*, the giant man of old ...a. (The jaw of the Java giant is larger than the gorilla's, but shows human characteristics.)
...HT: modern man.

PLATE XV

Dr. Franz Weidenreich and Dr. G. H. R. von Koenigswald examining a skull of one of the ea
giants of Java. On the table are skull fragments and teeth, some of them also belonging to
giants.

PLATE XVI

tinct elephants were believed to be the remains of giants, called
Raksasas, which guarded every temple in Java and Bali.

Dubois began to examine an old stratum, about four feet
thick, that had been re-exposed at just about the level of the
stream. It proved particularly rich in animal fossils. The omen
was good, for in November 1890 the doctor came upon a fossil
that he felt certain was prehuman. It was a fragment of a lower
jaw, with one tooth in place.

Work had to be halted during the wet season, but the following September Dubois eagerly resumed his digging in the
same stratum. He soon found an upper right molar tooth that
even at first sight looked human, or very close to it.

One month later and only about a yard away, Dubois
brushed the dirt from the find for which he had crossed half
the world. Embedded in the stone was some dark chocolate-
brown fossilized bone. The young doctor worked feverishly
with his hammer and chisel, hoping and yet scarcely daring to
hope, until a fine cranium emerged, a cranium like that of no
living creature. Almost the whole skullcap was there, harder
than marble and heavy in weight and portentousness.

"The amazing thing had happened," wrote G. Elliot Smith,
famous English anthropologist. "Dubois had actually found the
fossil his scientific imagination had visualized."

And yet Dubois was not sure. Perhaps the skull was that of
an ape. It was low, and there was a heavy bony ridge above
the eyes.

The rainy season again halted explorations. But again in
1892 Dubois was back. This time he made a new cutting, about
fifty feet away. To his utter amazement, Dubois there uncovered a completely human thigh bone—a left femur. If there
had been doubt about the humanness of the skull, Dubois, the
anatomist, could entertain none about the leg bone. Without
question it had belonged to a man or to some other creature
that had walked upright in the manner of man.

While the digging continued, Dubois pored over his find,

studying and measuring it in every possible way. He did not hurry, for a momentous decision was forming in his mind. Not until 1894 was he ready to publish the first scientific account of his discovery. Then he startled the world. For Dubois had decided that the skull and the leg bone belonged to the same creature, and he named it *"Pithecanthropus erectus,* a Human-

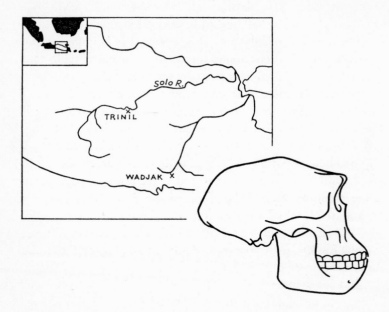

"PITHECANTHROPUS ERECTUS." THE SITE AT TRINIL WHERE HIS WORLD-FAMOUS BONES WERE UNEARTHED. IN THE LEFT CORNER, THE PITHECANTHROPUS DISTRICT OUTLINED ON A MAP OF THE ISLAND OF JAVA.

like Transitional Form from Java." "I considered it a link connecting apes and men," said Dubois.

Pitheko means ape in Greek, and *anthropos,* man. Thus Dubois drove home the point that he had found an erect-walking ape-man. The doctor had chosen the name with purpose. It was one that had been coined by the German scientist Haeckel for a hypothetical being that might link man with his anthropoid ancestors. Dubois, by taking it over, underlined his claim to having found the missing link.

For those unwilling to concede a relation between apes and men, the name and Dubois's claims were raw provocation. Scientists, for their part, were skeptical. It seemed suspicious that so significant a find should have been made in such an out-of-the-way place as Java, where others could not easily investigate all the circumstances. Here too was an amateur announcing the most important discovery in the history of man.

After trying unsuccessfully to find more materials, Dubois returned to Europe in 1895. The already famous bones of *Pithecanthropus erectus* were exhibited at the Third International Congress of Anthropology at Leyden. The leading anthropologists and paleontologists were there. Dubois later displayed the Pithecanthropus bones at scientific meetings in Liége, Paris, London, Dublin, Edinburgh, Berlin, and Jena.

Nevertheless, scientific skepticism did not abate. Was the skull simian or human? Was it normal or pathological? To what geological age did it belong? Could a thigh bone so unmistakably human be associated with a skull and teeth so clearly apelike?

Dubois, though he resented the questioning, defended his original theory. He made available pictures and measurements. He discussed the background of his discovery and his own theories about it. "I think," he said, addressing the Royal Dublin Society in 1896, "that *Pithecanthropus erectus* and the associated animals perished in a volcanic catastrophe." And Dubois sketched the rest of that ancient picture as he had put it together in his own mind and on the basis of his close observations. A volcanic eruption had probably killed Pithecanthropus and much of the life around him. The bodies, floating down the ancient river, had come to rest upon the Trinil beach. As decomposition set it, crocodiles seized upon the bones and dragged some of them a short distance away to gnaw on them. The marks of their teeth could be seen on some of the bones.

This could easily explain why the bones did not lie together, though they were not far apart. The jaw, skull, teeth, and thigh bones all were found within forty-six feet. In Dubois's opinion they undoubtedly were the bones of one being. He pointed out that while they were buried in one small area, "in 100 miles around nothing like them could be found."

Much of the controversy centered on the human or almost human thigh bone. It was 455 millimeters long, straight and slender, and quite unlike the same massive bones in the large apes. Dubois estimated on the basis of its size that Pithecanthropus must have stood about five feet eight, and weighed about 154 pounds.

Very significantly there was a marked development of the ridge to which the muscles of the thigh attach. This could only indicate an erect posture.

At Dublin, Dubois defensively explained his own conviction about this remarkably human bone: "No one can doubt that the femur belonged to a form with a very erect posture. Maybe the bending forward of the femur is not so strong as on the average in man. Had I found the femur alone I think I should have been misled to declare it to be the femur of a Man, by far the oldest man, but probably the first Tertiary Man. But the bone differs too from that of Man, and with the ape-like skull and teeth indicates a form transitional between Man and apes."

The teeth showed a strange mixture of human and ape characteristics. The molar roots were widely separated as in apes and in some primitive men, but the crowns, like those of a human, were wider from side to side than from front to back. The fragment of the lower jaw included the socket for the canine tooth. From the size and shape of this gap it was apparent that the canine tooth was not tusklike as in the apes, but of more human proportions. In addition, the chin region was not simian. Pithecanthropus had the beginnings of a chin.

His skull, however, was low and apelike, his forehead receding, and the brow ridges extended straight across as in the apes. From a study of the way the neck muscles would have had to attach to the skull, it seemed likely that the head was set on the neck in a very simian manner.

While scientists were puzzled and incredulous about this unheard-of combination of features, churchmen were outraged. Dr. John Lightfoot, chancellor of Cambridge, trumpeted that Adam and not the crude half-ape, half-human creature found in the Java back country was the first ancestor of man. To heighten the contrast, Dr. Lightfoot fixed the time of Adam's birth at 4004 B.C. The claim that the outlandish Java creature could have had anything to do with man was called rank heresy.

Hurt and discouraged by the double attack, Dubois, who had by then become a professor of geology at Amsterdam University, abruptly decided to withdraw the bones of Pithecanthropus from public inspection. He locked them in strongboxes in the Teyler Museum of Haarlem, his home town, and there they remained "incommunicado" for thirty years.

Pithecanthropus was a landmark, a turning-point, indispensable in the study of the origin of man. As the years went by, advances in anthropology made a new and closer study of the Java fossils even more necessary. Dubois nevertheless rejected all appeals to see the bones.

The second burial of Pithecanthropus became particularly critical in 1920. In that year a report was published of the finding of the first fossil skull in Australia. It was the spark that set off a wholly unexpected explosion. Suddenly and dramatically Dubois broke his long scientific silence. He announced for the first time that during his years in Java he had discovered not only Pithecanthropus but two other skulls. For thirty years he had said nothing about them! The anthropological world was staggered and shocked. Long delays in describing and publishing were frequent, but Dubois's secretiveness passed all bounds.

In 1889 a prospector looking for marble had found a skull near Wadjak, buried in one of the terrace-like deposits of a dried-up fresh-water lake. Dubois, who was then in Sumatra, heard about the find, rushed to Java, and purchased the skull. In the following year, 1890, he dug out a second one at the same site.

He carefully packed them away, for after he found Pithecanthropus he wanted nothing to detract from the fame of that discovery. The Wadjak skulls both had large brains. Dubois estimated their capacity at 1,550 cubic centimeters, or slightly more than the average brain size of modern Europeans.

Badly jarred, scientists felt that access to the hidden bones of Pithecanthropus and the new finds had to be obtained. Henry Fairfield Osborn, head of the American Museum of Natural History, called upon the president of the Dutch Academy of Sciences. Osborn compared Dubois's discovery of Pithecanthropus and the Wadjak skulls to the finding of a new planet by means of a secret telescope. To deny other scientists the right to look through the telescope and to insist that they accept the opinions of the discoverer alone put everyone in an untenable position, Osborn argued. He urged the president of the academy to appeal to Dubois to reopen his great finds to science.

It is not certain that Osborn's plea moved the stubborn Dutch physician to open his strongboxes, but shortly afterward, in 1923, Dr. Ales Hrdlicka, of the Smithsonian Institution, was invited to the Netherlands to see the original bones of Pithecanthropus and Wadjak. "It was the first time the precious specimens were shown to a scientific man after their long seclusion," Dr. Hrdlicka later reported. "We found Professor Dubois a big-bodied, big-hearted man who received us with cordial simplicity. He had all the specimens in his possession brought out from the strong boxes in which they are kept and demonstrated them to us personally and then permitted me to handle them to my satisfaction."

Having opened the door, Dubois continued gracious. Other scientists also were permitted to see the long-hidden bones, and later Dubois exhibited Pithecanthropus at an international meeting. He also released a cast he had made of the skull. It indicated a brain of about 900 cubic centimeters, well above the 300 to 650 cubic-centimeter range of the apes, and well below the 1,200 to 1,500 range of civilized man. In brain size Java man clearly was an in-between.

The shape of the brain and what could be seen of the markings of its convolutions on the brain case were even more revealing. Dr. Frederick Tilney, who made a close study of the cast and original material, expressed the opinion that Java man had so far advanced beyond his ape predecessors that he had developed the power of speech and had expanded his "visual and auditory sensibility." This plus his ability to walk upright and to use his hands freely—he did not have to depend on them for locomotion—placed him well along in the evolutionary advance. Just how far was to remain a matter of dispute for many years.

A tentative solution of the Pithecanthropus puzzle came in 1929. Or at least it was a solution that satisfied most of the experts. In that year another remarkable physician found another remarkable fossil skull, this time near Peking, China. I shall tell that story in another chapter, though the two finds and the work in China and Java thereafter intermingle so closely that separation is difficult.

The skull of Peking man—Sinanthropus—was more complete than the skull top from Java, which was broken off just above the ear. With more complete material, the scientists had no doubt that Sinanthropus was a true man—a primitive one certainly, but man. He had not only reached the human state anatomically; Peking man also knew the use of fire and implements. And his skull was amazingly like that of Pithecanthropus.

Franz Weidenreich, the noted authority on Peking man and other Asiatic finds, explained the effect of the Peking discovery on the status of Pithecanthropus: "In its general form and size [the Peking] skull agrees with the Java skull to such an extent that it identifies Pithecanthropus too as a true man, and a creature far above the stage of an ape."

At the very moment when everyone was convinced, Dubois, with his aptitude for the unpredictable, suddenly changed his mind. He announced that he had decided that Pithecanthropus was not an intermediate form—a man-ape—but a giant gibbon that finally transmuted into man. With his usual tenacity he stuck to this position—which again made Pithecanthropus unique and unmatched—until his death, in 1940.

Further confirmation of the Weidenreich verdict was to come later. Dubois, the brilliant, unaccountable, stubborn, pioneering, and secretive Dutch physician, had not found the missing link; he had not found man's ape ancestors; he had discovered the earliest man. So too did Columbus miss India and happen upon a new world.

The work that finally was to allay all doubts about the standing of Pithecanthropus began in 1930. In that year the Geological Survey of the Netherlands East Indies invited a young German paleontologist, G. H. R. von Koenigswald, to Java to search for more fossil remains of man.

Von Koenigswald had been born in Berlin, on November 13, 1902. As a schoolboy he had collected stones and fossils and had become fascinated by the evolution of the horse. By the time he was fourteen he was searching for fossil mammals. Von Koenigswald inevitably went into the study of paleontology, at Berlin, Tübingen, Cologne, and Munich. Three years after he finished his studies, in 1927, he eagerly accepted the offer of the post in Java.

Soon after his arrival, the survey began to excavate a high

level terrace of the same Solo River on whose banks Dubois had found Pithecanthropus. Among the twenty-five thousand bones taken from this treasure deposit were fragments of eleven human skulls and two shin bones. All the skulls had been broken in a peculiar way and it seemed probable that they had been used as "skull bowls." But they were not so old as Pithecanthropus.

One hot day the native workers on the terrace sent word that they had found what might be an older human skull. They left it untouched and called for assistance. Von Koenigswald and a colleague jumped on the first train—their headquarters were at Bandung—and went to Ngwai. From there they had to proceed on foot. Accompanied by a whole caravan of coolies, who carried their luggage on bamboo poles and on their bare shoulders, they pushed on through six miles of dense teakwood forests.

At the site, a thin gravel bed about sixty feet above the Solo River, was the skull. To protect it, the workers had covered it with a layer of earth. Von Koenigswald cautiously brushed the earth away and there, upside down, lay the upper part of a human skull, still partly covered with a cemented crust of sand. The young scientist was so excited that he overexposed all his pictures! It was the finest of the Solo skulls, but not the Pithecanthropus of which he dreamed.

West of Trinil and drained by the same Solo River was a region called Sangiran. There a vast dome had collapsed, exposing the Trinil formations around its whole inner slope. Every rainy season hundreds of bones, teeth, and jaws washed to the surface. Von Koenigswald felt it was the most promising site in Java and the one where he should find a second Pithecanthropus.

But these were the depression years. The budget of the geological survey had been so drastically slashed that von Koenigswald's job was abolished. Only by means of some grants was it possible for him to continue his work. Even so, he had just been married and was having a hard time. There was no money for collecting; but, with some friends, von Koenigswald nevertheless set out to explore Sangiran.

In the first years no Pithecanthropus materials came to light except one broken and doubtful tooth. Without the proper help the search was discouraging and difficult.

The first real help came when von Koenigswald was invited to a symposium on early man in Philadelphia in 1937, and given a Carnegie grant as a research assistant. The hunt for Pithecanthropus then could be reorganized. Hundreds of natives were enlisted. To encourage them to look for fossils, von Koenigswald not only bought every fossil they brought in, but even arranged festivals with *gamelans* and *rongengs*—native orchestras and dancing girls.

Not long afterward one of the men brought in a fragment that was unmistakably part of an ancient human skull. Von Koenigswald again hurried out to the site and on the dry banks of the river found a number of pieces that had been washed out of the sandstones and conglomerates in which the Trinil fauna were embedded.

Trailed by a bunch of excited natives, von Koenigswald crept up the hillside, collecting every fragment of bone he could find. He promised the men ten cents for every bit belonging to that human skull. "The result was terrible," lamented the paleontologist. "I had underestimated the business ability of my brown collectors. Behind my back they broke the larger fragments into pieces to increase the number of sales."

When the inch-by-inch search ended, von Koenigswald had forty fragments, thirty of which proved later to belong to the skull. They were very thick and could easily be fitted together. When they were, they formed a fine, nearly complete Pithecanthropus skullcap.

"It would be difficult to find without careful selection two modern skulls that resemble each other as much in detail as did the Trinil find and this new skull—except that the latter is more complete," said von Koenigswald. "Perhaps it should not be surprising that two individuals who had lived in the same age and the same place should be very much alike, and yet from our tremendous distance in time it was a little eerie to come upon two skulls which, as Weidenreich said, 'resemble each other as much as do two eggs.' "

With two Pithecanthropus skulls by which to judge, and with the important additional parts preserved in the new skull, most scientific doubts were removed. Pithecanthropus was given the rank of a true man, and no later developments have as yet changed that important standing.

Some of the few doubts not removed were those of Dubois. Von Koenigswald immediately informed his predecessor of the new find and sent him a photograph. The doctor promptly published the photograph, which had been intended only for his personal information, and implied that the new skull was "more or less of a fake."

Von Koenigswald continued to explore the rich Trinil formations; but he wanted a chance to compare his finds with those being made in China. In 1939, just as he was about to leave for Peking, one of his collectors brought him a fossil so baffling that he was doubly glad he had arranged the trip.

"Did you bring a surprise?" Weidenreich playfully inquired when he met von Koenigswald at the Peking station.

Von Koenigswald had: the fossil was a lower jaw so peculiar that he could not guess whether it had come from man or ape.

It was still in the matrix. When the stone was cleared away, the two scientists were certain that it was the jaw of a human, though one of unusual proportions and appearance. The well-preserved teeth were unusually large, though human in their pattern. On the other hand, there was a wide gap between the front teeth and the canines—exactly the kind of gap characteristic of the anthropoids and of all lower apes and monkeys. In addition the jaw projected in a way never seen in living man. "An upper jaw with human teeth and a simian gap was certainly a novelty," commented Weidenreich.

The jaw had been broken off, but the two scientists saw immediately that the break was fresh. That meant there should be a chance of finding more of it. Instructions were rushed off to the Malayan collector, and for four weeks the two waited with increasing anxiety.

At the end of that time a big rugged block of stone arrived. They sawed, chipped, and chiseled, and soon before them lay many pieces of a skull. It had been badly crushed long before it was fossilized, but the anthropologists put it together with little difficulty. They had the greater part of a brain case.

They had never seen one like it before. It had come from the same geological period as Pithecanthropus, and the well preserved rear portion closely resembled the two Pithecanthropus skulls. And yet the bone was thicker and more massive than any previously encountered in man.

At first the two surprised scientists decided that the two previous Pithecanthropus skulls must have been those of females, and the heavier new one that of a male. That seemed the only likely explanation they could hit upon.

The following year Weidenreich returned to the United States. Working at the American Museum of Natural History, he made a reconstruction that aroused his doubts about the male-female explanation of the size and thickness of the new skull.

In the meanwhile von Koenigswald was continuing the work in Java. In 1941 one of his collectors sent him part of an enormous human jaw. Although it was larger than that of a gorilla, it showed unmistakably human characteristics. Von Koenigswald could scarcely believe it. For days he carried a piece in his pocket to get used to the idea forming in his mind —the idea that it was the jaw of a giant.

He made a cast of the huge jaw and teeth—the critical ones still were in place—and sent it off to Weidenreich in New York. He named the man to whom it had belonged *Meganthropus paleojavanicus* (*megas* meaning "great," *anthropus,* "man," and *paleojavanicus,* "of old Java"), giant man of old Java. This was late in 1941.

On December 7 war suddenly came to the Pacific. Java was cut off from the free world as effectively as though time had turned back to the age of Pithecanthropus.

A few weeks after Pearl Harbor the cast of the new jaw arrived safely in New York. From the labels Weidenreich could see that von Koenigswald was establishing a new genus, the giant man of old Java. What more von Koenigswald would have said could not be learned, for communications were completely closed. It was impossible even to learn if the young scientist was still alive.

Under the circumstances, Weidenreich felt the scientific world should be informed about the gigantic new forms von Koenigswald had found. He applied to representatives of the Netherlands Indies for permission to publish the material in behalf of von Koenigswald.

While the war swept with awful momentum across the once quiet Pacific, the important but small news was told of the new giant ancestor of man. The jaw fragment far exceeded in height and thickness that of any known fossil or modern jaw, and likewise any known fossil or recent anthropoid jaw. Its pattern, however, was typically human. The teeth also testified to the human character of the gigantic jaw. Although they were enormous and proportionate to the jaw, they had the form of a man's teeth and not those of an ape.

Restudying the "surprise" jaw von Koenigswald had brought to Peking in 1939, Weidenreich then was convinced that it was not a large male Pithecanthropus as he and von Koenigswald had first surmised, but another early man, on the way from giantism. He renamed it *Pithecanthropus robustus.*

As Weidenreich pondered this unexpected appearance of giants among man's ancestors, he suddenly remembered the casts of three giant isolated teeth that von Koenigswald had given him a few years before.

Von Koenigswald had discovered the teeth, not in some deep prehistoric strata, but on the shelves of Chinese drugstores. The Chinese for centuries had prized pulverized fossil teeth, which they called dragon teeth, as a special and powerful medicine. Sufficient supplies always seemed to make their way into the shops. Knowing this, von Koenigswald always kept an eye on the Chinese drugstores in Java and made the rounds of the shops whenever he was in China. He even took a look into the Chinese drugstores in New York when he visited there.

In 1935, among the teeth of the rhinoceros, the three-toed horse, and numerous other mammals of the Tertiary period, he saw a molar of enormous proportions. Since it showed no relation to any known type of mammalian tooth, he thought that it might be that of a new giant ape. Two years later he found another huge upper molar in the drugstores, and later still a lower molar. All seemed to be of the same type, but before von Koenigswald could make a close study of them the war closed in.

Could the giant Chinese teeth have any connection with the giant Java jaw? Weidenreich mulled over this fascinating question. He decided on a thorough comparative study, a study that fully confirmed his hunch. The Chinese teeth too must have come from early giant men. In their crowns, in the size and arrangement of the cusps, they were the teeth of men, not apes.

"In other words," wrote Weidenreich, "the giant from the Hongkong chemist shop and the giant from central Java are in the same evolutionary line; the more primitive the forms are, the more gigantic are their dimensions."

Weidenreich could not resist playing with the idea of how large these early giants might have been. By comparing the teeth and bones with those of living animals and from careful anatomical measurements he decided that the Java giant was much larger than any living gorilla, and the Chinese giant was one and a half times larger still. That would have made him twice as large as a male gorilla! The Biblical words came inevitably to mind: "There were giants in the earth in those days" (Genesis vi, 4).

This scientific introduction of giants into the line of man's ancestry called for many explanations.

Weidenreich placed the giants first as the earliest and most primitive. The skull of the big Pithecanthropus, the one he renamed *Pithecanthropus robustus*, appeared a direct descendant of the giants. And Pithecanthropus a descendant of his. The giants and the near giants thus were connected with the normal-sized types in a descending line.

"I believe that all these forms have to be ranged in the human line and that the human line leads to giants, the farther back it is traced," said Weidenreich. "In other words the giants may be directly ancestral to man."

But did the line run back only to giants, or were there smaller men upon the earth in those days too? With only the meager data then available, Weidenreich hesitated to answer the questions. He did point out that the finding of both the giants and normal-sized Pithecanthropus in the same geological formation did not necessarily prove that both had lived at the same time.

Time and again for ages immemorial Java's volcanoes had poured out great streams of mud and lava that swept across the countryside, scooping up huge masses of soil and carrying it to new places. All of the first giant bones and those found later came from such areas and all were crushed and broken, as though they had been pressed and twisted and moved by great natural forces. But the first question had to be left to the future.

From the standpoint of structure, Weidenreich, one of the

world's authorities on human anatomy, did not find it difficult to understand how man could have arrived at his present form if he had descended from giants. The changes that occurred, he argued, were exactly those which would have been expected had there been a reduction in size. The case was most manifest in the human skull, but the same phenomena could be seen in

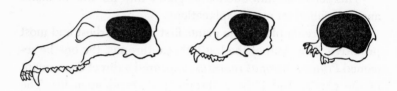

WHEN THE SKULL GROWS SMALLER, THE CRANIAL CAVITY TAKES UP A LARGER PROPORTION OF THE AVAILABLE SPACE AND THE FACE BECOMES SMALLER. THIS PHENOMENON CAN BE SEEN CLEARLY IN DOGS AS WELL AS IN MEN. THE "GIANT" RACES OF DOGDOM HAVE HUGE SNOUTS. THE INTERMEDIATE RACES, SUCH AS THE BULLDOG, HAVE ABOUT AN EVEN BALANCE IN BRAIN CAVITY AND FACE. IN THE DWARF RACES THE CRANIAL CAVITY OCCUPIES MOST OF THE SKULL AND THE FACE BECOMES ALMOST AN UNIMPORTANT ANNEX.

other mammals. Weidenreich considered the domestic dog a perfect example.

The great Dane, the St. Bernard, the Irish wolfhound, the "giant" races of dogdom, have elongated snouts that take up the whole front part of the skull. The cranial cavity occupies only the back part. In the dwarf races, like the Pekinese and the King Charles spaniel, the craniel cavity occupies almost the entire skull, and the face becomes only "an unimportant annex of the brain case proper." The in-between races, like the bull-dog, are intermediate in the proportion of face to brain case.

And thus it happened in man, Weidenreich suggested. As man grew physically smaller and more space had to be found for his brain, the face changed from a huge projecting one, with protuberant jaws and eyebrow ridges, to something of its present appearance. "The way in which this was done and the effect it had on the form, size, and mutual arrangement of the brain case and face are identical in man and dog," said Weidenreich.

The anatomist ruled out the possibility that the giants of old could be explained, as are the giants of today, by abnormal growth. Most of the giantism of the present is attributed to a disturbance in the pituitary gland. And not only does a young giant, generally born of normal-sized parents, grow to great height and size, but his jaws, hands, and feet enlarge even further. This is known as acromegalic giantism. Weidenreich held that the enlargement of the jaw of such a giant is very different from the kind of enlargement seen in the Java giant. Furthermore, the big chin of the acromegalic giant is completely absent in Meganthropus.

In addition, Weidenreich pointed out, the teeth of modern giants do not grow large along with the rest of the body; they are almost normal in size. The teeth of the Java giant, on the other hand, were in proportion to the jaw and skull—they were giant teeth too.

Weidenreich told this astounding story in a popular book, *Apes, Giants, and Man.*[3]

All the while, the most acute anxiety was felt for the man whose discoveries had opened this new vista. Word finally seeped through the Pacific blockade that von Koenigswald, his wife and daughter were alive, though in a Japanese concentration camp. Then reports came of the bombing of the city in which they were being held prisoner. All the news seemed black.

At the first moment of peace, Weidenreich and others made every effort to reach the von Koenigswalds. And then at last there was relief. All three were safe!

[3] Published by the University of Chicago Press, 1946.

When the Japanese seized Java, following the fall of Singapore, von Koenigswald, as a member of the Dutch military service, was immediately made a prisoner of war. For the first month of the occupation he was ordered to continue work in his own office. That offered a rare though dangerous opportunity. With great difficulty, von Koenigswald and his assistants concealed as much as possible of their most valuable materials. They put some important jaws among a lot of unimportant materials and substituted casts for some of the originals in their safe. Although the Japanese became suspicious, they never discovered the truth.

A friend hid the unmatchable tooth collection, including the giant teeth, in milk bottles.

The Japanese were deeply interested in the collections, but because they felt sure they would win the war and keep Java, they took fairly good care of the bones and the museum. Only one of the Solo skulls was removed. It was sent as a birthday present to the Emperor of Japan.

Von Koenigswald emerged from his prison camp—"I came back to life again"—to learn for the first time that his wife and daughter were also alive. "My happiness was complete," he said, "when I learned that all my precious specimens had been saved. Large parts of my collections, many of my books, and all of my clothes had been stolen, but Early Man survived the disaster."

With the aid of a Rockefeller Foundation grant, von Koenigswald came to the United States to work out some of his finds in collaboration with Weidenreich at the American Museum. He brought with him the invaluable original skull of *Pithecanthropus robustus*, the gigantic jaw of Meganthropus, the original giant teeth, the Solo skulls, and other materials. There was also his superb collection of isolated mammalian teeth. And before long even the Emperor's birthday-present skull was returned.

The whole collection was shown to the public in a special

exhibit at the museum in January 1948. Shortly afterward von Koenigswald went to the Netherlands to become professor of paleontology and historical geology at the State University of Utrecht. He took his superlative collection with him.

Before his departure a series of brilliant scientific studies of the amazing Java material was issued, though many of the finds have not yet been published. Man, as a result, could see farther, though still dimly, back into a past that is lost in the passage of thousands of years but is nevertheless vividly preserved in our body and brain.

Dubois had proved that it is possible to look deliberately—and successfully—for man's buried past. Von Koenigswald and Weidenreich had shown what those ancient remnants could mean. There were strong indications that the early men of Java had moved down into that land before its connection with Asia was broken, before Java became an island. Some of the innumerable animal bones that lay buried with Pithecanthropus and his fellow early men were strikingly similar to some of the fossil mammals of India.

Perhaps the tropical animals of India had followed the warmth to the lands of the south, through Burma, through the delta lowlands of Malaya, and into what is now the island of Java. Perhaps, under new conditions and in the semi-isolation of that island, they developed in new ways into the giants and primitive men unearthed by Dubois and von Koenigswald.

Perhaps another stream of these prehistoric migrants had turned north into China. The search for the origin of man turned to that vast land.

XIV

BLACK AND WEIDENREICH
CHINA: THE DISCOVERY
AND DISAPPEARANCE OF PEKING MAN

Not far from Peking is Chicken-bone Hill, and not far from Chicken-bone Hill lies low-rounded Dragon-bone Hill. The names of the hills held a clue to what might be hidden beneath their unrevealing surfaces, for traditionally the Chinese have called fossils chicken bones and dragon bones. And the proximity of the hills was important. It led scientists to one of the major discoveries that have thrown new light on the history of man.

Dr. J. G. Andersson, a Swedish geologist who went to Peking in 1914 as a mining adviser to the Chinese government, was one of the first to become interested in the fossil wealth of China. Up to that time, the Chinese had valued the ancient bones only for medicinal purposes.[1]

When Andersson and the Chinese Geological Survey began a systematic study of Chinese paleontology, they at first encountered little sympathy. The Chinese wanted no disturbance of the *feng-shui,* the spirits of the earth, wind, and water who

---

[1] Dr. Robert Broom, whose fossil finds in South Africa were to form another landmark, made this comment on the use of "dragon bones" for medicine: "The Chinese, as is well known, use fossil teeth as one of their principal medicines. Some western highbrows are inclined to sneer at the Chinaman's drugs, and say 'What virtue can there be in ground-up fossil teeth?' The Chinaman might reply that it never does any harm; which is more than can be said of some of the drugs in the British Pharmacopœia." Some Chinese families have for centuries been in the business of "mining" fossils to supply the drug trade.

guarded all graves, regardless of their age. Explorations had to be carried on with the greatest delicacy.

Roy Chapman Andrews, in his *Meet Your Ancestors*,[2] tells the story of Andersson's difficulties in trying to dig into one fossil deposit. The work had no sooner started than a large and very furious old lady thoroughly blocked all operations by seating herself squarely in the hole and refusing to move. Andersson tried persuasion. When it failed flatly, he turned to the subtler art of ridicule by borrowing an umbrella and gallantly holding it over her head to protect her from the sun. She only screamed the louder. The geologist then brought out his camera, explaining to the large audience that the lady undoubtedly would like to have her picture taken while sitting in the hole.

Her antipathy to the camera was even greater than her opposition to the disturbance of the past, and the old lady leaped from the diggings with a shriek of rage. Andersson technically had won the battle, but the ousted old lady continued to create such a ruckus that the geologist's native assistants advised him to retire from the scene.

Andersson then turned his attention to Chicken-bone Hill, long known, as its name picturesquely indicated, to be a source of fossil bones. One day when he and two other members of the geological survey were visiting the excavation there, a man brought them a few fossils from another place and said that he could show them more.

He led them to another hill, near the village of Choukoutien. The Chinese had always called it Dragon-bone Hill. The name, the setting, and the strata at once struck Andersson as promising.

On a later visit, Andersson picked up several bits of quartz that obviously did not belong to the strata there and could only have been brought in by man. To the geologist they indicated that there might be early stone implements about.

[2] Published by the Viking Press, New York, 1945.

Tapping the rock face, Andersson made an inspired guess: "In this spot lies primitive man. All we have to do is find him."

Dr. Otto Zdansky, a native of Sweden who had been with Andersson on the first visit to the hill, did some preliminary exploring. As he examined the stratified deposits, he was startled to come upon two primitive teeth that appeared surprisingly human. He labeled them "Homo sp?" and announced their discovery at a meeting held in Peking on October 22, 1926 in honor of a visit of the Crown Prince of Sweden.

The stir created by his report was strictly confined to scientific circles. Two teeth, even though they might hint of the presence of prehistoric man in China, were not enough to arouse the newspapers, alert though they were for "missing link" stories. But the scientists, and in particular one Peking physician who had come to China to search for man's beginnings, were profoundly interested and excited. The two worn, primitive molars were the first positive indication that early man might have existed in Asia north of the Himalayas. They were the first trace of him in that whole tremendous area.

The physician, Dr. Davidson Black, professor of anatomy at Peking Union Medical College, was another of those men fascinated by the history of the race and dedicated to filling in the gaps in the record. Dr. Black was a Canadian, born in Toronto on July 25, 1884. As a young medical student at the University of Toronto he became absorbed in the problems of human anatomy, and particularly in the field of neuroanatomy. This work, however, so much aroused his interest in biology that three years after he had received his degree in medicine, he took the unusual step of returning to the university to take an A.B. in biology.

In 1914 he went to Europe to study with G. Elliot Smith, the noted English anthropologist, and with German authorities. At the time Black arrived in Manchester, Smith was working on the restoration of the Piltdown skull, one of the most important remains of early man ever found, and the subject of an international controversy, of which I shall give an account in a later chapter.

Black plunged into the problems involved, and from that time on, the origin and early evolution of man occupied first place in his mind. The quest combined all those things he loved —adventure, discovery, geology, anatomy. As a friend said later, here was an opportunity for the full investment of Black's unique capital in life, and he knew it immediately and instinctively.

Black felt that man must have originated in Asia. When he was offered a post as professor of neurology and embryology at Peking, he eagerly accepted it as an opportunity to take up the search. One of his first acts was to acquire as complete a set as possible of the casts of all the significant fossil discoveries in the line of human descent—Pithecanthropus and all the others.

At first there were few who shared his enthusiasm for launching an Asiatic search for man's earliest ancestors. Finally he obtained a small sum of money and went to Jehol to search for fossils in the caves and river terraces of the Lwan River. But he found nothing.

Next Black went to Siam, for he thought that early man might have moved up into China from the south. Again he found nothing significant.

Andersson went straight to Black with the two bewildering teeth from Dragon-bone Hill. Black was sure that they had come from a human of exceptional antiquity, and he redoubled the efforts he had previously begun to instigate a scientific exploration of Dragon-bone Hill. He made so convincing a case that the Rockefeller Foundation provided the funds for a thorough investigation of the Choukoutien deposits, and for the first time a search for the origin of man was organized as a full-fledged scientific expedition.

At the outset a full understanding was reached with the Chinese Geological Survey. It was agreed that China, which of course claimed the site, should own all the specimens collected, while the expedition would study and describe them. Dr. Birgir Bohlin was brought from Sweden to supervise the field work under the general direction of Dr. Black.

Dragon-bone Hill, into which the workers drove their spades in April 1927, lies thirty-seven miles southwest of Peking. It is a low, rounding hill that stands just above some flat rocky terraces. It is quite unobtrusive in the wide-swinging arc of the beautiful Western Hills, hills in which are hidden both the Eight Great Temples and modern coal mines and quarries.

Quarrying operations had sliced away part of the valley face of Dragon-bone Hill. The white surfaces of the exposed limestone only seemed to accent the general red cast of the bald hill and of the countryside, for this was one of the red-earth districts of China.

Only a short distance below the hill nestled the small, scattered village of Choukoutien. Beyond the village stretched the great expanse of the Hopei plain, and across the plain ran both a railroad and the old sunken road along which camels still plodded on their slow way to Peking.

At some remote period in the past, water had honeycombed Dragon-bone Hill with caves, fissures, and passages. Animals and, if the strange primitive teeth were an indication, man, too, had taken shelter and lived in these protected recesses. But nature is ever changing. The caves filled up again—with debris, with the deposits of running water, and principally with the stone and earth that came sliding in when the roofs collapsed, as many of them did.

In time the fill hardened. Sometimes it became so hard and dense that it remained as a separate "dike" when the surrounding limestone weathered or was quarried away. Thus the "cave" at which work started appeared in 1927 only as a deep, high cleft in the hill—originally it had been about 150 feet wide, 150 feet high, and about 525 feet deep.

Work in the hard compacted stone was difficult; it had to be drilled and blasted. Tons upon tons of material had to be moved, and all of it sifted for possible loose teeth and small bones.

The unyieldingness of the stone, though, was as nothing compared to the other obstacles and dangers faced by the Choukoutien excavators. In that summer of 1927 antiforeign feeling flared up all over China. In the south the Russian agent, Borodin, and his corps of propagandists were in virtual command. Chinese soldiers had seized the British concession in Hankow. Nanking had been looted and many foreigners killed. Reports came in daily of additional kidnappings and murders.

The nationalist armies of Chiang Kai-shek, then moving on Shanghai, still were distant, and it was believed that a whole-sale massacre in the city was averted only by the arrival of British warships and troops. "Altogether it was a most un-healthy atmosphere in which to carry on scientific pursuits," said Andrews, who was in China at the time.

At Choukoutien, Bohlin was visited regularly by bands of Chinese soldiers. Although he and his workers were only thirty-seven miles from Peking, they were isolated for weeks at a time by the unsettled state of the country between the city and the hill. The danger was great, but no one was willing to call off the excavations. Great blocks of stone and smaller pieces that held promise of fossils were packed in more than five hundred boxes and sent off to Peking whenever conditions permitted. Even before detailed studies could be made, it was evident that a vast store of animal fossils had been collected.

The first season's work was scheduled to end on October 19, and no trace of early man had been found. A feeling of dis-appointment had set in when, on October 16, Bohlin discovered a human tooth embedded in the face of an exposure. It was close to the spot where the first two teeth had been collected.

Elated, Bohlin hurried to Peking to take it to Black. On the way, he was stopped a dozen times by soldiers, who little guessed that he carried a scientific treasure in his pocket. It was early in the evening when he reached Black. For the physician that was only the beginning of his best working hours. Long before, Black had discovered that he worked best and thought most clearly at night, and after his day at the college he customarily spent most of the night at his anthropology. He snatched what sleep he could in between.

On this night the two pored over the tooth until long after dawn. It was the first molar of an individual about eight years old, and definitely human. The physician compared it exhaustively with the teeth of modern Chinese children, with chimpanzee teeth and the teeth of Piltdown and Neanderthal man, all of which he had in his large collection.

The tooth differed so extremely in its essential characteristics that Black decided that it must have belonged to a race as distinctive as Pithecanthropus. On the evidence of the one molar he created a new genus of humanity, which he called *Sinanthropus pekinensis* (China man of Peking). Later this race was more commonly called Peking man.

Soon after the publication of his paper announcing the finding of Peking man, Black went to the United States and Europe on a vacation trip. With the permission of the geological survey he took the all-important tooth with him. To make certain that he would not lose it by some mischance, he carried it in an ingenious little receptacle chained to his waistcoat pocket.

The little brown tooth interested and impressed the authorities on evolution, but they were cautious. It was a small tooth upon which to base so large a classification.

Upon Dr. Black's return to China, work was resumed at Choukoutien. It looked then as though there were ten major strata in the cave. During the season of 1928 the workers reached some of the heavily fossiliferous middle beds.

From them came the right half of an adult jaw with three teeth in place, a portion of a child's jaw, some skull bones, and more than twenty teeth. Huge numbers of fossilized animal bones were among the material collected in 575 boxes during that season. There no longer was any question that this was one of the world's most important treasure-troves of early man. All of the finds of 1928 also confirmed Black's earlier conclusion that a distinct form of man had lived in the Peking foothills.

A further wealth of material came from Choukoutien during the season of 1929. Because heavy summer rains had hampered the work, the staff was anxious to press on as late as possible in the fall, though by November the weather had become bitterly cold.

Just before the work was scheduled to close, Dr. W. C. Pei (Pei Wen-chung), who was in charge of the excavations while Bohlin was away on an expedition to Turkestan, opened up two caves at the extreme end of the fissure. His assistants tied a rope around his waist and let him down into the first one. It looked interesting, but without waiting to explore further, Pei went on to the second, for it was then late in the afternoon.

On the floor was a large accumulation of debris. Pei stirred around in it. Suddenly, as he brushed away some loose material, there lay an unbelievable sight, a complete skull. It was partly covered by loose sand and partly embedded in a hard travertine (a porous stone formed by the deposits of water). A Sinanthropus skull! Pei telegraphed the momentous news to Black.

The next day, December 2, the skull and a large block of the matrix that had held it uncrushed and undisturbed throughout the centuries were cut out. A second, smaller block containing a small portion that had broken off was likewise cut away. Pei also packed a complete rhinoceros skull that lay near by.

Tenderly Pei and his assistants carried these remains of Sinanthropus to their camp. They wrapped them in layer after layer of Chinese cotton paper and, to protect them from jolting on the way to Peking, bound them in thick wrappings of cloth soaked in flour paste.

The weather was so cold the homemade plaster did not dry readily, and Pei would not risk the trip to Peking as long as there was any softness in the bulky priceless package. Three braziers were set up to dry it out. Finally on December 6 the skull was taken to Peking.

Black was a supremely happy man; all his hopes and dreams had been realized, for this beyond any doubt was the Sinanthropus he had pictured in his mind from the first meager evidence of the tooth. The jubilant physician could not keep the wonderful news to himself.

At a dinner the next night Roy Chapman Andrews noticed Black signaling him. A moment later he heard him say: "Roy, we've got a skull. Pei found it December 2."

There was no need to explain what kind of a skull. Andrews knew that it could only be that of Peking man. The two men and several other friends drove out to Black's laboratory the moment they could get away.

"There it was, the skull of an individual who had lived half a million years ago," Andrews recalled. "One of the most important discoveries in the whole history of human evolution. He couldn't have been very impressive when he was alive but, dead and fossilized, he was awe-inspiring."

While the two men stood there studying the skull and exclaiming over its almost incredible perfection—only the face was missing—Père Teilhard de Chardin, himself a noted discoverer of early man, came in.

To celebrate the great occasion, Andrews gave a party, a truly international party that symbolized in its own way the universality of Peking man. Eight nationalities—Swedish, American, Chinese, Canadian, German, French, Russian, and English—ate pig knuckles and sauerkraut and drank beer well into the night as they welcomed Peking man into the modern world.

The formal announcement to the world was made at a special meeting of the Geological Society of China on December

28, 1929. This time there was no absence of interest. The news flashed around the world.

At this first preliminary notice of discovery, Dr. Black said only that, judging from the shape and the delicacy of its modeling, the skull probably was that of an early adult or of an

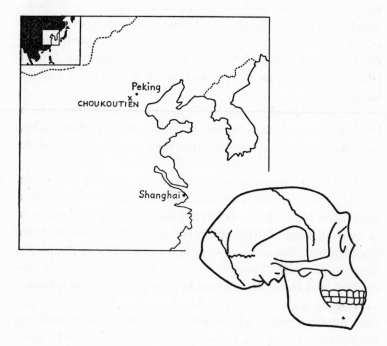

PEKING MAN. THE SITE AT WHICH HE WAS FOUND AND THE SINANTHROPUS AREA OUTLINED ON A MAP OF CHINA.

adolescent. He also expressed the opinion that it represented "a more generalized and progressive type" than Pithecanthropus.

The next step was to free the skull of Sinanthropus from the travertine that held it so tenaciously. The operation was a delicate one, taking time and skill. With a hacksaw the stone was cut away in slices one centimeter thick until the whole amazingly complete skull stood forth.

By this time it was evident that the work of preparing and studying the Peking discoveries and of continuing the field excavations was of such major and unequaled importance that it would have to be reorganized on a broader basis. With financing from the Rockefeller Foundation, the Cenozoic Research Laboratory was established as a special department of the Chinese Geological Survey. The survey also took formal title to Sinanthropus Hill in the hope of preserving it forever for science.

Sitting in his white coat in the laboratory office from which he directed operations, Black exclaimed to a visitor: "Why, man, just think of being paid for doing the job in the whole world you've always wanted to do!"

A growing stream of material came in, not only from the first big cave, but from five other diggings at the hill. Only a start could be made in classifying and studying the hundreds of cases of stone, fossils, and other materials shipped in from Choukoutien. But from some of that material came the pieces of another skull. They were small fragments, though uncrushed, and to the amazement of anthropologists accustomed to working with bits that stubbornly refused to fit together, they fitted as neatly as the pieces of a jigsaw puzzle. They formed the vault and a portion of the base of a second Sinanthropus skull.

A second special meeting of the Geological Society was called on July 30, 1930 to hear the announcement of the discovery of the second skull. The minutes of the meeting recorded: "As the discovery of Sinanthropus had aroused general public interest, the meeting was attended by an unusually large audience to hear Dr. Black's report and to see the second skull."

All night and every night Black worked at the laboratory, organizing, planning, keeping minutely detailed records of all the finds, making casts, drawings, and photographs. Only occasionally did he break off in the middle of the night for a short walk or stop at some restaurant for something to eat. During the days he tried to manage some modicum of sleep. This proved all the more difficult as anthropologists from all over the world began to converge on Peking to see the wonders of Dragon-bone Hill. Black was delighted and personally showed them around.

Black was a slender, thin-faced man whose energy and enthusiasm made his friends think of him as inexhaustible. As a high-school boy, when he carried supplies by canoe into some of the wilderness camps of the Hudson's Bay Company, the Indians had named him Mushkemush Kemit, "Little White Rat." His quiet, sudden movements made them think of the muskrat.[3]

One day while climbing around the hill at Choukoutien he suffered a heart attack. Later there was another. Black said nothing to his associates about the gravity of his condition. His last few weeks were spent putting his affairs in order and planning the next season's work at Choukoutien. Death came suddenly in 1934 in the laboratory that meant life to him.

The loss of the man who had envisioned and guided the big Choukoutien excavations was staggering, both personally and professionally, to all those who worked with him. Their sense of loss and grief and affection was poured out at a memorial meeting of the Geological Society and recorded in a memorial volume.

The Rockefeller Foundation considered long and carefully before it chose a successor. In 1935, with the approval of the Chinese Geological Survey, another anatomist and physician, Dr. Franz Weidenreich, was invited to carry on Black's work. His title became officially Visiting Professor of Anatomy at the

[3] On one expedition Black saved his life during a forest fire by standing in a lake with only his head above water for two nights and a day.

Peking Union Medical College and Honorary Director of the
Cenozoic Research Laboratory. At the time of his appointment
Weidenreich was serving as visiting professor of anatomy at
the University of Chicago.

The new head of the Sinanthropus research was born on
June 7, 1873 at Edenkoben, Germany. After studying medicine
and allied sciences at a number of German universities, he received his M.D. degree from the University of Strassburg in
1889. By 1904 he was professor of anatomy at Strassburg and
deeply interested in the blood-lymph system. That led to a
study of the tissues that are built up and fashioned by the units
carried in the blood stream—the muscular and connective tissues, the tendons, the ligaments, the cartilage, the bones and
teeth. From this it was only a natural progression to the jaws,
the skull, and the skeleton as a whole, and from that to the significance of these structures and hence to evolution. By 1914
Weidenreich had published fifty-five scientific papers.

Never a scientist of the laboratory only, he also took an
active part in politics. He served as a member of the municipal
council of Strassburg and was chosen president of the Democratic Party of Alsace-Lorraine, both sensitive posts during the
critical days of the First World War. When the French took
over Alsace-Lorraine at the end of the war, it followed inevitably that Weidenreich was dismissed from his post at the
university. Not until 1921 did he return to university circles as
professor of anatomy at the University of Heidelberg.

Just before the outbreak of the war in 1914 Weidenreich
had completed an important paper on the pelvis and hipbone of
the ape and the changes in them that made possible an upright
gait. The foot was another part of the anatomy with a revealing
evolutionary history. Weidenreich traced its development from
a grasping foot similar to that of a gorilla. A number of other
papers dealt with the evolution of the teeth and jaw. These detailed, exact, highly scientific studies underwrote with a huge
mass of material the contention of Darwin and Huxley that

ᴏᴠᴇ: Dragon-bone Hill. In the cleft, which was once a cave, the remains of Peking man were covered. The scoring guided the excavations. ʙᴇʟᴏᴡ: looking down into the excavation. At s level a wealth of Peking-man material came to light.

PLATE XVII

PLATE XVIII

LEFT: by 1937 the Dragon-bone Hill excavation was deep; many bones of Peking man and of the animals on which he fed had been found. RIGHT: the scoring on the excavation wall provided an accurate and permanent record of the location of each find. BELOW: excavators at their careful work. Every inch of this ancient, collapsed cave near Choukoutien was searched. Thousands of chipped stone tools, thousands of bones from extinct animals, and charcoal from the fires of Peking man were found.

PLATE XIX

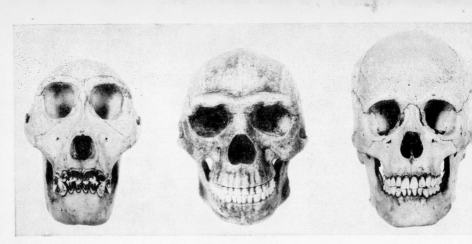

Mute testimony to evolution. From LEFT to RIGHT, gorilla, Peking man, modern man.

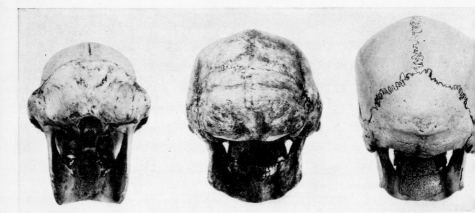

The same three from the rear.

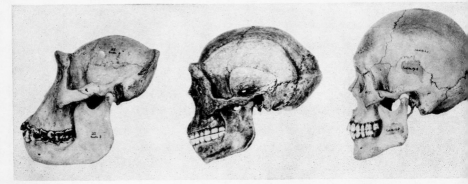

And a side view. As the size of the jaw decreases, the head becomes higher and the heavy brow ridges disappear.

PLATE XX

man is a descendant of an ancient anthropoid stock, but not of any recent genus of apes.

In 1928 Weidenreich was appointed professor of anthropology at the University of Frankfurt, a post that he held until 1935 and the rise of Hitler. As an expert on the origin and development of structure and race, he was an early victim of a regime obsessed by delusions of race.

So it was that at the age of sixty-two Weidenreich began a new career in China. The physician was a short, compactly built man, whose energy, like that of his predecessor, seemed boundless. As a young man his hobby was mountain-climbing and he had agilely clambered over many of the Alps. In China he scrambled over the excavations with the same quick ease. His bald head bobbing about the site was easy for workers to follow.

The political upheavals that had twice upset his whole world and were to do it again did not affect his disposition. The doctor was cheerful, even playful, and extremely devoted to his family and friends.

Soon after his arrival in China, Weidenreich started on a series of studies of Peking man, unsurpassed for thoroughness and scientific precision—*The Dentition of Sinanthropus, The Extremity Bones of Sinanthropus, The Skull of Sinanthropus.* The last is about the size of a telephone directory in a city of a million population. All these studies pointed directly to the conclusion already reached by Black: Sinanthropus was a true man, though a primitive one.

What placed him squarely in the human race, in Weidenreich's opinion, was, first of all, his ability to walk on two legs. "Apes, like man, have two hands and two feet, but man alone has acquired an upright position and the faculty to use his feet exclusively as locomotor instruments," said Weidenreich. "The apes stand and walk on all fours, or in other words, employ their hands for locomotion. Unless all the signs are deceiving, the claim may even be ventured that the change in locomotion and the corresponding alteration of the organization of the body are the essential specialization in the transformation of the prehuman form into the human form."

Thus Peking man and his close relative, Java man, walked into the human class.

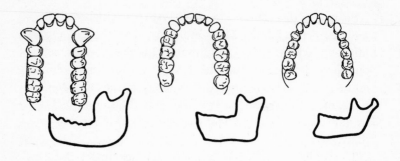

THE DENTAL ARCH AND JAW OF APE, PEKING MAN, AND MODERN MAN. THE TEETH OF THE APE ARE RANGED IN PARALLEL LINES AND THE JAW IS HEAVY. THE DENTAL ARCH OF PEKING MAN IS ROUNDED AND HIS JAW LIGHTER. MAN'S TEETH FOLLOW A WIDELY SPANNED ARCH AND HIS JAW IS LIGHTER STILL.

Weidenreich also emphasized that the teeth of Peking man were not the big projecting fangs of the ape. The crown of the first molar did not end in a sharp blade, nor did the first lower molar and the upper canine snap together like a pair of scissors. The teeth of Peking man were quite human in size, in shape, and in the way he chewed with them.

His dental arch, another revealing structure, was also on the human side. In the apes the teeth are arranged almost in two parallel lines; man's follow a widely spanned curve. Those of Sinanthropus slant, as though they were on the way to forming a curve.

A final test of Peking man's progress toward the standards

called human lay in the development of his skull. Gorilla—Sinanthropus—modern man—Weidenreich ranged their skulls in a haunting, striking row. Gorilla had virtually no forehead and a long, square jaw. The forehead of Sinanthropus began to round upward, and his jaw to recede. Man's forehead and skull had ballooned into roundness, and his jaw had pulled back even farther.

Turned to the rear, the three skulls told as dramatically of what had happened. The rear of Gorilla's skull was as short as a man's haircut. That of Sinanthropus came lower and rounded in toward the neck. Man's gave almost the impression of a ball.

In that higher, rounder head of Sinanthropus lodged a brain averaging about 1,000 cubic centimeters, one fourth smaller than the average brain of a man of today, but impressive when compared with the 450 cubic-centimeter average of the great apes.

With a brain so small could Peking man have had anything approaching human intelligence? The question was seriously debated. Two fine points were involved: does the size of the brain determine intelligence, and did Peking man show any traces of dawning human intelligence?

Characteristically Weidenreich marshaled fact rather than argument to establish his point that brain weight alone is no infallible sign of mental ability. If brain weight were the measure of intelligence, the elephant, with a brain weighing 5,000 grams, and one of the whales, with one of 10,000 grams, should lead all the rest. But another factor intervened. Despite his great brain, the whale has only one gram of brain substance for each 8,500 grams of body, while modern man has one gram of brain for each 44 grams of body.

Lest complacent human beings assume inherent superiority from the latter fact, Weidenreich pointed out that it is not definitive either. The capuchin monkey runs well ahead of man with one gram of brain for each 17.5 grams of body weight. "Neither the absolute nor the relative size of the brain can be used to measure the degree of mental ability in animal or human," cautioned Weidenreich.

The anatomist added that the mental ability of Peking man —and he implied of all men—may be judged only by the use

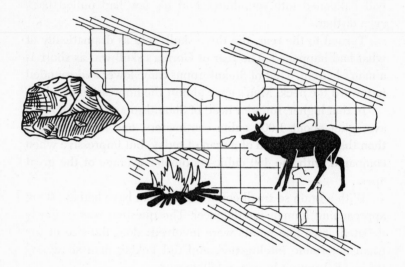

THE CHIPPED STONE TOOLS, THE FIRE, AND THE FOOD OF PEKING MAN OFFERED AGELESS PROOF OF HIS DAWNING HUMAN INTELLIGENCE.

made of it. "Cultural objects are the only guide as far as spiritual life is concerned," he explained. "They may be fallacious guides too, but we are completely lost if these objects are missing."

In the case of Peking man those objects were not missing. From the caves at Dragon-bone Hill came abundant proof that Peking man knew tools and fire.

Scattered through the layers of debris that had filled the

caves were thousands of chipped stone tools. One of the caves alone yielded more than two thousand artifacts—flaked choppers, boulders roughly shaped and edged, scrapers that might have cleaned the skins of animals, and hammer stones.

They were crude; perhaps they were stones that happened to break or chip in a way to fit the hand of Peking man rather than tools artfully shaped. And yet Peking man clearly had valued and selected them, for many of them were made of stone that did not occur in the caves. Some of the fossil bones also showed definite traces of having been shaped and used as crude tools.

Soft black layers mixed with charred bits of wood and bones told of Peking man's mastery of fire. Chemical tests scarcely were needed to prove that fires had burned at these points, but they were made and did verify the fact. In some cases hard layers of red and yellow clay underlay the charcoal of those ancient fires—hearths. Peking man probably had cooked some of his food.

From the stacks of bones about, it looked as though Peking man ate well. And venison must have been his favorite meat—more than seventy-five per cent of the fossil bones were those of the deer. But there also were bones of the wild boar, the bighorn sheep, the mammoth, the camel, the bison, the ostrich, and of such river-dwellers as the otter and the water buffalo. And all of the mammalian bones differed from those of living species. All were types that had long since vanished from the earth.

Near the big cave and about twenty feet below its lowest level, the excavators came upon what may have been Peking man's garbage dump. A layer of breccia (a stone made up of angular bits embedded in a matrix), several inches thick, was compacted of thousands of fragments of seed shells, bits of bone, and stone chips. The shells were those of the hackberry, a small fruit about the size of the wild cherry.

By his use of fire and tools and his mode of living, Peking man finally established his right to a place in the company of humans.

Dragon-bone Hill was to afford another glimpse of man making his way along the long road to civilization. Many ages after Peking man had vanished from the Western Hills, another group of men moved into another cave in Dragon-bone Hill. It seems probable that this cave was not accessible during the time of Sinanthropus, but was dissolved out of the limestone many thousands of years later.

The workers on the hill found it in 1931. When systematic exploration began, in 1933, a scene of violence was uncovered. Seven individuals, probably all members of one family, had met sudden death there in the upper cave in the hill. A round hole pierced one skull; the others had been fractured, apparently by the blows of blunt instruments.

One of the slain was a man of more than sixty years, an age not often reached in those hazardous days. A young man, two young women, an adolescent, a five-year-old, and an infant made up the remainder of the tragic group.

Some of their implements and ornaments lay around them, though they were few, almost as few as a migrating family might have carried on a journey. Among them were a bone needle, the polished antler of a deer, and a few beads from a necklace.

But an unimaginable wealth of fossil animal bones nearly filled the cave. Piled everywhere were the bones of thousands of hares, thousands of the complete lower jaws of Sika deer, and hundreds of whole skeletons of other deer, tigers, bears, hyenas, and ostriches. The hyenas, bears, and ostriches represented forms long since extinct, while the tiger and some of the others had disappeared from that part of Asia.[4]

[4] Weidenreich does not explain this huge accumulation of bones. He says only: "The most astonishing fact was the discovery of this unimaginable wealth of bones of fossil animals."

The cave and its violently murdered tenants seemed to belong to the period the geologists designate as Upper Paleolithic. It corresponded roughly to a culture that then was believed to have flourished in Europe between 20,000 and 100,000 years ago.

The findings of such a complete page from the past surpassed the wildest hopes of Weidenreich and his excavating team. At only one other place in the world—in Palestine—had there been a discovery of the same period that could match the upper cave at Choukoutien.

As Weidenreich began his studies, other amazing, nearly unexplainable features appeared. The skull of the old man looked something like that of a European—a primitive European, of course. One of the women, on the other hand, had a narrow head, remarkably similar to that of the Melanesians of New Guinea. Another peculiarity stumped the anthropologist. Across the forehead was a broad and shallow circular depression, a deformity that had nothing to do with the crushing blows that had killed her. Similar depressions are seen even in comparatively modern times in the skulls of women who carry heavy burdens by a strap running across the forehead.

As though enough problems had not been posed, the skull of the other woman displayed many of the distinctive traits of the modern Eskimo type.

A European, a Melanesian, and an Eskimo type lying dead in one close-knit group in a cave on a Chinese hillside! Weidenreich marveled.

After long study and investigation the anthropologist ventured the opinion that man may have split into different racial stems in even so early a stage of evolution as that represented by Pithecanthropus and Sinanthropus. He was convinced, though, that this held true only for the main races. He theorized that each of the latter might later have divided into subraces, originating as mere individual variations. "If this is true the presence of three 'racial' types in one and the same family is easy to understand," said Weidenreich.

Even more difficult and uncertain was the problem of the relation of the upper-cave people to Sinanthropus, two groups separated only by a few feet in space and yet by ages in time. Weidenreich would risk no more than a few observations. The lower molars of the old man of the upper cave were similar to those of Sinanthropus, and a type of tooth seldom found among the modern races of man.

Not beyond the realm of valid speculation was the possibility that the three curious types of the cave might explain another problem that long has baffled science.

Occasionally among the American Indians a primitive type appears that suggests an Australian or Melanesian native. To account for this anomaly some authorities have speculated that man may have moved to the American continent from Melanesia as well as from eastern Siberia. But there in the upper cave on Dragon-bone Hill were exactly the types that have appeared among the American Indians. If such types were in existence among the people who could have migrated from Asia, it would be unnecessary to postulate immigration from Australia or other parts of the world.

The two worn teeth that Zdansky picked up on Choukoutien Hill in 1921 had led far and wide. The discoveries that followed in their train traced the human race back very close to its beginnings. And these discoveries hinted at how long ago some of the fundamental racial differences might have originated.

Great theories often seem to hang upon very slender threads, or in this case upon a very few scraps of ancient bone. And yet that is the way of science. Detailed study, testing, and infinitely fine comparisons make it possible for the scientist to transmute his facts into theories that help to explain the world to itself. It was such scholarship that Black and Weidenreich supplied.

While Weidenreich carried on the scientific study of the

Peking finds, new fossils continued to pour in from Dragon-bone Hill. By late in 1941, the laboratory had the remains of more than forty Sinanthropus individuals.

But the times were growing increasingly uneasy. There were threats and reports of Japanese troop movements. By late

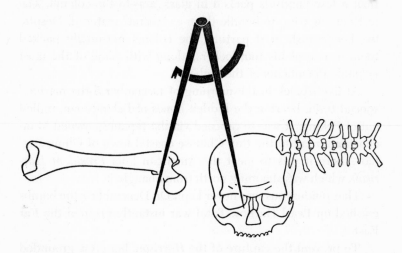

BY EXACTING STUDY OF THE REMAINS OF THE PAST THE HUMAN RACE WAS TRACED BACK ALMOST TO ITS BEGINNINGS.

November and early December those living at the center of the gathering storm could no longer misread the signs.

Weidenreich was in the United States on a visit. Dr. Wong Wen-hao, director of the geological survey, appealed to Dr. Henry S. Houghton, president of the Peking Union Medical College, to have the priceless Peking-man collection taken to safety. Wong was the custodian of the remains and wanted to save them from capture if the Japanese should move into Peking.

Somewhat reluctantly,[5] Dr. Houghton asked Colonel Wil-

[5] Dr. Houghton did not feel that the Americans should assume responsibility for the relics.

liam W. Ashurst, commander of the Marine detachment at the American Embassy in Peking, to send the Peking-man collection to safety in the United States with a Marine detachment leaving within a few days.

Dr. Houghton personally took the bones—scarcely more than a few handfuls packed in glass jars—to the colonel. The instructions were to handle them as "secret" material. Despite the hectic rush of departure, the colonel personally packed them in one of his foot-lockers, along with some of the most valuable documents of the embassy.

At five o'clock in the morning of December 5 the marines' special train, bearing the hidden bones of Peking man, pulled out of Peking. It was to proceed via the Japanese-owned Manchuria railroad to the tiny Chinese coastal town of Chinwangtao. There it was to meet the American liner *President Harrison*, which was steaming north from Shanghai.

That rendezvous was never kept. On December 7 the bombs crashed on Pearl Harbor. Total war instantly gripped the Far East.

To prevent the capture of the *Harrison*, her crew grounded her at the mouth of the Yangtze River.[6] The marine train with its special cargo and guards was immediately captured at Chinwangtao.

What happened from that moment on is clouded by rumor and the confusion of war. Only one fact is certain. From that day the remains of Peking man disappeared completely. Despite the efforts of three governments to find them, they have vanished from the world as completely as during the centuries when they lay hidden in the earth of Dragon-bone Hill.

According to one account, the Japanese loaded all the cases taken from the train on a lighter that was to take them to a freighter lying off Tientsin. The lighter, it is said, capsized, and

---

[6] The *Harrison* was later refloated and repaired by the Japanese. On her first voyage in the Japanese service she was sunk by an American submarine.

the remains of Peking man drifted away or sank to the bottom of the sea.

The other story is that the Japanese who looted the train knew nothing of the value of the scraps of bone and either threw them away or sold them to Chinese traders as "dragon bones." If so, they may long since have been ground into medicine.

The nine marines who had been on the train were later returned to Peking and, with Colonel Ashurst and the 250 men of his command, were sent to prisoner-of-war camps in Japan.[7]

By roundabout means Colonel Ashurst learned that the Japanese had taken millions of rounds of ammunition from the train and must have gone through everything aboard. "Perhaps they found the remains and just threw them away," said the colonel, now a retired brigadier general living in the South. "Like canned foods. The Japanese had no use for our foods they captured, so they just dumped them off the train. The Peking relics must not have looked like much. I hardly realized what they were."

A marine sergeant, interned in a concentration camp near Tientsin, reported that he later saw blankets and other marine equipment that had been on the same train. This too would indicate that the baggage had been captured by the Japanese.

It seems fairly certain that the Japanese did not secretly send the irreplaceable relics to Tokyo. After the end of the war the Looted Properties Division of the Far East Command searched Japan for them. Some boxes of artifacts from Choukoutien were found at Tokyo University, but they belonged to a later period than the time of Sinanthropus.

"I am pretty well convinced that what we got in Tokyo was all that the Japanese brought to Japan from China," said Dr. Frank C. Whitmore, Jr., scientific consultant to Allied headquarters, who directed the search in Japan for Peking man. "They kept exact lists of their loot, not knowing that we would

[7] The colonel was freed by American troops on September 12, 1945.

ever get those lists. We have accounted for all archeological items on the lists."

The Japanese, for their part, searched China for the Peking-man collection. No sooner did they move into Peking than they ransacked the city for the invaluable bones. They went over the college and the embassy with the proverbial fine-toothed comb. "They knew what they were looking for and knew that the relics had been in Peking," reported Miss Agnes Pearce, secretary of the China Medical Board. The controller of the college was taken into custody and questioned for five days. "The obvious inference is that if they searched in Peking, they must have searched the train at Chinwangtao," added Miss Pearce. "But we don't know."

Since the war, the Chinese Communist government seemingly has taken up the long search.

In the summer of 1951 Dr. Pei, who found the first famous skull, issued a loud statement charging that the United States had stolen the Peking-man treasure. The Communist press picked up the charge and blasted away at it. Early in 1952 Dr. Yang Chien-kien, head of the Chinese Institute of Anthropology in Peking, added to the furore by alleging that the vanished Peking-man collection is in the American Museum of Natural History in New York.

Dr. Harry L. Shapiro, chairman of the museum's Department of Anthropology answered that the accusations were only anti-American propaganda. The museum has only the casts of some of the skulls and bones which were made by Weidenreich and sent to a number of museums and experts. One collection of twenty such casts is on display in the museum's Hall of the Age of Man.

Behind the Red Chinese charges probably is the knowledge that Weidenreich joined the staff of the museum when the outbreak of war made his return to China impossible. There he finished his great work *The Skull of Sinanthropus Pekinensis*, *a Comparative Study on a Primitive Hominid Skull,*[8] and brought out his popular book *Apes, Giants and Man* [9] and the reports on von Koenigswald's Java giants. Even after suffering a heart attack early in 1947, he insisted upon spending a few hours each day at the museum. Death came on July 11, 1947 to "this brave and tenacious man who never gave in to adversities or difficulties."

The fate of Peking man—though not his scientific standing—remains one of the great international mysteries. To have emerged from the deep shadows of man's earliest years into world acclaim and the swirling violence of war, only to vanish completely—it was an odd and improbable end for Peking man.

[8] Published by G. E. Stechert, New York, 1943.
[9] Published by University of Chicago Press, 1946.

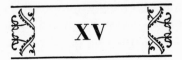

XV

DART AND BROOM

SOUTH AFRICA: APE-MEN

Many of the great land masses underwent the mauling of ice and the upheavals of mountain-making. But not South Africa. With a few exceptions, this huge tip of land has stood high and dry and little disturbed since the time when there were no forests on the earth and the primitive fish swarming in the Paleozoic seas were the most advanced form of life.

For millions of years South Africa has been a secure platform upon which life could develop. Thanks to this unusually stable background, the sprawling subcontinent between the Zambesi and the Cape might well have been considered a likely place to look for fossils dating far back, perhaps even to the misty unknown beginnings of man.

The obvious, however, is often both overlooked and ignored. The world took little notice when baboon and ape skulls of types that had long since disappeared from the earth began to be found in South African caves. There was genuine surprise when a quarryman named M. de Bruyn, working in a lime deposit near Taungs, blasted out a small skull that he recognized as unusual. It looked almost like that of a human. He sent it to Dr. Raymond A. Dart, professor of anatomy at Witwatersrand University, at Johannesburg.

As Dart cleaned it and studied it, his excitement grew. The face was almost complete. The lower jaw was there and also all the teeth, plus the whole of the right side of the brain cast. The teeth were milk teeth, with the first true molars just beginning to function. Clearly the skull was that of a young higher ape or apelike being, probably of a six-year-old. And it was a new type, Dart thought, allied to the ancestors of man.

The doctor rushed a notice of the discovery to London. In his preliminary report, published on February 7, 1925, was the following provocative—and prophetic—statement: "The specimen is of importance because it exhibits an extinct race of apes intermediate between living anthropoids and man."

Dart called attention to the human rather than the apelike character of the jaw, the teeth, the eye sockets, and the skull contours. He even dared to name the type of being the skull represented, *Australopithecus africanus* (South African ape).

The word "intermediate" and the claim that the little skull was that of a being between apes and men—what was popularly known as the missing link—irritated and amused anthropological circles. If Dart had announced the harnessing of perpetual motion, or the cracking of the atom, or the completion of a round trip to the moon, the skepticism could not have been profounder. All English and American anthropologists who expressed an opinion in print were unanimous—Dart had made a serious blunder. His little Taungs skull, they said, was only a variety of chimpanzee.

Privately they dubbed it "Dart's baby." Comments on Dart's "rush to get into print" verged on the vitriolic. His report had been made only six weeks after the skull had been placed in his hands. This was unheard-of haste. One important fossil find was kept secret for thirty years, no report was made on another skull for ten years, and the British Museum took seven years to produce a report on an important Rhodesian discovery.

A few, however, were sufficiently interested to go to South Africa for a closer look. The leading American anthropologist, Aleš Hrdlička, made the trip in 1925. He talked to Dart, investigated the site, did some digging, examined the skull, and was uncertain. "Just what relation this fossil form bears on the one hand, to the human phylum, and on the other to the chimpanzee and gorilla, can only be properly determined after the specimen is well identified, for which are needed additional and adult specimens," he cautiously wrote.

Another visitor, a local one, came to an entirely different conclusion. He was singularly well equipped to judge, for he himself had made amazing fossil discoveries in South Africa. From a one-time swampland he had dug the fossils that for the first time actually linked the reptiles and the mammals.

This fossil expert was Dr. Robert Broom. He had been born in 1866 in Paisley, Scotland, where his father, John Broom, was a designer of calicoes and Paisley shawls. As a youngster he was troubled with bronchitis and was sent to the seacoast for a year to live with his grandmother. There, at the age of six, the collecting instincts that must have been bred in him quickly came into the open. With a retired army lieutenant he hunted along the shore for crabs, shrimps, and innumerable other small marine creatures, which he kept alive in small bowls in his grandmother's house. In 1875 his father took a summer house near Linlithgow. John Broom by this time had become an enthusiastic field botanist, and he and his son Robert spent hours tramping along the banks of Scottish rivers, studying plant life.

Robert went to Glasgow University, where he became a junior assistant to the professor of chemistry and took his degree of doctor of medicine in 1889. He was a student of the great Lord Kelvin's, but courses in botany and anatomy aroused his passionate and enduring interest in the origin of mammals.

After graduation Broom went to Australia, ostensibly because it was believed the climate would be good for his health; actually his real hope was to study Australia's unique marsupials. In North Queensland, where he began his practice, he found the time to make a large collection of lizards. By 1895 he had published twelve scientific papers and had discovered a rich patch of bone breccia in the Wombeyan caves. Months of digging in the bone deposits produced some "very interesting" types of extinct marsupials.

Reports of strange mammal-like reptile fossils in South Africa began to reach the doctor. The lure was irresistible. In 1896 Broom left Australia and made his circuitous way to South Africa, arriving in Cape Town in January 1897.

Unfortunately he had no money to plunge into fossil-hunting. Out of necessity he took up medical practice in Little Namaqualand. In looking about, however, he caught a glimpse of the fossil-rich Karoo country. That was too much for him. He shifted his practice to a place within reach of it.

His medical practice went well, but seriously interfered with his investigation of the fantastic Karoo deposits. When he was offered an appointment as professor of geology and zoology at Victoria College in Stellenbosch, he took it eagerly. Since the post would permit him to give almost full time to the fossils, the sacrifice of the £1,000 income he was making in practice for the £450 salary of a professor mattered little. In seven years Broom more than doubled the number of known Karoo fossils and published ninety-six scientific papers. Only increasing financial necessity finally drove him back to medicine.

On a visit to London in 1906 Broom met Henry Fairfield Osborn. The head of the American Museum of Natural History persuaded him to make a hasty trip to New York to try to settle a question that had divided American experts—the affinities of the lower Permian Pelycosaurs, the huge lizard-like reptiles whose remains have been found in Texas and parts of the West.

Edward Drinker Cope was insisting that they were related to the South African mammal-like reptiles. Other authorities argued that they were closer to the Sphenodon of New Zealand. Broom spent almost the entire week he was in the United States going over the data in the museum. Upon his return to South Africa he published a paper holding that the American reptilians with their big sail-like backbones were closely related to the South African types, though a little more primitive and specialized. His conclusion has since been confirmed by many others.

Broom was very favorably impressed by America. When the government of South Africa showed no interest in his increasingly large collection of mammalian fossils, he packed them up and sent them to the American museum. He later went there to help in studying them.

A PELYCOSAUR AND SKULL

During the First World War, Broom joined a medical unit in a London hospital. In 1916, however, he returned to South Africa. In every moment that his medical practice left free, he delved deeper into the secrets of the reptile fossils. He was on the trail of one of the most basic questions: what was the origin of the mammals?

Science again was divided. Huxley had favored the view that the mammals had arisen from an amphibian ancestor. Cope argued for one of the mammal-like reptiles. Broom's masterly research in the one-time Karoo swampland virtually settled the issue in favor of the mammal-like reptiles.

Years later Field Marshal Jan C. Smuts, Prime Minister of the Union of South Africa, told the story of this achievement in his introduction to a book about Broom:

"His paleontological researches on the Karoo reptiles enabled him to bridge successfully the gap between the reptiles and the mammals. This gap long had remained the most considerable in animal paleontology. . . . In the Karoo reptilian fossils he found a rich horde of evidence which he carefully analyzed and correctly interpreted in a series of researches as masterly as any made during this century. The story of the evolution of life on this globe is perhaps the most enthralling romance in all science. Much of it remains obscure or unknown, but much more was debatable or unknown when Broom embarked on his Karoo researches."

Feeling sure that he had discovered the origins of the mammals, Broom often turned his thoughts to the origin of man. When he heard of Dart's discovery, it was not surprising that he hurried to Johannesburg.

There he spent several days studying the Taungs skull, and particularly the teeth. Their size and shape convinced him that the fossil child-ape was not closely related to such living anthropoids as the gorilla and the chimpanzee, but that in a number of characters it resembled man.

Dart was right, Broom decided with the quick-fire judgment that was typical of him. Furthermore, he felt certain that this was "practically the missing link," and the most important fossil find made up to that time. He wrote a paper saying so. In addition, Broom sent a section of the skull to William J. Sollas, the noted paleontologist of Oxford University, and was instrumental in winning him over to what Broom already was calling "our side."

With the exception of these few believers, the rest of the scientific world either joked about the "South African missing link" or forgot the subject for most of the next decade. The South African find joined the limbo of discoveries about which someone has been overenthusiastic. Dart himself was hurt by the treatment he had received, and felt discredited. He did not attempt to follow up his work with further explorations.

Dart and Broom, nevertheless, continued to study the Taungs skull. Closer examination only emphasized its humanness. The eyes and nose were like those of a human child and the milk teeth could have belonged to a six-year-old of today. The molar teeth, however, were a little larger. The incisors had been worn down, as they are in children of primitive races, though not in young apes.

In 1929 Dart removed the lower jaw from the upper. For the first time the two doctors could see the crowns of the teeth. Any lingering doubts that the little Australopithecus was related to man, rather than to the anthropoid apes, were removed, as far as they were concerned.

The lower milk molar in man is a grinding tooth with four well-developed cusps and usually two other small cusps. And so it was in the Taungs child. The orang, on the other hand, has only one large cusp and three small ones. The chimpanzee has one large main cusp and one small one; the gorilla, only one.

To Broom the fact that the large opening of the brain was situated more anteriorly than in the apes indicated that the little ape-man child must have walked or run on his hind feet.

A restoration drawing of the head disclosed an engaging child. Although there always is an element of imagination in such a restoration, the drawing was based on the most precise skull measurements. The eyes, head, and ears looked human, the nose was a flat little button, and the lips protuberant.

From what Dart and Broom knew of the country, they felt sure little Australopithecus and his relatives had lived in the Taungs caves. In the caves were many remains of the kind of animals on which the ape-men families might have fed—dassies, young antelopes, spring-hares, giant rodent moles, small baboons, tortoises, crabs, and lizards. Fifteen mammals eventually were identified. All were species that had disappeared from the world, and about half the genera to which they belonged were also extinct.

Unquestionably the Taungs deposits were taking the two physicians far back into prehistory. They hesitated to attempt to fix the time, but thought it possible the deposits belonged to the Upper Pliocene—say of two million years ago.

They were much surer that the land had then been a desert. The point was important, for all anthropoids of today live in forest or jungle. Broom suspected that the ape-men had captured the antelopes whose bones were in the caves only by waylaying them at waterholes. He saw no possibility that they could have run them down on foot.

He suggested too that they must have dug the moles and spring-hares from their holes, and killed the baboons by bashing in their heads with a stone. A large part of the baboon skulls found then and later were fractured as though by a blow from some blunt instrument.

Broom was not a man to be discouraged by opposition, or for that matter by the resistant darkness of centuries, the fastness of rock or other obstacles. He was consumed with eagerness to discover another Australopithecus and prove to the world that he and Dart were right. Unfortunately, he was still hampered in this desire by the necessity of making a living. His medical practice in the little town of Maquassi kept him well out of the range of the fossil caves.

Field Marshal Smuts, the scholarly Premier of the Union of South Africa, took care of this problem by offering Broom a post as curator of vertebrate paleontology and physical anthropology in the Transvaal Museum in Pretoria. "Gen. Smuts thought it was a pity that I should be spending my latter years in medical work to make a living when I might be devoting all my time to scientific work," Broom wrote later, in what was a simple statement of fact as far as both he and the general were concerned.

Broom gladly accepted, and at the age of sixty-eight again

made his avocation his vocation. For eighteen months he was occupied in continuing his collection of fossil reptiles. Not until 1936 was he ready to take up the trail of an adult ape-man.

Broom started work at some old lime workings about thirteen miles west of Pretoria. Some small fossil mammal bones had been taken out of it earlier and sent to New York for identification. The leading South African authority had maintained that it was impossible to describe them. "Like most mammalologists, he [the South African authority] was of the opinion that rats could not be described unless you could measure the length of their tails and count the number of mammæ; but I was not discouraged," said Broom.

The doctor insisted the fossil rats could be identified by studying the teeth. He proved right.

Continuing his work at the lime-works, Broom found and identified half a dozen new species of rats and moles. He also found some fossil remains of a small saber-toothed tiger, and a giant baboon jaw that at first aroused his hopes of another *Australopithecus*. When it was cleaned, however, it proved to be strictly baboon.

The Pretoria newspapers and others reported these discoveries, for Broom believed in co-operating with the press. He had always found, he said, that "he who works with the press gets far ahead of one who works in secret." He also was fond of reminding more reserved associates that many paleontological discoveries are made by amateurs and that "it is much better to have the public educated and interested than kept in ignorance."

As usual, the doctor's theory paid off. Two of Dart's students who had read the reports came to Broom to tell him about some small baboon skulls they had found in a cave at Sterkfontein, about thirty miles from Johannesburg. Broom was at once interested and aranged to go to the place with the students on the next Sunday.

To the people of that section it was no news that there were fossils about. Since the first mining camps had sprung up during the Witwatersrand gold rush of 1886, boys had been picking up fossil bones of antelope, monkeys, baboons, and perhaps ape-men. Years later, when Dr. George D. Barbour, of the University of Cincinnati, visited South Africa, he had lunch with a leading lawyer, who told him that as a boy he had played bowls with a "stone skull" that he had picked up in the fields near Sterkfontein.

By the 1930's the mining strike had yielded billions in gold and near-by Krugersdorp had grown into a thriving town. It had so far advanced in civic consciousness that in 1933 a guidebook had been issued urging visitors: "Come to Sterkfontein and find the missing link."

Broom arrived on August 9, 1936—though not in response to the forehanded invitation—and promptly did.

He and his student guides went first to a quarry where for many years a commercial company had been obtaining lime for its kilns. In breaks in the stone were many pockets of bone breccia, the composite deposit that contained the fossils.

It developed that G. W. Barlow, manager in charge of the quarrying and the caves, had once worked at Taungs and knew about the skull. Broom asked him if he had ever found anything like it at Sterkfontein. Barlow "rather thought" he had. He explained that he generally sold any "nice bones or skulls" to visitors who came to see the caves. The doctor begged him to keep a sharp outlook for anything like an ape-man skull, and Barlow promised that he would.

Three days later, Broom returned. Barlow handed him three small baboon skulls and the badly damaged skull of a saber-toothed tiger. Hunting through the debris where they had been blasted out, the doctor found more of the tiger skull and a "nice canine."

The following Monday Barlow produced a find that to Broom was more valuable than all the gold taken from the Witwatersrand mines.

"Is this what you are after?" asked Barlow, presenting the doctor with two thirds of a "beautiful fossil brain cast." (The stone bore the exact impress of the skull that once had lain there.)

It was. At first glance Broom sensed that it was the brain cast of an ape-man!

Since it had been blasted out only that morning, Broom feverishly dug into the debris. He worked for hours, until dark, but could find no more than the cast of the top of the head.

The next morning early he was back. And in three hours of digging, sifting, scraping, and moving big piles of rock he discovered all of the base of the skull, both sides of the upper jaw, and some fragments of the brain case.

When all the pieces were cleaned and assembled, Broom learned that, except for the lower jaw, he had most of the skull of a creature that obviously belonged to the same near-human family as the Taungs six-year-old. At first Broom named the new fossil *Australopithecus transvaalensis* (South African ape of the Transvaal). Later he decided that it belonged to another genus of the same family and renamed it *Plesianthropus transvaalensis* (near-man of the Transvaal). "To have started out to look for an adult skull of Australopithecus and to have found an adult of at least an allied form in about three months was a record of which we felt there was no reason to be ashamed," said Broom. "And to have gone to Sterkfontein and found what we wanted within nine days was even better."

Every week, and often twice a week during all of 1936, 1937, and part of 1938, the doctor continued to visit his fossil gold mine, for that is what it proved to be. All of the quarry boys were on the hunt for him, and whenever a blast blew out anything of likely interest, they stowed it away for the doctor or marked the place so he could dig it out himself. "Every visit cost me some shillings in tips," recalled Broom, "but it was worth it."

From the caves and quarry came many other parts of the

Sterkfontein ape-man—bits of skull, isolated teeth and parts of limb bones. And also the fossil bones of the animals on which the ape-men had fed—rats, moles, jackals.

Then came another memorable day. As Broom arrived one

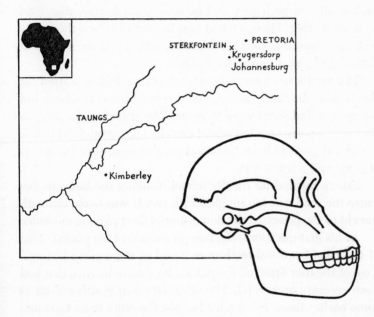

SOUTH AFRICAN APE-MAN. THE GOLD-MINE SECTION WHERE HIS BONES WERE DISCOVERED, AND THE AUSTRALOPITHECUS DISTRICT OUTLINED ON A MAP OF AFRICA.

fine June morning in 1938, Barlow greeted him with "I have something nice for you this morning." It was the palate of a large ape-man, with one molar in place.

Trying not to betray his excitement, Broom answered with restrained understatement: "Yes, that is a nice specimen. I'll give you a couple of pounds for it."

Barlow was pleased, but evasive about telling where the

palate had come from. The matrix was different from that of Sterkfontein, and the doctor felt sure it had been collected from some other site. He questioned the quarry boys; they had not seen it before. Broom dropped finesse. He told Barlow he had to know the source of the fossil; two of the teeth were freshly broken off and perhaps could be recovered. Barlow then held back no further. He explained that he had obtained the palate from a schoolboy, Gert Terblanche, who lived on a farm at Kromdraai, about two miles away.

The words were scarcely uttered before Broom started for the Terblanche farm. Gert, a fifteen-year-old, was at school, but his mother and sister were at home. The sister led the anxious doctor to a place on a hill where Gert had hammered the palate out of a deposit of bone breccia. Lying around were fragments of bone and a few teeth.

Broom hurried off for the school, walking the last mile because the road was too rough for his car. It was noon, but with the aid of the principal the doctor found Gert playing outdoors.

At his first questions, the boy pulled out of his pocket "four of the most beautiful teeth ever found in the world's history." Two of the four fitted on the palate; they were the two that had been recently broken off. The other two had weathered off at some earlier time. The doctor bought the teeth from Gert and transferred them to the greater safety of his pocket.

Gert said he had another piece of the skull hidden away. The problem was to get him out of school and to his hiding-place before dark might halt any necessary investigations.

Broom suggested to the principal that he be allowed to talk to the teachers and children about their caves and how bones got into them. For more than an hour he lectured to them, illustrating his points with the clever blackboard sketches he often made at the museum. The principal was so pleased that he dismissed the whole school well before the closing hour at two in the afternoon. The boy and the doctor rushed off. When they reached the hill, Gert dug into his cache and drew out "a fine jaw with some beautiful teeth."

During the next few days the two sifted all the ground around the spot where the skull had been embedded and recovered a number of scraps of bone and tooth. When all the pieces were cleaned and joined, Broom again had a wonderful surprise. He had the greater part of the left side of a skull and the lower right jaw with many of the teeth well preserved.

The skull differed in some important respects from that found at Sterkfontein. The face was flatter, the jaw more powerful, and the teeth larger. In this way it was more apelike. In other ways, particularly in the form of the teeth, it was more human. Some people began to be convinced. The *London Illustrated News* captioned its picture: "The Missing Link No Longer Missing."

The differences were so marked that the doctor decided his Kromdraai man must have belonged to a different genus, and he named him *Paranthropus robustus* (robust near-man). Some English anthropologists who were then more sympathetically following the South African discoveries thought Broom was nevertheless running wild in identifying two new genera on the basis of skulls that they considered only adult forms of the Taungs "ape."

"Of course," Dr. Broom said, "the critics did not know the whole of the facts. When one has jealous opponents one does not let them know everything."

What the critics did not know was that each of the three skulls was associated with different animals. Fossil remains of horses were abundant at Kromdraai. None were found in the Sterkfontein quarry. The Kromdraai jackal, baboon, and sabertooth tiger were distinctive. At Kromdraai there was a giant dassie; at Sterkfontein only a small one. At Sterkfontein a big wart-hog was uncovered; at Kromdraai, none. And yet the two places were only two miles apart.

To Broom there was nothing remarkable in finding three different genera ape-men in the Transvaal. He calmly predicted that many more would appear when the rich deposits were investigated more fully in the next fifty years or so! If the Taungs cave should prove to be 2,000,000 years old, Sterkfontein about 1,200,000, and Kromdraai 800,000, the doctor suggested it would not be surprising to find a number of types of primitive men.

The war stopped the work in the caves. The enforced halt gave Broom and his assistants their first real chance to sort, study, measure, and describe the amazing mass of material they had collected. In 1946, in consequence, Broom and his assistant, G. W. H. Schepers, were able to publish their book, *The South African Fossil Ape-Men*. It gave a full and scientific account, along with photographs, of all the remains found up to that time.

The scientific world, which had relegated the ape-men to the category of pseudo-science ten years earlier, was awakened with a shock. There was no longer any denying that the South African discoveries were of prime importance, though anthropology still might differ over their interpretation. Many were won over. The National Academy of Sciences in Washington awarded Broom its Daniel Giraud Elliot Medal for the most important work in biology published in 1946.

Soon after the end of the war, General Smuts sent for Broom. The venerable South African statesman recognized, Broom later reported, "that we were discovering the origin of man and that the work in the caves must be carried on." The general offered the doctor government support and whatever money might be needed for further explorations. Shortly afterward Smuts left for a trip to England and America, and the promising prospect he had outlined suffered a bad upset.

Broom was just about to resume work when he received a letter from the Historical Monuments Commission of South

Africa informing him that he would be permitted to excavate only under certain conditions.

The doctor's version of the commission's intervention does not disguise his outrage at the whole proceeding: "The Historical Monuments Commission which believes that it has dictatorial rights to decide who is to be allowed to hunt for fossils and how the work is to be done, intervened and warned me that I would not be allowed to excavate except under conditions which I regarded as insulting.

"I was to be allowed to work only in collaboration with a 'competent field geologist' who was to be consulted whenever a blast was contemplated. To continue on such terms was impossible and I had to wait until Gen. Smuts returned from America. When he came back at Christmas, he phoned me again. He seemed very angry and told me to carry on."

Broom resumed operations at Kromdraai. He had been on the job for three months when he received a "permit" from the commission to continue his work there. Nothing was said about Sterkfontein.

The doctor's reaction was immediate and also his action. He dropped his explorations at Kromdraai and ostentatiously began work at Sterkfontein without a permit. By provoking this defiance, the commission, as it turned out, did Broom a great favor. At Sterkfontein the doctor decided to look a little farther into the site where *Plesianthropus transvaalensis* had been found. No more blasting had been done there, since the lime was poor, and Broom reasoned that it might be possible to find some other parts of the skeleton.

No further parts of *P. transvaalensis* showed up, though Broom found the crushed snout of an adolescent Plesianthropus and six fine unworn teeth. That cheered him up. A day or two later he came upon part of the skull of a baby, with a few milk molars. The doctor felt even more encouraged.

Supreme encouragement was to come only a little later. On

April 18, only two weeks after the permitless resumption of
work at Sterkfontein, the doctor and his assistants blasted out
a large piece of what looked like unpromising breccia. As the
smoke blew away, they saw a sight almost unbelievable to an
anthropologist. A whole, a perfect skull was exposed, standing
out like an ivory inlay in the darker rock.

The blast had split it in two—an immaterial matter. The
base of the skull was in the block that had broken away. The
upper half was exposed in the wall. Small lime crystals had
formed in the brain case, which sparkled as though it were
lined with diamonds. "I have seen many interesting sights in
my long life," the doctor said. "This was the most thrilling of
my experience."

The first need was to have this remarkable discovery photographed *in situ*. As no one in the party had a camera, Broom
phoned the editor of the Johannesburg *Star*. Within an hour
and a half a reporter and a photographer had covered the thirty
miles and were at the spot. Dr. Broom was photographed in
one of the climactic moments of his life kneeling against the
mottled rock of the cave and pointing to what looked like a
strange white nodule in the dense stone. The other piece of
skull, white in its chunk of stone, lay on a ledge just above.

Broom's assistants and nearly everyone else who worked in
the dusty caves and quarries customarily wore khaki shirts and
shorts, pith helmets, and heavy shoes. Broom strode into this
rough setting each day in a carefully tailored business suit, a
wing collar, striped tie, and well-polished shoes. At night when
the others straggled out dirty, disheveled, and sweaty, he
emerged as crisply immaculate as on his morning arrival. It was
a measure of the greatness and pressure of April 18 that the
doctor had removed his coat. He is shown in the pictures in
shirt sleeves, but the sleeves were not rolled up; the cuffs, fastened with gold links, were fresh, unsmudged, uncrumpled,
unwilted.

After the photographs were made, the block of stone hold-

ing the base of the skull was gently carried to a car. With crow-
bars the workers then pried loose the large block holding the
top of the skull. In a little more than an hour "the most valuable
specimen ever discovered," to use Broom's words, was safe in
the Transvaal Museum.

The skull was that of an adult female Plesianthropus.
Around the museum she promptly became known as Mrs. Ples.
Mrs. Ples would scarcely have been considered a beauty by
modern standards. Her jaw was heavy and underslung, her
nose flat. And yet there was about her an unmistakable quality
of humanness.

Few dispute, as Broom said flatly, that the skull is one of
the finest fossils ever discovered. The doctor for his part did
not hesitate to rate it as more important than the skulls of Java
and Peking man or the jaw of Heidelberg man.

The earlier finds definitely were men; dawn men, primitive
men, it is true, but human. Mrs. Ples and her contemporaries
were beings not yet fully human; they were the links, the long-
denied and long-sought transitions between the anthropoids
and men. They were the hitherto missing proof of the unbroken
descent of life at one of the critical stages of evolution, the
jump from anthropoid to hominid—to the human race.

In both Europe and America interest was intense. Mrs. Ples
created a sensation. The effect in South Africa was one of sensation compounded, for the finding of the astoundingly complete fossil had not only broken anthropological precedent—it
had broken the law.

The doctor's flouting of the Historical Monuments Commission had become too obvious to overlook. The commission
held a full meeting at which it condemned his action, and voted
to send a protesting delegation to General Smuts. The doctor
was charged with ignoring the strata in the caves and thus
destroying valuable evidence that might later be needed for
dating the specimens.

Broom insisted that there was no truth whatever in the

allegations, but he was forced temporarily to halt operations at Sterkfontein. "It was manifest that the press and probably a large part of the people were on my side," the doctor declared. "Here I had made a discovery that had put South Africa in the news all over the world and now I was forbidden to do any more work except under conditions which I considered insulting."

To break the stalemate, B. V. Lomdaard, professor of geology at Pretoria University, was appointed to investigate. His decision largely was favorable for the doctor: there were no strata to be disturbed in the place where he was working, and no harm had been done. Broom duly received a permit to work at Sterkfontein.

His reaction was characteristic: "So they had to allow me to continue, though still under absurd conditions to which I pay no attention."

The doctor next unearthed an almost perfect male jaw. It supplied one further highly meaningful clue to the relative apeness and humanness of the ape-men. The telltale canine tooth was larger than in man, but had been ground down in line with the other teeth, just as in man. Such a wearing down of the canine is never found in the males of the anthropoid apes.

On August 1, 1948 came a third major discovery, one to rank with the skull and the jaw. A nearly perfect pelvis was found embedded in a slab of stone. As the doctor realized at once, and later scientific studies confirmed, it provided final proof that the ape-men had walked on two legs rather than on all fours.

When Broom had only skulls, which looked a little like chimpanzee skulls, many doubted their human relatedness. When he came upon some bits of thigh bone that looked almost human, the doubters intimated that he had got fragments of human skeletons mixed with his chimpanzee skulls. The

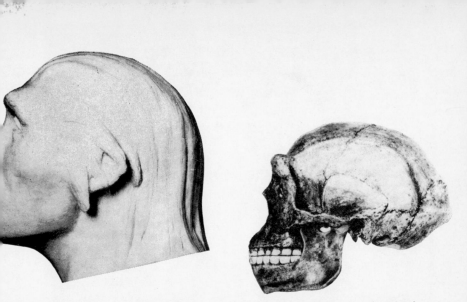

ng woman. Reconstruction of the head and skull of a woman who lived in the Choukoutien
cave.

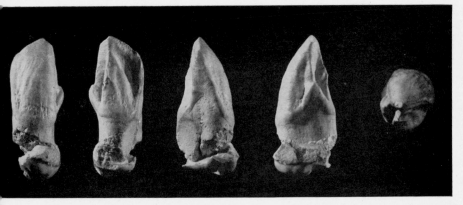

h of a later South African ape-man. Teleanthropus was more advanced than the earlier ape-
and had reached the same evolutionary stage as Pithecanthropus.

PLATE XXI

PLATE XXII

Kromdraai *Sterkfontein*

Swartkrans

On the low ridges surrounding this gentle South African valley man's earliest ancestors were found. From ancient caves at Sterkfontein, Kromdraai, and Swartkrans came the remains of the ape-men, the beings who are a major link between the anthropoids and the most primitive humans,

One of the most thrilling sights ever to greet a searcher for early man. A lucky blast at Sterkfontein in 1947 uncovered a perfect whole skull of an ape-man. Dr. Robert Broom and his assistant and successor, John T. Robinson, examine their extraordinary find.

Looking down into part of the Swartkrans excavation. At this site giant-sized ape-men, almost as large as the Java giants, were found. The long rods are rock drills for explosive charges, which do little damage if carefully controlled. All fine material is sifted for bone fragments.

PLATE XXIV

outside the Swartkrans excavation. Native boys are breaking up bone breccia, looking for il specimens. In the background Dr. Broom is examining specimens that show bone.

hand of Dr. Broom points to the crushed skull of a child still in place in the Swartkrans vation.

PLATE XXV

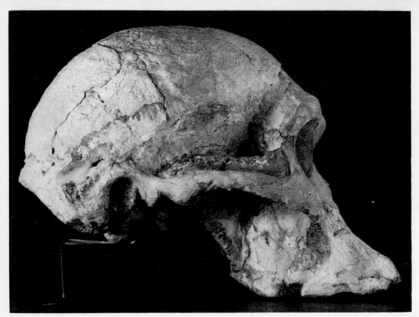

The complete skull of *Plesianthropus transvaalensis* (near man of the Transvaal). Actually this was a woman, known around the laboratory as "Mrs. Ples."

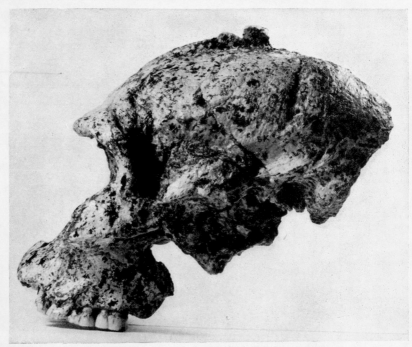

The incomplete skull of one of the big ape-men, from the Swartkrans excavation. Skull was a little crushed during fossilization; the braincase was flattened and the face forced forward.

PLATE XXVI

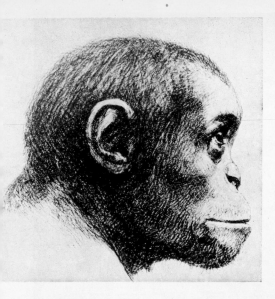

The Taungs six-year-old ape-man, the world's first clue that a link between the anthropoids and humans had been found.

...ey at Swartkrans examining a deposit of bone breccia, a rock compounded of ... fragments.

PLATE XXVII

Adolph Knopf. Chairman of the Committee on the Age of the Earth.

Kenneth Page Oakley. His new system fluorine dating cut the time of modern ma

Willard F. Libby. His work with Carbon-14 re-dated the last twenty-five thousand years.

Sherwood L. Washburn. He emphasized periment to test what happened in evolu

PLATE XXVIII

pelvis was another matter. It was scarcely half the length of a chimpanzee pelvis and so decidedly different from that of a gorilla that even a layman could see at a glance that it was in another class. It closely resembled the human pelvis, though when it was cleaned and studied minutely, it was evident that it was not quite human either.

"What we can now say is that the pelvis is not in the least anthropoid, and that it is nearly, but not quite human," the doctor summed up. More nearly than any of the other discoveries, the pelvis fossil put the ape-men in between the anthropoids and man, and perhaps fairly close to the ancestral stock from which man is descended.

At this time a University of California expedition headed by Wendell Phillips arrived in South Africa. Broom was delighted with the suggestion that the expedition would work with him and finance the costs if he would open a new cave.

A promising spot in a cave at Swartkrans, about one mile from Sterkfontein, was selected. Again success came fast. Within a few days Broom and his new co-workers had discovered the teeth and jaw of still another type of ape-man.

The teeth of the "Swartkrans ape-man" were nearly fifty per cent larger than those of *Paranthropus robustus,* and for this reason he was named officially *Paranthropus crassidens* (coarse-toothed). The massiveness of the jaw and teeth inevitably invited comparisons with the early giant men found in Java by von Koenigswald. Stories flashed around the world: there had been giants in South Africa too. Broom, however, was cautious on the point.

As had happened many times before, however, evidence to lessen doubts was soon forthcoming. While Broom was visiting in the United States in 1949, his assistant, J. T. Robinson, found another nearly perfect lower jaw. It also was massive. Some separate teeth that also came to light at Swartkrans looked remarkably like the teeth of the Java giant. "It almost seems to confirm the view of the noted paleontologist Dr. Weidenreich that there were giants on the earth in those days," Broom said then.

Upon his return from the United States, Broom again plunged into work. Honorary degrees, awards, and medals had come to him, for the world's recognition was then his. One great national and international honor had topped them all. In celebration of his eightieth year, November 30, 1946 through November 30, 1947, the Royal Society of South Africa arranged for a major scientific gathering and for the special publication of a *Robert Broom Commemorative Volume.*

The high point of the meeting was a dinner at which the doctor spoke. "Either God has been on my side, or I have been on God's side," said the doctor, and the suspicion swept some of his listeners that he firmly believed the first alternative was the correct one.

A trip to the caves was planned as an important part of the celebration. Most of the scientists dressed for the expedition in what is almost their uniform, khaki and stout shoes. The doctor, however, in fitting observance of the occasion, wore not only his usual wing collar and striped tie, but a tail coat. At the end of the day the usual Broom phenomenon was repeated. The doctor left looking as though he were ready to step into a receiving line; the others, all in their field regalia, were bedraggled.

Many of the leading figures of anthropology contributed scientific chapters to the commemorative volume, including William King Gregory of Columbia University, Charles L. Camp of the University of California, Dart, Weidenreich, L. B. S. Leakey, explorer of East African fossils, W. E. Le Gros Clark of Oxford, and Broom himself. General Smuts wrote the foreword.

The doctor and his aide supplied a chapter on some new types of mammal-like reptiles. Broom also complied the bibliography of his work. "It seems better," he said, refusing any truck with false modesty, "that a scientist should compile his own bibliography than that he should leave the work for another to do after he is dead." Broom listed more than four hundred publications.

During this last and most famous phase of his career the tall, spare doctor suffered no diminution of his energy and determination. His nose was large and jutting, his chin pointed and firm; the strong bony structure of his face seemed almost as evident as that of some of his skulls. His hair was gray, with a suggestion of curl in it, and his eyeglasses seemed to settle comfortably beneath heavy dark brows.

For all his drive and inclination for controversy, Broom always had a disposition that drew friends and admirers. Part of his attractiveness lay in his wry humor. When a friend met him on his way to a lecture with three or four skulls tucked under his arm, the doctor made a face and muttered: "Alas, poor Yorick, I knew him well."

He delighted in the fact that two rodents were named for him, *Gebrillus pæba broomi* and *Otomys unisulcatus broomi.* He was equally honored when a friend and associate named a bat *Pipstrellus Kuhli broomi.*

That a man with a medical career and such a completely absorbing subprofession could also have had hobbies seems improbable, but Broom was given to improbables. The doctor's hobbies were part of his uncanny instinct for collecting. He amassed a large and valuable collection of old Transvaal stamps.

He also was able to detect a fine work of art almost as surely as a hidden fossil. During one visit to London he noticed a small water-color sketch signed "J. Reynolds" in a heap on an art-dealer's barrow. His quick judgment told him that it was genuine, but he hurried to the British Museum to check the signature. It was as he thought. He went back immediately, only to find that someone had purchased the sketch a few minutes after he had left. The dealer, however, offered him three others, all signed, and apparently as genuine as the first. He wanted eighteen shillings for them. When the doctor found that he had only fifteen shillings in his pocket, the dealer let him have them for that amount. Among the three was a sketch of Lady Hamilton, made in 1875, the year before she went to Naples.

Broom thereafter got considerable enjoyment out of the thought that he had acquired an original portrait of Lady Hamilton by Sir Joshua Reynolds for five shillings. Through other such happy finds, the art collection displayed on the walls of the doctor's office was valued at about seven thousand pounds.

The doctor's instinct in the choice of a wife was equally sure. Without a murmur Mrs. Broom lived in the country townships to which her husband's work took him, and accepted all the other tribulations of marriage to so ardent a scientist and collector.

No life could have been fuller, and few men have made more significant scientific contributions to anthropology. Even before Broom died, on April 6, 1951, at the age of eighty-four, scientific appraisal of his work was making certain of his recognition as the man who discovered the immediate origin of man and mammals.

Although many scientists studied the South African finds, the first scientific appraisal of them appeared in the *1949 Yearbook of Physical Anthropology.* The principal evaluation was made by Wilfrid E. Le Gros Clark, professor of anatomy at Oxford University.

When Clark began his studies, Broom had found the remains of more than thirty individual South African ape-men or Australopithecinæ. Among the thirty were infants, juveniles, and adults, both young and aged. The fossils had come from several different sites and were in an excellent state of preservation. Never before had anthropology had such a wealth of material with which to work. Years would be required to complete the scientific studies of the materials on hand.

In a summary at the beginning of his report, Clark held: "From all of this material it is evident in some respects that [the Australopithecinæ] were definitely apelike creatures with small brains and large jaws. Indeed, in the general proportions of braincase and facial skeleton they represent a simian level of development not very different from that of the modern large apes.

"But in the details of the construction of the skull, in their dental morphology, and in their limb bones, the simian features are combined with a number of characters in which they differ from recent or fossil apes and at the same time approximate quite markedly to the Hominidæ [the family that includes modern man]. All those who have had the opportunity of examining the original material are agreed on these hominid characters; the real issue is the question of their evolutionary and taxonomic significance."

Not to make any loose comparisons, Clark compiled photographic records of ninety skulls of modern large apes from collections at Oxford and the British Museum. He then meticulously compared them with the South African skulls. Looking at the bareness of a skull, the layman is inclined to wonder what a scientist can see in it. To the scientist, however, it is as full of information as a combined master road map and encyclopedia. To illustrate the type of thing the anthropologist looks for, here are a few of the comparisons made by Clark:

► The occipital torus is lower and the occipital condyles (both part of the joining of skull and neck) farther forward than in apes. These features indicate a poise of the head very different from that of the ape and approaching in some degree that characteristic of man.

► The supraorbital and frontal regions contrast strongly with those of the chimpanzee and are markedly different from those of the gorilla.

► The position of the brain case relative to the upper part

of the face has been estimated by what may be called the supraorbital height index, that is $\dfrac{FB}{AB} \times 100$. (Clark divided the skull into precise measurement areas and thus could accurately compare the various areas). In 25 gorilla skulls the corrected

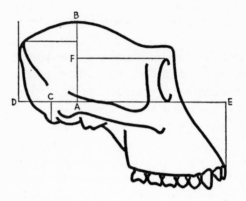

FOR STUDY THE SCIENTIST LAYS OUT THE SKULL IN PRECISE MEAS-UREMENT AREAS. HE THEN CAN MAKE ACCURATE COMPARISONS. BY MEASURING THE HEIGHT OF THE SKULL IN RELATION TO THE UPPER PART OF THE FACE, FB OVER AB, CLARK DETERMINED THAT THE SKULL HEIGHT OF THE APE-MAN WAS OUTSIDE THE RANGE OF THE APES AND WITHIN THE LIMITS OF MAN.

average of this index is estimated at not higher than 50. In a series of 15 female gorilla skulls, the maximum index was found to be 50. In 38 chimpanzees it is 47.1. In 25 orang skulls, 49.2. The supraorbital index of the Australopithecinæ skull No. 5 (Mrs. Ples) is 68, and here again it surpasses the range of variation in the ape skulls examined and comes within the limits of the Hominidæ.

Many such comparisons were made. The words used generally are enlightening only to the expert. Clark, however, superimposed an outline of a chimpanzee skull on a drawing of the skull of Mrs. Ples. He did the same thing with the skull of an orang. At once the striking difference was made clear to anyone. Point by point it could be seen how completely different Mrs. Ples was from either the chimpanzee or the orang.

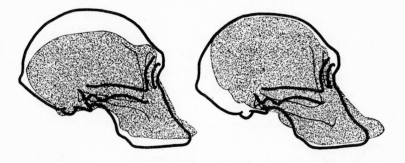

THE APE-MEN OF SOUTH AFRICA HAD SMALL BRAINS AND LARGE JAWS, LIKE THE APES. BUT HOW DRAMATICALLY THEY DIFFERED FROM THE APES WAS SHOWN WHEN CLARK SUPERIMPOSED THE SKULL OF A CHIMPANZEE ON THE SKULL OF AN APE-MAN (LEFT). AT THE RIGHT THE SKULL OF AN ORANGUTAN IS SUPERIMPOSED.

The most detailed study was also made of the teeth of both groups—their size, their shape, their structure, their placement, the wear shown.

After this exacting comparison Clark concluded: "It is apparent that the Australopithecine dentition (permanent and deciduous) shows a great many characters in which it is clearly distinguished from that of the anthropoid apes and at the same time shows remarkable similarities with that of man."

Were the teeth of the South African ape-men anything like those of Java and Peking man? Using all the available data, Clark decided that they were.

"There is no question but that the dentition of the Pithecanthropus group [Java man and Peking man] is a hominid type of dentition," he reported. "And now it appears that this is no less the case with the Australopithecinæ. But if this is so, and if the commonly accepted criteria of dental morphology are applied in the present instance, it is difficult to avoid the conclusion that the Australopithecinæ should be placed in the category of the Hominidæ. Such a conclusion does not conflict with the evidence of the skull: on the contrary it is clearly consistent with it."

Turning to comparisons of the limb bones, Clark found them much more on the human than the ape plan.

The pelvis, as Broom had pointed out, was so decidedly human that Clark felt compelled to examine the charge that it might simply have become mixed with the ape-man bones. He emphasized that it was found within a few yards of several skulls and teeth and that Broom reported to him that all of the Sterkfontein remains found during 1947 and 1948 came from an area measuring about fifteen feet by fifteen feet. Apart from the close association, Clark cited the "intrinsic evidence of the pelvis itself" as proof that it belonged to the ape-man. Though the bone was predominantly human, he, like Broom, was impressed by features that were not to be seen in modern man.

The Oxford professor expressed the opinion that the pelvic bone only clinched the evidence previously given by the set of the skull and the limb bones: the ape-men stood and walked very much like men.

The small size of the brain—it is smaller by two hundred to four hundred or more cubic centimeters than those of Java and Peking man—was not considered by Clark as interfering with the conclusions drawn from the skull and limb skeletons. "It is obviously to be presumed," he commented, "that the earliest representatives of the hominid sequence would certainly have had a brain of no greater volume."

If a hypothetical picture could be constructed of the an-

cestral forerunners of Homo at a stage in evolution when the
brain volume was about six hundred cubic centimeters, Clark
ventured the opinion that those ancestors might have looked
very much like the South African ape-men.

His verdict: "It seems a reasonable inference that the
Australopithecinæ either represent a group of early hominids
which occupied a position quite close to the main line of later
hominid evolution, or else they represent only slightly modified
descendants of such a group.

"As between these two possible alternatives, a decision
must depend partly on the geological age of the South African
fossils and this still remains very uncertain." [1]

Clark predicted that it may be some time before the full
significance of "these astonishingly primitive hominids" is recognized. Relatively few have been able to examine the original
material. The Oxford professor added too: "I have the impression that some critics are reluctant to accept the evidence at its
face value just because it is so abundant and so consistent, because it seems, in fact, 'almost too good to be true.' "

By all the evidence, men at last had met their ancestors.

Another conviction was also growing. The impressive South
African ape-man fossils pointed directly to the possibility that
man originated in Africa.

At the Wenner-Gren International Symposium on Anthropology, in New York in 1952, Père Pierre Teilhard de Chardin,
one of the world's experts on early man and his origins, set
forth the thesis: "It becomes difficult not to accept the idea that
the Dark Continent is precisely the one which during the upper Cenozoic acted as the main laboratory for the zoological
development and earliest establishment of man on this planet.

"It apparently is in the depths of Africa (and not on the

[1] Dr. Kenneth Page Oakley, of the British Museum (Natural History), went to South Africa in 1953 to study the possibility of applying
his fluorine test to the ape-men and animal fossils. Such tests have helped
to determine the age and geological sequence of some of the most important British fossils.

shores of the Mediterranean or on the Asiatic plateau) that the primeval center of human expansion and dispersion must have been located, long before this center shifted in much later times, toward (or even split between) Eurasia and America."

The French priest added that around this fundamental proposition the whole of anthropology's perspective on the "biological and historical processes of hominization" is being broadened and readjusted.

There seems to be every prospect that man soon will have to acknowledge a new birthplace and homeland of his kind.

The fossil discoveries in South Africa, Java, and China supplied a new answer to that ever tantalizing question: how and where did man originate? The greatest gaps in the record were filled in. The important links are no longer missing. And a start can now be made on the main outlines of the evolutionary story of man.

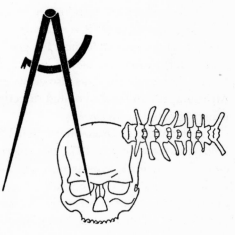

Part III

A CHANGED THEORY OF MAN'S EVOLUTION

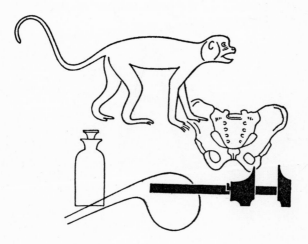

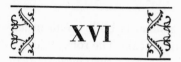

XVI

KNOPF

URANIUM AND THE AGE OF THE EARTH

As CONVINCING NUMBERS of man's early ancestors began to emerge from their long obscurity, another question came more forcefully to the forefront than ever before. How old is man?

The point has always aroused man's curiosity. Just as someone whose birth records have been lost may have a sense of uncertainty about his place in the world, so does man feel unsure because he cannot date his own beginnings. The urge to know is deep.

More than this, the question of how old we humans are is a crucial one to the whole theory of evolution and to many related branches of science. Has there been time for the infinitely slow changes that Darwin assumed were the basis of evolution? Or, put the other way round, if man has been in existence for a shorter time, could he have changed as much as the fossil records show he has? The questions are basic, and in the end the theory of evolution must stand or fall by the answers to them. Either evolution is possible in the time that has passed, or it is impossible.

But the problem of how old man is and of the time available for his evolution is one that so far has never been directly answerable.

Recorded dates begin a mere four thousand or five thousand years ago. One of the first reliable ones is that of the eclipse of the sun that occurred in 2238 B.C., immediately before the capture and destruction of Ur by the Elamites. Beyond that earliest written moment in time, scientists until recently have been forced to rely upon comparisons, sequences, and indirect evidences.

In that way geologists built up an order of past ages and an approximate time scale. The rocks that lay deepest were the oldest—provided, of course, they were undisturbed. They could

RECORDED TIME IS BRIEF. RENAISSANCE DOME, ROMAN ARCH, PYR-AMID—MAN'S MONUMENTS AND HIS WRITTEN DATES SOON END.

be placed in the three oldest geologic ages, the Archeozoic, the Proterozoic, and the Paleozoic. The rocks formed on top of these older layers were assigned to the Mesozoic, and the more recent, the top deposits, to the Cenozoic. That provided a geologic time scale.

By examining the fossils found in these various layers of rock, a timetable also was worked out for life. It showed life's progression in time from the simplest algæ buried in the oldest rocks, on up through the fish, the reptiles, the mammals, and man. Thus life could be roughly timed too.

But to say that the fossil remains of man are found only in the recent Cenozoic deposits did not solve the problem of how old man is. For how many years ago were the more recent rocks laid down? That was difficult to decide.

In the first fifty years of this century the ideas of science about when the different geologic eras occurred and how long they and their subdivisions lasted changed radically and profoundly. The change was far greater than that brought about in the world of 1492 by the discovery of America. The whole concept of time was modified.

THE AGE OF THE EARTH IS MULTIPLIED BY TWENTY. IN THE OPENING YEARS OF THE TWENTIETH CENTURY THE AGE OF THE EARTH OFTEN WAS SET AT 100 MILLION YEARS—REPRESENTED BY DASH-SIZE LINE AT TOP. NOW URANIUM DATING HAS FIXED THE AGE OF THE EARTH AT MORE THAN 2 BILLION YEARS—REPRESENTED BY LONG LINE.

It was altered because new techniques suddenly disclosed that the earth was far older than anyone had thought before 1900. The age of the earth was not doubled or tripled, but multiplied twenty times!

Necessarily, the time allowed for the geological eras and their subdivisions also was changed, for the length of the part was dependent on the length of the whole.

Science was staggered by the stupendous change. To round up the new ideas, to appraise them, to provide a new perspective, the National Research Council in the late 1920's set up a special committee on the Age of the Earth. A Californian who had shaped a brilliant career in geology at Yale was chosen to head it: Adolph Knopf.

Knopf was born in San Francisco in 1882, and early showed his interest in geology. He took his B.S., M.S., and Ph.D. degrees at the University of California, the last in 1909. After working with the U. S. Geological Survey in Alaska and the West, he joined the faculty of Yale as an associate professor of geology. That was in 1920. He progressed up the academic ladder until in 1938 he became Sterling professor of geology. He held that chair until his retirement, and his return to the West, in 1951.

As chairman of the National Research Council committee, Knopf invited a number of outstanding geologists to work with him. Out of their studies, in 1931, there came a large volume: *The Age of the Earth.* It went into the background of the changes, into the new timing techniques; and it gave the world its first complete scientific evaluation of where it then stood in time.

The picture was a startling one, made all the more so by a review of what had been thought before, and of why the old ideas had crumbled before the new.

When the *Beagle* sailed around the world, Darwin saw the unmistakable evidence of the majestic pace at which the forces of nature had shaped and reshaped the continents and sea basins, and he knew that the world was very old. Old enough, he assumed, for life to have evolved from its simplest beginnings up to man. He did not attempt, however, to estimate how much time was entailed.

During the latter part of the nineteenth century, others undertook this trackless task. One ingenious means after another was devised for measuring the age of the earth.

Lord Kelvin based one estimate on the time required for the earth to cool from a molten mass to its present well-encrusted form—some forty million years. His reasoning and his mathematics seemed unassailable. And yet evolution at the rate envisioned by Darwin and his followers could not have taken place within that constricted time. Something was wrong. The Darwinians chafed at the tight bonds Lord Kelvin had clamped upon them, but saw no means of escape. Not until several years after the opening of the new century, and the discovery of a new kind of timing, did the fatal flaw in Lord Kelvin's reasoning become evident. Then his estimate of forty million years from molten mass to present-day earth collapsed almost overnight.

Joly was another to venture into this unknown of unknowns. His base of departure was the salt in the sea. By computing the amount of salt washed into the sea each year and dividing it into the salt in the world oceans, he arrived at an earth age of eighty to ninety million years.

Two assumptions underlay his figures. The first was that the rate at which salt is carried into the oceans and other waters had remained constant through all time. Obviously it had not. At times erosion had cut greedily into the land, dissolving the rocks and leaching out their chemicals. In other eras the process had been slow. Joly's second assumption—that sodium has been steadily accumulating in the oceans—proved equally untenable.

Another scientist fixed upon an age of fifty-seven million years, based on the separation of the moon from the earth.

Nor did geologists neglect what seemed like the most evident measurement of the earth's age, the thickness of its sedimentary rocks. From the very beginning, as soon as the earth's crust had firmed, the rains began wearing away the land and transporting it down to the seas.

The silt, along with the shells, skeletons, and limy remains of unimaginable millions of sea creatures, settled to the bottom. Grain by grain, film by film, layer by layer, the sediments accumulated on ocean and lake floors. In time they compacted into stone. When the seas later receded and the former sea floors were elevated, the one-time sediments came to form much of the covering of the earth.

If it were possible to calculate how much time had been consumed in the formation of the earth's sedimentary deposits, a fairly accurate estimate could be made of the earth's age. Many a scientist tried, and the estimates ranged all the way from twenty-five million years to one hundred million.

But here again there was a major flaw. No one could be certain of how thick the sedimentary rocks lay. Every time a calculation was made based on one thickness, still greater depths were discovered. According to the latest findings, the greatest thickness of the rocks is now believed to be about fifty-eight miles. No one is certain, however, that the sedimentary layer will not prove to be somewhat deeper. A fantastic pad of the rock formed in water lies over the earth's core.

There was another fallacy in trying to tell time by the sedimentary rocks. Not all were laid down at the same rate. Some reliable recent studies have indicated that enough grains of sand may be piled up on a sea bottom to form one foot of sandstone in 450 years. But it may take 900 years to build up one foot of shale from the slowly settling muds, and 2,250 years to compile one foot of limestone from the myriad shells and bodies of the minute inhabitants of the water.

And not only were the rates of formation different for the different kinds of stone, but they undoubtedly varied in different periods of the past and in different areas of the world. As a time clock the sedimentary rocks were unsatisfactory and frustrating. One geologist called estimates based on the thickness of the sedimentary strata not worth the paper they were written on. Somewhat sadly Knopf concurred; "this judgment is unfortunately true in the main," he said.

Only in a limited, though remarkable way has dependable time information so far been wrested from the layering of the rock. And such as there is exists only because a few exceptional rock formations almost literally carry their own dates in years impressed upon them.

Some Miocene shales at Oeningen, Switzerland, speak in a unique way of the passage of a year. At the bottom of each layer of these shales are the blossoms of poplar and camphor trees, certain harbingers of the spring. Lying over them is a thin film filled with the winged ants and the summer's fruit of the elm and poplar. And completing the layer—or varve, as it is called—is a zone studded with the autumn fruit of the camphor tree, the wild grape, and the date plum.

Layer by layer these shales marvelously record the passing of the seasons and the years. Each year's story is fixed forever in the format of the stone. Age and rate of deposition are an open secret for anyone to read.

Unfortunately the shales of Oeningen are still alone in the perfection of their recording of the passing seasons. But there is a growing belief that other rocks also must record what went on upon the earth at the time of their formation, if science could only discern it.

In Wyoming and Colorado are vast deposits of "Green River" oil shales, which may help to establish the point—and also supply the United States with an almost unlimited new source of oil. The shales are very thinly layered. Each layer consists of two laminæ, one of which contains more carbonaceous material than the other. It is believed that the more carbonaceous layer was formed during the summer, when leaves and stalks washed down into the two fresh-water lakes where the shales were deposited. During the rest of the year there was less organic matter to drift down to the bottom.

The two laminæ are thought to represent the sediment deposited in one year. Since each layer or varve, averages $\frac{1}{2000}$th of a foot in thickness, and the beds are 2,600 feet thick, it would seem that some five million years passed in their formation.

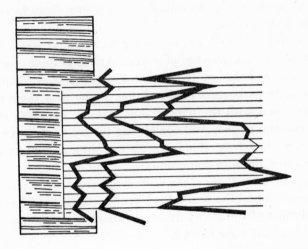

VARVE AND VARVE READING. ON THE LEFT, TYPICAL VARVES OR LAYERS OF STONE. THE FIRST ZIGZAG LINE SHOWS VARIATIONS IN THE AMOUNT OF SEDIMENTARY MATERIAL DEPOSITED IN DIFFERENT YEARS. THE OTHER TWO VARVE READINGS ARE COMPARATIVE.

These great cliffs, almost mountains of oil shales, make up about one third of the deposits laid down in their geological age, the Eocene. And yet it is impossible to jump to the conclusion that they account for one third of Eocene time. The studies that might justify such an estimate for this important subdivision of the Cenozoic have not yet been made. There is high hope, however, that studies of these and other rocks formed in telltale annual varves may in the future help to date part of the past.

While science tried unsuccessfully to tell the age of the earth by studies of its cooling, of the salt in the ocean, and of the

thickness of the sedimentary rocks, wholly unexpected assistance came from physics. Physics discovered the strange phenomenon of radioactivity. And suddenly there was a new and
direct clue to the age of the earth.

Uranium, the first radioactive material to come to the
world's attention, was found as an oxide in 1789 and named for
Uranus, the father of the gods. Very appropriately, the geologist Arthur Holmes thought, "for in its own right uranium is
a trinity and two of its members are the parents of a numerous
progeny of descendants."

But more than a century passed before Roentgen learned
that uranium compounds gave off rays capable of penetrating
black paper and making an impression on a photographic
plate. This new and puzzling characteristic was called radioactivity. Evidently it was inherent in the uranium atom itself.

Then Mme Curie found that thorium also possessed radioactive properties, and that pitchblende, the natural ore of
uranium, was four or five times more radioactive than could be
accounted for by its content of uranium and thorium. The story
of how the famous Polish-born scientist laboriously separated
one ton of pitchblende and, in the last seemingly useless bit of
residuum, found radium is one of the classics of science.

Sir Ernest Rutherford and Hans Geiger devised an electrical
method of counting the particles expelled. They were able to
magnify the passage of each particle so that it would give a
kick to the needle of an electrometer.

From all this brilliant pioneering, it became clear that
uranium and its radioactive elements were unstable. They were
constantly breaking down, disintegrating, losing their radioactivity. What was left when the spark was gone was a different substance, one distinct from its parents in physical and
chemical properties. It was lead! Uranium turned into lead!

What was equally important, it made this transition at a
fixed rate. Later, science was to learn that this rate is one of the
steadiest things known; changes in neither space, time, tem-

perature, nor other conditions seem to affect it in the slightest. Once started, it continues without stop or deviation. Here, then, was something solid to tie to, a clock free of all the vagaries and variations of other measurable processes.

And at the end of four and one half billion years, half of uranium's radioactivity was gone!

The uranium from which our lead has come must therefore have been present when the earth was born, when it was wrenched from its parent, the sun. The life of uranium encompassed the entire history of the globe. Uranium was a time-piece ticking off earth's history, and science at last had a reasonably accurate measure of the earth's age.

But in the early years of this century not all of this was as clear as it later became. B. B. Boltwood, a Yale radio-chemist, in 1906 was the first to glimpse uranium's possibilities for telling time. Boltwood was impressed with the disintegration theory. He also had noticed that lead is present in nearly all radioactive minerals. Perhaps—at that time he had to say perhaps—lead was the final disintegration product of uranium.

Boltwood set out to check. He found first of all that the amount of lead per gram of uranium varies in different minerals. That suggested another idea—he would line up the minerals according to their lead-uranium ratio.

The results were revealing, enlightening. The greater the amount of lead, the older was the geological formation from which the ore came. The theory was substantiated; whether you started with the answer and worked forward or began at the beginning and progressed down to the answer, it checked. Age and lead were measurably linked.

The physicists went eagerly to work. Although the process that became known as lead or uranium dating was not to be perfected for a number of years, it was at once apparent that the oldest rocks were possibly twenty times older than science had thought. It looked as though at least two thousand million years had been consumed in changing uranium into lead in the oldest radioactive minerals. Hence the earth had to be at least two thousand million years old! The earlier estimates fixing the age of the earth under one hundred million years went crashing.

As research continued and knowledge of radioactivity rapidly increased, the first estimates of an almost unimaginable age became only surer.

Most radioactive minerals contain three radioactive elements, U 238, U 235, and thorium. Each produces a lead of a different atomic weight, lead 206, 207, and 208, and at a different rate.

Thus three examinations for age were possible. The physicists saw a way to obtain three independent determinations from a single mineral. One is based on the ratio between U 238 and the radiogenic lead derived from it. The second is based on the ratio between the thorium in the mineral and the lead that comes from it. The third, in a sense, is a cross-check. It is made by obtaining the ratio between the lead derived from the uranium and that from the thorium.

"If all three determinations agree," Knopf pointed out, "assurance is rendered trebly sure. As the most ancient minerals were formed as much as 2,000 million years ago such a threefold check on determinations of age is highly welcome."

Samples of radioactive minerals were collected from all over the world. In the method used by Alfred O. Nier, first at Harvard and later at the University of Minnesota, lead ions are produced by bombarding lead-iodide vapor with electrons. The ion currents then are measured with an electric tube amplifier. An analysis can generally be obtained in two days, and the results rechecked if desired.

Although the method proper is an absolute one—that is, sure and precise—it is beset by many complexities. Interpretation of the results coming from the apparatus is often far from easy.

In some cases the ages shown by a test of the three different leads are in remarkable agreement, and the interpretive problem is at a minimum. Nier reported one Parry Sound uranianite that showed an age of 1,003 million years on the basis of its uranium lead, an age of 945 million years on its thorium lead, and one of 1,030 million years on the ratio between the two. A Connecticut samarskite checked in respectively at 253 million years, 266 million, and 280 million, plus or minus a possible error of 15 million years.

On the other hand, some minerals show disconcerting differences on the three lead tests. One of the most disturbing was an unusual Swedish marine-oil shale known as kolm. Kolm is one of the few ancient radioactive minerals that can be precisely placed in a geologic sequence. Embedded in it are trilobites and other fossils dating back to the earliest appearance of life on earth, or at least to its first appearance in the rocks. The little animals whose skeletal remains drifted down through the waters and into the kolm were the dominant inhabitants of the seas at a time when no life had yet crept out of the sheltering waters onto the harsh land.

The uranium in the kolm seems to have been precipitated out of the sea water and into the stone at the time the stone was forming. The lead that came from the uranium ran up an age of 380 million years on tests. But the lead derived from thorium indicated an age of 770 million years. Scientists considered the latter figure manifestly too large. Something seemed to be wrong.

For a while the trouble could not be fathomed. Then it was discovered that one of the intermediate radioactive products was radon, a gas with a half-life [1] of only a few days. If some

---

[1] A half-life is the length of time in which one half of the radioactive atoms in a material will have exploded and become non-radioactive. For example, radiophosphorus has a half-life of fourteen days. If at a given time a given amount has 100 million explosions per second, there will be only 50 million explosions per second at the end of fourteen days. With each subsequent fourteen-day period that passes, the number of explosions will again be reduced by one half.

of this fleeting gas had diffused away, the amount of lead derived from the uranium would have been reduced and the
whole comparison with the thorium lead badly thrown off. It
looked as though this was what had happened. By solving two
simultaneous equations, the probable age of the Swedish kolm
was fixed very reliably at 440 million years.

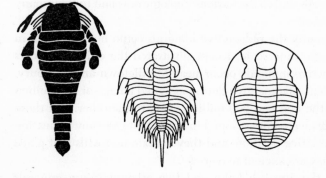

TRILOBITES. THESE ANIMALS WERE DOMINANT INHABITANTS OF
THE SEAS AT A TIME WHEN THERE WAS NO LIFE ON THE LAND.
THEIR FOSSIL REMAINS ARE FOUND IN SOME OF THE MOST ANCIENT
ROCKS.

Some of the age records piled up by lead dating sounded
almost as fantastic as their total years. Knopf reported one of
the oldest, a uranianite from Sinyaya Pala, Karelia, Soviet Union. On the basis of the tests it had been around for some 1,852
million years.

Like most of the other extremely old radioactive minerals,
the Russian uranianite occurs in what the geologists call peg-
matite dikes. The dikes are veins or masses of mineral intrusive
in still older rocks, rocks that must have been there when the
radioactive minerals were formed. It is thus that the geologists
and physicists calculate that the earth must be at least 2,000
million years old. And it may be even older.

Geologists were at first startled and upset by the cataclysmic action with which the physicists wiped out the world they had pictured. Not until the 1930's was it possible to reconcile the two. The bringing together of the two was one of the major accomplishments of Knopf's committee.

That done, a further problem became acute. If the earth had to be given an age of 2,000 million years, how much time was to be allotted to the various geologic eras and to their many subdivisions?

Frequently the radioactive minerals could not be placed in the geologic time scale. Knopf illustrated the difficulty. Veins of radioactive minerals occur near Middletown and Danbury, Connecticut. Radioactive dating assigned an age of 350 million years to the one and 260 million years to the other. But these pegmatites were not arranged in strata that gave any indication of their relative position, and they contain no fossils that place them. They are ancient mavericks.

Only the Swedish kolm and two other uranium minerals have so far supplied clues to their geologic position. A pitchblende from Joachimstal, Bavaria, and a thorite from Norway both showed a radioactive age of 230 million years. In both cases the surrounding rocks and the fossils buried in them pointed to their origin in early Permian times—that is to say, at the very end of the Paleozoic. Upon this basis, science now infers that the Paleozoic era ended about 200 million years ago.

A firm start also has been made in fixing time at the other end of the scale. Many years ago a great "thrust," a tongue of stone more than fifty miles long, cut through the mountains of the Front Range of Colorado. On it and seemingly related to it in origin is some pitchblende that on several tests has shown an age of nearly 60 million years.

The big thrust and some mountain changes that immediately preceded it have long been regarded as marking the beginning of the Cenozoic period. Thus if the pitchblende is 60 million years old and the preceding activity can be estimated at

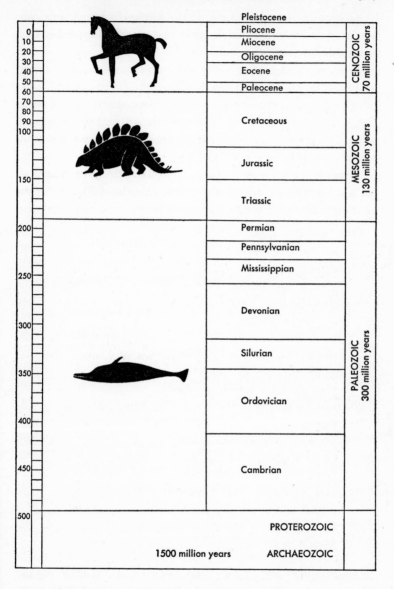

Pleistocene		
Pliocene		CENOZOIC 70 million years
Miocene		
Oligocene		
Eocene		
Paleocene		
Cretaceous		MESOZOIC 130 million years
Jurassic		
Triassic		
Permian		PALEOZOIC 300 million years
Pennsylvanian		
Mississippian		
Devonian		
Silurian		
Ordovician		
Cambrian		
PROTEROZOIC		
1500 million years	ARCHAEOZOIC	

THE GEOLOGIST'S CHART OF THE TIME OF THE EARTH AND THE LIFE
THAT LIVED UPON IT IN THESE PERIODS.

10 million years, the opening of the modern geologic era can be dated at 70 million years ago. The pitchblende dates this turning-point in time.

With the dates of the Cenozoic and the Paleozoic fairly well fixed by lead dating, the length of the intervenient Mesozoic period can be figured by the simple process of subtracting. If the Paleozoic ended 200 million years ago and the Cenozoic began 70 million years ago, the Mesozoic must have stretched over the 130 million years in between.

Upon this underpinning, fragile-seeming to the layman and yet solid to the scientist with his full knowledge, Knopf drew up a new outline of the timing of the major geologic eras:

> 2,000,000,000 to 500,000,000 years: the Archeozoic and Proterozoic. At least three fourths of geologic time, 1,500 million years, passed during these two periods. This great span of time went by before any life other than algæ became abundant on this planet, or at least left any record in the rocks.
>
> 500,000,000 to 200,000,000 years: the Paleozoic. In this stretch of 300 million years, seas and lands changed many times, and life advanced from the simple little algæ up to the primitive reptiles.
>
> 200,000,000 to 70,000,000 years: the Mesozoic. During this 130 million years the Rockies and the Andes and other great mountains were upthrust, and evolution continued on from the first dinosaurs through the birds and into the age when the reptiles ruled the earth.
>
> 70,000,000 years to the present: the Cenozoic. In this most recent and still continuing era came repeated advances and retreats of the great polar icecap, and the rise of man.

In allotting 300 million years to the Paleozoic, 130 million to the Mesozoic, and 70 million to the Cenozoic, Knopf set up approximately a 5:2:1 ratio for the division of time since life began its upward climb.

But fixing the grand divisions of time is not enough. To assign man to his place and to date other important epochs such as the ice age or the coal-forming era, a finer breakdown is necessary. The subdivisions as well as the grand divisions must be defined in time.

So far dating by radioactivity has not been carried far enough to fill in the whole calendar. It is as though the seasons had been sketched in, but the duration of the days and weeks had not been determined. Other means still must be used to date the various subdivision stages. One of the best available is the evolution of the horse. By studying the likely length of time required to change little eohippus into Equus, scientists have worked out a time schedule for the various subdivisions of the Cenozoic. On the basis of these and other studies, Knopf suggested the following division of the latest geologic era:

PLEISTOCENE	1	*million years*	
PLIOCENE	11	"	"
MIOCENE	17	"	"
OLIGOCENE	11	"	"
EOCENE	20	"	"
PALEOCENE	10	"	"
	70	"	"

It is hoped that radioactive and other absolute methods of dating will eventually make such estimates more exact.

"We can say that a solid framework for the absolute length of geologic time and its major sub-divisions has been constructed by the combined labor of geologists, chemists and physicists," Knopf summed up. "The highly important details such as the length of the sub-divisions from Cambrian through Pliocene, not a single one of which has yet been determined, remain as tasks for the future."

But the fixing of the "absolute length" of time and of its major subdivisions was enough to remake the concept of time. Dating with uranium and lead has stretched time, almost in the way a musician extends the bellows of an accordion. And the beginnings, the gray shadowy beginnings, have been stretched the most.

How vastly these changes have altered thought about man's period can perhaps be most dramatically highlighted by the way in which they have affected the time theories of one man.

When Sir Arthur Keith, the great English paleontologist, brought out the first edition of his *Antiquity of Man* in 1914, he drew up a timetable for man. He based it on the time estimates of the later geological ages published by W. J. Sollas in 1900. By studying the rate at which the rivers laid down their deposits and estimating the thickness of the accumulations—a method long since discredited—Sollas fixed the duration of the Pleistocene at 400,000 years and the Pliocene at 500,000 years.

Keith also drew a genealogical tree, showing how men and apes and other groups had branched out from the main trunk of life. He had the modern human branch separating from its ancestral stem about two million years ago. But Keith felt that most men, in considering the antiquity of their race, think not of the date at which the human lineage separated from the anthropoids, but of the period at which man reached some approximation to his present status and intelligence.

"From what we know and what we must infer of the ancestry of Eoanthropus (Piltdown Man), of Neanderthal, and modern man, we have reasonable grounds for presuming that man was approaching the human standard in size of brain by the commencement of the Pliocene period," Keith wrote. In this way he fixed the age of modern man at about one million years.

By 1925, when he prepared a completely revised edition of his *Antiquity of Man*, Keith felt compelled to change his estimates. Many important discoveries of man's early tools and culture convinced him that he had overestimated the age of modern man. Regretfully, but yielding to what he considered the evidence, Keith cut his previous estimates in half. He allowed only 200,000 years for the Pleistocene and 300,000 for the Pliocene. Keith also felt that there was a very good chance that this time would have to be further reduced.

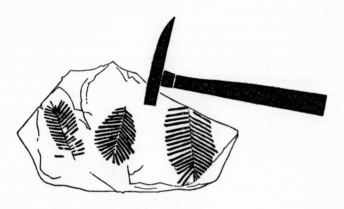

FOSSIL FERNS AND GEOLOGIST'S HAMMER

"If such a small sum is left at our disposal," he wrote, "then we shall have to conclude that evolutionary changes have moulded man during the Pleistocene at a much more rapid pace than we have hitherto conceived possible.

"I feel as Huxley did, when Lord Kelvin reduced the time limit at the disposal of evolutionists, that there must be a mistake somewhere."

Keith's misgivings proved well founded. Although the duration of the subdivisions of geologic time remain to be settled, there is no longer any question about their greater magnitude, and Keith's 1925 estimate of 200,000 years for the Pleistocene has been increased to 1,000,000, and his 300,000 for the Pliocene has been raised to something in the neighborhood of 11,-000,000 years.

And yet this imposing stretching of time at the recent end of the earth's timetable was as nothing. Radioactive dating had made a much vaster change in the whole grand backdrop of time against which man moves. At the beginning of this century, man's time was thought to be about 1/100th of the earth's time. In the new universe whose outlines were drawn by Knopf, man's span was reduced to 1/2000th of the whole. Man's sojourn on this planet became a mere moment.

Thus the rays emitted by a once little-known mineral enormously expanded the age of the earth and relatively reduced man's lifetime upon it.

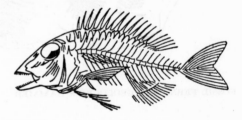

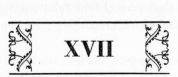

XVII

OAKLEY

FLUORINE AND THE AGE OF EARLY MAN

If AGE could only be read in the bones—anthropologists long have beguiled themselves with this dream. If there were some aging process inherent in the bones, or some other way in which the remains of men and animals could bespeak their own antiquity, a little more of the dimness that veils the past might be cleared away.

As things have always stood, the closest study of the structure of fossils taken from the earth, the most precise comparisons with other remains, the most exacting investigations of the strata or sites in which they were embedded, told only of relative ages. By comparisons, the anthropologist and geologist were able to say that the elephant, for example, from which these bones came probably lived before this rhinoceros, or this human skull probably precedes another, or, in technical terms, this fossil tooth is from the Mesozoic, that from the Cenozoic.

But to say that a fossil dated from the Cenozoic was not to fix its age in years except in the roughest way. Had historians been in the same plight, they would have been forced to tell their students: we know that Washington came before Lincoln, but we cannot determine whether he was born one hundred, two hundred, or two thousand years earlier.

Since exact answers have always been impossible, scientists have always disagreed about the dating of the bones yielded up by the ground. Controversies over every important find have raged for years. A better system for the placing of human fossil remains in their correct time-relations was sorely needed; it was fundamental to understanding their significance.

In 1802 an Italian chemist named Morichini detected traces of fluorine in the tooth of a fossil elephant found near Rome. It was an interesting clue to a possible change in the bone.

$$OH \geq F \gg Cl$$

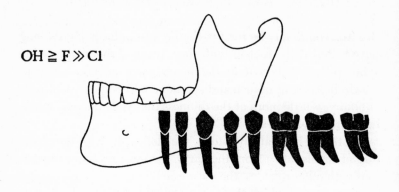

FLUORINE IS ABSORBED BY TOOTH AND BONE.

The French scientist Gay-Lussac held, however, that the "fluoric acid" probably had been absorbed by the animal during its lifetime. Two other French investigators came to a different conclusion. They ran some tests with new ivory and tooth enamel. There was no fluorine in them. "This singular circumstance seems to indicate that fluoric acid exists in the earth . . . that during the long continuance of these substances [ivories] in the earth they combine with fluoric acid," they reported.

More refined methods later disclosed that fluorine is absorbed by the teeth during life, but that bone buried in the earth is likely to absorb still more fluorine if it is exposed to fluorine-bearing waters.

An English chemist, James Middleton, was sufficiently impressed with this finding to read a paper before an 1844 meeting of the Geological Society of London claiming that fossil bones contain fluorine in proportion to their antiquity. He compared the fluorine content in some fossil bones with the fluorine in the bones of a 2,000-year-old Greek skeleton. In this way he estimated the age of one of his fossils at 7,700 years and the other, from Eocene beds in France, at 24,000 years.

This daring attempt at geochronology was not taken seriously and was largely forgotten until the principle was revived about fifty years later by the French mineralogist A. Carnot. Carnot analyzed a number of fossil bones, ranging from recognized Paleozoic age to recent. By averaging his findings he worked out a table indicating the fluorine content to be expected in the various geologic ages:

RECENT	0.3	*per cent*
PLEISTOCENE	1.5	" "
TERTIARY	2.3	" "
MESOZOIC	3.4	" "
PALEOZOIC	3.7	" "

The averages, unfortunately, concealed a crucial point. Bones and teeth in some localities had a much higher fluorine content than in others, for the amount of fluorine in ground waters varies widely. Much depended on where the fossil had been buried. The permeability of the matrix—the material in which the bones were embedded—also affected the amount of fluorine that might be absorbed. For these reasons Carnot's work, though interesting, was considered of no practical or scientific importance.

Later research has indicated, however, that Carnot himself understood this difficulty. In fact, he used fluorine dating to establish the relative, not the absolute, age of a human bone that had been unearthed at Billancourt, France. But few of his contemporaries realized the significance of this distinction, and it probably was for this reason that his work was entirely forgotten during the succeeding half century.

Two unrelated events during World War II rearoused interest in the old fluorine data. The Geological Survey of Great Britain undertook a survey of the phosphate resources of the country, and also a study of the effect of fluoridated water in reducing tooth decay in children.

A young geologist and anthropologist, Dr. Kenneth Page Oakley, was assigned to the work. He had been born at Amersham in 1911 and from his boyhood had been interested in prehistoric man, fossils, and rocks. There was nothing surprising in the fact that he took his degree at University College, London, in anthropology and geology. During the war he was transferred to the geological survey from his post at the British Museum (Natural History).

When Oakley came to the United States for scientific meetings, his American colleagues at first looked at him with a puzzled air; he resembled someone familiar to them. Then the answer occurred to them. He looked amazingly like Lincoln in his younger years.

As the British scientist delved back into the history of fluorine for the war survey, he saw its weaknesses as a tool for the general dating of fossils, but it struck him that it might be useful for sorting bones of different ages that might have become mixed together in the same deposit. "Animal or human bones which have been lying in a gravel bed for 200,000 years are likely to have fixed considerably more fluorine than a human skeleton interred in the same grave, say 2,000 years ago," he explained.

Thus if the bones in the same deposit showed the same fluorine content, it might be assumed that they had been in the ground for approximately the same time; or, if their fluorine content differed, that they had not come there simultaneously.

Oakley also saw that if there were associated animal bones that clearly belonged to the same geologic age as the bed, it would be pretty definitely possible to arrive at a new and more accurate age estimate for the human remains. At the time he did not know that Carnot had touched upon the same idea.

Oakley's proposal was discussed at a meeting of the British Association for the Advancement of Science in 1947, and at the Pan African Congress on Pre-History in the same year.

Dr. L. S. B. Leakey, curator of the Coryndon Museum of Nairobi and the discoverer of many East African fossils, was at the African meeting. He was trying to determine the age of some human skull fragments from the Kanjera-Kanam region of Kenya. Oakley suggested that if they were fluorine-tested along with some animal bones from the same site, light might be thrown on his problem. Leakey gladly accepted the offer and sent Oakley samples of both.

On this, its first test, fluorine dating failed. The Kanjera beds from which the fossils were taken were made up of volcanic ash, an ash exceedingly rich in fluorine. So rapidly did the bones absorb it that they early reached the saturation point. No separation according to time was possible. Too much fluorine too fast played havoc with the first trial.

Oakley recognized that fluorine testing was virtually doomed to failure on any bones from the tropics or other regions where conditions were likely to produce extremely rapid and variable mineralization. He decided to try again with fossils from a different kind of ground.

In 1948, some new fossil finds had again directed attention to a famous skeleton in the British closet: the Galley Hill skeleton. Arguments about its antiquity had been heatedly going on since the time of its discovery in 1888.

The controversial skeleton was unearthed about eight feet below the surface by a workman digging in a gravel pit at Galley Hill, Kent. It looked very ancient. With excitement running high, the headmaster of the adjoining school was summoned to see and advise about the strange bones protruding from the gravel face.

Before anything could be done, Robert Elliot, a printer and amateur archæologist, came out to the pit on one of his regular expeditions in search of flints. The workman who discovered the bones was in his pay and led him to the skeleton. Without any further ceremony, Elliot proceeded to dig it out.

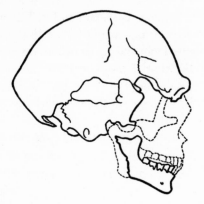

THE GALLEY HILL SKULL

A few days later Elliot took the bones to London, to E. T. Newton, a paleontologist. Newton was deeply interested and offered to study and mend them; but Elliot refused. He wanted to make his own study and description of them and went home with the bones. Somehow, he failed to get around to it.

In 1912, when a physician, Dr. Frank Corner, offered to buy the Galley Hill bones for one hundred pounds, Elliot parted with them. The new owner promptly deposited them on loan to the British Museum, and there they remained until 1948, when the doctor's widow withdrew them. Only a few small pieces of bone and some of the material that originally had adhered to the skeleton was left in the museum.

During the thirty-six years that the Galley Hill skeleton

rested uneasily in the museum, one group insisted that it was the remains of a very early man. Another group argued that the Galley Hill find was nothing more than a comparatively modern man who had been buried in the ancient gravels.

Elliot and the headmaster testified that the gravel deposits where the skeleton was found looked undisturbed to them. They saw no evidences of a burial. Sir John Evans, on the other hand, argued that whole skeletons seldom are discovered unless there has been a burial. On this circumstantial evidence alone, he was suspicious of the antiquity of Galley Hill man.

The Galley Hill skeleton had ardent proponents and opponents, with the latter probably outnumbering the former. The upshot was that the disputed skeleton was placed in what was known as a "suspense account."

In the summer of 1948, M. F. Ashley Montagu, an American anthropologist, went to England to study the Galley Hill region. He began a thorough restudy of the case at just about the time the museum decided to try to get at the truth about the skeleton by subjecting the few bits still in its possession to the new fluorine test.

The test was carefully made. In addition to samples taken from the Galley Hill bits, other samples were taken from twenty-two animal bones that had been found in the vicinity —no animal bones appeared in the deposit.

Bones from Galley Hill animals long identified with the Middle Pleistocene period showed from 1.7 to 2.8 per cent of fluorine. Upper Pleistocene fossils from the same district ranged from 0.9 to 1.4 per cent in fluorine content; those from the Holocene (recent) from 0.5 to 0.3.

The bones of Galley Hill man averaged 0.4 per cent! "Far from being Middle Pleistocene, the Galley Hill skeleton is a comparatively recent burial," Oakley announced. Galley Hill man thus stood revealed as a very late comer.

Montagu, working in conventional ways, had come to the same conclusion. His reanalysis of Galley Hill's bones indicated that they were not especially primitive. The absence of other bones in the gravel pit was significant too. Most of the gravel had undergone a complete decalcification (a washing away of the calcium) that would have destroyed any bones there when the process was taking place. Hence the bones of Galley Hill man must not have been there at the time.

The two findings were in striking confirmation of each other. Galley Hill man was permanently demoted.

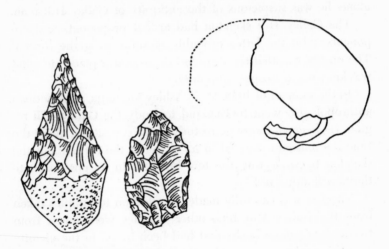

THE FLINT TOOLS OF SWANSCOMBE MAN, AND ALL THERE IS OF HIS ANCIENT SKULL

The Galley Hill results were all the more significant when another skull, known as the Swanscombe skull, was discovered only a few miles away. The structure of the skull proper and the animal bones associated with it indicated great age. This was borne out when it was subjected to the fluorine test. One sample from the skull disclosed a fluorine content of 1.9 per cent and another 2 per cent.

"The contemporaneity of this skull with the associated Acheulian hand-axe industry is completely confirmed," Oakley reported. "It is in fact the oldest known human cranium in Europe (it being understood that the Heidelberg mandible is older)." Oakley later estimated the age of the Swanscombe skull as not much more than 100,000 years.

As the fluorine test proved its worth in separating the ancient from the merely old, hope grew that here at last science might have a time tool for at least partially dating the past. In a number of scientific reports Oakley set out all the facts. At the same time he constantly cautioned against expecting more of fluorine than it could do. He warned again and again that it could not be used to draw comparisons between the ages of material found in different parts of the world. And he emphasized repeatedly that its usefulness lies in distinguishing between objects found at the same site and thus subjected to the same fluorine-bearing waters.

But one of the most baffling and contested cases of conjecturing the age of a skull lay well within the field marked out for fluorine dating. In 1908 Charles Dawson, an English lawyer who spent his spare time collecting early stone implements, fossils, and other natural-history materials, was walking along a road on the Piltdown common.

The common was a Sussex moorland, lying about 120 feet above sea level, and about a mile west of the river Ouse. From it, in the distance, it was possible to catch a glimpse of the English Channel. This was an ancient land, and in the vicinity the first English eoliths—stones of dawn—the first crude implements used by primitive man, had been found.

Suddenly Dawson noticed that the road was being repaired with some peculiar brown flints. He knew they were unusual in the district, and asked where they had come from. When he learned that they had been dug from a gravel bed on a near-by farm, he went to see the place.

The gravel pit was not much more than a shallow trench,

about four feet deep, lying between a hedge and a road leading to a farmhouse. The gravel was in strata, clearly laid down by running water, and had been cemented together by an oxide that had stained everything a deep brown. It looked to Dawson like the kind of place that might yield fossils. He asked the workmen to keep a sharp outlook for anything of the kind.

When Dawson stopped by a few days later, one of the men handed him a thick piece of human skull bone. A search failed to disclose any other remains. Nevertheless, Dawson continued to visit the pit. One day in 1911 he saw another piece of skull, including a part of the left brow ridge, lying on one of the rain-washed dumps. It was another part of his first find!

Dawson no longer had any doubts about the importance of his discovery. He enlisted the co-operation of Sir Arthur Smith-Woodward, noted paleontologist of the British Museum. Together they made a thorough and systematic search of the gravel spoil heaps. Their reward came in the spring of 1912 when they uncovered another large portion of the skull—a remarkable skull.

The human bones came from the lowest and darkest layer of the gravel. In that same layer were some very crude stone implements (eoliths), some of them blunted and rounded by rolling and washing in the ancient bed of the Ouse—the river had once flowed across the common. Also scattered through the gravel were bits of the teeth and bones of long-extinct elephants, hippopotamuses, a mastodon, rhinoceroses, horses, red deer, and beaver.

Although the bones of this strange assortment of animals—this was England—lay close together, it was certain they had not all lived at the same time.

One of the elephants, *Elephas planifrons,* and the mastodon undoubtedly belonged together, in one of the early warm, lush intervals that came between the ice invasions of the Pleistocene. The later species of elephant and the hippopotamus had flourished in the tropical jungles that covered England in another and later glacial interlude. The beaver probably belonged to a still more recent time.

Did Piltdown man belong to the time of the oldest animals or to the period of some of the others? Upon the answer depended a vast difference in his age.

ANOTHER ENGLAND. "ELEPHAS PLANIFRONS," A HIPPOPOTAMUS, AND BEAVER, ALL OF WHOSE BONES RESTED BESIDE THOSE OF PILTDOWN MAN ON THE PREHISTORIC PILTDOWN COMMON.

The authorities clashed. One faction cited impressive evidence to prove that the man whose skull lay buried in the gravel pit must have gone back to the Lower Pleistocene; perhaps he was the hunter of *Elephas planifrons* and the mastodon. Others were equally firm in placing him with the later-comers of the Middle or Upper Pleistocene.

Study of the Piltdown skull did not solve the enigma, for it was a most unusual skull. The jaw looked like that of an ape; the brain case like that of an early man. Comparisons showed that the jaw was almost indistinguishable from that of a young chimpanzee. The chin did not jut out like that of a human, but fell away like an ape's. A canine tooth, which turned up in the gravels soon after the skull, was a massive, projecting tusk, far more apelike than human.

And yet the experts could not get away from the human-ness of the brain case. It appeared human whether the fragments were studied separately or were put together. The pieces included a large part of the left side of the head and jaw, and part of the right.

Working with these bits and pieces, Sir Arthur Smith-Woodward reconstructed a being whose forehead was fairly high, but whose chinless jaw projected as in an ape. He named this peculiar man *Eoanthropus dawsoni* (Dawn man of Dawson).

But this was not the last of Eoanthropus's skull. Sir Arthur Keith, another distinguished anthropologist objected that a mistake had been made in putting the bones of Dawn man together. The reconstructed head seemed a little lopsided, and Sir Arthur argued that the skulls of primitive man and apes are markedly symmetrical.

Keith decided to try a restoration himself. He fitted the fragments together in such a way that Piltdown man had a much roomier brain case, one that might have held a brain of 1,500 cubic centimeters. Smith-Woodward had given Piltdown man a brain capacity of only 1,070 cubic centimeters, a decidedly subhuman amount.

Which was right? Keith's critics charged that it was impossible to join a few fragments, as Keith had, and come out with the correct form. They challenged Keith to try to put together a modern skull from a few equally incomplete pieces.

Keith accepted the dare. The contest was on. A group of anatomists cut a skull-cast of an ancient Egyptian woman into a few fragments no more revealing than those of the Piltdown skull. Keith went to work.

Unlike all the king's horses and all the king's men in the scarcely more famous case of Humpty-Dumpty, the anthropologist succeeded. In two days Keith had the Egyptian skull reconstructed in virtually its correct form. He successfully estimated its brain capacity to within twenty cubic centimeters of the right figure. His only mistake was in assuming that the skull was masculine, and providing it with the male's projecting brow ridges.

After this dramatic episode, the study of the Piltdown skull proceeded more quietly. Some further readjustments brought fairly general agreement upon a brain capacity of about 1,400 cubic centimeters. This put Eoanthropus well within the brain range of modern man. In fact it made him the first modern man known.[1]

With these clues, Piltdown man was given a forehead of almost human proportions. To reconstruct what the remainder of the face must have been was a difficult problem, for the experts had only the forehead, the brow ridges, some of the nasal bones, and part of the lower jaw with which to work.

While this puzzle was being studied, Dawson found three fragments of a second Piltdown skull only two miles distant from the first site. Clearly they belonged to the same type of being, and luckily provided some further clues to the shape of the face.

When the two were put together, the anthropologists concluded that Eoanthropus's face was not overlong nor unduly projecting. Although the skull was thick, the nose flat, and the jaw massive, it was an essentially human face that looked out on the world again.

[1] Eoanthropus probably was a woman.

For some, however, the combination was too much. The South African man-apes had not yet been dug from their caves to accustom the world to a combination of human and apelike characteristics in a single individual or group. Skeptics insisted that the jaw probably was that of an ape, and the skull a human one that somehow had become mixed in the same deposit.

One scientist dryly commented that it would be a miracle if a primitive man left his brain case and not his jaw in the very spot where an anthropoid had left his jaw and not his brain case. He added further that the miracle would be even more dazzling if another anthropoid had deposited his canine tooth in the same busy spot.

There seemed, nevertheless, to be no solution on the traditional basis. After the most thorough study of the Piltdown bones and of all the surrounding circumstances, the experts were irreconcilably split.

It was in this stalemate that Oakley proposed a fluorine test. He hoped a fluorine determination might shed enough light on the age of the skull to settle the major points in the dispute. Furthermore, all the requirements for a successful use of fluorine seemed to be met—a mixture of remains in the same bed, and conditions under which fluorine fixation would have been slow.

In October 1948 the Keeper of Geology of the British Museum authorized the sampling of the precious Piltdown specimens. With a dentist's drill, a tiny bit of material was dug out of every available bone and tooth in the Piltdown and neighboring deposits, and seventeen samples were taken from the Eoanthropus bones and teeth.[2]

One of the most difficult feats was getting enough material from the highly important canine tooth. Chemists who made the complicated fluorine tests asked for twenty milligrams of powdered bone or tooth with which to work and about one

[2] Strangely enough, after the drill bit through the discolored surface of the teeth, the dentine was as white as new.

hundred milligrams if possible.[3] Of the canine, they managed with a scant three milligrams. But large or small, samples were obtained and the tests completed.

Once more the results were striking. All of the bones of Piltdown man showed approximately the same fluorine content. And so did the remains of the "second individual" found more than two miles away.

There had been no "miracle" mixing of bones. Jaws and cranium could have belonged to the same being; the jaw was not that of an ape and the skull that of a man.[4] Both were quite certainly contemporary. And so one important point in the long-standing Piltdown dispute was settled.[5]

Of even greater significance, the fluorine content of the Eoanthropus bones was low. It averaged only 0.2 per cent. The bones could not have been in the gravels for very long.

In startling contrast, the bones of the older elephant and of the mastodon—the Lower Plesitocene remains—showed 1.9 to 3.1 per cent of fluorine. In the many millennia since they had lain in the brown Piltdown gravels, a great deal of fluorine had crept deep into their cells.

The bones of the hippopotamus and the other elephant had a fluorine content of 0.8 to 1.5 per cent. Their placement in one

[3] Most of the analyses were made in the Department of the Government Chemist. The Piltdown samples were analyzed by Dr. C. R. Hoskins.

[4] Oakley emphasizes that it is still possible that the remains represent two creatures, though this does not now seem likely.

[5] The same type of problem arose in Java. Additional human-like thigh bones were found in the vicinity where Pithecanthropus had been discovered. Were they the leg bones of Pithecanthropus or of some later man? Bergman and Karsten in 1952 applied the fluorine test to samples taken from the Pithecanthropus skull and from the newly found thigh bones. Both showed virtually the same flourine content. It could be said conclusively that the new unbiased evidence proved that both were contemporaneous. This did not mean that the bones came from the same individual, but that they came from men who had lived at approximately the same time.

R. A. M. Bergman and P. Karsten: *The Fluorine Content of Pithecanthropus and Other Specimens from the Trinil Fauna.* Proceedings of the Royal Netherlands Academy of Science, sec. B, Vol. LV, No. 2 (1952).

of the more recent interglacial periods seemed to be entirely correct.

Of all the bones found with Eoanthropus, only those of the beaver showed the same fluorine percentage, 0.2. Eoanthropus —called the First Englishman in Smith-Woodward's book about the discovery—and the beaver probably had lived on the Ouse at approximately the same time. Oddly enough, this had been the original opinion of Dawson. From his study of the condition of the bones of the two, he had decided that they were the only contemporaries of all those whose remains had come to rest in the Piltdown gravels.

Oakley felt the fluorine results were supported by the geological history of the beds and fitted in well with the geological records. He pointed out that the gravels gave many indications of having been reworked several times in the course of the river's meandering. He suspected that the bones of Piltdown man did not reach their final resting-place until the final rearrangement of the gravel, probably during the last warm interlude before the glaciers stretched down finally from the north.

The fluorine content of the Eoanthropus bones was so exceptionally low that it approached the percentage of a modern deposit; and Oakley felt compelled to ask whether Eoanthropus could have lived after the last glaciation.

Upon the evidence of the beaver, he rejected such a possibility. The beaver must have lived in the Ouse when the river ran across the Piltdown moor. And that was before the last advance of the glaciers. The gouging and scouring of the ice rearranged the topography of the whole area. After the retreat of the ice, the Ouse shifted to a bed some distance from the common and far below it. Thus, if the bones of Piltdown had come to rest in the Ouse gravels when the river ran across the moor, he must have lived in the last interglacial epoch.

Oakley at first attempted no closer dating of Piltdown man. At the Wenner-Gren International Symposium in New York in

1952, however, he expressed the opinion on the basis of further study that Eoanthropus had lived not much more than 50,000 years ago. Before the fluorine test was applied to the remains of Piltdown man, many authorities had suggested that they were about 500,000 years old and perhaps a million!

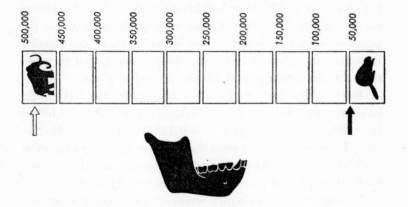

DID PILTDOWN MAN LIVE IN THE TIME OF THE MASTODON, 500,000 OR MORE YEARS AGO, OR DID HE BELONG TO THE TIME OF THE BEAVER, AROUND 50,000 YEARS AGO? FLUORINE DATING PLACED HIM DEFINITELY WITH THE BEAVER AND THUS GAVE HIM—THE FIRST MAN OF ACCEPTED HUMAN INTELLIGENCE—AN AGE OF NOT MUCH MORE THAN 50,000 YEARS.

Tremendous consequences hinge upon this finding. It means, no less, that modern man is much younger than science previously had thought. For Piltdown man is the first man known with a completely modern-sized brain case. None of his known precursors—Swanscombe man, Peking man, Java man, or any of the others—had reached that status, though some maintain that Swanscombe man approached it.

To date the arrival of modern man at about fifty thousand years ago instead of the one million previously set for him shakes anthropology, history, and the theory of evolution.

Oakley had changed man's perspective.

The English scientist himself drew no implications from his work. He calmly continued his testing of other remains that had also long baffled anthropologists.

Mlle G. Henri-Martin asked Oakley to test the remarkable Fontéchevade skulls. They had been found under a stalagmitic sheet that clearly separated them from other more recent remains of man discovered in the upper levels of the famous French cave. Although few seriously questioned that they belonged to an earlier period, Oakley agreed to a test.

Bone drilled from two skulls found under the stalagmitic layer averaged 0.4 and 0.5 in fluorine content. Animal bones from the same level ranged from 0.5 to 0.9 in fluorine. On the other hand, bones taken from the upper part of the cave generally showed only 0.1 per cent of fluorine. In fact, the average for the lower bones was 0.5 and for the upper ones, 0.1.

Taking full note of his own warning against comparing fluorine dates from different deposits, Oakley in his 1950 report to the Viking Fund could not resist quoting some comparisons made by a Dutch scientist who studied both the Swanscombe and the Fontéchevade deposits.

At Swanscombe all of the vole teeth examined by the Dutch scientist belonged to extinct species.[6] At Fontéchevade she failed to find any extinct species among a fairly large collection. "Taking this fact into consideration with the new paleontological data, I think one may now rest assured that the Swanscombe skull certainly belongs to an earlier inter-glacial than the Fontéchevade skull," Oakley said.

At the New York Symposium, Oakley estimated the age of the older Fontéchevade skulls at not much more than 50,000 years, the same age given Piltdown man. "It may well be of

[6] The vole is a small lemming-like animal, also somewhat resembling the chipmunk.

considerable significance that Piltdown Man and Fontéchevade Man appear to be of approximately the same age," he commented.

From his growing experience, Oakley recommended against undertaking a long and difficult series of fluorine determinations unless the circumstances or a preliminary test should show them to be necessary.

A fragment of a human skull discovered at a considerable depth in Suffolk was brought to him. From the same level came the horn-core of a *Bos primigenius,* which without much doubt belonged to the deposit. Was the human skull as old?

Two preliminary tests cleared the point. The human skull had a fluorine content of 0.1; the horn of 1.5 per cent. No further inquiry was needed. The skull was so obviously recent, and the fluorine finding checked so thoroughly with geological observations, that there was no need to go farther.

On the other hand, Oakley is cautious when his preliminary results flatly contradict extensively held beliefs. It had always been assumed that an ancient skull found in a Thames deposit at Lloyd's site in London was associated with the bones of a Pleistocene elephant and rhinoceros which lay with it. The skull proved to have a fluorine content of only 0.3 per cent, while the elephant femur and the rhinoceros ulna respectively showed 1.3 and 1.1 per cent.

This large difference in fluorine content could not be attributed to variations in the permeability of the surroundings in which they lay. The skull and the rhinoceros bone both were embedded in the same type of clay, but they differed notably in fluorine content. On the other hand, the rhinoceros and elephant bone registered about the same fluorine content though the elephant bone lay in sand. Nevertheless, Oakley suggested further analyses.

Another skull, known as the Walbrook skull, was discovered

in the gravels of another Thames terrace. It checked in with a promising 0.7 per cent of fluorine, but since no animal bones were found with it, no valid comparisons could be drawn. Oakley emphasized again that animal fossils of recognized periods are needed for the interpretation of a fluorine examination.

On some further tests Oakley laid several other famous ghosts.

In 1863 a jaw had been unearthed at Abbeville in France. Because it looked so modern—the term was relative—it was "put on the shelf." Oakley wondered if the decision had any backing in fact, and obtained permission from the director of the Musée de L'Homme in Paris to sample it, along with some other fossil bones from the vicinity of Abbeville. The doubts about the jaw in this case apparently were well founded. On Oakley's test the jaw showed a mere 0.1 per cent of fluorine, and the mandible, 0.2. All of the animal bones were well over 1 per cent.

The same archæologically sad assessment of youth was levied against other fossil fragments of which the experts had once held high hopes. They had been found at Ebbsfleet, near Swanscombe, in 1902. But they averaged only 0.3 per cent fluorine as compared with more than 1 per cent for the twelve animal bones taken from the same site.

The use of fluorine to measure the relative time and age of bony remains has a solid base in chemistry.

Fluorine, in the form of fluorides, occurs in most ground waters that pass through sedimentary formations. It is thus very widespread. When the fluorine ions come in contact with the crystalline mineral matter in teeth or bones, they are locked in. One by one, the submicroscopic units of the hydroxyapatite that make up the teeth are converted into fluorapatite. In the chemists' words, they occupy the hydroxyl position in the apatite crystal lattice. Fluorapatite is a relatively stable mineral, much less soluble and more resistant to weathering than the original material of the teeth or bones.[7]

Thus, once the fluorine is fixed, it probably is there to stay. Any acids in the soil strong enough to dissolve fluorapatite will almost certainly destroy the bones first. Since any fluorine in the teeth or bones stays there, and any additional fluorine ions loose in the ground water may be absorbed, the fluorine content of a bone will almost certainly increase with time. And a measurement of time is interred with the bone.

Fluorine dating is not the ultimate answer to the anthropologist's hope for a method that will let him read the age of a bone in the bone's own structure. But it is a step in that direction. For the first time a definite though limited means has been devised for an impartial, scientific appraisal of a bone's relative age.

In its first few experimental years, fluorine dating settled some moot archæological questions. It also has overturned some of the best-made estimates of modern man's time upon the earth. Oakley's work has said—though he has not uttered the words—that modern man is younger than he thinks. Modern man, as a consequence, is pictured not as an ancient of a million years ago, but as a late-comer of the last fifty thousand years. And the difference matters mightily.

[7] It probably is for the same reason that it is effective in protecting living teeth against decay.

LIBBY

CARBON-14 AND THE REDATING OF THE

LAST 25,000 YEARS

MANY THOUSANDS OF YEARS AGO a fine spruce forest grew in a region now known as Two Creeks, Wisconsin. It might have gone the unnoticed way of most forests if the weather had not grown colder, and if the great icecap that covered the northern top of the continent had not begun a new push to the south. The great mass of ice ground down upon the spruce forest, snapping off the trees, shoving over the stumps, and leaving them, like so many matchsticks, all pointed to the southwest, the direction of the glacier's movement.

This ancient and far from unique contest between ice and wood again might have gone forever unmarked except that the glacial advance that mowed down the Wisconsin forest was the last of our time. After this final thrust the climate grew warmer, the ice melted, and the part of the continent that is now Canada and the United States became habitable for man. By the most careful studies, scientists judged that this turning-point in history occurred about twenty-five thousand years ago.

And this verdict might have stood undisputed if a tall quiet physical chemist at the University of Chicago had not proved, in 1950, that ancient bits of organic matter, like the fossilized wood of the Two Creeks spruce trees, carry their own dates written within them.

The chemist, Dr. Willard F. Libby, reduced some few ounces of the ancient wood to pure carbon, and spread it in one of the world's most sensitive Geiger counters. Because the carbon—carbon-14—was radioactive, the counter began to click. It was almost as though the carbon were counting out its own age. And its age proved to be 11,000 years, not the 25,000 previously supposed by science.

AN ANCIENT WISCONSIN SPRUCE FOREST WAS BOWLED OVER BY THE LAST ADVANCE OF THE ICE ON THIS CONTINENT. ALL OF THE TREES FELL POINTING TO THE SOUTHWEST, THE DIRECTION OF THE GLACIER'S MOVEMENT. BY MEASURING THE RADIOACTIVITY OF THE CARBON IN THE FOSSILIZED WOOD, LIBBY WAS ABLE TO DETERMINE ITS AGE, AND THUS THE DATE WHEN THE MOVING ICE DESTROYED THE FOREST.

When a small group of scientists were told of what had happened, they reacted with startled excitement. For they suddenly realized that the radiochemists who had found a way to measure the age of the earth by radioactivity might also have found a means of measuring the age of many of the remains of life that were buried anonymously in the earth. Perhaps this oldest dream of archæology could be realized.

If the method could be proved, it would mean that any scrap of charcoal from a fire at which prehistoric man had warmed himself could be dated—and hence that the man who had made the fire could be dated.

It would mean that the time of long extinct animals could be determined, perhaps from a bit of horn or antler, or from the dung, or possibly even from the bones.

It would mean that the time of great climatic changes could be fixed.

It would mean that changes which had occurred anywhere in the world could be compared, for the standard of measurement would be the same.

It would mean that a new calendar for the past—up to twenty-five thousand years—could be written.

And other almost unbelievable prospects of solving hitherto unsolvable problems of the past unrolled before archæologists, geologists, and other scientists.

G. Evelyn Hutchinson, director of graduate studies in zoology at Yale University, did not hesitate to call the discovery of Carbon-14 "one of the most remarkable scientific accomplishments of the decade." The decade had included the atom bomb. The board of nine distinguished scientists who nominated Libby for the 1951 Research Corporation Award termed it "one of the greatest contributions of the century to archæology."

Libby did not start out deliberately to solve the unreachable problems of archæology and geology, or to affect the timing of man's history on the earth. He could scarcely have been more removed than he was from such bizarre concerns as the age of the tomb of Snefru, the excavations at Tayinat, the puzzling contents of the Adena mounds, or the explosion of Mount Mazama.

Up to the time when he discovered Carbon-14's potentialities, Libby was completely absorbed in the cold—though some would argue equally bizarre concerns of nuclear chemistry and physics.

The discoverer of the new dating tool was born on a farm near Grand Valley, Colorado, on December 17, 1908. After growing up to college age, he entered the University of California with the intention of becoming an engineer. He enrolled in some courses in chemistry, because they were required, but remained because he was captivated by the untold possibilities of that science as he saw them. Engineering soon was dropped.

After taking his Ph.D., Libby was appointed to the faculty of California, and from 1933 to 1941 gradually became more and more interested in the problems of radioactivity. He began to investigate new types of natural radioactivity. His activities from 1941 to 1945 he describes as "war research" in New York. This typical understatement modestly covers an important part in the development of the atom bomb—with the Manhattan District. At the end of the war he joined the faculty of the University of Chicago as a professor of chemistry, sharing an office suite with Dr. Harold C. Urey, Nobel prize-winner and one of the principals in the bomb project.

About six feet two inches tall, lean, with thin blond hair that tends to ruffling, blue eyes, and the chemist's strong hands, Libby stayed close to his laboratory and his science. He resumed work at once on two parallel interests: natural radioactivity in the lighter chemical elements, and the measurement of extremely weak radioactive sources.

Of all the elements that might become radioactive, carbon was far and away the most important. It was at the base of the living process, and of paramount interest to biology.[1] Libby put two of his graduate students on its trail.

All the while, Libby himself was pondering the effect of

[1] Ordinary stable carbon has an atomic weight of 12, and can be called Carbon-12. There is also a Carbon-13 as well as radioactive Carbon-14.

cosmic rays on the chemical elements of the atmosphere. Since V. F. Hess discovered cosmic radiation in 1911, there had been constant conjecture about what effect these mysterious rays from outer space might have upon the earth. The total energy received from cosmic radiation is small—no more than that from starlight. But the specific energy per constituent particle is several thousand times greater than the greatest energy produced so far in man's atomic piles or cyclotrons. It was conceivable therefore that cosmic radiation might alter the earth's atmosphere in detectable ways.

Libby suggested in a paper, published in 1946, that both radioactive carbon and radioactive hydrogen (tritium) might be created in the outer atmosphere by cosmic-ray bombardment.

The earth is surrounded by an envelope of nitrogen. About five miles out from the surface on which we live, the cosmic rays with their charge of several billion electron volts collide with its outer layers. Since the nitrogen is "reactive," the result is a small atomic explosion.

The nitrogen atom is split. Out of its smashing comes one particle of radioactive carbon—Carbon-14—and one of hydrogen.

Through the vast natural movements of the air, the radioactive carbon is mixed evenly with the ordinary carbon dioxide of the atmosphere. Although there is only an infinitesimal amount of the radiocarbon—about one part in a trillion—all the atmospheric carbon dioxide is rendered radioactive.

Carbon dioxide is the stuff plants breathe and photosynthesize into their food; it is literally their breath of life. Since all living plants are constantly taking in the essential CO_2, the radioactive along with the inert, it must follow, Libby argued, that all plants are radioactive.

And since animals eat the plants and man eats both the plants and the animals, they in their turn would have to be radioactive. On the basis of this reasoning, Libby daringly predicted that all living things would be radioactive.

In addition, he predicted that radiocarbon would be found in the sea; for an exchange occurs between the carbon dioxide in the atmosphere and the dissolved bicarbonate and carbonate ions in the oceans.

As he followed this logic through, Libby asked a further question. How much Carbon-14 is there in the world—a staggering question to the layman—and does the C-14 in the atmosphere, in the ocean, and in living things account for all of it?

He turned first to the question of the world supply. By calculating the number of cosmic-ray neutrons generated in one square centimeter at the top of the atmosphere, and by multiplying that figure by the surface of the earth, Libby arrived at the total production of Carbon-14. Out of the unseen, out of the unknown, out of the blue came production figures as specific as those issued by a government bureau on the industrial output of, say, coal.

It was elementary that radioactive carbon, like all other radioactive substances, would disintegrate at a fixed, unshakable rate. Laboratory studies already had indicated that the still-to-be-materialized Carbon-14 would have a half-life of something less than 6,000 years. That meant that half of its radioactivity would be gone at the end of 6,000 years, half of the remainder at the end of another 6,000 year period, half of that at the end of a third period, and virtually all of it after approximately 25,000 years.

With his figures on total production at hand, and with a fairly close estimate of how long each particle would last, Libby was able to compute how much Carbon-14 should be in existence in the world. His answer: 81 metric tons (as later adjusted to more exact half-life figures).

Libby did not have to labor through the next few steps. His mind flew to the answer. Not all of the 81 tons would be in the atmosphere, in the ocean, and in living things. Another part would lie buried in the remains, the organic remains of all the plants, animals, and humans that had lived during the preceding 25,000 years.

This had to follow from another fact. During life, the Carbon-14 taken in with food just about balances that lost by disintegration. At death, however, intake ceases abruptly. From then on, there is only disintegration at a fixed rate. Libby saw that by measuring how much radioactivity remains in any dead organic matter, it would be possible to tell how old that matter might be. The earth's buried past could be dated.

"Once you ask the question, where is the Carbon-14, and where does it go, it's like one, two, three," said Libby. "You have dating."

But in 1947 this was only a theory. No one had proved that the nitrogen atom is split into C-14 far out in space. No one had detected C-14 in anything living or dead. The theory was unproved at every point.

Libby did not hesitate, however, to put it to the most stringent test. He proposed the means for doing so, and promptly went about the business.

By one of the curious gyrations that mark the development of Carbon-14 dating, the scene of action then shifted from outer space to the sewers of Baltimore. If Carbon-14 was present in organic matter, one of the best places to look for it would seem to be in decomposing organic matter that had been alive only a short time before. That suggested sewage, and the methane gas derived from it.

With the assistance of A. V. Grosse, of the Houdry Process Corp., Libby secured samples of methane from a Baltimore sewage plant. It was processed and tested in a highly sensitive Geiger counter. The gas was radioactive! [2]

[2] For comparative purposes, methane from petroleum—another carbon product—also was run through the counter. Like all petroleum, it was millions of years old and should long ago have lost all its radioactivity. It had.

What was more, the amount of C-14 found in the sewage methane was very close to what Libby had predicted. He had forecast what the answer would be, and that was what it was! Evidently Libby's whole line of reasoning had been correct.

Thus gas from the Baltimore sewers established that Carbon-14 is formed by cosmic-ray action in the outer atmosphere and is mixed through living matter.

With this proof in hand, Libby and his associate, E. C. Anderson, in 1947 announced the discovery of Carbon-14 in nature.

But the gas had been collected at sea-level Baltimore. Would there be the same amount of Carbon-14 in living matter from the highest mountain peaks, where the neutron bombardment produced by cosmic rays is at a maximum, or at the equator, where it is at a minimum?

To determine whether heights or depths or latitude or longitude affect the concentration of C-14, Libby began a world-wide assay of living radiocarbon. Co-operating scientists in nearly all parts of the world except China and Russia sent him materials for testing—spruce from the Yukon, honeysuckle leaves from Oak Ridge, North African brier, oak from Palestine, *Sterculia excelsa* from a nine-thousand-foot peak in Bolivia, ironwood from the Marshall Islands, eucalyptus from New South Wales, beech from Darwin's Tierra del Fuego, seal oil collected by the Byrd expedition to the Antarctic.

Regardless of where they came from, these far-flung samples of nature in some of her most diverse aspects clicked out an average of 15.3 "disintegrations" per minute in the University of Chicago's Geiger counter. That was the rate registered by the Baltimore sewage.

Another conclusion could be drawn: living things contain a constant amount of Carbon-14 irrespective of their geographical distribution, and Carbon-14 is evenly distributed throughout the world.

Libby was ready for another crucial test. Would non-living

organic matter show the anticipated loss of radioactivity, and would the loss register in fewer clicks on the Geiger counter? Would the fewer clicks correspond to the period of death? In brief, could the age of non-living matter be measured?

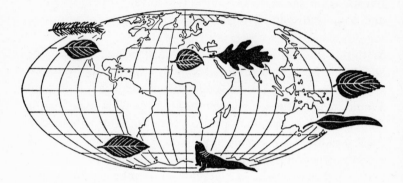

ORGANIC MATERIALS FROM ALL LATITUDES AND LONGITUDES, FROM MOUNTAIN PEAKS AND SEA LEVEL PROVED THAT ALL LIVING THINGS ARE RADIOACTIVE. IN THE WORLD-WIDE ASSAY WERE SPRUCE FROM THE YUKON, HONEYSUCKLE LEAVES FROM OAK RIDGE, BRIER FROM NORTH AFRICA, OAK FROM PALESTINE, IRONWOOD FROM THE MARSHALL ISLANDS, EUCALYPTUS FROM NEW SOUTH WALES, BEECH FROM TIERRA DEL FUEGO, AND SEAL OIL FROM THE ANTARCTIC.

The counter was pitted first against samples of known historic age. Donald Collier, of the Chicago Natural History Museum, cut a few ounces of wood from an inconspicuous deck plank of the big crescent-shaped mortuary boat of Sesostris III. It was well established that this Pharaoh of Egypt had been thus handsomely equipped for his journey into the after-world about 3,750 years ago. On Libby's counter, the wood showed enough of a loss of radioactivity to indicate an average age of 3,621 years, plus or minus a possible error of 180 years.[3]

[3] All C-14 dates are presented with the scientist's familiar ±. It is the standard way of figuring the degree of error of a measurement. If a

Libby and his associate in this testing, Dr. James R. Arnold, also tested a bit of corewood from the "Centennial" sequoia, a redwood giant felled in 1874. Exactly 2,905 rings marking annual cycles of growth could be seen between the innermost portion of the sample and the outside of the tree. Three C-14 tests were run, one indicating an age of 3,045 years, one 2,817 years, and the third 2,404 years. The average was 2,710. So the counter checked, too, against a record of nature.

Into the counter also went pinewood from the floor of a *hilani* (palace) of the Syro-Hittite period at Tayinat, Syria. It had a known age of 2,625 years. On three runs in the counter, the floor wood registered an average age of 2,531 years. Again there was a close check.

The results were still within range on what was believed to be a 4,575-year-old cypress beam from the tomb of Snefru, at Meydum, Egypt. It showed a counter age of 4,802 years.

Where the age was known or approximately known, the counter came uncannily close. Whether the Geiger counter—an instrument that perhaps typifies the middle of the twentieth century—was tested against the historic time of Snefru or against the naturally recorded age of an Arizona redwood, it proved itself. Once again the Carbon-14 method survived, and brilliantly, the strictest kind of test.

As word seeped out about this new and amazing way of dating the past, interest in archæological circles was intense. Libby for his part needed the help of men who knew the past. So the unusual step was taken of calling an inter-science conference to discuss the development of a new scientific method. The meeting was held on January 9, 1948. Libby explained what he was doing and asked for aid in systematically collecting samples that would not only test Carbon-14 against

---

date is given as, say, 2,400 ± 200 years, this means that from the evidence of the measurement alone, the chance is 68 per cent that the true value is between 2,200 and 2,600 years. To ease the reading of many figures, the plus and minus signs will be omitted from this point on, unless some special reason requires their use.

known dates, but against the unknown, against the great mass of material that preceded written history.

At the request of the conference, the American Anthropological Association in February 1948 named a committee to work with Libby and to appraise the new dating tool. It was made up of Frederick Johnson, of the Peabody Museum, Andover, Massachusetts, chairman; Froelich Rainey, of the University of Pennsylvania Museum; and Donald Collier, of the Chicago Museum. The Geological Society of America later appointed Richard Foster Flint, of Yale University, to work with the committee. The committee thus became a joint interest of the two societies.

Under the title of Committee on Radioactive Carbon 14, the group decided on nothing less than a test of the new method against the major archæological remains of the last twenty-five thousand years in all parts of the world. Some of the broadest and most difficult problems were included—the rise and fall of civilizations in the Near East, the first appearance of man on the North and South American continents, the end of the ice age all over the world.

The committee arbitrarily divided the job into ten parts and assigned an expert to each. The ten subchairmen, nine archæologists and one geologist, were to collect samples for testing, and in the end to prepare a critical report on the results obtained.

Soon a new stream of material, as odd, as improbable, as fantastic as any ever to reach a laboratory, began to roll into Chicago.

In the meanwhile Libby had made great advances on two other essential parts of Carbon-14 dating. First he worked out a more precise half-life for Carbon-14. The procedure was a long and complex one, using radioactive carbon dioxide obtained from the Atomic Energy Commission, for the Carbon-14 produced in an atomic pile is exactly the same as that produced by the

hale deposits at Rifle, Colorado. Note the mine to which the zigzag road at the left leads, lant at the right, and the housing area in the valley.

hales. Their layering may afford a clue to time. Sealed in them is the bulk of the nation's erable shale oil.

PLATE XXIX

Search for the Piltdown man. The gravel from this shallow bed beside an English road was meticulously sifted.

Piltdown man, the first man known to have reached the intelligence of modern man. His brain was equal in size to those of men living to-day. He lived just before the last ice age, not much more than fifty thousand years ago.

PLATE XXX

Photographs: Scientific American

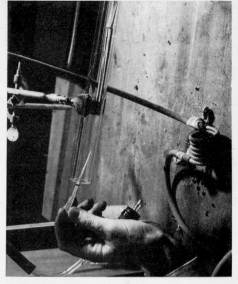

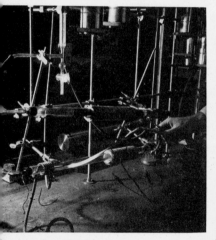

bon-14 test of age. A bit of ancient wood
from a block. It is placed in a tube to
uced to pure carbon. Through controlled
stion, carbon dioxide is formed. Oxida-
completed, the carbon dioxide is con-
, and pure carbon is obtained for testing.

PLATE XXXI

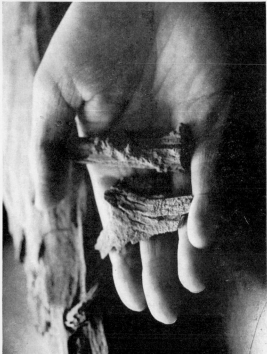

ABOVE: Willard F. Libby with Geiger counter holding the pure carbon of the sample (see plate 31). The counter will be inserted in the center of the battery of eleven other Geiger counters. By measuring radioactive loss of sample, Libby can determine its age. LEFT: wood dating back to the last ice age. Carbon-14 fixed its age at about eleven thousand years.

PLATE XXXII

smashing of the nitrogen atom in the outer atmosphere. To make certain exactly how long radioactive carbon lives, more than one hundred measurements were made. In the end Libby concluded that C-14 has a half-life of 5,568 years, plus or minus an error of 30 years. This meant the half-life was probably accurate to within 50 years and almost certainly to within 100 years.

The techniques for preparing and measuring the samples also were refined. Standards had to be set for the materials themselves. An obvious prerequisite, but one that had to be emphasized continually, was that the sample must contain only the carbon atoms present at the time of death. Any C-14 that might have crept in later through contamination by radioactive materials, or by chemical absorption or otherwise, would make the material appear younger. Warnings were issued against wrapping samples in cotton or any other radioactive organic material.

Libby soon found that charcoal, or charred organic material such as heavily burned bone, was best for dating. Such carbon is not very likely to be altered, no matter how long it has been in the ground or under what conditions.

Wood, grasses, and even peat proved reliable on the same score. Some twigs and leaves that had moldered in the ground for more than ten thousand years, most of the time soaked in underground waters, showed the same Carbon-14 content as well-preserved pieces of wood found with them. The water seemingly had no effect on the C-14.

Shell that looked powdery or chalky was regarded with suspicion. Such a state indicated it might have picked up additional C-14 later. Unburned bone also proved a poor prospect, both because its carbon content is low and because it is likely to have suffered alteration.

Once a sample was accepted and cleaned—dirt brushed away, rootlets removed—the Libby group worked out a very exact procedure for reducing it to pure carbon.

As Libby puts it when he is talking as scientists do around the laboratory, they also had to "polish up" the Geiger counter and "work it down." To detect radioactivity at the low level existing in nature, to find the one Carbon-14 particle in a trillion, the most sensitive counters known had to be used.

The pure carbon of the sample then was spread on the wall of the eight-inch cylinder that is the heart of the counter. With this kind of arrangement, known as the screen wall counter, Libby had an instrument able to pick up the weakest radiation.

Another problem also had to be solved: that of keeping out cosmic radiation and any other radiation from the laboratory or equipment. To shut it away, Libby stacked steel eight inches thick all around the counter. The slabs were piled up at the sides, and above and under the counter, like so many big legal tomes. The steel barrier reduces the cosmic-ray penetration from 500 counts per minute to 100. To cut this radiation still further, Libby packed the counter cylinder in a battery of eleven Geiger counters, each about eighteen inches long and two inches in diameter.

The effect is not unlike that of a piece of pipe surrounded by eleven smaller pipes, and all of it housed in a cozy little steel cave. All of the apparatus fits easily on the top of a table of about ordinary kitchen size.

Despite the steel and the Geiger battery, enough radiation still managed to get through to set the counter clicking at the rate of about five counts a minute. This is known as the background count; it goes steadily on in a noisy chirp. The five counts simply are deducted from whatever is being measured. Thus a wood sample registering 11.7 counts per minute would have a measurement of 6.7 counts. To make certain that the background stays steadily at the given counts and does not shift, as it does when there is an atomic explosion anywhere in this country, it is tested repeatedly.

With this "polished up" and "worked down" counter Libby was able to measure even the weakest radiation of natural carbon, to about a two-per-cent error, in forty-eight hours. Even greater accuracy might have been possible if the sample had been run longer, but the added certainty was not found important enough to justify the additional time of the scientists.

So Libby was ready with a precise technique and an apparatus of the greatest sensitivity to measure the chunks of old wood, the boxes of peat, the bits of horn, the ancient rope sandals, and the other incredible variety of material that came into his laboratory under a wide assortment of postmarks.

This miscellany of the past was almost as surprising to the archæologists who sent it as to the physical chemist who received it. Archæologists had seldom, if ever before, collected the kind of material Libby wanted. No one had ever dreamed that the charcoal from one of prehistoric man's fires could be anthropologically useful. Or that fossilized dung could have an archæological value. The archæologists traditionally gathered any flints that early man had chipped, or any bones left from the animals he had eaten, but, after carefully noting such byproducts as the carbon and dung, discarded them in the field. But the collectors learned rapidly. They reopened old diggings, and resifted museum reserves. Each of the ten subchairmen sent in dozens of specimens.

The generalization that "history begins at 3,000 B.C." had been current for years; but despite the lack of written records going back more than 5,000 years ago, archæology, geology, and the related sciences had formed many accepted estimates of the time of still earlier events. In the third stage of the testing, it was these dates, some careful and well substantiated, some admittedly little more than guesses, and others only a convenient way of showing that one occurrence probably was earlier than another, that were put to the test.

Egyptologists long had dated the opening of the first dynasty, an important turning-point in the ancient history of Egypt, at 4,700 to 5,100 years ago. To test this estimate, a collector obtained some wood from a beam in the tomb of He-maka, a vizier in the reign of King Udimu of the first dynasty. In Libby's counter this wood showed an age of 4,883 years.

In Palestine a bitter dispute had centered on the "Dead Sea Scrolls," an ancient copy of the Book of Isaiah, found, wrapped in linen, in a cave in Palestine. A piece of the linen, still strong and showing its beautiful weaving, was submitted to Libby. He gave it an age of 1,917 years, and thus confirmed the ancient authenticity claimed for the scroll.

The remarkable animal paintings found in a cave at Las-caux, France, were unquestionably the work of prehistoric man and yet their time was most uncertain. Collectors for the committee searching for testable organic material in the cave found what had been an early hearth in one corner. Charcoal from the hearth dated at 15,516 years, and though there was no certainty that it came from the fires of the men who had made the life-like animal paintings, it supplied a firm date from which to work forward or backward in further research.

Some mud from Lake Knocknacran, in Ireland, which almost certainly traced back to the last advance of the glaciers, registered an age of 11,787 years.

A wooden platform built by early man around the marshy edges of a lake, long since gone, near Starr Carr, in England, dated 9,488 years.

During the winter when the ice was thick on Upper Linsley Pond, Connecticut, Edward S. Deevey, Jr., of Yale University, bored out a section of mud in such a way that each layer was kept intact. In Libby's counter the deeper layers showed significantly less radioactivity than the upper ones:

DEPTH IN METERS	AGE IN YEARS
5.5	976
8.05	1800
9.15	5159
11.65	8323

More than six feet down from the surface in Gypsum Cave, Las Vegas, Nevada, excavators had found some dung of the great sloth. Libby gave it an age of 10,455 years.

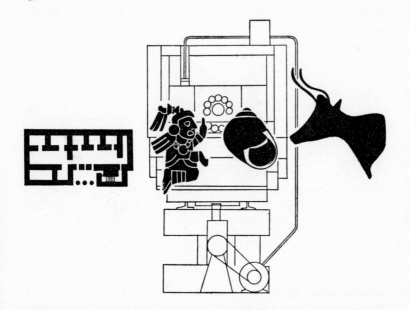

A FANTASTIC PROCESSION OF MATERIALS WENT THROUGH LIBBY'S COUNTER—WOOD FROM A LARGE "HILANI" OR PALACE AT TAYINAT, SYRIA, MAYAN REMAINS, A LAND SNAIL FROM THE WORLD'S OLDEST KNOWN VILLAGE, AT JARMO, IRAQ, CHARCOAL FROM THE FAMOUS LASCAUX CAVE.

And so the materials went through the counter, a fantastic procession. Seemingly inconsequential as they were, mud, peat, charcoal, bits of linen, they and many other carefully selected samples like them began to piece together a changed story of early man and his environment.

The fossil wood from the Two Creeks spruce trees had fixed the date of the last advance of the polar icecap. It also fixed a new date, an amazingly recent one, for man's first appearance in the northern part of this continent, for obviously humans had not obtained a foothold in a land engulfed by ice. Man then had come upon the scene in the north less than 11,000 years ago. Only 11,000 years ago instead of the 25,000 previously set!

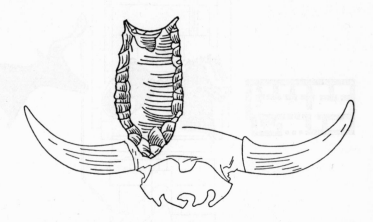

FOLSOM ARROWHEAD AND THE SKULL OF AN EXTINCT FORM OF BISON WITH WHICH THE ARROWHEADS ARE OFTEN FOUND. CARBON-14 DATING OF SOME OF THE CHARRED BISON BONE FIXED ITS AGE AT ABOUT 10,000 YEARS. THIS MEANT THAT THE MAN WHO MADE AND SHOT THE ARROWHEAD AND PROBABLY ROASTED AND ATE THE BISON WAS ABROAD IN THE LAND ABOUT 10,000 YEARS AGO.

This startling finding had immediate repercussions. It meant that a shorter time than anyone had thought had elapsed between the early men who moved in with the melting of the ice, and the Indians who held sway in the wilderness of America when the first European explorers reached this land. The revision closed a gap between the older and younger cultures that had sorely puzzled archæologists.

Other evidence soon supported this new timing of the appearance of North American man. Until 1927, archæologists knew very little about the earliest inhabitants of this continent. In that year a peculiar kind of fluted arrowhead was found at Folsom, New Mexico, in association with the remains of an extinct kind of bison. If man had lived there at the time of the bison, which he had apparently hunted and killed, he must have been an early-comer to this continent. And other "Folsom" arrowheads were found with other and similar bison bones in different parts of the country. Not only did "early man" live in the Southwest; apparently he had spread widely.

On the basis of this surprising material, archæologists concluded that Folsom man dated back to the end of the ice age, then believed to be about twenty-five thousand years ago. Others disagreed and favored a more recent time. As a consequence, estimates of man's beginnings here varied as much as fifteen thousand years.

Some charred bone from a "Folsom" site at Lubbock, Texas, was sent to Libby. The counter set its age at 9,883 years. Since there was every indication that the bison had been killed by an arrow of Folsom man, and probably roasted and eaten by him too, Folsom man could be dated by Carbon-14 evidence at about ten thousand years.

Evidently these early men lived on the west coast too. In a cave in Oregon, a cave that had collapsed many years ago, L. S. Cressman, of the University of Oregon, found nearly two hundred pairs of perfectly preserved woven fiber sandals. They were skillfully and intricately made, the rope-like fiber criss-crossing in a handsome pattern between rows of small, tightly tied knots. From the standpoint of design, they were as well shaped as any beach or house slipper of today. Their age on Libby's test was 9,053 years.

No similarly early evidence of man appeared on the east coast. The earliest trace of occupation there came from the wood of a fish weir (fish trap) uncovered under Boylston Street in downtown Boston. It was dated 5,000 years ago.

Frederick Johnson, the chairman of the Carbon-14 Committee, noted that the dates for "early man" supplied through work on the first materials furnished by the committee were "too few to justify conclusions," but he added: "The consistency of them as a whole may well indicate what the future has in store." Johnson said further: "In general the oldest remains, especially Folsom, appear to be about 10,000 years old."

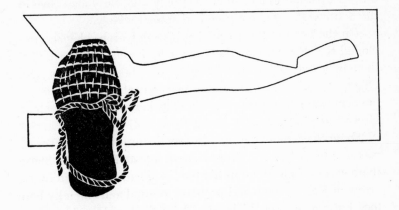

SANDALS OF 9,000 YEARS AGO. IN THE BACKGROUND, THE OREGON CAVE IN WHICH THEY WERE FOUND.

To the south, in Mexico and South America, man also was present and flourishing at the same period. On the edges of what had been a swamp in ancient times, but was a bull-ring in modern ones, the fossilized remains of an early man had been discovered at Tepexpán, Mexico. In the same clay were the bones of an extinct elephant. Helmut de Terra, who was in charge of the collection of Mexican samples for the committee, was able to obtain some peat from the same site. Libby found it had a Carbon-14 age of 11,300 years, and that corresponded closely with de Terra's estimate of 11,000 to 12,000 years for

Tepexpán man. Other samples—bits of the burned bone of the sloth and horse that were associated with human artifacts—placed man at the Straits of Magellan some 9,000 years ago.

Were the great geologic and climatic changes in South America synchronous with those of Europe and North America? Did the movements of men follow at about the same time everywhere? The radiocarbon dates seemed to lend support to that significant hypothesis.

Libby's counter also clicked out the story of man's transition from a roving hunter into a town dweller and farmer.

At Jarmo, in Iraq, a University of Chicago expedition dug deep into an ancient site. At Levels Seven and Eight they came upon the remains of the earliest village yet discovered. The people who had lived there had not even developed the very early art of pottery; they were "pre-ceramic." Quantities of materials were brought back for Libby to date, but the first to be timed were the shells of two land snails. The shells showed an age of 6,707 years, a somewhat more recent date than the expedition had expected, but one that it accepted willingly.

Man's prowess as a farmer was evidenced by some corncobs from another part of the world. At Bat Cave, Arizona, excavators discovered primitive corncobs at a level six feet below the surface. Succeeding layers traced corn's progress from a simple, primitive grain almost to the modern grain at the top.

Libby was able to draw up the following timetable for the Bat Cave corn and for the wood associated with it—and incidentally to demonstrate once more that Carbon-14 dating could sort materials in their right order, according to their level in the ground:

	DEPTH IN FEET	AGE IN YEARS
cobs	0–1	1,752
wood	1–2	1,907
wood	2–3	2,239
wood and corn	3–4	2,249
wood	4–5	2,862

Carbon-14 dating also helped to fix the time of the great Inca civilization in Peru and of the Aztec and Mayan ages in Mexico. Some Carbon-14 dates for the Mexican and South American materials were more recent than those previously assigned; others were older. In this way the counter tended to close a troublesome gap in Central and South American dawn history. Carbon-14 dates also held out an exciting possibility of correlating the Mayan and Christian calendars. Many of the events of ancient Mexican history can be placed in the Mayan calender, but all authoritative efforts to fit them into the Christian calendar have so far failed.

The materials flowing into Chicago continued to date man's world as well as man, and often as surprisingly. In Europe, too, the ice had crept down from the north to overwhelm the land and turn it into a frozen tundra. Geologists had studied its records in Scandinavia and northern Europe and had traced the separate glaciers that had covered England and Ireland.

In a north German wood some birch trees had grown just before the last advance of the ice and, like the spruce trees in Wisconsin, were bowled over and buried by the relentless movement of the frozen mass. Samples of their wood were sent to Libby and also specimens of peat and mud from lakes gouged out by the glaciers and later filled with their melting waters. The German birch dated 10,800 years; the English mud, 10,851 years; and the Irish glacial mud, 11,310 years.

Not only were these dates extremely interesting for the way they fixed the last advance of the glaciers in Europe. They strikingly suggested that the last period of glaciation came at about the same time in both Europe and America. "The essential agreement of the dates implies that de-glaciation of Northern Europe was contemporaneous with that of North America," concluded Flint and Deevey in their article "Radiocarbon Dating of Late-Pleistocene Events." [4] Deevey is director of the Geochronometric Laboratory of Yale University.

[4] Published in the *American Journal of Science*, Vol. CCXL, pp. 257–300 (1951).

Deevey added in another publication, in a discussion of the nearness of the European continental and English glacier dates: "Radiocarbon dating carries chronologies across the North Sea as easily as it does across the Atlantic."

Many of the dates counted out by Carbon-14 confirmed long-standing judgments of archæologists and geologists. About these there is little question.

Others abruptly upset well-established and long-accepted theories, to some of which a man had given a lifetime of work. What has tended to happen in the latter case is well told by Deevey: "According to one's point of view, it is refreshing or discouraging to recall the number of instances in which a direct challenge offered by a radiocarbon date to a previously published stratigraphic assignment has resulted in the significant modification or withdrawal of previously published statements and cherished views. At the same time in some instances acceptance of the radiocarbon dates requires a mental balancing of probabilities that is suspiciously close to special pleading."

Still other Carbon-14 dates seemed flatly to contradict well-authenticated points of fact. Through the most thorough and careful studies, archæologists had decided that the Adena or early woodland period in Indian culture preceded another stage known as the Hopewell. Carbon-14 dates exactly reversed this accepted order, to the surprise and disbelief of many archæologists.

A problem that arose in Peru demonstrated the same kind of difficulty. One sample from an Inca mound, dated by Carbon-14 at 4,257 years, lay below another sample dated at 4,380 years. Since the deposits seemed to be undisturbed, the older sample should, of course, have been the deeper. Something seemed to be wrong.

Some of the ten subcommittee chairmen, in discussing the dates for their sections of the work, in the formal committee report, *Radiocarbon Dating*,[5] pointed out that there are possi-

---

[5] Published in July 1951 by the Society for American Archæology.

bilities of error in Carbon-14 dates as well as in the earlier judgments of archæologists. Each, however, accepted the over-all validity of Carbon-14 dates.

And no one was dogmatic about the points of disagreement. James B. Griffin, of the University of Michigan Museum of Anthropology, the man in charge of the collection of the hotly disputed Adena-Hopewell samples, noted: "Perhaps the familiar cultural pattern is being repeated of the old archæologist not being able to learn the new physics, or perhaps we are merely repeating Hooton's lament at learning the tree ring dates for Pecos after his laboriously calculated estimates of its life span."

The top committee of four, in its formal summary in the report, emphasized that "conclusions concerning the general validity of the method must be based on the over-all consistency of all, or at least large numbers of dates."

The whole committee added its impressive verdict: "The method is valid and the dates accurate within the expectable error. . . . Certain glaring discrepancies in isolated samples and for a few series such as the Hopewell-Adena samples, are due possibly to mistaken attribution of archeological or geological contexts, to custodial errors or to contamination of the samples subsequent to excavation."

Libby, with all the precision of the atomic chemist, checked and re-checked the method. "There's nothing wrong with it from the physical side," he said. "Now we have to await the final opinion of the archæologists."

Johnson, Rainey, Collier, and Flint displayed little doubt about what the final decision of their respective sciences will be: "There is but little question that the method of dating established by Libby and his associates is firmly established. There has become available a means world-wide in scope and which can provide dates for certain types of material and in certain ranges which are more accurate than any known system covering similar ground. It is to be recognized, however, that the method is by no means perfected."

Johnson, in a chapter contributed to the book in which Libby in 1952 made his full report of the method, underlined this verdict: [6]

"The salient conclusion which may be reached is that the initial experiment, if that is what it may be called, was successful from the archæological and geological point of view. There is great promise that a valuable tool for the constructing of a chronology has been developed. Its value rests not only upon the measurement of dates of events which have been impossible to secure within a given range of accuracy heretofore, but also upon the institution of a chronological scale world-wide in scope.

"As inevitable refinements are made, the course of events in all continents may be directly compared. Once this becomes possible, the value and usefulness of interpretations of the significance of events will be immeasurably enhanced."

Equally solid testimony, not only to the acceptance of Carbon-14 dating, but to the rare enthusiasm with which it has been received, came in another way. Many of the leading universities of the world hastened to establish Carbon-14 laboratories, where they will carry on with the methods developed by Libby.

Yale, Michigan, Columbia, Chicago, and Pennsylvania in this country, and Cambridge and Copenhagen abroad, had laboratories in operation early in 1952. In addition the U. S. Geological Survey and the government of New Zealand set up C-14 laboratories as an indispensable part of their study of their lands.

To Libby this was a development devoutly to be welcomed. The Chicago chemist was eager to get on with his work on other radioactive materials; in 1950 he announced the presence

[6] Willard F. Libby: *Radiocarbon Dating* (University of Chicago Press, 1952).

of tritium, the radioactive isotope of hydrogen, in heavy water.

Anxious as he was to turn Carbon-14 dating over to the appropriate sciences, Libby kept his own counter going. Partly for further checking on the method, partly to work on additional refinements, partly to assist any new laboratory over beginning hurdles, and partly, he wryly admitted to friends, because "once you get used to a mummy a week, it's hard to break off." [7]

But the man who found the way to date the past in the atomic collisions of the outer atmosphere will leave most of the dating to others. Others will work out the retimed picture of the world's last twenty-five thousand years and decide upon its final meanings.

The new techniques, absolute in the sense that they remove much of the vagary of human judgment and partiality, thus have signally and dramatically cut the time of modern man.

Carbon-14 is shortening the time distance that separates the men of today from their ancestors who lived in caves and chipped stone arrowheads. It is reducing the gap between them to a fleeting ten thousand years.

Fluorine dating is showing that the first creatures who could be called modern men—*Homo sapiens*—did not evolve a million years ago, but only a brief fifty thousand years back.

Lead dating is vastly expanding the age of the world, but relatively decreasing man's span in it.

These are radical, fundamental changes. And they have posed a new evolutionary problem.

---

[7] By further concentration of samples, Libby hopes to be able to date back to 30,000 years.

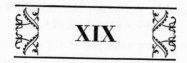

XIX

WASHBURN

EVOLUTION AND EXPERIMENT

THE DILEMMA was acute. Could modern man have evolved from the stage of the South African ape-men in the brief period of one million years? Could the last-lap transition from the underslung jaw and beetling brow of Piltdown man have been made in the last fifty thousand years?

The answer seemed to be no, if each difference between these ancestors and the men of today had to be accounted for by natural selection working in the way and at the pace Darwin had assumed. Then no million years could possibly have sufficed.

Evolution as it had been understood would have been impossible within the new time scheme. Or, if the changes had come about as science had thought, then there must be some error in the new timing.

Thus evolution in 1950 again was confronted with a serious time problem.

A young associate professor of anthropology at the University of Chicago, Dr. Sherwood L. Washburn, proposed a way out of the impasse. But first of all he acknowledged the difficulty: "This new situation has been called a statistical and mathematical absurdity. If each one of the differences between the ape-men and ourselves is based upon a separate element of genetic construction of the individual, it is true it becomes mathematically impossible to change the ape men into modern men in the time that seems to be implied in the actual record."

Washburn was in an excellent position to understand and diagnose the trouble. Although the time dilemma had been sharply defined only since 1950, he had been at work for several years on studies of how man physically changes. The work already had shown that there are probably fewer basic, genetic differences between early men and modern men than appear on the surface. It indicated too that the few big genetic differences might well have been achieved within the available time, and that the other smaller differences could have followed along, almost automatically.

Washburn had come upon these ideas in the laboratory, by experimenting with animals, and not by staring at or measuring fossils. Early in his career he had decided that he would attempt an experimental study of evolutionary changes. Of course the actual changes could not be brought under the microscope. But, Washburn reasoned, you could by operation produce the same kinds of changes that did occur ages ago, and then see what would happen.

Obviously no animals exactly like those that lived in the past were still alive to work with. Nevertheless, many of the structures that were present in the animals of the ancient world were still to be found—and little changed—in living animals. Any one part, say the jaw, could be studied, changed, and studied further.

"The missing links were not fossils," said Washburn. "Fossils are fragments of individuals who once lived and were successful. The implication of the doctrine of natural selection is that structure mirrors function, and that it is successful function that survives.

"To a certain extent function is reflected in the bones. But you cannot solve this puzzle by looking only at the bones, for the answer is not there. The answer lies in how the man or the animal functioned, and that lies in the experimental laboratory. There you can study comparable parts."

It was not surprising that Washburn should propose a new

and active approach to the study of evolution. On the contrary, that might have been expected. He is a scientist who likes theories that can be backed by verifiable facts, and he does not operate in well-worn ruts.

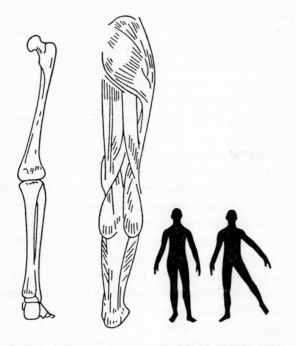

THE BONES TELL MUCH ABOUT FOSSIL MAN. THEY "MIRROR FUNC-TION." BUT THE MUSCLES ARE THE "DOING THINGS," AND MUST BE STUDIED TO KNOW HOW MAN MOVED AND CHANGED.

Washburn was born in Cambridge, Massachusetts, in 1911, the descendant of a long line of New England clergymen. *Life* once published a photograph of his distinguished father, the former dean of the Episcopal Theological School, standing against a stained-glass window containing figures of the Washburn Puritan ancestors.

"But," said one of his colleagues, "it is impossible to associate Sherry Washburn with anything so immobile as a stained glass window."

He must have been one of the liveliest of children. At the age of thirteen, he and his brother were climbing the Alps, conquering one peak after another. During his school days he once had a summer job with the Harvard Museum of Natural History. When the museum tidied up, he salvaged enough material to establish his own museum of natural history at Groton.

In time he went on to Harvard and its department of anthropology. He interrupted his graduate work there to go with a college expedition to collect gibbons in Siam and monkeys in Borneo. Washburn also studied at Oxford before returning to Harvard to take his doctorate. He then went to the School of Medicine of Columbia University as an instructor in anatomy and at once turned to studying rats, mice, and monkeys to find out what happens when a change occurs in a bone or a muscle. This was information of great interest to plastic surgeons.

Next came an expedition to Uganda to collect an even one hundred monkeys and apes. Upon his return in 1947, Washburn accepted an appointment to the faculty of the University of Chicago. An associate, who was introducing him at a university dinner added: "We have never been the same since, and I hasten to add with rejoicing that we hope never to be again."

This young professor is short, slender, quick, intent when the subject is anthropology, relaxed when it is something other. When he presides at a meeting or rises to speak, a roomful of anthropologists sits up with a new sort of anticipatory attention. It is not that Sherry Washburn is given to the startling, but that things are bound to start moving in one way or another, and that way is likely to be fresh and challenging.

The jaw muscle probably has changed more than any other muscle in human evolution. Besides, it long had been recognized that the jaw muscle might affect the form of the brain case; Darwin had called attention to this possibility. In addition, the jaw is one of the parts of the anatomy that most frequently survive in fossil form. For all these reasons it was a likely starting-place for the kind of studies Washburn planned. Rats were chosen for investigation.

Rats are born in an undeveloped state and do not at first have a constant temperature. An obstetrician had discovered that because of this peculiarity they could be anesthetized very easily by placing them on the tray of a refrigerator. The cold sends them into a kind of hibernation.

While the newborn rats were comatose, Washburn operated on twenty-two of them. Being extremely careful to damage no other muscle or tissue, he removed the jaw muscle on one side. In ten he also separated the long muscles from the nuchal crest, a ridge across the back of the head. The rats recovered rapidly and were soon back with their mothers, nursing happily, or so it seemed.

When they were about four months old and fully grown, they were sacrificed and their skeletons studied. A notable change had come about in the head. On the side that had not been operated, the rats had the usual deep creases and heavy brow ridges—the same kind of ridges and creases seen in the skull of Neanderthal man and some of the other early men, and taken as a sign of their primitiveness. On the other side, the operated side, the skull of the rats was smooth, very much as the skull of modern man is smooth.

One side of the rats' head was Neanderthal, so to speak, and the other was modern. The bony structure was entirely unlike, and yet the only change had been in the muscle. The muscle apparently controlled the form of the skull; the ridges and creases seemingly were superstructures created to withstand the pull of the powerful jaw muscle.

Imagine for a moment that someone looking for fossils had dug deep into the ground and come upon two such halves of a skull. Comparing feature for feature, the scientist would compile a long list of descriptive differences. It might look as though the two skull halves were separated by many ages in evolution. Nothing would betray that one piece seemed to be primitive and the other modern because one muscle had been severed.

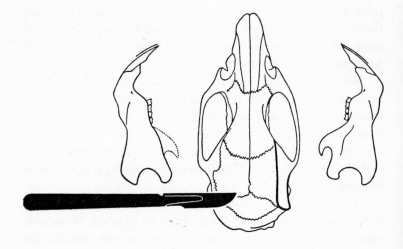

RAT SKULL AND JAW. IF THE JAW MUSCLE IS REMOVED IN BABY RATS, THE USUAL HEAVY "PRIMITIVE" RIDGE ON THE SKULL DOES NOT DEVELOP. IN THIS RAT THE MUSCLE WAS REMOVED ONLY ON THE LEFT SIDE. NOTE THE ABSENCE OF THE RIDGE ON THAT SIDE (CENTER VIEW OF SKULL). IN THE SIDE VIEW (LEFT SECTION) THE DOTTED LINE INDICATES THE ABSENCE OF THE RIDGE OR CREST. COMPARE THIS WITH THE CREST ON THE UNOPERATED SIDE OF THE JAW (AT RIGHT). ONE SIDE OF THE RAT'S HEAD THUS BECAME SMOOTH AND "MODERN." THE OTHER, UNOPERATED SIDE REMAINED KNOBBY AND "NEANDERTHAL."

Washburn was not surprised that the operation had affected the skull of the rats, but he was astonished at how marked the difference was. He set out to check these interesting results in every way possible. Would a change in the bone produce equally striking alterations? In a long series of experiments, he removed certain bones and certain parts of the bones in the same region of the head. The method was one developed to teach plastic surgeons what parts of the bone must be replaced and what parts can be left to take care of themselves.

To his continuing surprise, Washburn found that it made relatively little difference what was done to the bone. Other bones would grow back and fill in. In the end, removal of even large sections made little difference to the animal. The rats got along as well as normally.

But the slightest change in the muscle always made a tremendous difference. "The muscles are 'doing' things," Washburn explains. "The bones are relatively inert and take care of themselves to a surprising extent.

"We started to study bone and muscle. When we were through we had decided the bone was relatively unimportant as long as it was there, and that the muscles were exceedingly important."

It was a long jump, however, from rats to men. Washburn sought some intermediate group in which to check his findings. The monkey seemed likely to provide some of the unusual, hidden information he needed, and Washburn set off for Uganda. The one hundred apes and monkeys he collected were of three different types.

His camp was set up deep in the monkey territory. Early in the morning the native hunters went out to collect the animals. Washburn spent the hot days dissecting and preparing them. Every significant muscle was meticulously studied and weighed. Some of the skulls were furrowed with a great crease across the forehead; there were bony ridges around the eyes, and an extremely wide flat nose. Others had smooth contours.

"If these skulls had been found as fossils," said Washburn, "one would have been tempted to call the first a Peking Man monkey and the other a modern type. But as it happens both are of the same species and lived at exactly the same time."

The big knobby "primitive" skull was that of a large male. The smooth "modern" one belonged to a female. But among the monkeys there also were some juvenile males who had none of the heavy protuberances. Their jaw muscles, Washburn discovered, weighed about the same as those of the female.

Only one difference could be found between the skull of the young male and that of the female. He had huge canine teeth —the teeth the males use in fighting.

"We know that the differences between males and females are dependent upon a relatively small number of genetic differences," Washburn explained. "I don't know how many, but the number is not great. If such differences can be produced, there is no reason why a relatively small number of changes could not change a Neanderthal-like man into a more or less modern form."

A comparison of the weight of the jaw muscles he had removed from the monkeys underlined Washburn's point. Whenever the muscle weighed more than 32 or 33 grams, typical "primitive" creases appeared in the skull. If the muscle weighed only 10 or 12 grams, there were none. The heavier muscles also produced changes in the structure of the nose, the eyes, and the cheek.

In humans, three great buttresses carry the pressure of the teeth up into the face. Various combinations of muscles affect each of the buttresses differently and produce varied patterns of bony growth.

Many anthropologists rule Neanderthal man out of the direct human line and insist that his was a branch that came to naught. It is argued that modern man could not have descended from a creature with such huge brow ridges, heavy cheeks, and massive jaws. According to Washburn's analysis, the "primitive" features that shocked many of the early students of Neanderthal man into thinking that he was some kind of idiot, or perhaps some unusually thick-headed enemy from abroad, can be accounted for by his great jaw and the heavy muscles that must have attached to it.

Despite his forbidding appearance, Neanderthal man had a brain of near-human size. Washburn likes to say jokingly that if he had been enrolled in college today he might have done well, and probably would have been considered an invaluable asset to the football team.

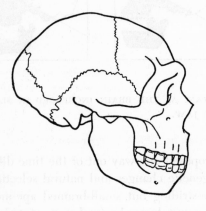

NEANDERTHAL SKULL

Since the brain reached modern or near-modern size with such predecessors as Neanderthal man and Piltdown man, almost the only important change in man has been a decrease in the size of the features. The modern jaw has become a little less underslung, the eyebrows somewhat less beetling, and the nose not quite so broad. In the long range of evolution such changes are minor; they are only the finishing touches, the top dressing.

"Just less face, less teeth, less bones, less muscle will account for these changes," Washburn wrote. "And if this is correct, the genetic dilemma is solved.

"We know from work on laboratory and on domestic animals that to produce more or less of a structure already there is easy. It is hard to get a different pattern."

APE, FOSSIL MAN, AND MAN. AS THE BRAIN INCREASED IN SIZE, THERE WAS LESS FACE AND JAW.

And so Washburn proposed one way out of the time difficulty. A relatively few genetic changes and natural selection could transform the free-striding but small-brained ape-men into the still free-striding but larger-brained men of today. Evolution in this way could well have been accomplished in the lesser span allowed by the new timing.

Other, new laboratory work said that natural selection also may have moved faster than was generally thought. Few attempts had been made to watch natural selection at work. The experiment of di Cesnola with the praying mantis and the recent work with bacteria and fruit flies were the exceptions rather than the rule.[1] When Dr. Lee R. Dice, of the Laboratory of Vertebrate Biology of the University of Michigan, decided to try to study the seldom-seen process under the carefully controlled conditions of the modern laboratory, it was an unusually interesting prospect.

[1] See Chapters x and xi.

Dice put a barn owl in a cage, in a light and setting that exactly paralleled that of nature, and let it prey on mice. Half of the mice matched the floor of the cage in color; half contrasted. And the owl captured almost twice as many of the mice that were conspicuously colored. Those which matched the background had a much better chance of escaping his swoops, and this was true whether the background was light or dark. To eliminate chance, the experiment was repeated under both conditions.

MICE CONTRASTING WITH THEIR BACKGROUND WERE EASILY CAPTURED BY THE OWL. THEY HAD A POOR CHANCE OF SURVIVING. THOSE MATCHING THEIR BACKGROUND WERE FAR MORE LIKELY TO ESCAPE THE PREDATORY OWL.

The Dice laboratory also undertook similar experiments with a penguin, a night heron, and a sunfish. In one experiment 470 fish were placed in a pool with a dark background. The penguin caught 201 that were light-colored and therefore conspicuous. He took only 73 that matched the background.

The sunfish was offered a chance at mosquito fish. When

the background of the pool was gray, he captured 137 contrastingly colored dark fish. When the background was changed to black, he caught 29 grays and only 8 blacks.

If the owl had been preying on the mice in nature instead of in the laboratory, the concealingly colored ones would have replaced the conspicuously colored ones in seven or eight generations of mice. Man would have seen the results—as perhaps he did see them in the white mice that inhabit white beaches, in the dark ones that live on lava backgrounds, in the dun ones that live in the desert. Man would have understood how this came about; he probably would not have guessed that the concealingly colored mice could have taken over so rapidly.

But if there were relatively few genetic changes necessary and if evolution sometimes moved fast, the progress from ape-man to man might well have been made within a million years and the finishing touches might well have been applied within the last fifty thousand.

This way of looking at natural selection and genetic change is new and little known. Unlike some of the older theories of how and when man evolved, it is wide open to verification. The work of Washburn and Dice can be repeated and expanded by others. The way has been opened for a new experimental approach to the study of evolution.

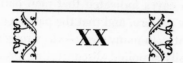

EVOLUTION REVISED
A NEW TIME AND A NEW WAY

SINCE 1950 the scientific evidence has pointed inescapably to one conclusion: man did not evolve in either the time or the way that Darwin and the modern evolutionists thought most probable. The physicists and the geologists by 1950 had clearly shown that the world is older and man is younger than anyone had dared to estimate before.

By that year, the men who dug into the ancient caves of South Africa and China, looking for traces of early man and the part-human, part-anthropoid races that had preceded him had succeeded. All the major steps in the evolution of man were for the first time filled in; the hitherto missing link had been found. But the missing link was not what science had expected; no one had imagined a being with the head of an ape and the body of a man.

What did it mean? The physicists and geologists and fossil-hunters did not say. They merely presented their dates and materials. Oakley indicated only that Galley Hill man was relatively modern and that Piltdown man instead of going back some one million years belonged to a period of about fifty thousand years ago.

The question was insistent: what did it mean? How did the new findings affect the theory of evolution? This was a problem for the anthropologist, because the whole problem of man's origins and evolution was affected.

The surprising and almost unbelievable fossils that came from the banks of the Solo River, from Dragon-bone Hill, and from the Sterkfontein caves indicated that man had developed according to a new pattern, and that the pattern given him in the past—and currently, in many cases—was wrong at some critical points. The fossils supplied disconcerting proof that the development of the body came first, and the typical development of the brain later—that we had human bodies long before we reached human intelligence.

At first, such evidence from the ground was disbelieved, as evidence is likely to be when it runs counter to what the world has always thought.

When Eugène Dubois found an undeniably human leg bone close by the skull of *Pithecanthropus erectus,* the world cried: "They can't belong together." The ridicule heaped upon his find, in large part because of this "discrepancy," drove the Dutch physician into his thirty-year retreat.

The skepticism was almost as strong when similar bones began to be found with the skulls of Peking man.

Broom ran headlong into the same feeling that there must be a mix-up when he discovered human-like pelvic bones in the same deposits with the unquestionably apelike skulls of the South African ape-men. For a number of years his work was not taken seriously because he ventured to claim that the apelike creatures could have had near-human bodies and walked like men.

The conviction that the first men began as replicas, however crude and primitive, of modern man was so deep that the evidence to the contrary long was discredited and discounted. It was a staple belief that many millions of years ago some of the anthropoids developed better brains, and that as they became smarter they came down out of the trees and gradually evolved into modern man.

Weidenreich was perhaps the first authority to point out that man's development might have followed a different course. In 1941 he wrote: "Little is known about the development of other parts of the skeleton, but it can be taken as definitely established that the erect posture and all that is connected with its adoption were attained long before [man reached his definitive form]. Thus the subsequent change of the skull, and above all that of the brain case, morphologically viewed, crowns the transformation in the true sense of the word, both in time and position."

But not until after the publication of the South African monographs and their appraisal by Clark of Oxford did science generally begin to grant that the body reached human form long before the brain.

Laboratory work at the University of Chicago and Harvard strongly confirmed the new pattern of evolution evinced by the fossils. Washburn, at Chicago, made a close study of the different body "complexes" of man and the apes.

In the arms, the ribs, and the shoulder girdle, he found, the two are very much alike. The important middle part of the body had changed little; there men still were essentially apes. The specialist can recognize the technical differences between the shoulders of modern man and the ape, but the differences are not great.

The most noticeable departure is in the hands, which Washburn, from the long-term anthropological viewpoint, considered of lesser importance. Once man had become a biped, selection inevitably would have favored a hand differing from that of the tree-living primates. Even so, the human hand still shows a remarkable amount of the primitive grasping adaptation, particularly in the long fingers and nails.[1]

As Washburn and a number of other anthropologists now see it, the middle part of the body, the trunk and arms, began to take on its essential form millions of years ago, at the time when the earliest primates climbed up into the trees. The story as they trace it goes, in outline, something like this:

The development of the ability to grasp with the hands and

[1] To this day the ability to grasp with the hands and the feet is the one ability all primates have in common.

feet set the first primates apart from all the other primitive mammals and made it possible for them to take up life in the trees.

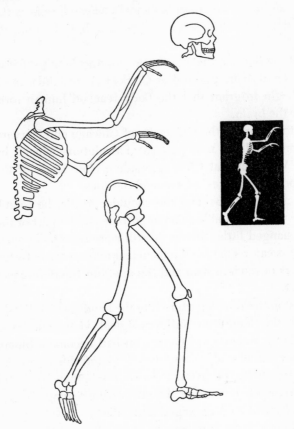

THE THREE GREAT BODY "COMPLEXES" OF MAN. EACH SECTION EVOLVED DIFFERENTLY. THE ARMS, SHOULDERS, AND RIBS CHANGED LITTLE. IN THIS MIDDLE PART OF THE BODY MEN STILL ARE ESSENTIALLY APES. THERE WAS AN ALL-IMPORTANT CHANGE IN THE PELVIS-LEGS COMPLEX, A CHANGE THAT STARTED MAN ON A DISTINCTIVE LINE OF EVOLUTION. MAN'S ABILITY TO WALK ON TWO LEGS FREED HIS HANDS FOR THE USE OF TOOLS. THE DEVELOPMENT OF THE THIRD GREAT COMPLEX, THE BRAIN, THEN FOLLOWED.

But life in the leafy green world above was a fairly restricted, though safe one. Without the great ranges over which the ground-living animals could move and mix, the tree-living primates came to differ widely from each other.

Many of them developed differences in the senses. In the trees, the strong sense of smell, the ears that cocked to the least sound, the hair that stood on end at the threat of danger, were not so important as on the ground. The monkeys with better eyes and color vision were the ones that survived and left descendants. And gradually the brain changed from a primitive "smell-brain" to a more advanced "sight-brain."

The monkeys thus equipped became abundantly successful in the Old World tropical forests and in most of the other areas to which they spread.[2]

Some of the numerous small bands of primates then began to develop a different mode of locomotion. Instead of hopping or running along, holding fast with hands and feet, they would swing along with a different motion of the arms. This mode of progress, called brachiation, involved anatomical changes in the wrist, elbow, shoulder, and thoracic region.

And thus the apes arose, and the shoulder, arms, and ribs took on the form that has been carried along almost unchanged to all of us today.

Washburn points out that no monkey anywhere in the world has such arms and shoulders. But every essential detail of this "complex" is shared by man and ape. He believes this crucially important change occurred about ten million years ago.

As the eons rolled by, the story continues, some of the apes that ate a more varied diet came down to the ground to live. Like their present-day descendants, they could take a few steps

[2] The older, more primitive forms soon were replaced, except where they were especially protected, or retreated to a nocturnal life. The safety of the island of Madagascar, for example, saved the lemurs. The tarsiers, the lorises, and the galagos found refuge in the night.

upright, perhaps even while holding a stick in one hand. But when they wanted to cover space, down went the knuckles and they proceeded on all fours.

GIBBON, GORILLA, AND SPIDER MONKEY. THE GIBBON AND GORILLA SWING ALONG WITH THE ARMS—BRACHIATE. THE MONKEY, LACKING THE ARM AND SHOULDER DEVELOPMENT OF THE APES AND MAN, RUNS ALONG HOLDING FAST WITH ARMS, LEGS, AND, IN THE CASE OF THE NEW WORLD MONKEY, WITH THE TAIL TOO.

About a million years ago there came what many anthropologists regard as the most important of all the changes in the evolution of man, a change that forever afterward was to set man apart from his anthropoid ancestors.

Some of the big ground-living apes were born with a different kind of pelvis. It meant that they could walk upright, on two legs! For the first time, in all of time, the hands were free. They no longer had to be used for locomotion. These ground-living apes could use tools, for any implement held in the hands no longer had to be dropped every time more than a few steps were taken. "The fact that we number more than a few thousand bipeds living in the Old World tropics is due to the development of tools," said Washburn.

From this point on, all was changed; a new future had been cast. Natural selection was on a new basis, for a premium had been placed on brains as well as brawn. The most intelligent of the biped man-apes, the ones that could most effectively use

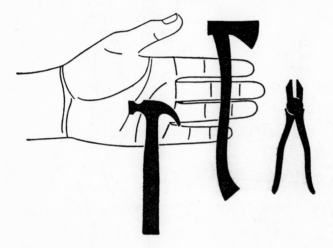

HAND AND TOOLS

sticks and stones to beat off their enemies and kill their food, were the survivors and the parents of the next generation.

The pelvis that precipitated this all-important turn in evolution has a number of functions. It not only connects the legs and trunk in such a way that it controls gait; it gives origin to many muscles and serves as a bony birth canal.

How any living creature stands and moves depends in large part upon the length of the pelvis and upon the angle at which it is inclined. In the apes it is long and slanting. In the ape-men and men it is shorter and more nearly upright.

Washburn believes that this whole vital evolutionary cycle began when some of the big ground-living apes were born with

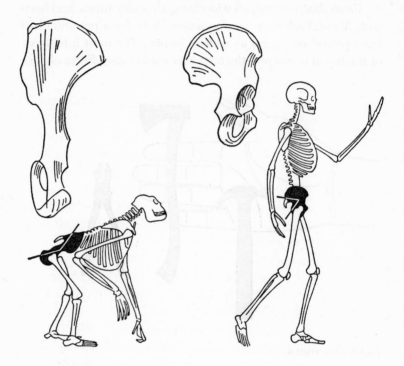

ONE GREAT CHANGE FOREVER AFTERWARD SET MAN APART FROM HIS ANTHROPOID ANCESTORS. IT WAS IN THE PELVIS. THE APES, WITH THEIR LONG SLANTING PELVIS, CAN TAKE ONLY A FEW STEPS UPRIGHT AND MUST USE THE HANDS FOR LOCOMOTION. MAN, BECAUSE OF HIS SHORTER PELVIS, CAN STAND AND WALK—HE IS A BIPED. HIS HANDS ARE THEN NO LONGER NEEDED FOR LOCOMOTION.

a shorter pelvis. When this basic genetic change occurred, the bone had to take on a more upright position to assure a safe birth for offspring. And once the pelvis is brought into such a position, the thigh muscles that attach to it are directly affected.

These muscles make the human step.

Washburn argues that the real difference between the walk of man and ape is not in the extent of the motion, but in the ability to finish the step with a drive. The muscle that provides the drive and swings back the thigh is the gluteus maximus, the muscle that arises from the posterior part of the pelvis. When the pelvis is short, the gluteus maximus pulls hard. A vigorous step is possible.

Negative evidence of how important the muscle is appears when it becomes paralyzed. A man who suffers such an accident cannot walk normally, though he can get around easily with a flexed gait similar to that of the apes. "The paralysis of the single muscle makes the human type of bipedal locomotion impossible," wrote Washburn. "It shows that the form and function of this particular muscle is critical in the evolution of man's posture and gait."

Carrying this argument back to what may have happened when the first apes began to walk, Washburn maintains that since selection is for function, the animals able to walk and use the hands most freely were the ones to survive. Hence selection favored the new type of pelvis. "It is my belief," the Chicago anthropologist concludes, "that this single change is the thing that initiates human evolution."

And the evidence backs up this theory with enlightening and revealing regularity. No living ape ever has been found with a human-type pelvis. Nor has any man or any of the fossil remains of man ever been discovered with an ape-type pelvis. In Java, in China, in South Africa, the pelvic bones found with the fossils placed in the human line were either human or near-human in type. There has been no exception, though the world long wanted to believe otherwise.

To put the point to the final test, Washburn has proposed a bold and intriguing experiment. He would like to operate on a laboratory ape and change its pelvis, much as the pelvis must have changed in evolution. If the operation succeeded, the ape would be able to walk on two legs! Its hands would be freed for the use of tools. The studies that could be made as this one animal relived in part a change through which the human race passed about a million years ago would hold exciting possibilities.

Preliminary studies have indicated that the operation is anatomically possible. Only the lack of laboratory funds has halted work along this amazing and promising line.

It was only after the trunk and the pelvis and legs had developed much as they are today that the brain began the spectacular growth that eventually was to change ape-man and primitive man into modern man. Until the 1940's science assumed that the growth of the brain always came first. Supposedly it was a better brain that enabled the mammals as a group to triumph over the reptiles when the two contended for the control of that ancient world of sea and jungle.

And supposedly it was again the development of a better brain that led the apes out of the trees and onto the ground. Even Weidenreich, though he recognized that the evolution of the body came first, rated the development of the brain as the primary factor in evolution.

The faith in the priority of the brain was first seriously jarred in 1948. In that year Professor Tilly Edinger of Harvard showed that the growth of the brain tends to follow in evolution. The earliest mammals, their fossil remains revealed, had brains no more advanced than those of the reptiles. Only later, after they had become typical mammals, did the brains reach modern mammalian proportions.

The horse, which Edinger studied in particular, attained its characteristic form, its long legs and teeth, well before the brain reached its final size.

And so it was with man. A comparison of the brain capacity of man and his forerunners sharply etches the pattern:

	CRANIAL CAPACITY
Chimpanzee and gorilla	325–650 (cubic centimeters)
South African ape-men	450–650
Java man	790–900
Peking man	900–1,200
Piltdown man	1,300–1,400
Neanderthal man	1,100–1,500
Modern man	1,200–1,500

The South African ape-men—despite their near-human bodies and upright posture—were in the brain range of the apes.

"There is no doubt that all human fossils described so far have human pelves and limb bones, and the man-apes were remarkably human in these features," Washburn emphasized. "Therefore it appears that the differences in the brain between apes and man, just as those in dentition, were attained after full human status had been achieved in the limbs and trunk."

In its final evolution the change in the brain was large. Between the ape-men and the emergence of modern man, the brain more than doubled in size. It grew from the 650-cubic-centimeter maximum of the apes and the ape-men to the modern top average of 1,500 cubic centimeters.

Some of the Neanderthal men of Europe had a brain capacity very close to that of modern man, if not within the modern range. They were well along the way. And there seems to be little question that Piltdown man had a brain of modern size, if it is recalled that the final reconstruction gave him a brain capacity of 1,400 cubic centimeters. Modern man had arrived.

It is at this point that the question of time enters and becomes critical. Until Oakley came along with his fluorine test, it was generally assumed that Piltdown man—probably the first to achieve the full intelligence of modern man—went back to a period of about one million years ago. That was the date accepted for the first appearance of modern man, and the family trees in the textbooks show modern man branching off from his anthropoid forebears at about that point.

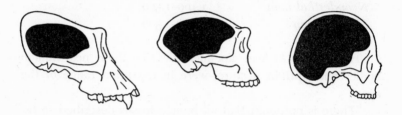

THE GROWTH OF THE BRAIN. THE APE (LEFT) HAD A BRAIN AVERAGING LESS THAN 650 CUBIC CENTIMETERS. PRIMITIVE MAN REACHED A BRAIN OF 900 TO 1,200 CUBIC CENTIMETERS. MODERN MAN OFTEN HAS A BRAIN OF 1,500 CUBIC CENTIMETERS. THE BRAIN OF MODERN MAN IS MORE THAN TWICE AS LARGE AS THAT OF THE APE.

But Oakley proved that Piltdown man was not contemporaneous with the elephants and mastodons that roamed the English countryside 500,000 or more years ago. On the contrary, he clearly was associated with the beavers who had lived in the river Ouse when it flowed across the Piltdown common about 50,000 years ago, just before the last ice age began. This took Piltdown man, probably the first being who rightfully could be called a man, out of the remote past and brought him very close to modern times.

It should be remembered, too, that many of the other fossils that once appeared to date man with a fairly sizable brain back in the shadowy stretches of 500,000 to 1,000,000 years ago were also shown to belong to comparatively recent years.

How recent? Here Carbon-14 comes in. Although the Carbon-14 dates do not go beyond 25,000 years, they clearly indicate that the ice last extended down from the north both in Europe and in North America about 11,000 years ago. If this is correct, geologists hold that the final glaciation began less than 50,000 years ago.

This is an assumption, unsupported as yet by any absolute system of dating, but with the date of the final advance of the ice fixed, and with all the wealth of evidence left by the glaciers themselves, there is little speculation in estimating the duration of the last ice age.

The new timing indicates therefore that humans who had the requisite intelligence to be called men did not reach that high status until about 50,000 years ago. Modern man, then, is only about 50,000 years old.

The 50,000 years, of course, are approximate. But even if this estimate should later be enlarged to 75,000 or 100,000 years, modern man still would be the veriest of newcomers by all evolutionary standards. And if our 50,000-year tenure of the earth must be adjusted, the chances are that it will be shortened. Unpublished work and studies now going on in a number of universities are tending to pull the time of man's emergence as man even closer to today.

At the same time, the work of Washburn, Dice, and others demonstrated that man could have made the steep climb from ape-man to modern man in the shorter time now allotted.

In the light of these new understandings, much that has been taught about the time of man and his development must now be changed. Books must be rewritten and courses revised. For the new timing, the new fossil finds, the new pattern of evolution are bringing about a new and major revision in the theory of the origin of man.

The theory of evolution is not being weakened by this correction of past errors and misconceptions and by the opening of new understandings. On the contrary, the basic truths developed by Darwin and the brilliant succession of evolutionists who came after him are strengthened.

Science can make again for its goal: the unattainable but approximate truth about man, his origins and evolution.

SELECTED BIBLIOGRAPHY

MAN'S ORIGINS

DARWIN

DARWIN, CHARLES: *The Voyage of the Beagle.* New York: E. P. Dutton & Co.; 1950.
In England this famous and unmatchable account of Darwin's five-year trip around the world was published under the title *Journal of Researches into the Geology and Natural History of the Various Countries Visited by H. M. S. Beagle.* A reprint of this edition was published in New York in 1952 by Hafner.

——: *The Diary of the Voyage of H. M. S. Beagle,* edited from the manuscript by Lady Nora Barlow, granddaughter of Darwin. Cambridge: The University Press; 1933.
Here are Darwin's own vivid and unfolding impressions as he jotted them down from day to day.

BARLOW, NORA: *Charles Darwin and the Voyage of the Beagle.* London: Pilot Press; 1945. Darwin's *Beagle* notebook and his affectionate, descriptive letters home.

DARWIN, CHARLES: *The Origin of Species.* New York: The Modern Library; 1936.
This classic which changed the world's thought offers rich, rewarding, and not difficult reading. But if time is lacking Chapters i–vi and xv will provide the most important parts of Darwin's theory.

——: *The Descent of Man.* New York: The Modern Library; 1936.
The Descent of Man and *The Origin of Species* are here pre-

sented in a single inexpensive volume. Darwin's great array of evidence to prove that man is descended from an earlier simpler form is contained in the brief 167 pages of Part One. Part Two, the bulk of the book, deals with sexual selection.

HOOTON, ERNEST A.: *Up from the Ape.* Revised edition. New York: The Macmillan Co.; 1946.
A modern statement of the descent of man.

HUXLEY, JULIAN: *Evolution, the Modern Synthesis.* New York: Harper & Brothers; 1942.
In this collection of essays by leading scientists, Huxley, the grandson of T. H. Huxley, Darwin's great defender, brilliantly analyzes the theory of natural selection.

HUXLEY, THOMAS H.: *Man's Place in Nature.* London, New York: D. Appleton; 1863 and 1896. Now out of print.
Thirteen months after the publication of *The Origin of Species,* Huxley made it clear that evolution applied to man too, a fact only hinted at by Darwin.

WEST, GEOFFREY: *Charles Darwin, a Portrait.* New Haven: Yale University Press; 1938.
This well-known biography of Darwin is particularly interesting for its account of the remarkable Darwin family.

LAMARCK

LAMARCK, JEAN-BAPTISTE-PIERRE-ANTOINE DE MONET, CHEVALIER DE: *Histoire naturelle des animaux sans vertèbres.* Paris: Desray; 1815–22

——: *Recherches sur l'organisation des corps vivans.* Paris: l'auteur; 1802.
Here is a concise statement of Lamarck's theories. For clarity it is not surpassed in any of his later works.

NORDENSKIÖLD, ERIK: *The History of Biology.* New York: Alfred A. Knopf; 1928.
This standard history contains useful and interesting chapters on Lamarck and many other leading biologists and evolutionists.

PACKARD, ALPHEUS SPRING: *Lamarck, the Founder of Evolution.*
New York: Longmans, Green & Co.; 1901.
> The most complete biography of Lamarck.

GIARD

BOHN, GEORGE: *Alfred Giard et son œuvre.* Paris: Mercure de
France; 1910.
> A valuable and warmly written appraisal of the work of Giard
> by one of his pupils.

GIARD, ALFRED: *Œuvres diversés—reunies et reéditeés par les soins
d'un group d'élèves et d'amis.* Paris: Laboratoire d'Evolution des
Êtres Organisés; 1911–13.
> A collection of Giard's writings.

——: *Controverses transformistes.* Paris: Naud; 1904.
> The evolution controversy in France.

COPE

OSBORN, HENRY FAIRFIELD: *Cope, Master Naturalist.* Princeton:
Princeton University Press; 1931.
> A warm and authoritative account of the life and work of Cope
> by a friend.

SIMPSON, GEORGE GAYLORD: *Life of the Past.* New Haven: Yale
University Press; 1953.
> An expert and fascinating story of what is known now about
> some of the fossil wealth with which Cope worked earlier.

DE VRIES

DE VRIES, HUGO: *Species and Varieties.* Chicago: Open Court Publishing Co.; 1905.
> This translation of a series of lectures which de Vries gave at
> the University of California is an excellent, readable story of
> the botanist's great work and the mutation theories he drew
> from it.

——: *The Mutation Theory.* Chicago: Open Court Publishing Co.; 1909–10.

MENDEL

Iltis, Hugo: *Life of Mendel.* London: George Allen & Unwin; 1932.
   This is one of the few biographies of Mendel, the discoverer of the laws of heredity. It is written by a fellow townsman who gave a lifetime to the task.

HALDANE

Haldane, J. B. S.: *Adventures of a Biologist.* New York: Harper & Brothers; 1940.

——: *The Causes of Evolution.* London: Longmans, Green & Co.; 1932.

——: See chapter by Haldane in *Evolution, the Modern Synthesis,* edited by Julian Huxley.

FISHER

Fisher, Ronald Aylmer: *Genetical Theory of Natural Selection.* Oxford: Clarendon Press; 1930.
   This is a difficult and technical book, but a brilliant demonstration of how mathematics settled the dispute over the roles of natural selection and mutation in evolution.

WRIGHT

Wright, Sewall
   Wright's work is set forth principally in a series of publications not written for the layman.

Dobzhansky, Theodosius: *Genetics and the Origin of Species.* Third edition. New York: Columbia University Press; 1951.
   An up-to-date and scholarly discussion of population genetics, including the work of Wright, Haldane, and Fisher.

Huxley, Julian: *Evolution in Action*. New York: Harper & Brothers; 1953.
In a fine readable style, Huxley presents some of the materials and problems dealt with by Haldane, Fisher, and Wright.

MAN'S BURIED RECORD

DUBOIS AND VON KOENIGSWALD. JAVA

Von Koenigswald, G. H. R.: "Search for Early Man." In *Natural History Magazine,* published by the American Museum of Natural History, January 1947.
Here von Koenigswald tells the fascinating story of his discoveries and adventures in Java.

Weidenreich, Franz: *Apes, Giants, and Man*. Chicago: University of Chicago Press; 1946.
A popular, easily readable account of the discovery of the Java giants and their significance.

BLACK AND WEIDENREICH. CHINA

Andrews, Roy Chapman: *Meet Your Ancestors*. New York: The Viking Press; 1945.
The early part of the work in China.

Weidenreich, Franz: Anthropological Papers. Memorial volume, compiled by Sherwood L. Washburn and Davida Wolffson. New York: The Viking Fund; 1949.

DART AND BROOM. SOUTH AFRICA

Broom, Robert: *Finding the Missing Link*. London: C. A. Watts & Co.; 1950.
Broom's own colorful, readable story.

——: "The Ape-men." In *Yearbook of Physical Anthropology—1949,* pages 65–9. New York: The Viking Fund; 1949.
Broom inimitably tells of some of his most famous discoveries.

A CHANGED THEORY OF MAN'S EVOLUTION

KNOPF

KNOPF, ADOLPH: *The Age of the Earth.* National Research Council. Bulletin 80; 1931.

JEPSEN, G. L., *et al.: Genetics, Paleontology & Evolution.* Princeton: Princeton University Press; 1949.
An excellent summary of the changes brought about by uranium dating.

OAKLEY

OAKLEY, KENNETH PAGE: "The Fluorine Dating Method." In *American Yearbook of Physical Anthropology,* pages 44–9. New York: The Viking Fund; 1949.

——: "Dating Human Fossil Remains." In *Anthropology Today,* pages 143–57. Chicago: University of Chicago Press; 1953.
In this international symposium of anthropologists Oakley tells of the new dating of Piltdown man and some of the other key fossils.

KEITH, SIR ARTHUR: *The Antiquity of Man.* Two volumes. Philadelphia: J. B. Lippincott Co.; 1929.
A full and authoritative account of the major fossils finds of early man.

——: *An Autobiography.* New York: Philosophical Library; 1950.
Dating, fossils finds, and reminiscences of many of the leading evolutionists.

LIBBY

LIBBY, WILLARD F.: *Radiocarbon Dating.* Chicago: University of Chicago Press; 1952.
Scholarly, detailed, including interesting tables of materials dated.

JOHNSON, FREDERICK: *Radiocarbon Dating.* Memoirs of the Society for American Archaeology. Salt Lake City: Society for American Archaeology; 1951.

The official report of the appraisal committee appointed by the American Anthropological Association and the Geological Society of America.

WASHBURN

WASHBURN, SHERWOOD L.: "The New Physical Anthropology." In *Transactions of the New York Academy of Sciences,* Series 2, Volume XIII, Number 7, pages 298–304; May 19, 1951.

INDEX